Adobe® Photoshop® CS2

CLASSROOM IN A BOOK®

www.adobepress.com

Adobe® Photoshop® CS2 Classroom in a Book® for Windows® and Mac OS.

Adobe Systems Incorporated, 345 Park Avenue, San Jose, California 95110, USA

Adobe Press books are published by Peachpit Press, Berkeley, CA. To report errors, please send a note to errata@peachpit.com.

Printed in the U.S.A.

ISBN # 0-321-32184-7

9 8 7 6

Writer: Anita Dennis
Design Director: Andrew Faulkner, afstudio design
Designer: Alison O'Gara, afstudio design
Production: Jan Martí, Command Z

We offer our sincere thanks to the following people for their support and help with this project: Martin Boliek, Russell Brown, Laura Kersell, Julieanne Kost, Jack Lewis, Jan Martí, Jill Merlin, Steve Muller, John Nack, Alison O'Gara, Todd Ritola, Karen Seriguchi, Lee Unkrich, and Christine Yarrow. We couldn't have done it without you.

Working with Selections page 131

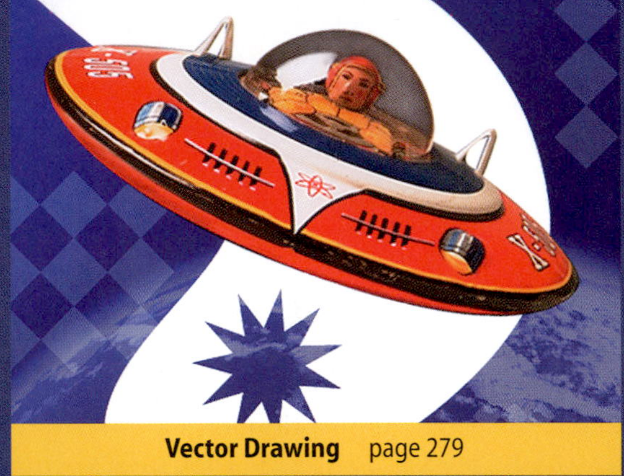

Vector Drawing page 279

Layer Basics page 157

Advanced Layers page 313

Digital Photography page 219

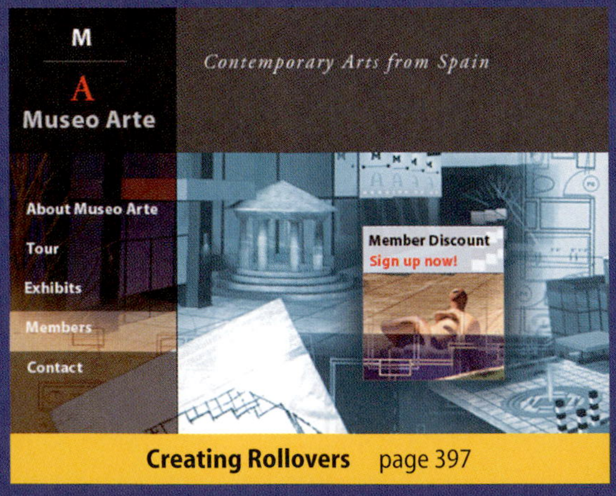

Creating Rollovers page 397

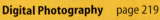

From the Authors

Welcome to Adobe® Photoshop® CS2 Classroom in a Book. Whether you just purchased your first digital camera and want to learn the basics of the world's leading imaging software application, or you're a graphic designer who spends six hours a day in Photoshop and you need to maximize your productivity, this book is for you.

In the 16 lessons of this book, you will learn everything from compositing images into artistic montages, to processing camera raw digital photographs, to producing Web animations. We've consolidated content from the previous edition, offering a streamlined, hands-on training course that will teach you Photoshop fundamentals, as well as how to use many of the exciting new features in Photoshop CS2, in concise, colorful, comprehensive exercises.

Plus, we've included some fun stuff—for example, Photoshop guru Russell Brown will show you how to experiment with layers while making a profound fashion statement in his entertaining QuickTime movies. (Be sure to check out his QuickTime movies on the book's CD.) In addition, Photoshop evangelist Julieanne Kost shares some of her best power-user tips, and we've included some "extra-credit" assignments for students who want to challenge themselves further. (For details about what's new in this edition of the book, see page 2.)

Good luck and have fun!

Andrew Faulkner and Anita Dennis

Contents

Getting Started

1 Getting to Know the Work Area

2 Using Adobe Bridge

5 Working with Selections

6 Layer Basics

7 Masks and Channels

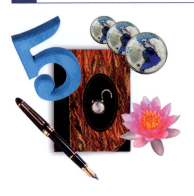

10 Vector Drawing Techniques

11 Advanced Layer Techniques

12 Advanced Compositing

13 Creating Links Within an Image

14 Creating Rollover Web Visuals

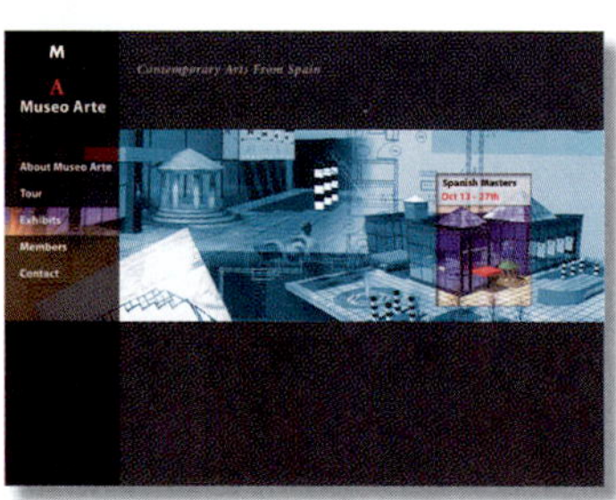

15 Animating GIF Images for the Web

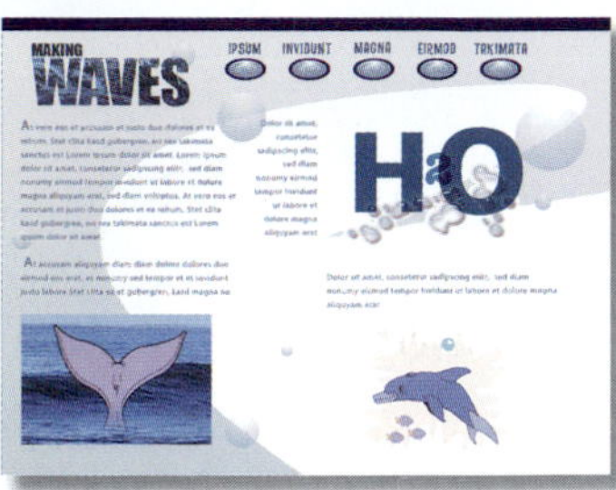

16 Producing and Printing Consistent Color

John Nack
Photoshop Product Manager
Adobe Systems, Inc.

Hello Photoshop fans,

Thank you for purchasing Adobe Photoshop CS2 Classroom in a Book, *the official training workbook for the world's best image-editing program. I am particularly excited about this edition because it showcases many of the groundbreaking features new to Photoshop CS2. For example, Lesson 8 shows you the ins and outs of the new Camera Raw dialog box, as well as the revolutionary new Vanishing Point feature, which lets you transform, clone, and paint objects in perspective. And Lessons 9 and 10 give you a taste of using Smart Objects, which let you nondestructively transform, rotate, and warp layers, as well as keep vector artwork editable in Photoshop. There are lots of great new features in Photoshop CS2, and this Classroom in a Book will get you up to speed using them.*

Good luck with your learning, and thanks,

John Nack

John Nack
Adobe Photoshop Product Manager

Getting Started

Adobe® Photoshop® CS2, the benchmark for digital imaging excellence, delivers a new level of power, precision, and control, as well as exciting new features and next-generation enhancements. Included with Photoshop CS2 is ImageReady™ CS2, which offers a versatile set of tools for creating and optimizing visual content for the Web, and Adobe Bridge®, the new visual file browser that provides both workaday productivity as well as creative inspiration. Photoshop CS2 pushes the boundaries of digital image editing and helps you turn your dreams into designs more easily than ever before.

About Classroom in a Book

Adobe Photoshop CS2 Classroom in a Book® is part of the official training series for Adobe graphics and publishing software developed by experts at Adobe Systems. The lessons are designed to let you learn at your own pace. If you're new to Adobe Photoshop, you'll learn the fundamental concepts and features you'll need to master the program. And, if you've been using Adobe Photoshop for a while, you'll find that *Classroom in a Book* teaches many advanced features, including tips and techniques for using the latest version of the application and for preparing images for the Web.

Although each lesson provides step-by-step instructions for creating a specific project, there's room for exploration and experimentation. You can follow the book from start to finish, or do only the lessons that match your interests and needs. Each lesson concludes with a review section summarizing what you've covered.

What's new in this edition

New lessons in this edition include information on many new features, such as new chapters on typography, Adobe Bridge, and digital photography. The digital photography lesson includes exercises on using such new features as the Camera Raw dialog box and the Vanishing Point filter. Other lessons incorporate other new features, such as support for Smart Objects and the new Spot Healing Brush tool.

In addition to covering the new features of Adobe Photoshop CS2, this edition of *Adobe Photoshop Classroom in a Book* features a number of new and exciting changes itself. First, if you're a regular student of the Classroom in a Book series, you've probably already noticed that this edition is in four colors. Being able to see the screen captures and image windows in full color will help you more easily compare what's on our pages to what's on your screen, which will help you follow steps and complete exercises more easily. In addition, this edition of *Classroom in a Book* features some tips and techniques from two of Adobe's own experts, Photoshop evangelist Julieanne Kost and senior creative director Russell Brown. Look for Julieanne's tips and Russell's tutorials through the pages of the book.

Prerequisites

Before you begin to use *Adobe Photoshop CS2 Classroom in a Book*, you should have a working knowledge of your computer and its operating system. Make sure that you know how to use the mouse and standard menus and commands, and also how to open, save, and close files. If you need to review these techniques, see the documentation included with your Microsoft® Windows® or Apple® Mac® OS X documentation.

Installing Adobe Photoshop

Before you begin using *Adobe Photoshop CS2 Classroom in a Book*, make sure that your system is set up correctly and that you've installed the required software and hardware. You must purchase the Adobe Photoshop CS2 software separately. For system requirements and complete instructions on installing the software, see the *InstallReadMe* file on the application CD.

What's on the CD*

Here is an overview of the contents of the Classroom in a Book CD

Lesson files . . . and so much more

The *Adobe Photoshop CS2 Classroom in a Book* CD includes the lesson files that you'll need to complete the exercises in this book, as well as other content to help you learn more about Adobe Photoshop and use it with greater efficiency and ease. The diagram below represents the contents of the CD, which should help you locate the files you need.

Lessons

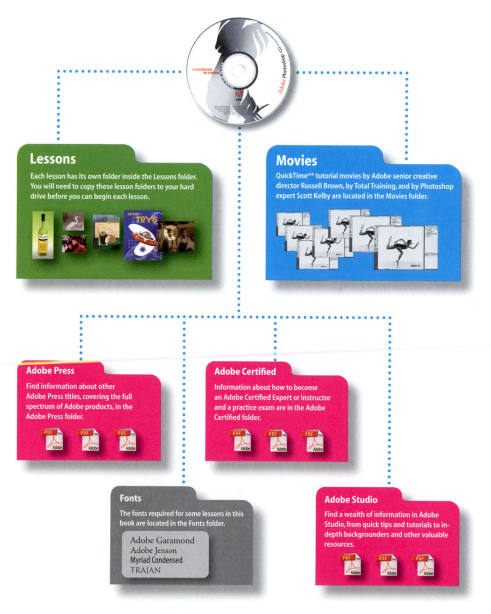

Each lesson has its own folder inside the Lessons folder. You will need to copy these lesson folders to your hard drive before you can begin each lesson.

Movies

QuickTime** tutorial movies by Adobe senior creative director Russell Brown, by Total Training, and by Photoshop expert Scott Kelby are located in the Movies folder.

Adobe Press

Find information about other Adobe Press titles, covering the full spectrum of Adobe products, in the Adobe Press folder.

Adobe Certified

Information about how to become an Adobe Certified Expert or instructor and a practice exam are in the Adobe Certified folder.

Fonts

The fonts required for some lessons in this book are located in the Fonts folder.

Adobe Garamond
Adobe Jenson
Myriad Condensed
TRAJAN

Adobe Studio

Find a wealth of information in Adobe Studio, from quick tips and tutorials to in-depth backgrounders and other valuable resources.

*** The latest version of Apple QuickTime can be downloaded from www.apple.com/support/downloads/quicktime652.html.*

Photoshop, ImageReady, and Bridge use the same installer. You must install all three applications from the Adobe Photoshop CS2 application CD onto your hard disk; you cannot run the programs from the CD. Follow the onscreen instructions.

Make sure that your serial number is accessible before installing the application; you can find the serial number on the registration card or CD sleeve.

Starting Adobe Photoshop

You start Photoshop just as you do most software applications.

To start Adobe Photoshop in Windows:

1 Choose Start > All Programs > Adobe Photoshop CS2.

2 In the Welcome Screen, click Close.

To start Adobe Photoshop in Mac OS:

1 Open the Applications/Adobe Photoshop CS2 folder, and double-click the Adobe Photoshop program icon.

2 In the Welcome Screen, click Close.

Installing the Classroom in a Book fonts

To ensure that the lesson files appear on your system with the correct fonts, you may need to install the *Classroom in a Book* font files. The fonts are in the Fonts folder on the *Adobe Photoshop CS2 Classroom in a Book* CD. If you already have these on your system, you do not need to install them.

Use the following procedure to install the fonts on your hard drive.

1 Insert the *Adobe Photoshop CS2 Classroom in a Book* CD into your CD-ROM drive.

2 Install the font files using the procedure for the version of your operating system:

• Windows: Drag the fonts from the CD to your hard disk and place them in your Adobe common fonts folder (typically C:\Program Files\Common Files\Adobe\Fonts).

• Mac OS: Open the Fonts folder on the CD. Select all of the fonts in the Fonts folder and drag them into the Library/Fonts folder on your hard disk. You can select and drag multiple fonts to install them, but you cannot drag the entire folder to install the fonts.

Copying the Classroom in a Book files

The *Adobe Photoshop CS2 Classroom in a Book* CD includes folders containing all the electronic files for the lessons in the book. Each lesson has its own folder; you must copy the folders to your hard disk to complete the lessons. To save room on your disk, you can install only the folder necessary for each lesson as you need it, and remove it when you're done.

To install the *Classroom in a Book* lesson files, do the following:

1 Insert the *Adobe Photoshop CS2 Classroom in a Book* CD into your CD-ROM drive.

2 Browse the contents and locate the Lessons folder.

3 Do one of the following:

• To copy all the lesson files, drag the Lessons folder from the CD onto your hard disk.

• To copy only individual lesson files, first create a new folder on your hard disk and name it **Lessons**. Then, drag the lesson folder or folders that you want to copy from the CD into the Lessons folder on your hard disk.

If you are installing the files in Windows 2000, you may need to unlock the lesson files before you can use them. If you use Windows 2000 and encounter locked files, proceed to Step 4.

4 (Windows 2000 only) Unlock the files you copied:

• Right-click the folder that contains the locked files, such as Lessons, and choose Properties from the contextual menu.

• In the Attributes area of the File Properties dialog box, deselect (uncheck) the Read-only check box, and then click Apply.

• In the Confirm Attributes Changes dialog box, select the option "Apply changes to this folder, subfolders, and files."

• Click OK to close the Confirm Attributes Changes dialog box, and click OK again to close the File Properties dialog box.

This final step is not necessary for Windows XP or Mac OS users.

Note: As you complete each lesson, you will overwrite the start files. If you want to restore the original files, recopy the corresponding Lesson folder from the Adobe Photoshop CS2 Classroom in a Book *CD to the Lessons folder on your hard drive.*

Restoring default preferences

The preferences files store palette and command settings information. Each time you quit Adobe Photoshop, the positions of the palettes and certain command settings are recorded in the respective preferences file. Any selections you make in the Preferences dialog box are also part of this type of application file.

At the beginning of each lesson in this book, you will be told to reset the default preferences, using a three-key combination. This deletes any options you may have selected in the Preferences dialog box.

You can ignore the instructions to reset your preferences. If you do so, be aware that the tools, palettes, and other settings in your Photoshop CS2 application may not match those described in this book, so you may have to be slightly more resourceful in finding things. With that in mind, you should be able to do the lesson without other difficulties.

Saving your monitor-calibration settings is a simple procedure that you should perform before you start work on this book; the procedure is described in the following section. If you have not custom-calibrated your color monitor, this procedure is unnecessary.

Saving the options you may have selected in the Preferences dialog box is beyond the scope of this book. If you are not sure how to do this yourself, get help from your network administrator. Otherwise, you can simply keep a record of preferences that you've customized, and then restore them manually after you finish these lessons.

To save your current color settings:

1 Start Adobe Photoshop.

2 Choose Edit > Color Settings.

3 In the Color Settings dialog box, examine the Settings menu.

- If the Settings menu is Custom, go on to Step 4 of this procedure.
- If the Settings option is anything other than Custom, click OK to close the dialog box. You do not need to do anything else.

4 Click the Save button. (Be careful to click Save, *not* OK.)

The Save dialog box opens. The default location is the Settings folder, which is where you want to save your file. The default file extension is .csf (color settings file).

5 In the File Name field (Windows) or Save As field (Mac OS), type a descriptive name for your color settings, preserving the .csf file extension. Then click Save.

6 In the Color Settings Comment dialog box, type any descriptive text that will help you identify the color settings later, such as the date, specific settings, or your workgroup.

7 Click OK to close the Color Settings Comment dialog box, and again to close the Color Settings dialog box.

To restore your color settings:

1 Start Adobe Photoshop.

2 Choose Edit > Color Settings.

3 In the Settings menu in the Color Settings dialog box, select the color-settings file you defined in the previous procedure.

4 Click OK.

Additional resources

Adobe Photoshop CS2 Classroom in a Book is not meant to replace documentation that comes with the program or to be a comprehensive reference for every feature in Photoshop CS2. Only the commands and options used in the lessons are explained in this book. For comprehensive information about program features, refer to any of these resources:

- Photoshop Help, which is the complete version of the user guide built into the Adobe Photoshop CS2 application. You can view it by choosing Help > Photoshop Help. For more information, see Lesson 1, "Getting to Know the Work Area."
- The Adobe Web site (www.adobe.com), which you can view by choosing Help > Photoshop Online if you have a connection to the World Wide Web.
- Adobe Studio (http://studio.adobe.com), where you can find a wealth of tips, tutorials, plug-ins, actions, and other design inspiration and instructional content.

- The *Adobe Photoshop CS2 User Guide*, which contains most of the material included in the Help system. If the User Guide book is not included in your Photoshop CS2 package, it is available for purchase at www.adobe.com. The Help system that is already built into the application contains all the information in the *User Guide*, plus additional information not included in the printed version.

- The Total Training Video Workshop CD, which comes in the Adobe Photoshop CS2 product box. These training videos contain 60 minutes of instruction by experienced industry leaders on both new and key features in Photoshop CS2.

Adobe Certification

The Adobe Training and Certification programs are designed to help Adobe customers and trainers improve and promote their product-proficiency skills. There are three levels of certification:

- Adobe Certified Expert (ACE)
- Adobe Certified Instructor (ACI)
- Adobe Authorized Training Center (AATC)

The Adobe Certified Expert program is a way for expert users to upgrade their credentials. You can use Adobe certification as a catalyst for getting a raise, finding a job, or promoting your expertise.

If you are an ACE-level instructor, the Adobe Certified Instructor program takes your skills to the next level and gives you access to a wide range of Adobe resources.

Adobe Authorized Training Centers offer instructor-led courses and training on Adobe products, employing only Adobe Certified Instructors. A directory of AATCs is available at http://partners.adobe.com.

For information on the Adobe Certified programs, visit www.adobe.com/support/certification/main.html.

As you work with Adobe Photoshop, you'll discover that there is often more than one way to accomplish the same task. To make the best use of the extensive editing capabilities in Photoshop, you must first learn to navigate the work area.

1 Getting to Know the Work Area

Lesson overview

In this lesson, you'll learn how to do the following:

- Open Adobe Photoshop files.
- Select and use some of the tools in the toolbox.
- Set options for a selected tool using the tool options bar.
- Use various methods of zooming in and out on an image.
- Select, rearrange, and use palettes.
- Choose commands on palette and context menus.
- Open and use a palette docked in the palette well.
- Undo actions to correct mistakes or to make different choices.
- Customize the workspace.
- Jump from Photoshop to ImageReady.
- Find topics in Photoshop Help.

This lesson will take about an hour and a half to complete. Before starting Adobe Photoshop, locate the Lesson01 folder on the *Adobe Photoshop CS2 Classroom in a Book* CD, and copy the folder into the Lessons folder that you created on your hard disk for these projects (or create it now). As you work on this lesson, you'll overwrite the start files. If you need to restore the start files, copy them again from the *Adobe Photoshop CS2 Classroom in a Book* CD.

Starting to work in Adobe Photoshop

The Adobe Photoshop work area includes the command menus at the top of your screen and a variety of tools and palettes for editing and adding elements to your image. You can also add commands and filters to the menus by installing third-party software known as *plug-in modules.*

Photoshop works with bitmapped, digitized images (that is, continuous-tone images that have been converted into a series of small squares, or picture elements, called *pixels*). You can also work with vector graphics, which are drawings made of smooth lines that retain their crispness when scaled. You can create original artwork in Photoshop, or you can import images into the program from many sources, such as:

- Photographs from a digital camera.
- Commercial CDs of digital images.
- Scans of photographs, transparencies, negatives, graphics, or other documents.
- Captured video images.
- Artwork created in drawing programs.

For information on the kinds of files you can use with Adobe Photoshop CS2, see "About file formats" in Photoshop Help.

Starting Photoshop and opening a file

To begin, you'll start Adobe Photoshop and reset the default preferences.

Note: *Usually, you won't reset the defaults when you're on your own. However, while you're working in this book, you'll reset them each time so that what you see onscreen matches the descriptions in the lessons. See "Restoring default preferences" on page 6.*

1 On the desktop, double-click the Adobe Photoshop icon to start Adobe Photoshop and then immediately hold down Ctrl-Alt-Shift (Windows) or Command-Option-Shift (Mac OS) to reset the default settings.

If you don't see the Photoshop icon on your desktop, choose Start > All Programs > Adobe Photoshop CS2 (Windows) or look in either the Applications folder or the Dock (Mac OS).

2 When prompted, click Yes to confirm that you want to delete the Adobe Photoshop Settings File, and then click Close to close the Welcome Screen.

The Photoshop work area appears as shown in the following illustration.

***Note:** The following illustration shows the Mac OS version of Photoshop. On Windows, the arrangement is the same, but operating system styles may vary.*

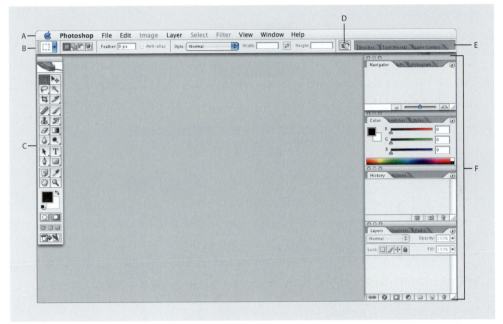

***A.** Menu bar **B.** Tool options bar **C.** Toolbox **D.** Adobe Bridge button **E.** Palette well **F.** Floating palettes*

The default work area in Photoshop consists of a menu bar at the top of the screen, a tool options bar below the menu bar, a floating toolbox on the left, floating palettes, and one or more image windows, which are opened separately.

3 Choose File > Open, and navigate to the Lessons/Lesson01/Project1 folder that you copied to your hard drive from the *Adobe Photoshop CS2 Classroom in a Book* CD.

4 Select the 01End1.psd file and click Open.

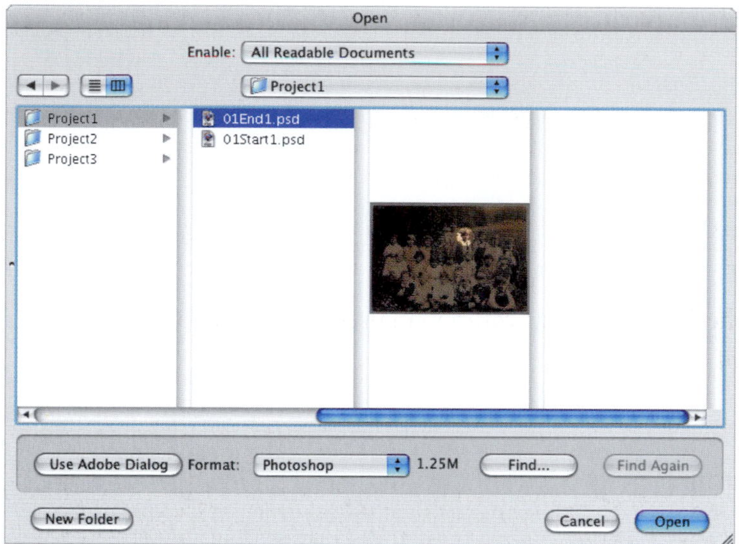

The 01End1.psd file opens in its own window, called the *image window*. The end files in this book show you what you are creating in the different projects. In this end file, an old school photograph has been enhanced so that one student in the class appears spotlighted while the rest of the picture appears to be in shadow.

5 Choose File > Close, or click the close button on the title bar of the window in which the photograph appears. (Do not close Photoshop.)

Opening a file with Adobe Bridge

In this book, you'll work with different start files in each lesson. You may make copies of these files and save them under different names or locations, or you may work from the original start files and then copy them from the CD again if you want a fresh start. There are three start files for this lesson, each of which is in its own Project folder.

In the previous exercise, you used the classic method of opening a file. Now you'll open another file using the Adobe Bridge visual file browser, which helps take the guesswork out of finding the image file that you need.

1 Click the Go to Bridge button ( ) on the tool options bar.

Adobe Bridge opens, displaying a collection of palettes, menus, buttons, and panes.

Note: You can also open Adobe Bridge by choosing File > Browse.

2 In the Folders palette in the upper left corner of Bridge, navigate to the Lessons/Lesson01 folder on your hard drive and select the Project1 folder nested within it.

When you select the Project1 folder, thumbnail previews of the folder contents appear in the right pane of Bridge.

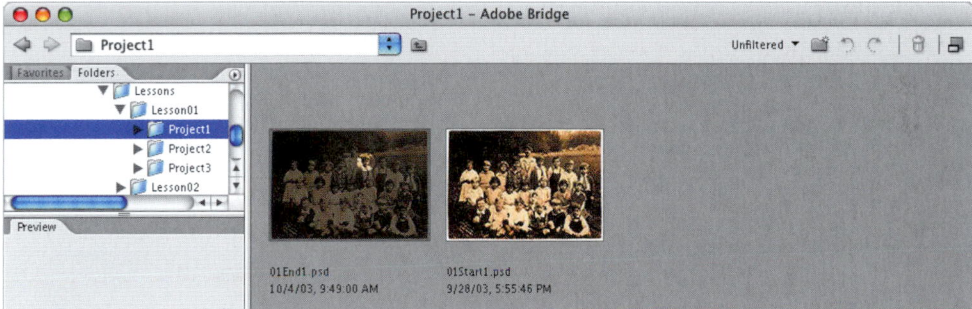

3 Select the 01Start1.psd file and open it by double-clicking its thumbnail, or use the Bridge menu bar and choose File > Open.

The 01Start1.psd image opens in Photoshop.

Adobe Bridge is much more than a convenient visual interface for opening files. You'll have the chance to learn more about the many features and functions of Adobe Bridge in Lesson 2, "Using Adobe Bridge."

Note: Leave Bridge open for the moment, as you may use it to locate and open files later in this lesson.

Using the tools

Photoshop provides an integrated set of tools for producing sophisticated graphics for print, Web, and mobile viewing. We could easily fill an entire book with details on the wealth of Photoshop tools and tool configurations. While that would certainly be a useful reference, it's not the goal of this book. Instead, you'll start gaining experience by configuring and using a few tools on a sample project. Every lesson will introduce you to more tools and ways to use them. By the time you finish all the lessons in this book, you'll have a solid foundation for further explorations of the Photoshop tool set.

Selecting and using a tool from the toolbox

The toolbox—the long, narrow palette on the far left side of the work area—contains selection tools, painting and editing tools, foreground- and background-color selection boxes, and viewing tools.

Let's start by using the Zoom tool, which appears in many other Adobe applications, including Illustrator, InDesign, and Acrobat.

Note: For a complete list of the tools in the toolbox, see the toolbox overview on page 48.

1 Examine the status bar at the bottom of the image window and notice the percentage listed on the far left end. This represents the current enlargement view of the image, or zoom level.

A. Zoom level B. Status bar

Note: In Windows, the status bar may appear across the bottom of the work area.

2 Move the pointer over the toolbox and hover it over the magnifying-glass icon until a tooltip appears, identifying the tool by name and providing its keyboard shortcut.

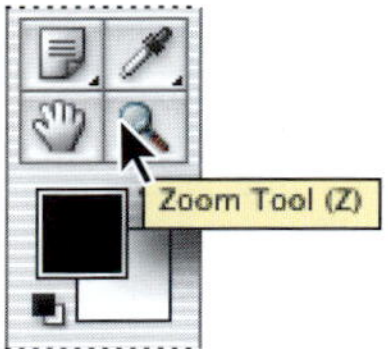

3 Select the Zoom tool by either clicking the Zoom tool button (🔍) in the toolbox or by pressing Z, the keyboard shortcut for the Zoom tool.

4 Move the pointer over the image window. Notice that it now looks like a tiny magnifying glass with a plus sign (+) in the center of the glass.

5 Click anywhere in the image window.

The image enlarges to a preset percentage level, which replaces the previous value in the status bar. The location you clicked when you used the Zoom tool becomes the center of the enlarged view. If you click again, the zoom advances to the next preset level, up to a maximum of 1600%.

6 Hold down the Alt key (Windows) or Option key (Mac OS) so that the Zoom tool pointer appears with a minus sign (–) in the center of the magnifying glass, and then click anywhere in the image. Then release the Alt or Option key.

Now the view zooms out to a lower preset magnification. Examine the photograph and decide which child you want to spotlight.

Note: *There are other ways to zoom out. For example, you can select the Zoom In (🔍) or Zoom Out (🔍) mode on the Zoom tool options bar. You can choose View > Zoom In or View > Zoom Out. Or, you can type a lower percentage in the status bar and press Enter (Windows) or Return (Mac OS).*

7 Using the Zoom tool, drag a rectangle to enclose the area of the image that includes the child you want to spotlight.

The image enlarges so that the area you enclosed in your rectangle now fills the entire image window.

You have now tried three ways of using the Zoom tool to change the magnification in the image window: clicking, holding down a keyboard modifier while clicking, and dragging to define a magnification area. Many of the other tools in the toolbox can be used with keyboard combinations. You'll have opportunities to use these techniques in various lessons in this book.

Selecting and using a hidden tool

Photoshop has many tools you can use to edit image files, but you will probably work with only a few of them at a time. The toolbox arranges some of the tools in groups, with only one tool shown for each group. The other tools in the group are hidden behind that tool.

A small triangle in the lower right corner of a button is your clue that other tools are available but hidden under that tool.

1 Position the pointer over the tool at the top of the left toolbox column until the tooltip appears, identifying it as the Rectangular Marquee tool ([]) with the keyboard shortcut M. Then select that tool.

2 Select the Elliptical Marquee tool (○), which is hidden behind the Rectangular Marquee tool, using one of the following methods:

- Press and hold the mouse button over the Rectangular Marquee tool to open the pop-up list of hidden tools, and select the Elliptical Marquee tool.

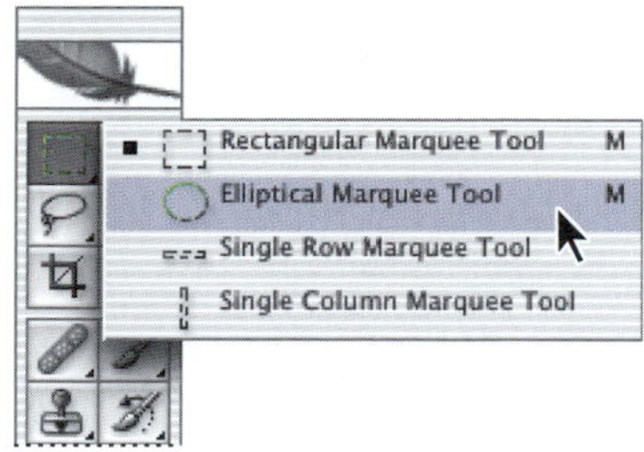

- Alt-click (Windows) or Option-click (Mac OS) the tool button in the toolbox to cycle through the hidden marquee tools until the Elliptical Marquee tool is selected.
- Press Shift-M, which switches between the Rectangular and Elliptical Marquee tools.

3 Move the pointer over the image window so that it appears as crosshairs (-¦-) and move it to the upper left side of the child's head.

4 Drag the pointer down and to the right to draw an ellipse around the child and then release the mouse button.

An animated dashed line indicates that the area inside it is *selected*. When you select an area, it becomes the only editable area of the image. The area outside the selection is protected.

5 Move the pointer inside your elliptical selection so that the pointer appears as an arrow with a small rectangle (▷⬚).

6 Drag the selection so that it is accurately centered over the child.

When you drag the selection, only the selection border moves, not pixels in the image. When you want to move the pixels in the image, you'll need to use a different technique, which you'll learn a little later. There's more about making different kinds of selections and moving the selection contents in Lesson 5, "Working with Selections."

Using keyboard combinations with tool actions

Many tools can operate under certain constraints. You usually activate these modes by holding down specific keyboard keys as you move the tool with the mouse. Some tools have modes that you choose on the tool options bar.

The next task is to make a fresh start at selecting the child. This time, you'll use a keyboard combination that constrains the elliptical selection to a circle that you'll draw from the center outward instead of from the outside inward.

1 Make sure that the Elliptical Marquee tool (○) is still selected in the toolbox, and deactivate the current selection by doing one of the following:

- In the image window, click anywhere outside the selected area.
- Choose Select > Deselect.
- Use the keyboard shortcut Ctrl-D (Windows) or Command-D (Mac OS).

2 Position the pointer in the center of the child's face.

3 Press Alt-Shift (Windows) or Option-Shift (Mac OS) and drag outward from the center of the face until the circle completely encloses the child's face.

4 Carefully release first the mouse button and then the keyboard keys.

If you are not satisfied with the selection circle, you can move it: Place the pointer inside the circle and drag, or click outside the selection circle to deselect it and then try again.

Note: *If you accidentally release one or both of the keys prematurely, the tool reverts to its normal behavior (unconstrained and drawing from the edge). If, however, you haven't yet released the mouse button, you can just press the keys down again, and the selection changes back. If you have released the mouse button, simply start again at Step 1.*

5 In the toolbox, double-click the Zoom tool (🔍) to return to 100% view. If the entire image doesn't fit in the image window, then click the Fit Screen button on the tool options bar.

Notice that the selection remains active, even after you use the Zoom tool.

Applying a change to a selected area

In order to spotlight the selected child, you'll want to darken the rest of the image, not the area inside the current selection. Since the area within the selection is protected from change, you'll invert the selection, making the rest of the image active and preventing the change from affecting the one child's face.

1 Choose Select > Inverse.

Although the animated selection border around the child looks the same, notice that a similar border appears all around the edges of the image. Now the rest of the image is selected and can be edited, while the area within the circle is not selected and cannot be changed while the selection is active.

***A.** Selected (editable) area **B.** Unselected (protected) area*

2 Choose Image > Adjustments > Curves.

The keyboard shortcut for this command, Ctrl-M (Windows) or Command-M (Mac OS) appears by the command name on the Adjustments submenu. In the future, you may just press that keyboard combination to open the Curves dialog box.

3 In the Curves dialog box, make sure that the Preview option is selected. If necessary, drag the dialog box to one side so that you can see most of the image window.

The Preview option shows the effect of your selections in the image window, so the picture changes as you adjust settings. This saves you from having to repeatedly open and close dialog boxes as you experiment with different options.

4 Drag the control point in the upper right corner of the graph straight down until the value shown in the Output option is approximately 150. (The Input value should remain unchanged.)

As you drag, the highlights are reduced in the selected area of the image.

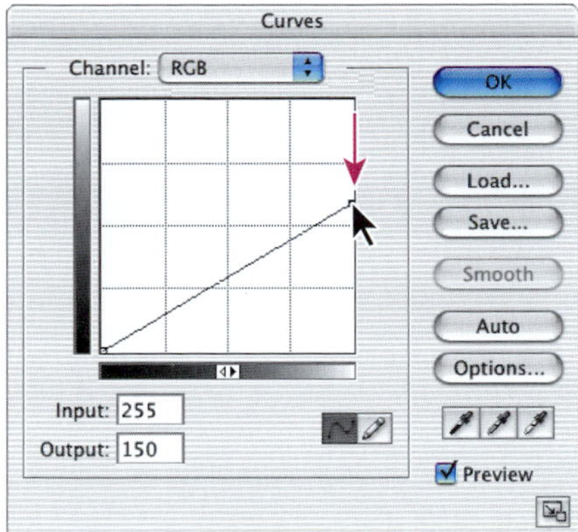

5 Examine the results in the image window and then adjust the Output value up or down until you are satisfied with the results.

6 Click OK to close the Curves dialog box.

7 Do one of the following:

- If you want to save your changes, choose File > Save and then choose File > Close.
- If you want to revert to the unaltered version of the file, choose File > Close and click No when you are asked if you want to save your changes.
- If you want to do both of the above, choose File > Save As, and then either rename the file or save it to a different folder on your computer, and click OK. Then choose File > Close.

You don't have to deselect, because closing the file cancels the selection.

Congratulations! You've just finished your first Photoshop project. Although the Curves dialog box is actually one of the more sophisticated methods of altering an image, it isn't difficult to use, as you have seen. You will learn more about making adjustments to images in many other lessons in this book. Lessons 3, 4, and 8, in particular, address techniques like those used in classic darkroom work, such as adjusting for exposure, retouching, and correcting colors.

Zooming and scrolling with the Navigator palette

The Navigator palette is another speedy way to make large changes in the zoom level, especially when the exact percentage of magnification is unimportant. It's also a great way to scroll around in an image, because the thumbnail shows you exactly what part of the image appears in the image window.

The slider under the image thumbnail in the Navigator palette enlarges the image when you drag it to the right (toward the large mountain icon) and reduces it when you drag to the left.

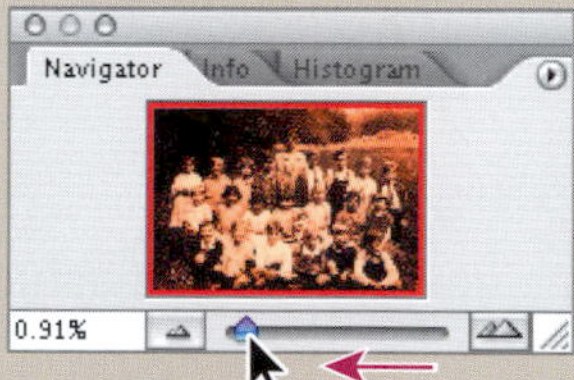

The red rectanglar outline represents the area of the image that appears in the image window. When you zoom in far enough that the image window shows only part of the image, you can drag the red outline around the thumbnail area to see other areas of the image.This also is an excellent way to verify which part of an image you're working on when you work at very high zoom levels.

Using the tool options bar and other palettes

You've already had some experience with the tool options bar. In the previous project, you saw that there are options on the tool options bar for the Zoom tool that change the view of the current image window. Now we will learn more about setting tool properties on the tool options bar, as well as using palettes and palette menus.

Previewing and opening another file

The next project involves a promotional postcard for a community project. First, let's preview the end file so we can see what we're aiming to do.

1 Click the Go to Bridge button on the tool options bar.

2 In the Bridge Folders palette, click the Project2 folder.

3 Select the 01End2.psd file in the thumbnail preview area so that it appears in the Preview palette.

4 Examine the image and notice the text that is set against the cloudlike area across the lower part of the image.

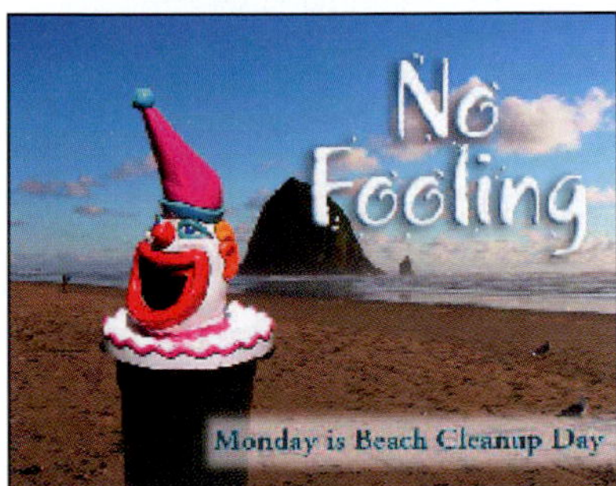

5 Select the thumbnail for the 01Start2.psd file and double-click to open it in Photoshop.

Setting tool properties on the tool options bar

With the 01Start2.psd file open in Photoshop, you're ready to select the characteristics for the text and then to type your message.

1 In the toolbox, select the Horizontal Type tool (T).

The buttons and menu on the tool options bar now relate to the Type tool.

2 On the tool options bar, select a font you like from the first pop-up menu. (We used Adobe Garamond, but you can use another font if you prefer.)

3 Specify **12 pt** as the font size. You can specify 12 points using the font-size pop-up menu, by typing directly in the font-size text box and pressing Enter (Windows) or Return (Mac OS), or by scrubbing the font-size menu label.

You can place the cursor over the labels of most numeric settings on the tool options bar, in palettes, and in dialog boxes in Photoshop, and the "scrubby slider" appears. Dragging this pointing-finger slider icon to the right increases the value; dragging to the left decreases the value. Alt-dragging (Windows) or Option-dragging (Mac OS) changes the values in smaller increments; Shift-dragging changes them in larger increments.

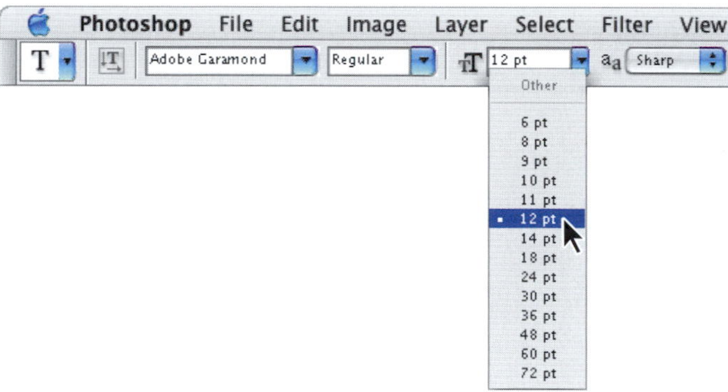

4 Click once anywhere on the left side of the image and type **Monday is Beach Cleanup Day.**

The text appears with the font and font-size formatting that you selected.

5 In the toolbox, select the Move tool (▸✢) at the top of the column on the right.

Note: *Don't select the Move tool using the V keyboard shortcut, because you're in text-entry mode. Typing V will add the letter to your text in the image window.*

6 Position the Move tool pointer over the text you typed and drag the text into the misty white rectangle near the bottom of the image, centering the text inside it.

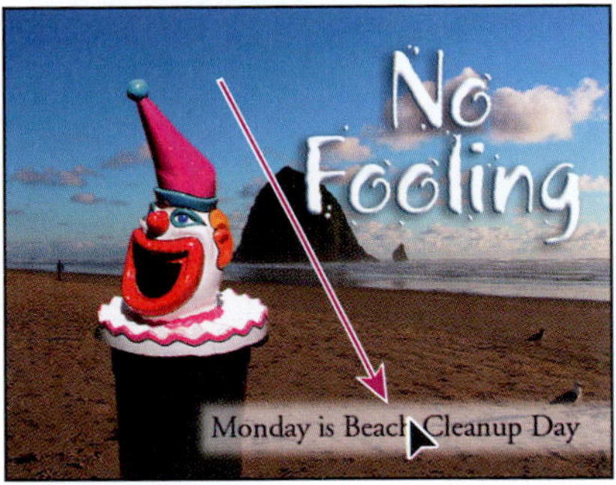

Using palettes and palette menus

The text color in your image is the same as the Foreground Color swatch in the toolbox, which is black by default. The text in the end-file example was a dark blue that coordinates nicely with the rest of the image. You'll color the text by selecting it and then choosing another color.

1 In the toolbox, select the Horizontal Type tool (T).

2 Drag the Horizontal Type tool across the text to select all the words.

3 In the Color palette group, click the Swatches tab to bring that palette forward.

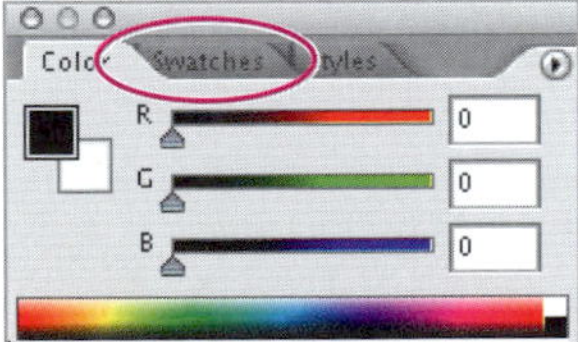

4 Select any swatch. The color you select appears in three places: as the Foreground Color in the toolbox, in the text color swatch on the tool options bar, and in the text you

typed in the image window. (Select any other tool in the toolbox to deselect the text so that you can see the color applied to it.)

Note: *When you move the pointer over the swatches, it temporarily changes into an eyedropper. Set the tip of the eyedropper on the swatch you want, and click to select it.*

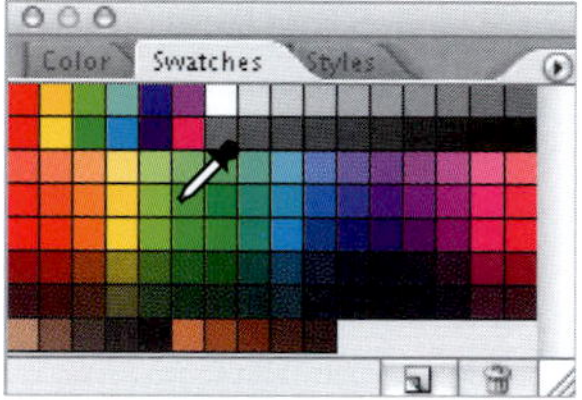

That's how easy it is to select a color, although there are other methods in Photoshop. However, you'll use a specific color for this project, and it's easier to find it if you change the Swatches palette display.

5 Make sure that the Horizontal Type tool is not still selected. Click the arrow (◉) on the Swatches palette to open the palette menu, and choose the Small List command.

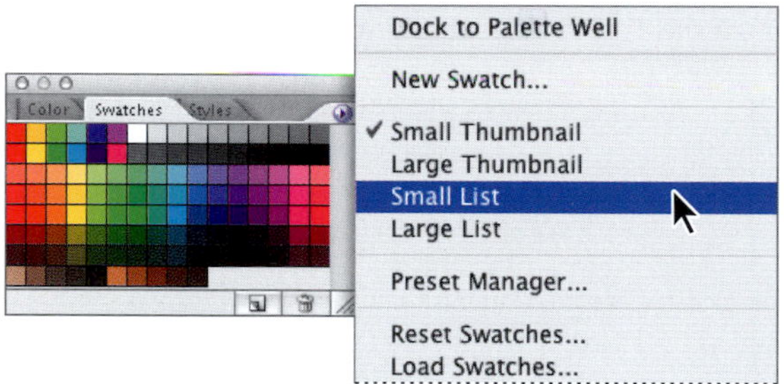

6 Select the Type tool and reselect the text, as you did in Steps 1 and 2.

7 In the Swatches palette, scroll down to near the bottom of the list to find the Darker Cyan swatch, and then select it.

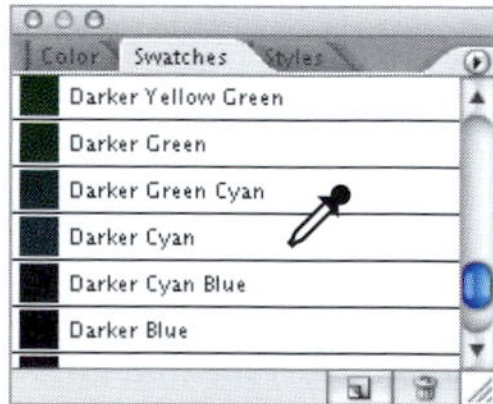

Now the text appears in the Darker Cyan color.

8 Select the Hand tool (✋) to deselect the text. Then click the Default Foreground and Background Colors icon (■) on the toolbox to make Black the foreground color.

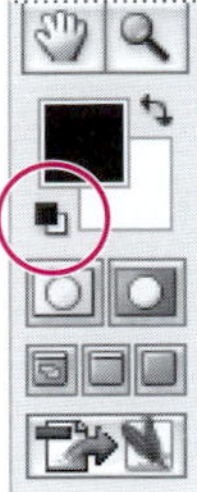

Resetting the default colors does not change the color of the text, because the text is no longer selected.

9 You've finished the task, so close the file. You can either save it, close it without saving, or save it under a different name or location, as you did for your Project1 file.

It's as simple as that—you've completed another project. Nice job!

Undoing actions in Photoshop

In a perfect world, you'd never make a mistake. You'd never click the wrong item. You'd always perfectly anticipate how specific actions would bring your design ideas to life exactly as you imagined them. In a perfect world, you'd never have to backtrack.

For the real world, Photoshop gives you the power to step back and undo actions so that you can try other options. Our next project provides you with an opportunity to experiment freely, knowing that you can reverse the process.

This project also introduces you to layering, which is one of the fundamental and most powerful features in Photoshop. There are many kinds of Photoshop layers, some of which contain images, text, or solid colors, and others that simply interact with layers below them. The file for this next project has both kinds of layers. You don't have to understand layers to complete this project successfully, so don't worry about that right now. You'll learn more about layers in Lesson 6, "Layer Basics," and Lesson 11, "Advanced Layer Techniques."

Undoing a single action

Even beginning computer users quickly learn to use and appreciate the familiar Undo command. As we will do each time we start a new project, we'll begin by looking at the final result.

1 Click the Go to Bridge button and navigate to the Lessons/Lesson01/Project3 folder.

2 Select the 01End3.psd file so that you can see the results you'll achieve in this exercise. After you've studied it in the Preview pane, double-click the 01Start3.psd file thumbnail to open it in Photoshop.

Notice the listings in the Layers palette. The Tie Designs layer is a clipping mask. A clipping mask works somewhat like a selection in that it restricts the area of the image that can be altered. With the clipping mask in place, you can paint a design over the man's tie without worrying about any stray brush strokes disturbing the rest of the image. The Tie Designs layer is selected, because it's the layer you'll be editing now.

3 In the toolbox, select the Brush tool (🖌), or press B to select it by its keyboard shortcut.

4 On the tool options bar, click the Brushes tab in the palette well to temporarily open the Brushes palette.

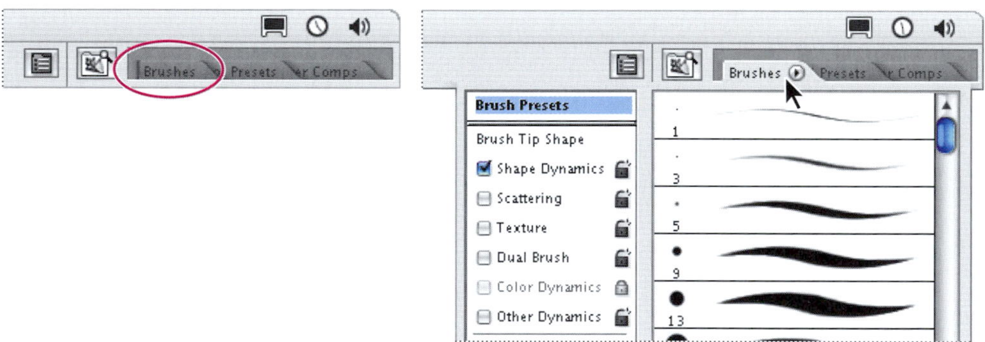

5 Scroll down the list of brushes and select the Soft Round 35-pixel brush. (The name will appear as a tooltip if you hover the pointer over a brush.)

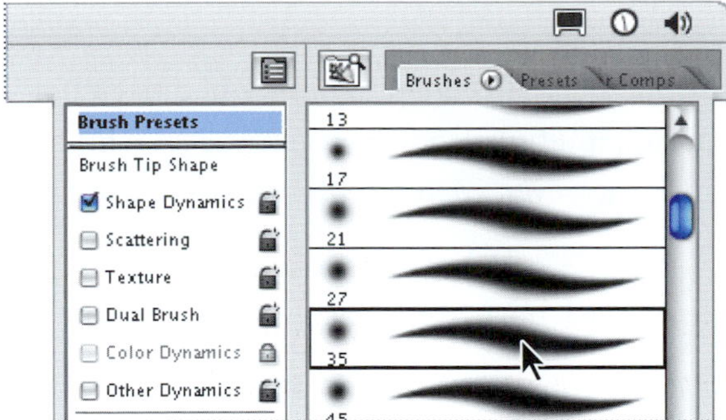

If you want to try a different brush, that's OK, but select a brush that's reasonably close to 35 pixels—preferably between 20 and 50 pixels.

6 Move the pointer over the image so that it appears as a circle with the diameter you selected in Step 5. Then draw a stripe anywhere in the yellow tie. You don't have to worry about staying within the lines, because the brush won't paint anything outside the tie clipping mask.

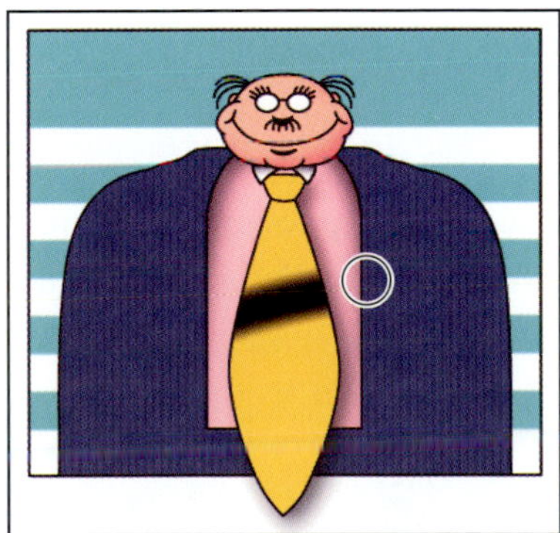

Oops! Your stripe may be very nice, but the design calls for dots, so you'll need to remove the painted stripe.

7 Choose Edit > Undo Brush Tool, or press Ctrl-Z (Windows) or Command-Z (Mac OS) to undo the Brush tool action.

The tie is again a solid yellow color, with no stripe.

Note: *You'll get more experience with clipping masks in Lesson 10, "Vector Drawing Techniques," and in Lesson 11, "Advanced Layer Techniques."*

Undoing multiple actions

The Undo command reverses only one step. This is a practicality because Photoshop files can be very large, and maintaining multiple Undo steps can tie up a lot of memory, which tends to degrade performance. However, you can still step back through multiple actions using the History palette.

1 Using the same Brush tool settings, click once over the (unstriped) yellow tie to create a soft dot.

2 Click several more times in different areas on the tie to create a pattern of dots.

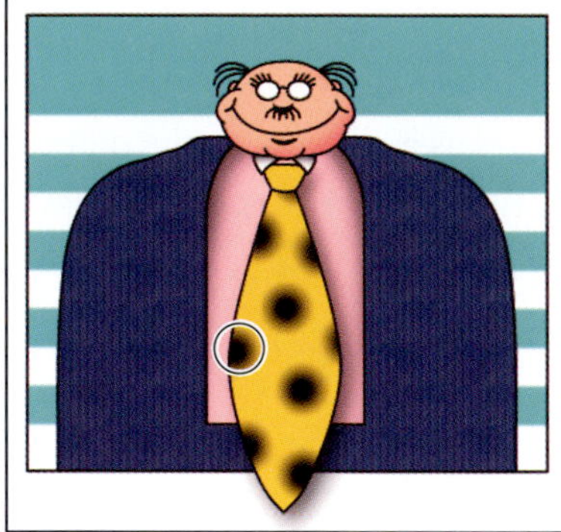

3 Using the History palette tab, drag it from its palette group to a position next to the other palettes. Then, drag down the lower right corner of the History palette to expand it so that you can see more steps. (This isolating and resizing is only for convenience.)

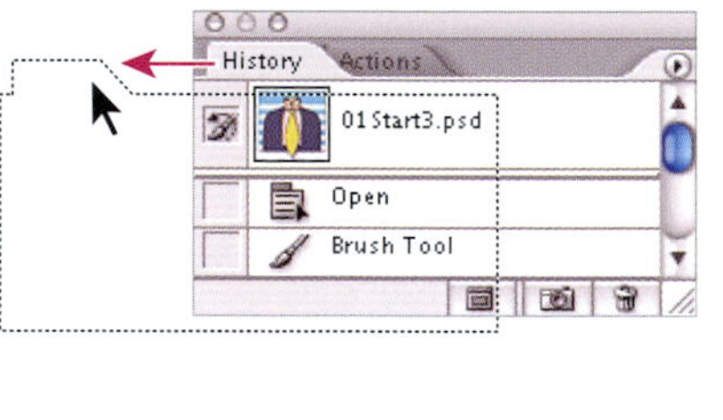

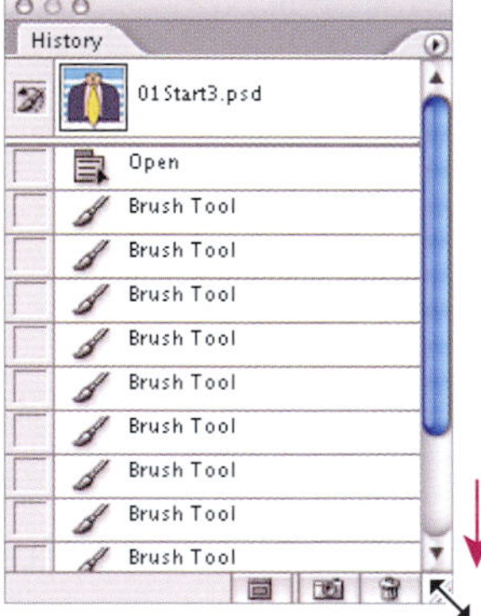

You can also expand the History palette by clicking the minimize/maximize button (Windows) or the green zoom button (Mac OS) on the palette title bar. This resizes the palette so that all the current history states are in view.

The History palette records the recent actions you've performed in the image. The current state is selected, at the bottom of the list.

4 Click one of the earlier actions in the History palette, and examine the changes this causes in the image window: Several previous actions are undone.

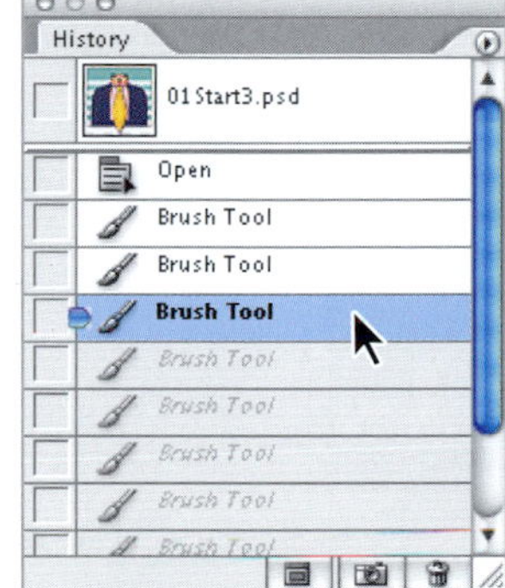

5 In the image window, create a new dot on the tie with the Brush tool.

Notice that the History palette has removed the dimmed actions that had been listed after the selected history state and has added a new one.

6 Choose Edit > Undo Brush Tool or press Ctrl-Z (Windows) or Command-Z (Mac OS) to undo the dot you created in Step 5.

Now the History palette restores the earlier listing of dimmed actions.

7 Select the state at the bottom of the History palette list.

The image is restored to the condition it was in when you finished Step 2 of this exercise.

By default, the Photoshop History palette retains only the last 20 actions. This is also a compromise, striking a balance between flexibility and performance. You can change the number of levels in the History palette by choosing Edit > Preferences > General

(Windows) or Photoshop > Preferences > General (Mac OS) and typing a different number in the History States option.

You'll explore the History palette more in Lesson 4, "Retouching and Repairing."

Using a context menu

Context menus are short menus that are appropriate to specific elements in the work area. They are sometimes referred to as "right-click" or "shortcut" menus. Usually, the commands on a context menu are also available in some other area of the user interface, but using the context menu can save time.

1 If the Brush tool (🖌) is not still selected in the toolbox, select it now.

2 In the image window, right-click (Windows) or Control-click (Mac OS) anywhere in the image to open the Brush tool context menu.

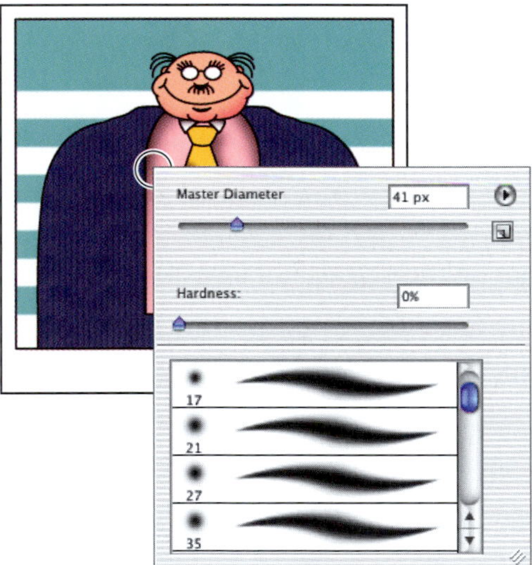

Context menus vary with their context, of course, so what appears can be a menu of commands or a palette-like set of options, which is what happens in this case.

3 Select a finer brush, such as the Hard Round 5-pixel brush. You may need to scroll up or down the list in the context menu to find the right brush.

4 In the image window, use the selected brush to create smaller dots on the tie.

Note: Clicking anywhere in the work area closes the context menu. If the tie area is hidden behind the Brush tool context menu, click another area or double-click your selection in the context menu to close it.

5 Place additional dots on the tie.

6 As it suits you, use the Undo command and the History palette to backtrack through your painting actions to correct mistakes or make different choices.

When you finish making changes to your tie design, give yourself a pat on the back because you've finished another project. You can choose File > Save if you want to save your results, or File > Save As if you want to save it in another location or with a different name, or you can close the file without saving.

More about palettes and palette locations

Photoshop palettes are powerful and varied. You rarely would have a project in which you needed to see all palettes simultaneously. That's why they're in palette groups and why the default configurations leave some palettes unopened.

The complete list of palettes appears on the Window menu, with check marks by the names of the palettes that are open at the front of their palette groups. You can open a closed palette or close an open one by selecting the palette name on the Window menu.

You can hide all palettes at once—including the tool options bar and toolbox—by pressing the Tab key. To reopen them, press Tab again.

You already used the palette well when you opened the Brushes palette for Project3. You can drag palettes to or from the palette well. This is convenient for bulky palettes or ones that you use only occasionally but want to keep handy.

Other actions that you can use to arrange palettes include the following:

- To move an entire palette group, drag the title bar to another location in the work area.
- To move a palette to another group, drag the palette tab into that palette group so that a black highlight appears inside the group, and then release the mouse button.

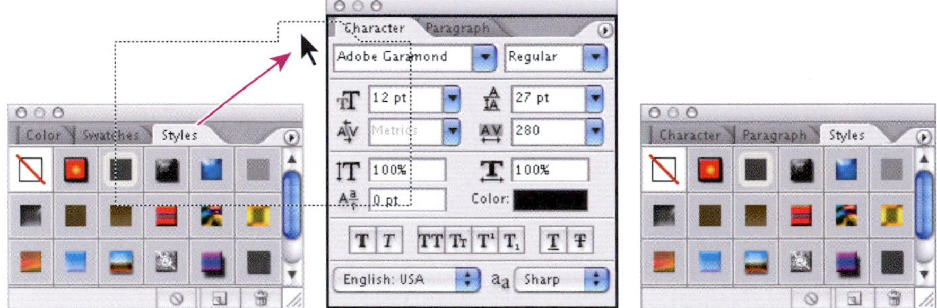

- To dock a palette in the palette well on the tool options bar, drag the palette tab into the palette well so that the palette well is highlighted.

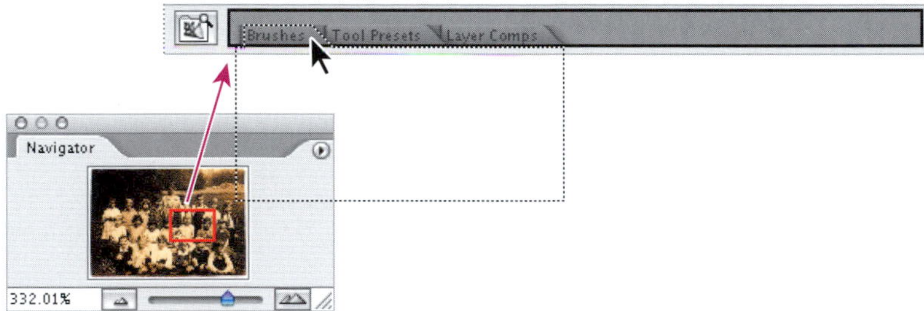

Expanding and collapsing palettes

You can also resize a palette to see more or fewer of the available options it contains, either by dragging or clicking to toggle between preset sizes.

- To change the height of a palette, drag its lower right corner.
- To expand a palette to show as much as possible of its contents, click the minimize/maximize button (Windows) or the zoom button (Mac OS). Click a second time to collapse the palette group.

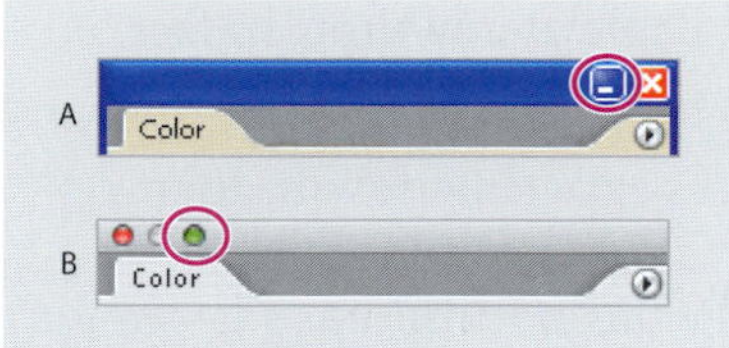

A. Windows B. Mac OS

- To collapse a palette group so that only the title bar and tabs are visible, double-click a palette tab or palette title bar. Double-click again to restore it to the expanded view.

Notice that the tabs for the various palettes in the palette group and the button for the palette menu remain visible after you collapse a palette.

***Note:** You cannot resize the Color, Character, and Paragraph palettes.*

Special notes about the toolbox and tool options bar

The toolbox and the tool options bar share some characteristics with the other palettes:

- You can drag the toolbox by its title bar to a different location in the work area. You can move the tool options bar to another location by dragging the grab bar at the far left end of the palette.
- You can hide the toolbox and tool options bar.

However, there are other palette features that are not available or do not apply to the toolbox or tool options bar:

- You cannot group the toolbox or tool options bar with other palettes.
- You cannot resize the toolbox or tool options bar.
- You cannot dock the toolbox in the palette well. (The same is true for the tool options bar, because the palette well appears on the tool options bar.)
- The toolbox and tool options bar do not have palette menus.

Customizing the workspace

It's great that Photoshop offers so many ways to control the display and location of the tool options bar and its many palettes, but it can be time-consuming to drag palettes around the screen so that you can see some palettes for certain projects and other palettes for other projects. Luckily, Photoshop lets you customize your workspace, controlling what palettes, tools, and menus are available at any time. In fact, it comes with a few preset workspaces suitable for different types of workflows—tone and color correction, painting and retouching, and so on. Let's experiment with them.

Note: *If you closed 01Start3.psd at the end of the previous exercise, open it—or open any other image file—to complete the following exercise.*

1 Choose Window > Workspace > Color and Tonal Correction. If prompted, click Yes to apply the workspace.

If you've been experimenting with opening, closing, and moving palettes, you'll notice that Photoshop lines up the floating palettes along the right edge of the workspace. Otherwise, it may appear that nothing changes in the workspace. As you're about to see, however, Photoshop has colored many of the menu commands that are commonly used for color and tonal corrections.

2 Click the Window menu, and drag over the other menus to see that color and tonal-correction commands now appear orange.

3 Choose Window > Workspace > Web Design. If prompted, click Yes to apply the workspace.

4 Click the Window menu, and drag over the other menus to see that Web design–related commands now appear purple.

For times when presets don't suit your purposes, you can customize the workspace to your specific needs. Say, for example, that you do lots of Web design, but no digital video work.

5 Click the Image menu and drag down to see the Pixel Aspect Ratio subcommands.

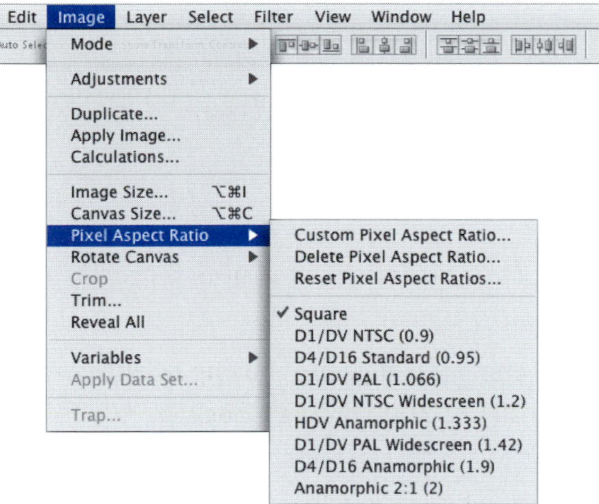

These subcommands include several DV formats that many print and Web designers don't need to use.

6 Choose Window > Workspace > Keyboard Shortcuts & Menus.

The Keyboard Shortcuts and Menus dialog box lets you control availability of the application and palette menu commands, as well as create custom keyboard shortcuts for menus, palettes, and tools. For instance, you can hide commands that you use infrequently, or highlight commonly used commands to make them easier to see.

7 In the Menus tab of the Keyboard Shortcuts and Menus dialog box, choose Menu For: > Application Menus.

8 Toggle open the Image menu command by clicking its right-pointing triangle.

When it's open you will see the Image menu commands and subcommands, including Mode, Adjustments, and Duplicate.

9 Scroll down to Pixel Aspect Ratio and click the eye icon to turn off visibility for all of the DV and video formats—there are eight of them, beginning with D1/DV NTSC (0.9) through Anamorphic 2:1 (2).

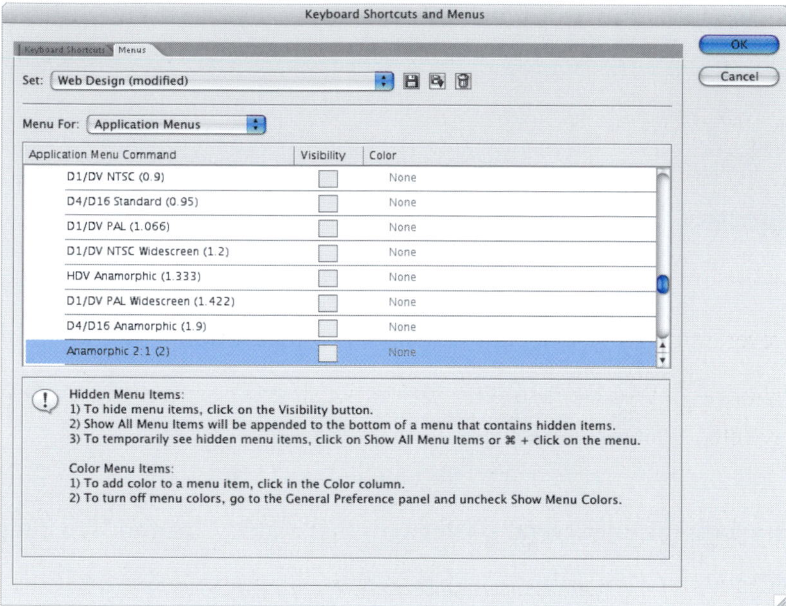

10 Now scroll up to the Image > Mode > RGB command, and click None in the Color column. Choose Red from the pop-up menu.

11 Click OK to close the Keyboard Shortcuts and Menus dialog box.

12 Click the Image menu command and scroll down: The Image > Mode > RGB command is now highlighted in red, and the DV and video formats are unavailable from the Pixel Aspect Ratio subcommand.

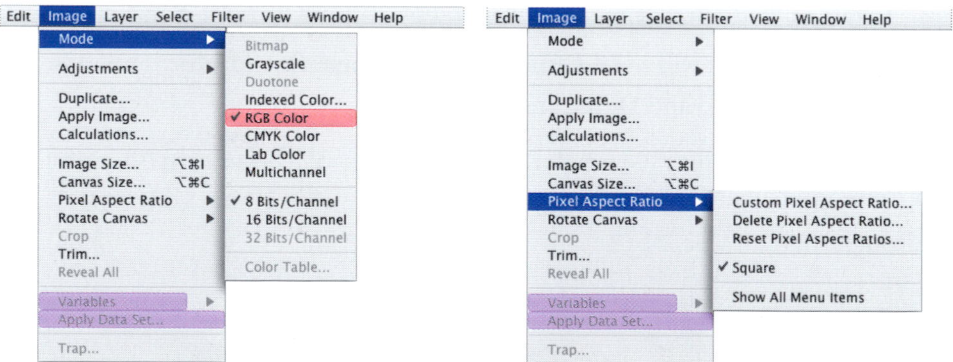

You can save this workspace by choosing Window > Workspace > Save Workspace. In the Save Workspace dialog box, give your workspace a name; make sure the Menus,

Palette Locations, and Keyboard Shortcuts boxes are checked; and then click Save. Then, your custom workspace will be listed in the Window > Workspace submenu.

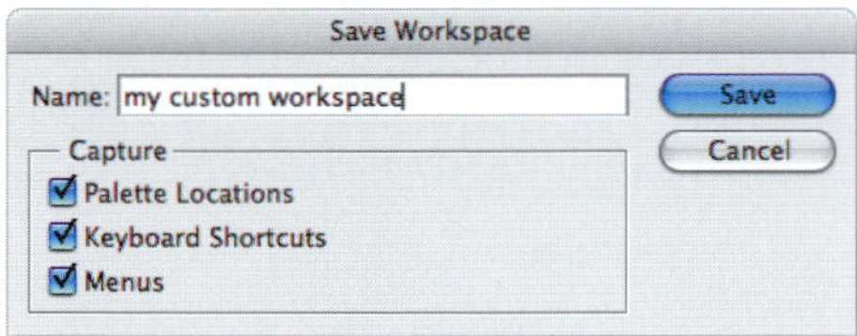

For now, however, return to the default workspace configuration.

13 Choose Window > Workspace > Default Workspace. When prompted, click Don't Save to not save changes to the menu file.

Jumping to Adobe ImageReady

Adobe ImageReady is a companion application to Photoshop that lets you create moving elements, such as animations and rollovers, and other image content for Web and mobile authoring. ImageReady contains many tools that are familiar to Photoshop users and some that are unique. Because ImageReady is Web-focused, it automatically reduces high-resolution images to 72 dpi. So it's a good idea to always work on high-resolution content in Photoshop, but you can easily jump between the applications to access the unique features of each application, yet still maintain a streamlined workflow.

1 Switch to ImageReady by clicking the Edit in ImageReady button ( ) in the Photoshop toolbox. If the ImageReady Welcome Screen appears, click Close.

Note: *To reset preferences as you open ImageReady, hold down Ctrl-Alt-Shift (Windows) or Command-Option-Shift (Mac OS) when you click the Edit in ImageReady button ( ). When asked if you want to delete the preferences, click Yes.*

You can jump between Photoshop and ImageReady to transfer an image between the two applications for editing without closing or exiting the originating application. Also, you can jump from ImageReady to other graphics-editing applications and HTML-editing applications you may have installed on your system. For more information on jumping to other applications from ImageReady, see Photoshop Help.

2 In ImageReady, click the Edit in Photoshop button ( ) in the toolbox to return to Photoshop.

Each time an image in Photoshop or ImageReady is updated with changes made in a jumped-to application, a single history state is added to the Photoshop or ImageReady History palette. You'll learn more about how to use the History palette later; see "About snapshots and History palette states" on page 118 of this book.

You'll learn about creating Web-ready content in ImageReady in Lessons 13, 14, and 15.

Using Photoshop Help

For complete information about using palettes, tools, and other application features, refer to Photoshop Help. Photoshop Help includes all the topics in the printed *Adobe Photoshop CS2 User Guide,* and more. It includes the complete list of keyboard shortcuts, how-to tips, tutorials, and explanations of Photoshop, ImageReady, and Bridge concepts and feature descriptions.

Photoshop Help is easy to use, because you can look for topics in several ways:

- Scanning the table of contents.
- Searching for keywords.
- Using the index.
- Jumping to related topics using text links.

First, you'll try looking for a topic using the Contents palette.

1 Choose Help > Photoshop Help.

Note: *You can also open Photoshop Help by pressing F1 (Windows) or Command-/ (Mac OS).*

The Adobe Help Center opens. The topics for the Help content appear in the left pane of the floating window.

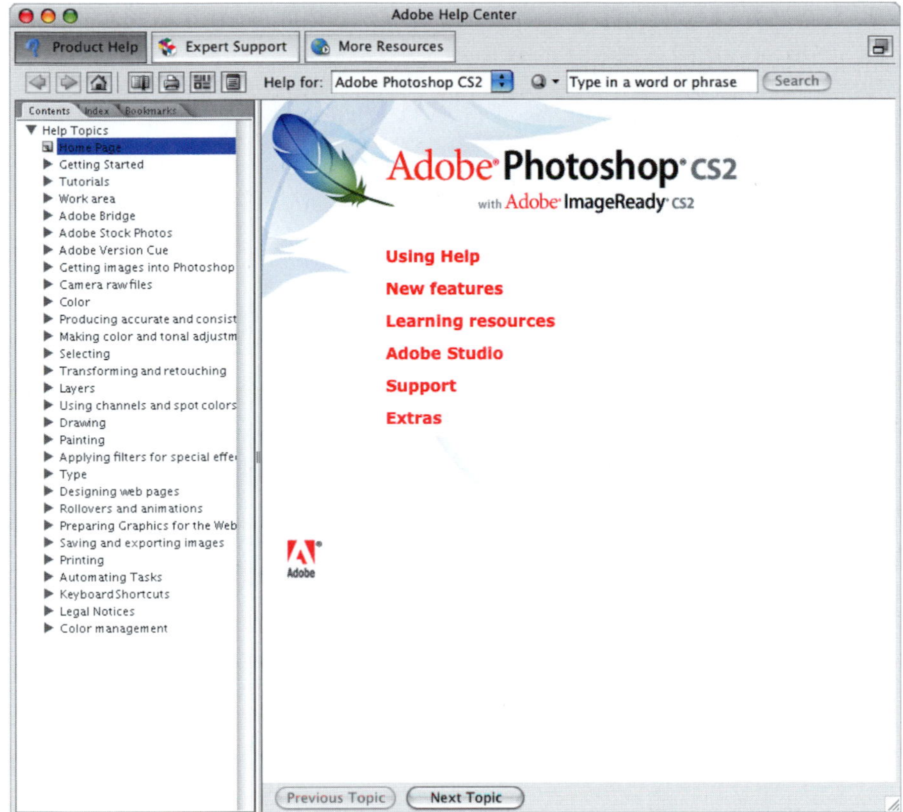

2 In the Contents tab of the left pane of the Help window, scroll down to skim through the Help contents. They are organized in topics, like the chapters of a book.

3 Depending on your platform, do one of the following:

• Windows: Near the top of the list of topics, click the right-pointing triangle to toggle open the topic *Work area*, and then toggle open the *Tools* topic.

• Mac OS: Near the top of the list of topics, click the right-pointing triangle to toggle open the topic *Looking at the Work Area*, and then toggle open the *Using Tools* topic.

4 Click *About tools and the toolbox* to select and view that topic. An explanation of Photoshop tools and the toolbox appears. In Windows, you'll also see a diagram of the toolbox, with each tool called out by name.

Some Help Center entries include links to related topics. Links appear as red, underlined text. The mouse pointer changes to a pointing-finger icon (☝) when positioned over a link. You can click any text link to jump to that related topic.

5 Scroll down (if necessary) and depending on your platform, do one of the following:

- Windows: Click the *Selection tools gallery* text link.
- Mac OS: Click the *Toolbox overview (1 of 3)* text link.

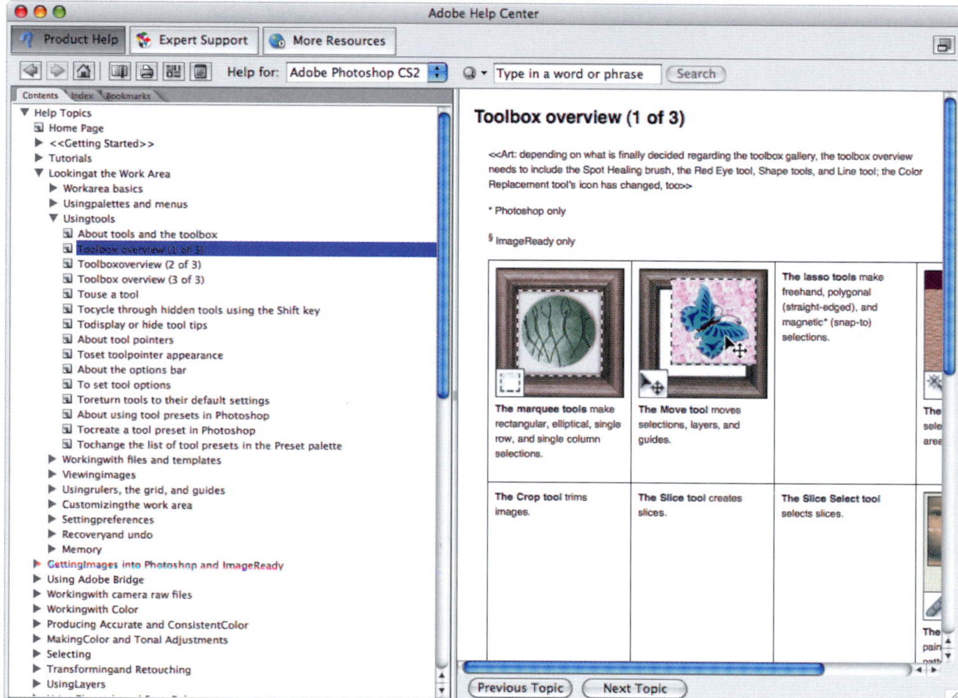

6 Click Next Topic one or two more times to see information the rest of the tools.

Using Help Center keywords, links, and index

If you can't find the topic you're interested in by skimming the Contents page, you can try searching on a keyword.

1 At the top of the window, type a keyword in the search text box, such as **lasso**, and click the Search button. A list of topics appears in the left pane. To view any of these topics, click the topic name.

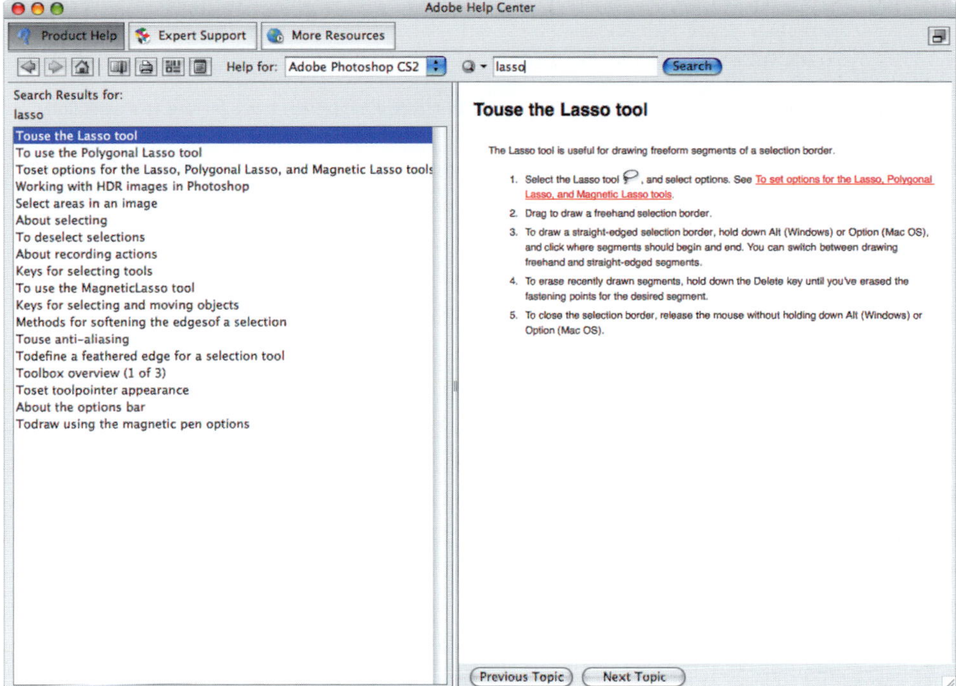

You can also search for a topic using the index.

2 Click the Return to Home Page button (🏠) at the top of the window.

3 In the left pane, click the Index tab to bring that palette forward. An alphabetical list of letters appears in the left pane.

4 Click a letter, such as "T," to display index entries for that letter.

Index entries appear alphabetically by topic and subtopic, like the index of a book. You can scroll down the list to see all the entries that begin with the letter "T."

5 Click an entry to open the topic about that entry. If there is more than one entry for a topic, click the triangle to toggle open visibility for all of the entries, and then click the entry that you want to read.

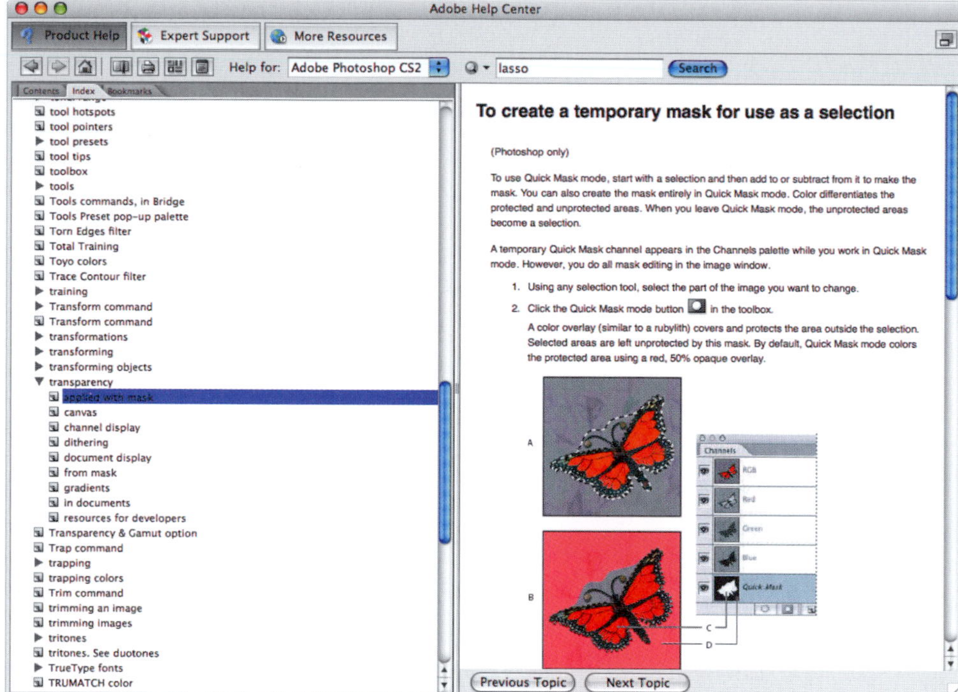

6 When you have finished browsing, choose Adobe Help Center > Close (Windows) or Adobe Help Center > Quit Adobe Help Center (Mac OS) to close Photoshop Help.

Using Adobe online services

Another way to get information about Adobe Photoshop and to stay abreast of updates is to use Adobe online services. If you have an Internet connection and a Web browser installed on your system, you can access the Adobe Systems Web site (www.adobe.com) for information on Photoshop and other Adobe products. You can also be notified automatically when updates are available.

1 In Photoshop, choose Help > Photoshop Online, or click the icon ( ) at the top of the toolbox.

Your default Web browser launches and displays the Photoshop product page on the U.S. Adobe Systems Web site. You can explore the site and find such information as tips and techniques, galleries of artwork by Adobe designers and artists around the world, the latest product information, and troubleshooting and technical information. Or, you can learn about other Adobe products and news.

Now, you'll return to Photoshop and set it up so that you can automatically receive software updates.

2 Close your browser.

3 Return to Photoshop, and choose Help > Updates. In the Adobe Updater dialog box that appears, click the Preferences button.

4 In the Adobe Updater Preferences dialog box, check the box "Automatically check for updates every month." Then, decide whether you want updates to be downloaded automatically, or whether you want to be alerted before updates are downloaded.

If you choose to not automatically check for updates every month, you can still manually go to Adobe's Web site (as in Step 1) and check for Photoshop updates.

5 Click OK to save your changes.

Congratulations again; you've finished Lesson 1.

Now that you're acquainted with the basics of the Photoshop work area, you can explore more about the Adobe Bridge visual file browser, or jump ahead and begin learning how to create and edit images. Once you know the basics, you can complete the *Adobe Photoshop CS2 Classroom in a Book* lessons either in sequential order, or according to the subject that most interests you.

Toolbox overview

The marquee tools *make rectangular, elliptical, single row, and single column selections.*

The Move tool *moves selections, layers, and guides.*

The lasso tools *make freehand, polygonal (straight-edged), and magnetic* (snap-to) selections.*

The Magic Wand tool *selects similarly colored areas.*

The Crop tool *trims images.*

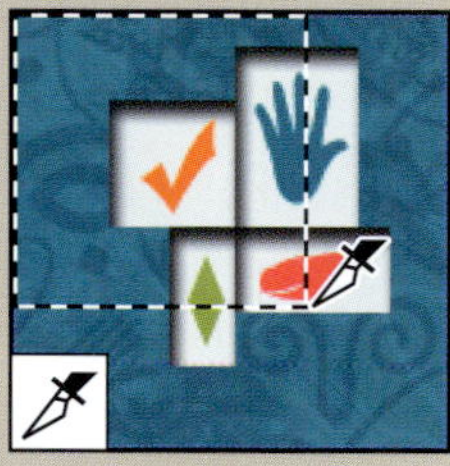

The Slice tool *creates slices.*

The Slice Select tool *selects slices.*

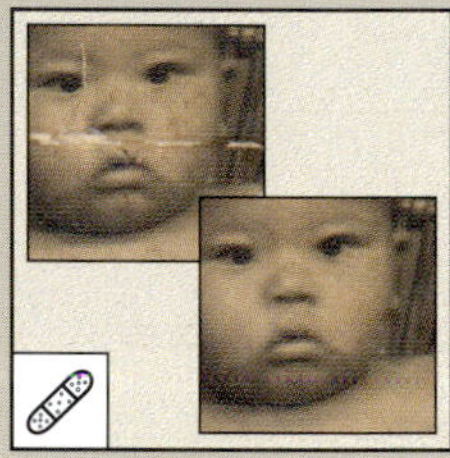

The Healing Brush tool* *paints with a sample or pattern to repair imperfections in an image.*

The Spot Healing Brush tool* *quickly removes blemishes and imperfections from photographs with a uniform background.*

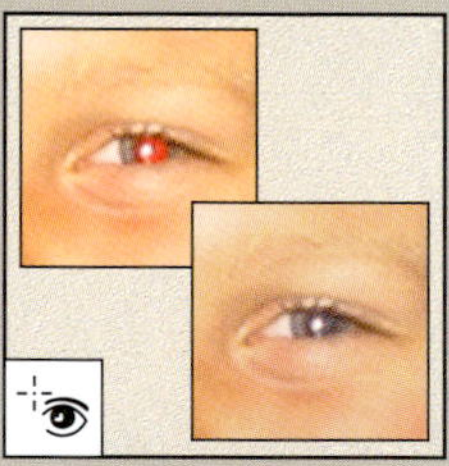

The Red Eye tool* *removes red-eye in flash photos with one click.*

The Patch tool* *repairs imperfections in a selected area of an image using a sample or pattern.*

The Color Replacement tool* *substitutes one color for another.*

** Photoshop only* *§ ImageReady only*

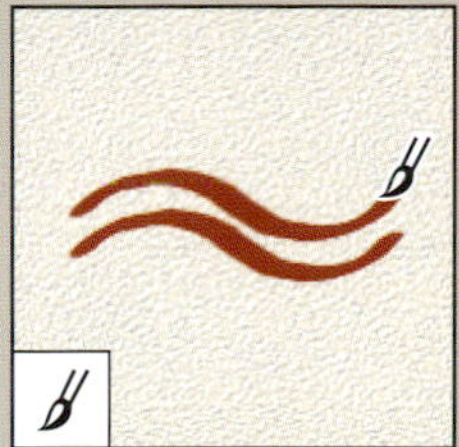
The Brush tool *paints brush strokes.*

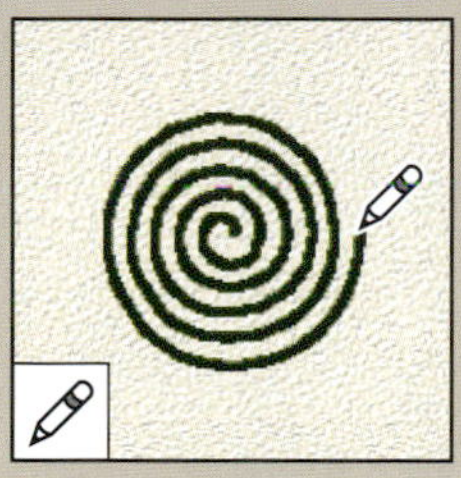
The Pencil tool *paints hard-edged strokes.*

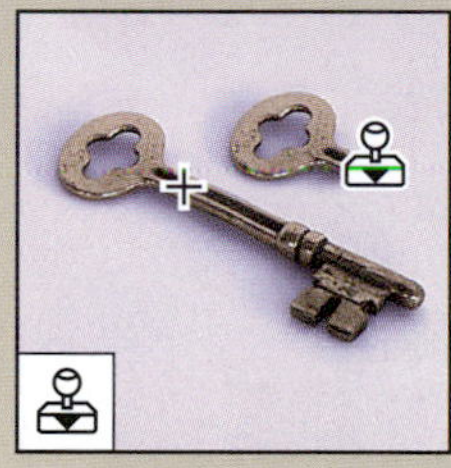
The Clone Stamp tool *paints with a sample of an image.*

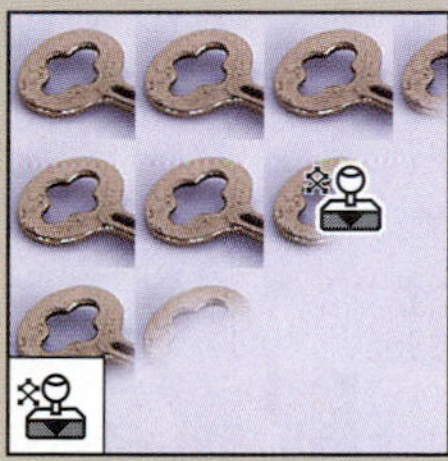
The Pattern Stamp tool* *paints with a part of an image as a pattern.*

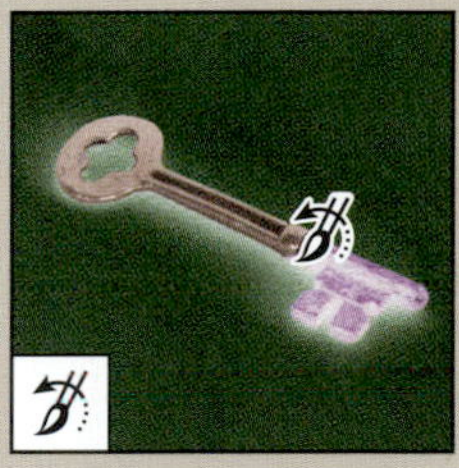
The History Brush tool* *paints a copy of the selected state or snapshot into the current image window.*

The Art History Brush tool* *paints stylized strokes that simulate the look of different paint styles, using a selected state or snapshot.*

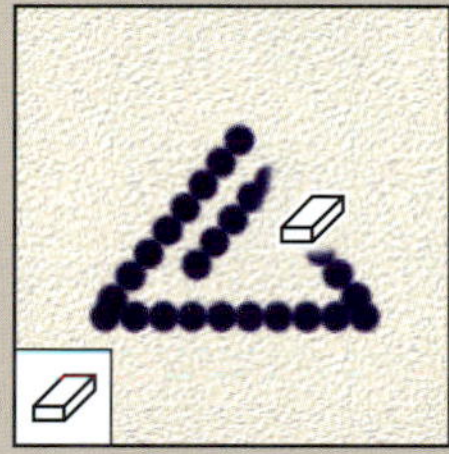
The Eraser tool *erases pixels and restores parts of an image to a previously saved state.*

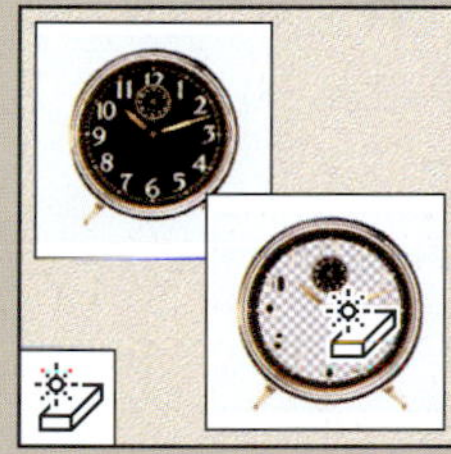
The Magic Eraser tool *erases solid-colored areas to transparency with a single click.*

The Background Eraser tool* *erases areas to transparency by dragging.*

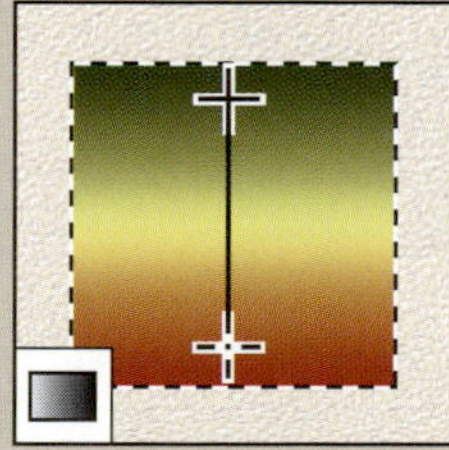
The Gradient tool* *creates straight-line, radial, angle, reflected, and diamond blends between colors.*

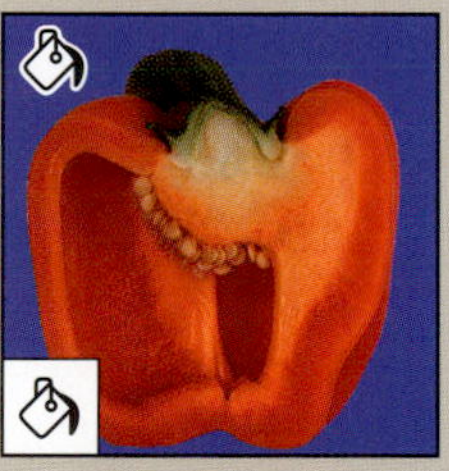
The Paint Bucket tool *fills similarly colored areas with the foreground color.*

The Blur tool* *blurs hard edges in an image.*

Toolbox overview (continued)

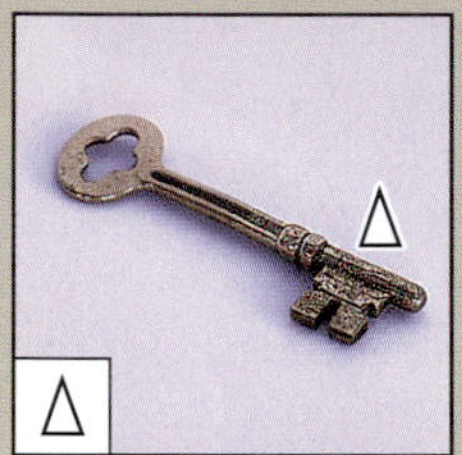
The Sharpen tool* *sharpens soft edges in an image.*

The Smudge tool* *smudges data in an image.*

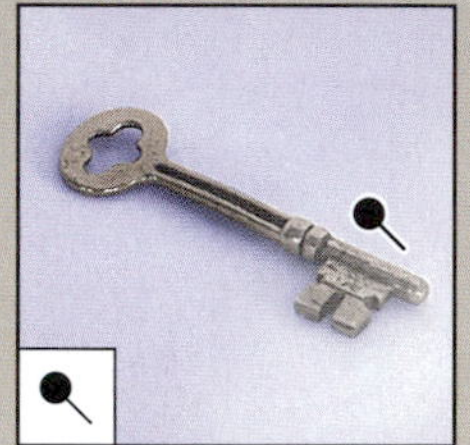
The Dodge tool* *lightens areas in an image.*

The Burn tool* *darkens areas in an image.*

The Sponge tool* *changes the color saturation of an area.*

The path selection tools* *make shape or segment selections showing anchor points, direction lines, and direction points.*

The type tools *create type on an image.*

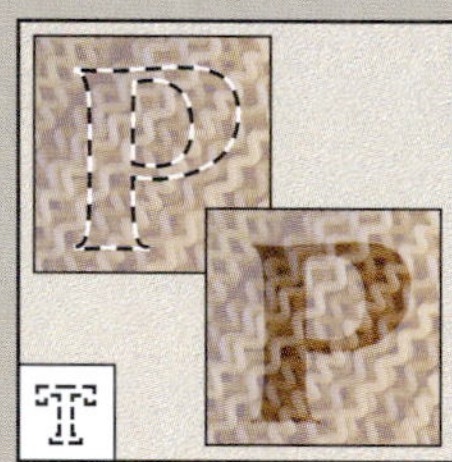
The type mask tools* *create a selection in the shape of type.*

The pen tools* *draw smooth-edged paths.*

The Custom Shape tool* *makes customized shapes selected from a custom shape list.*

The annotations tools* *make notes and audio annotations that can be attached to an image.*

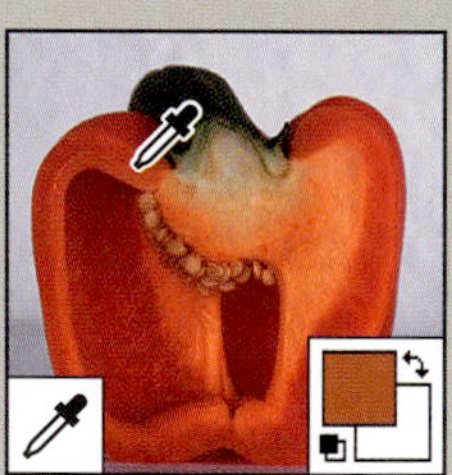
The Eyedropper tool *samples colors in an image.*

** Photoshop only* *§ ImageReady only*

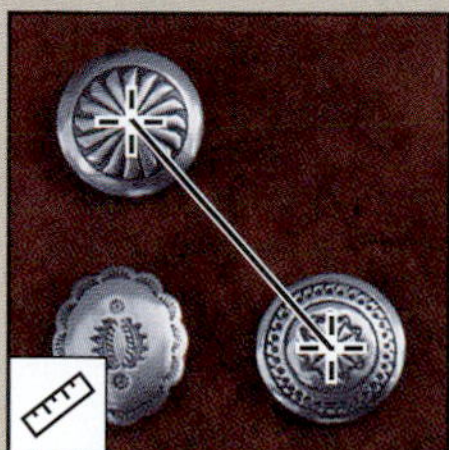

The Measure tool* *measures distances, locations, and angles.*

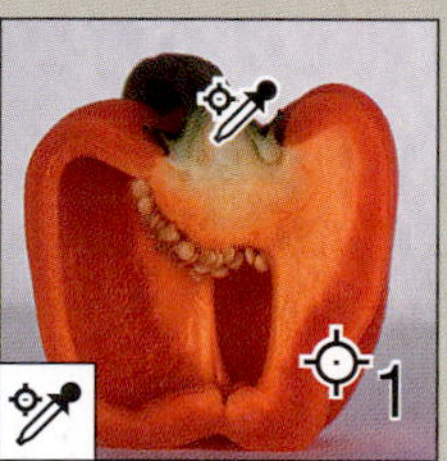

The Color Sampler tool* *samples up to four areas of the image.*

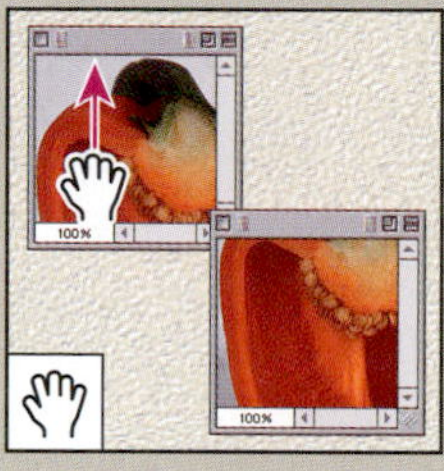

The Hand tool *moves an image within its window.*

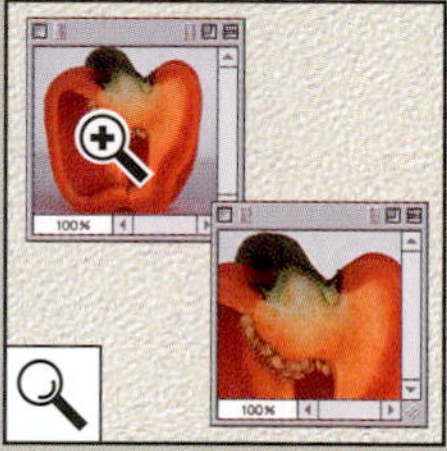

The Zoom tool *magnifies and reduces the view of an image.*

The image map tools§ *define image map areas in an image.*

The Image Map Select tool§ *selects image maps.*

The Toggle Image Map Visibility tool§ *toggles between showing and hiding image maps.*

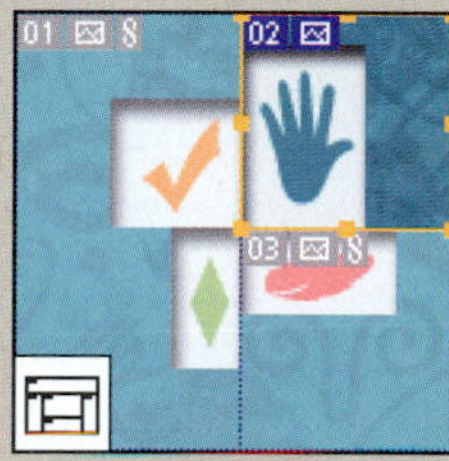

The Toggle Slices Visibility tool§ *toggles between showing and hiding slices of an image.*

The Preview Document tool§ *previews rollover effects directly in ImageReady.*

The Preview In Default Browser tool§ *previews animations in a Web browser.*

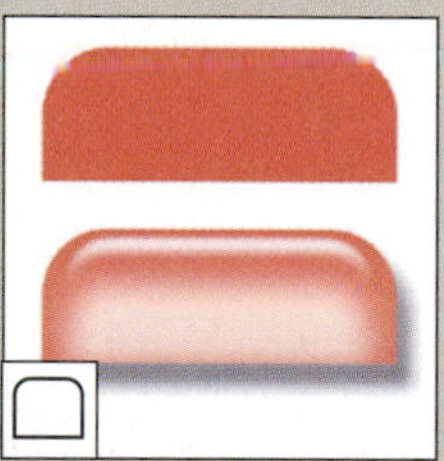

The Tab Rectangle tool§ *draws a rectangle with rounded upper corners.*

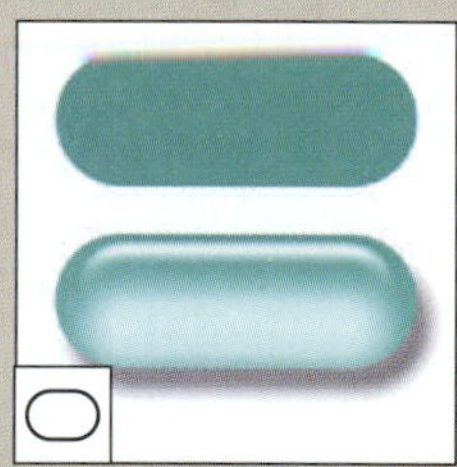

The Pill Rectangle tool§ *draws a rectangle with all corners rounded.*

Review

Review questions

1 Describe two types of images you can open in Photoshop.

2 How do you open image files using Adobe Bridge?

3 How do you select tools in Photoshop?

4 Describe two ways to change your view of an image.

5 What are two ways to get more information about Photoshop?

Review answers

1 You can scan a photograph, transparency, negative, or graphic into the program; capture a digital video image; or import artwork created in a drawing program. You can also import digital photos.

2 Click the Go to Bridge button on the Photoshop tool options bar to jump to Bridge; locate the image file you want to open, and double-click its thumbnail to open it in Photoshop.

3 Select tools in the toolbox, or press the tool's keyboard shortcut. A selected tool remains active until you select a different tool. To select a hidden tool, use either a keyboard shortcut to toggle through the tools, or hold down the mouse button on the tool in the toolbox to open a pop-up menu of the hidden tools.

4 Choose commands from the View menu to zoom in or out of an image, or to fit it onscreen; or use the zoom tools and click or drag over an image to enlarge or reduce the view. You can also use keyboard shortcuts or the Navigator palette to control the display of an image.

5 The Photoshop Help system includes all the information in the *Adobe Photoshop CS2 User Guide* plus keyboard shortcuts, task-based topics, and illustrations. Photoshop also includes a link to the Adobe Systems Photoshop Web page for additional information on services, products, and tips pertaining to Photoshop.

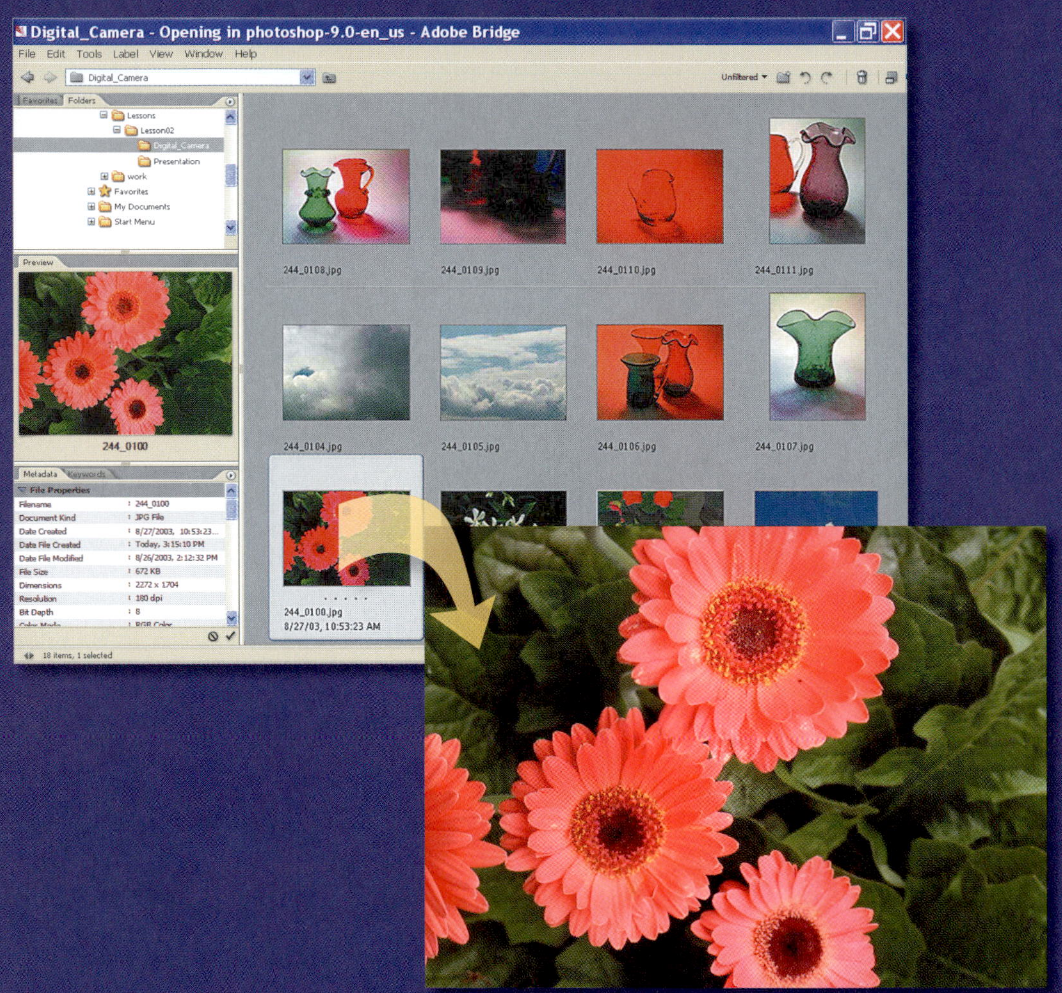

When you're hunting for specific pictures in your stash of image files, Adobe Bridge is your new best friend. It helps you save time with features that organize files so that you can both see and search for exactly the files you need. It also offers a royalty-free stock photography service and automates routine tasks with built-in scripts.

2 Using Adobe Bridge

Lesson overview

In this lesson, you'll learn how to do the following:

- Identify and resize Adobe Bridge palettes and panes.
- Rotate, resize, and view thumbnail and preview image files.
- Sort and rearrange thumbnails in the Bridge browser window.
- Delete and batch-rename files in Adobe Bridge.
- Assign star rankings, colored labels, metadata, and keywords to image files.
- Search for image files based on criteria you define.
- Create a Web gallery of images selected in Adobe Bridge.
- Search for and download stock photography from Adobe Bridge.

This lesson will take an hour to an hour and a half to complete. Copy the Lesson02 folder from the *Adobe Photoshop CS2 Classroom in a Book* CD into the Lessons folder on your hard drive that you set up earlier. As you work, you'll overwrite some of the start files. To restore these original files, recopy them from the CD.

Getting started

You've already had a brief introduction to Adobe Bridge in Lesson 1, "Getting to Know the Work Area." If you've completed that lesson, you know that the permanent Go to Bridge button (▣) on the Photoshop tool options bar takes you directly to Adobe Bridge. In this lesson, you will explore Adobe Bridge in depth. The aim of the first project for the lesson is to organize a motley collection of photographs.

Adobe Bridge shares some functionality with your desktop regarding files and folders. The changes you apply to files in Adobe Bridge change the files themselves, not merely the Adobe Bridge view of them. At the end of the lesson, you'll experience how easy it can be to find specific images on your computer, as well as to browse and purchase stock photography using Adobe Bridge.

1 Start Photoshop and then immediately hold down Ctrl-Alt-Shift (Windows) or Command-Option-Shift (Mac OS) to restore the default preferences. (See "Restoring default preferences" on page 6.)

2 When prompted, click Yes to confirm that you want to reset preferences, and Close to close the Welcome Screen.

3 Click the Go to Bridge button ( ) on the tool options bar to open Adobe Bridge.

***Note:** You can also open Adobe Bridge by double-clicking its application icon on the desktop or by clicking it in the Dock (Mac OS), or by choosing Start > All Programs > Adobe Bridge (Windows).*

The Bridge browser window is the dashboard for a creative workflow. It provides the starting point for you to browse, locate, and preview your assets.

Viewing and editing files in Adobe Bridge

The left side of the browser window displays palettes that you can rearrange, resize, and group within Adobe Bridge, using the same techniques as with Photoshop palettes. The palettes in Adobe Bridge help you navigate, preview, search, and manage information for your image files and folders.

Customizing Adobe Bridge views and spaces

The ideal arrangement and relative sizes of items and areas of Adobe Bridge depend on your work style and preferences. Depending on the tasks you're doing, it may be important to see what images are in a file; at other times, viewing information about the file may take priority. You can customize Adobe Bridge to increase your efficiency in these different situations.

In this procedure, you'll try out some of the custom views you can use in Adobe Bridge. The default configuration of Adobe Bridge areas appears in the following figure, although you won't see these particular thumbnails onscreen yet.

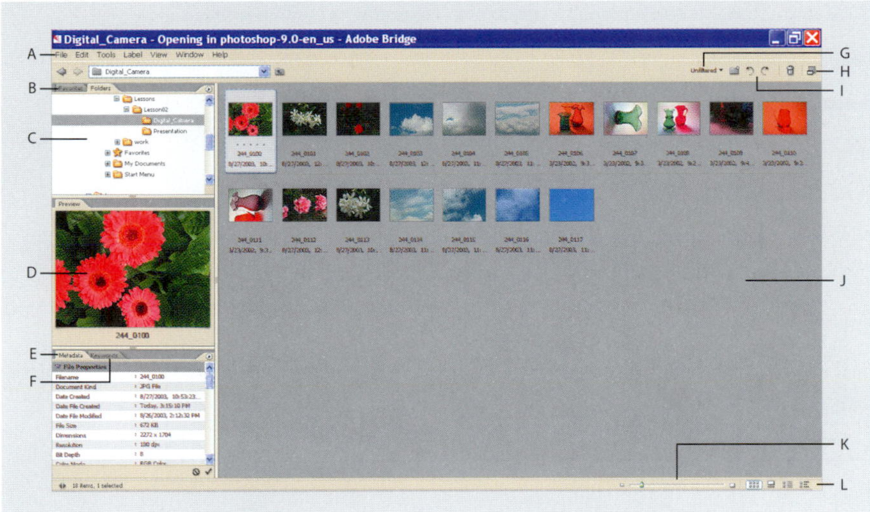

A. *Menu bar* ***B.*** *Favorites palette* ***C.*** *Folders palette* ***D.*** *Preview palette* ***E.*** *Metadata palette* ***F.*** *Keywords palette* ***G.*** *Filter view menu* ***H.*** *Compact mode button* ***I.*** *Rotation buttons* ***J.*** *Thumbnail preview pane* ***K.*** *Thumbnail slider* ***L.*** *View option buttons*

Note: *If you do not see the tabbed palettes on the left side of the browser window, click the Show/hide panels button (◂▸) in the lower left corner.*

1 Click the Folders tab in the upper left corner of the Bridge browser window to bring that palette forward, and navigate to the Lessons/Lesson02/Digital_Camera folder that you copied to your hard drive from the *Adobe Photoshop CS2 Classroom in a Book* CD. To navigate, either click the arrows (Mac OS) or plus signs (Windows) to open nested folders in the Folders palette, or double-click the folder thumbnail icons in the thumbnail preview area on the right side of the browser window.

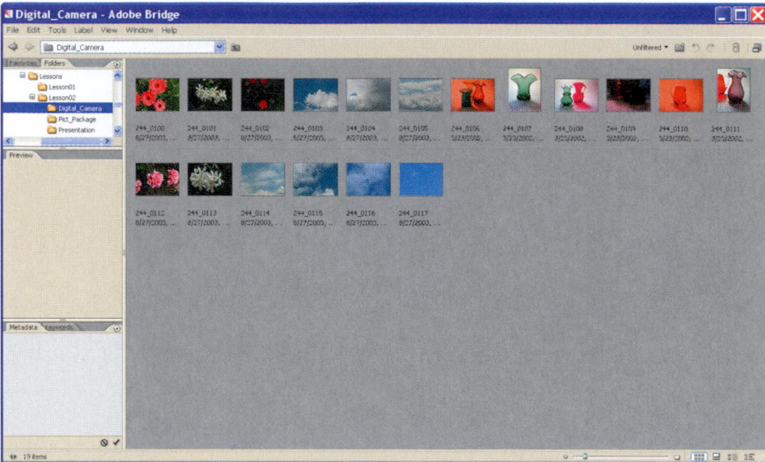

The Bridge preview pane updates interactively, showing you thumbnail previews of asset files. Adobe Bridge displays previews of image files such as those in PSD, TIFF, and JPEG formats as well as Adobe Illustrator vector files, multipage Adobe PDF files, and Microsoft Office documents.

2 At the bottom of the browser window, drag the thumbnail slider to reduce and then enlarge the thumbnail previews. Then, choose the Details view, then the Filmstrip view.

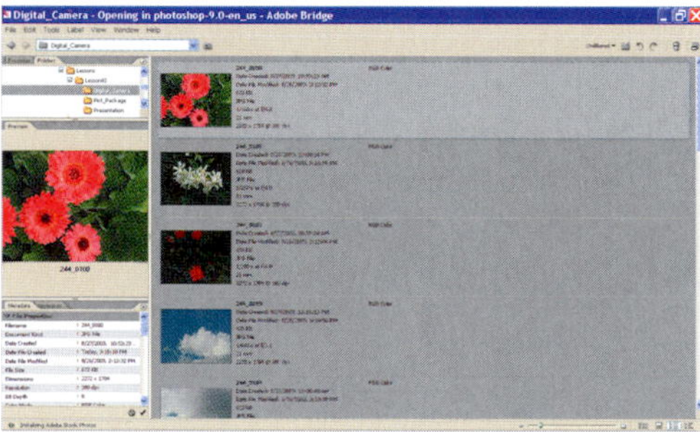

Details view

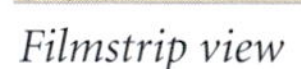

Filmstrip view

Note: *Adobe Bridge also offers a Versions and Alternates view for those who work with Version Cue CS2. For more about Version Cue, see the "Understanding Adobe Version Cue CS2 File Manager" white paper on the* Adobe Photoshop CS2 Classroom in a Book *CD.*

3 Choose Window > Workspace > Lightbox. Then, in succession, choose the File Navigator, Metadata Focus, and Filmstrip Focus workspaces.

Adobe Bridge can be customized to suit virtually any workflow or preference.

4 When you're finished experimenting, reset to the default workspace (press Command-F1 on the Mac or Ctrl-F1 in Windows).

5 Select any thumbnail by clicking it once.

A larger preview appears in the Preview palette, filling the available area.

6 Enlarge the Preview palette by dragging the horizontal and vertical bars that separate it from the other panes of the browser window. The pointer appears as double lines with arrows (⇹) when positioned over the bars.

7 Continue to adjust the panes, palettes, and thumbnails in Adobe Bridge until the arrangement suits you.

Adobe Bridge modes

You can work in Photoshop with Adobe Bridge open in Full Mode in the background, at the ready for you to jump to and use to locate and open files. Or you can switch to Compact or Ultra-Compact mode by clicking those buttons in the upper right corner of the Bridge browser window. Both compact modes display Bridge as a floating palette over Photoshop. Ultra-Compact mode (▤) displays only the Go Back and Go Forward buttons as well as the Recent Folders menu. Compact mode (▣) shows thumbnail previews of the selected folder. As soon as you start to navigate to a folder in Ultra-Compact mode, Bridge automatically switches to Compact mode so that you can see thumbnail previews. Both modes provide a button to toggle back to Full mode (▢).

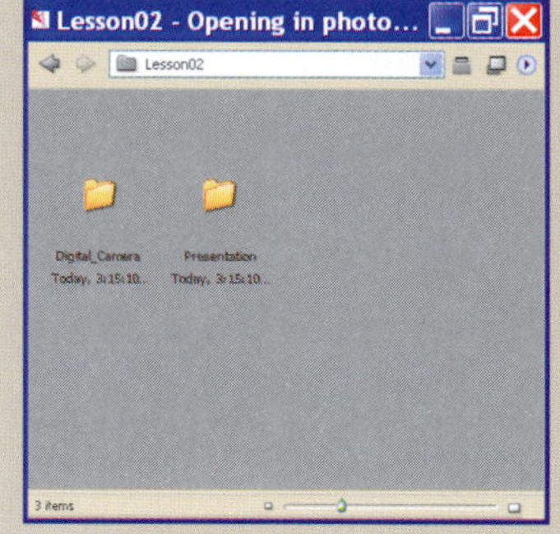

Compact mode

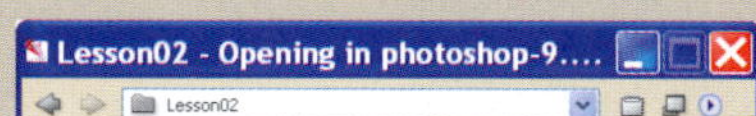

Ultra-Compact mode

Rotating and opening images

In addition to controlling the workspace and appearance of image previews in Bridge, you can also change the orientation of selected images and open them in Photoshop. Rotating the thumbnail previews in Adobe Bridge does not affect the resolution or quality of the files, but the rotation *is* permanent unless or until you undo it.

1 Select the 244_0107.jpg thumbnail in the Lesson02/Digital_Camera folder.

2 Click the Rotate 90° Counterclockwise button (↶) at the top of the browser window.

3 In the thumbnail preview pane, select the 244_0111.jpg thumbnail.

4 Click the Rotate 90° Clockwise button (↷).

5 (Optional) To open any .PSD, .TIF, or .JPG image at any time into Photoshop from within Adobe Bridge, double-click its thumbnail preview.

Note: *Adobe Bridge will also automatically open .AI files into Adobe Illustrator, .PDF files into Adobe Acrobat, .INDD files into Adobe InDesign, and .DOC and .XLS documents into Microsoft Word and Microsoft Excel, respectively, if you have those applications. You can control file associations in Adobe Bridge preferences.*

You can select multiple thumbnails in Adobe Bridge and open or rotate them together. Select the files by using the usual methods: Click and then Shift-click, or drag the cursor across image thumbnails, to select contiguous files; or Ctrl-click (Windows) or Command-click (Mac OS) to select discontiguous images.

Deleting images

You can use Adobe Bridge to remove files or folders from your system exactly as you would remove them from your desktop. Deleting images in Adobe Bridge sends the files to the Recycle Bin (Windows) or Trash (Mac OS).

Using Adobe Bridge to examine your images, you can confidently select and delete files that you no longer need or that you find unsatisfactory.

1 Select the thumbnail for 244_0109.jpg, which is poorly composed, out of focus, and underexposed—a real loser.

2 Click the Delete Item button ( ) at the top of the Bridge browser window. When a message appears asking you to confirm this action, click OK.

At this point, the deleted file is not yet removed from your computer, although it is not visible in Adobe Bridge. You can find and retrieve deleted files by switching to the desktop and dragging them out of the Recycle Bin (Windows) or Trash (Mac OS). When you empty your desktop trash container, the files will be permanently deleted from your computer.

Rearranging and renaming image files

You can rearrange thumbnails in Adobe Bridge as freely as you might move negatives or slides on a light table. You can also use a batch-renaming process to give image files friendlier but well-organized filenames. In this exercise, you'll rearrange the thumbnails according to subject matter—colored glass containers, flowers, and cloudy skies—and then rename them.

1 In the thumbnail preview area of the browser window, drag the thumbnails of cloudy-sky photographs one by one until they are next to each other.

2 Select the first sky thumbnail in the group and then Shift-click the last sky thumbnail to select the entire group.

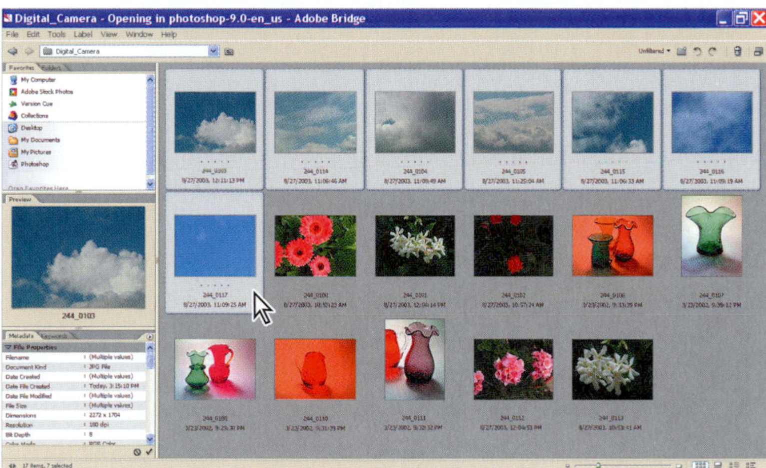

3 Choose Tools > Batch Rename.

4 Under New Filenames in the Batch Rename dialog box, choose Text from the Current Filename pop-up menu, and type **Clouds** in the text field.

5 Click the plus button (⊕)at the far right side of the New Filenames area, and choose Sequence Number from the pop-up menu. Make sure the default, 1, is selected for the starting sequence number, or type **1** now.

6 Click the plus button to create a third criterion, and then choose New Extension from the pop-up menu. Type **jpg** (no period necessary) into the extension text field. (This preserves the .jpg file extension in the filename.)

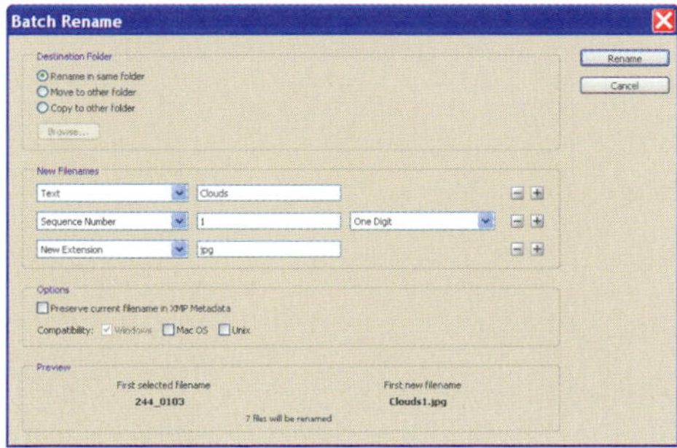

7 For Compatibility, select the check boxes for other operating systems: Windows, Mac OS, and Unix. (The operating system you are using will be dimmed but checked.)

8 Review the sample in the Preview area to make sure that it reads "Clouds1.jpg," and then click Rename.

9 Choose View > Sort > By Filename to arrange the thumbnails in alphanumeric order.

10 Using the techniques described in Steps 1–8, select and batch-rename the remaining photographs according to the subject matter pictured: flowers and ornamental glassware. When you set options in the Batch Rename dialog box, type **Plants** instead of *Clouds* to name the flower images, and type **Glass** for the glassware images. Otherwise, use the same options as in Steps 5–7.

The Batch Rename command behaves differently depending on what is selected when you choose the command: If no thumbnails are selected, the naming scheme you specify in the Batch Rename dialog box applies the name change to all the files in the selected folder. If several—but not all—thumbnails are selected, the command renames only the selected files.

***Note:** You can also rename a single file in Adobe Bridge in the conventional manner—that is, by clicking the filename in the thumbnail preview area and typing to overwrite the existing name.*

Embedding information for easy identification

Adobe Bridge gives you numerous tools for retrieving the images you need to find. This is critical when you have a large number of stored images and no time to waste on browsing through hundreds or thousands of files.

In this section, you'll work with three more ways to embed information in files so that you can quickly find them later: rankings, metadata, and keywords.

Ranking and sorting image files

Adobe Bridge has a star-ranking feature that you can use to group and sort image thumbnails. This gives you an alternative way to organize images in the thumbnail preview area. In this exercise, five stars will stand for the best and most usable images, three stars for medium-quality images, and one star for the poorest-quality or least desirable photographs. How many stars you assign to each image is a personal judgment, so there are no right or wrong answers for star rankings, and—as opposed to the real world, perhaps—no one will take offense at your choices.

1 Make sure you have large, clear thumbnail previews, and then click to select one that's of particularly good quality, such as the red glass pitcher.

2 Click one of the dots that appear below the image thumbnail. When you click, the dot turns into a star. Click to turn all five dots into stars.

3 Select additional high-quality files, including one or two images in each category (glass, flowers, and skies).

Note: *Use Ctrl-click (Windows) or Command-click (Mac OS) to select discontiguous thumbnails, if desired.*

4 Choose Label > ***** to apply the five-star ranking to all selected images at once. Click OK to dismiss the XMP warning dialog box if it appears.

5 Choose View > Sort > By Rating to rearrange the thumbnails so that the best images are grouped together. Toggle off View > Sort > Ascending Order to have the five-starred images appear at the top of the thumbnail preview area.

6 Continue to assign five-, three-, and one-star rankings to all the files in the folder, either by ranking them individually (as in Steps 1 and 2) or in multiples (as in Steps 3 and 4).

***Note:** You can delete stars at any time by selecting the thumbnail, moving the cursor over the stars, and clicking the gray circle with a slash through it (⊘) that appears to the left.*

7 Choose View > Sort > By Rating again to arrange the files in reverse alphabetical order of their rankings.

Quality is not the only consideration by which you might want to rank images. You can use star rankings to indicate anything—subject matter, client, project name, or time of day, for example. Indeed, if you want to organize your images by multiple factors—say, by quality and by project, you can also apply colored labels your images. Yellow labels might be applied to assets that will be used for a Web project, for example, while red labels could indicate that the image will be used for a print brochure.

8 Click to select the thumbnail of any image, such as the red pitcher, and then choose Label > Yellow. Click OK to dismiss the XMP warning dialog box if it appears.

A yellow label appears behind the five-star ranking of the thumbnail preview.

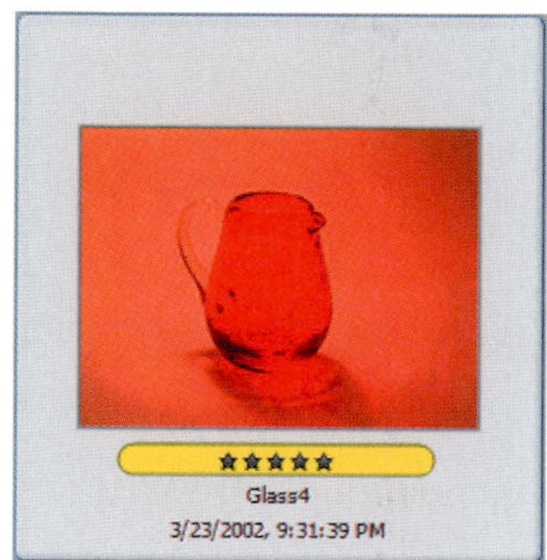

9 Continue to assign colored labels—yellow or otherwise—to additional files in the folder, either by selecting them individually or in multiples and then choosing a color from the Label menu.

Note: *You can also apply colored labels by selecting one or more thumbnails and Control-clicking (Mac OS) or right-clicking (Windows) and choosing Label and a color from the contextual pop up menu.*

10 Choose View > Sort > By Label to arrange the files in the thumbnail preview area by their colored labels.

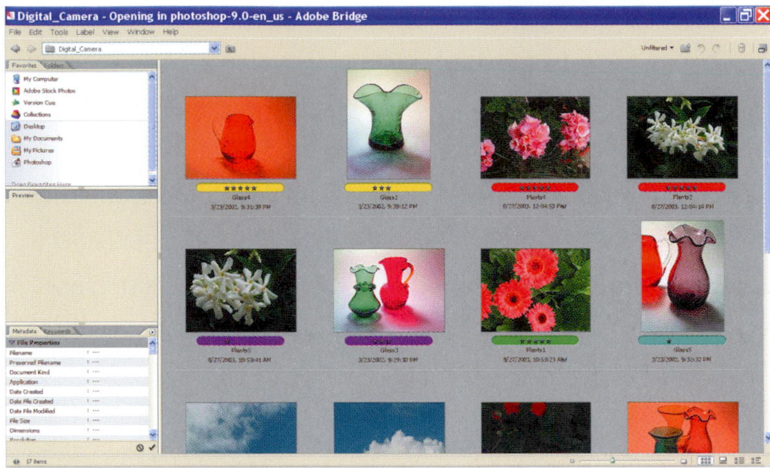

In addition to sorting your view by rankings and labels, you can filter the view to see only those thumbnails of a specific ranking or color. Let's experiment with those filters now.

11 Choose Show 5 Stars from the Unfiltered pop-up menu to show thumbnails of only those thumbnails with a five-star ranking.

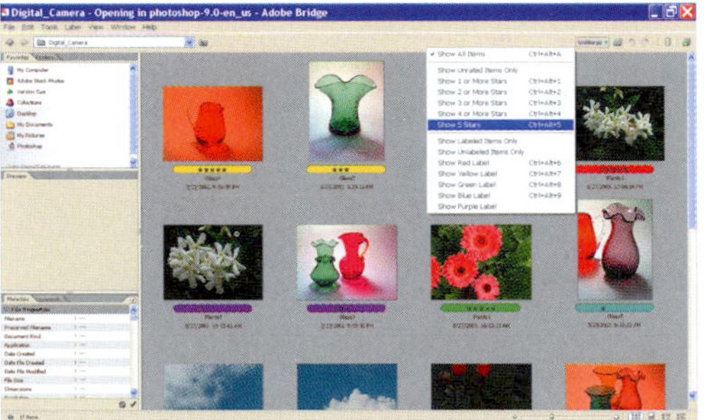

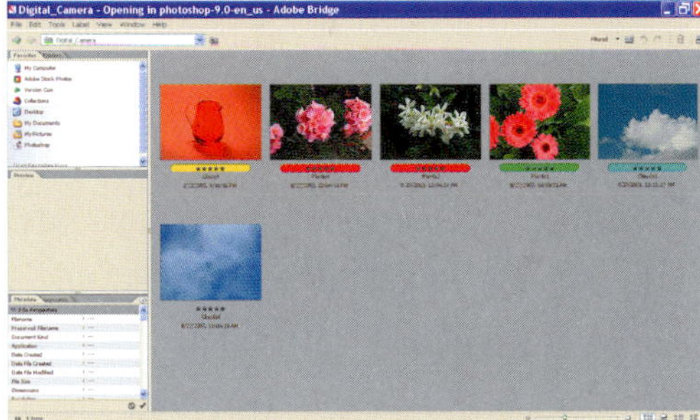

12 Choose Filtered > Show Red Label.

13 Choose Filtered > Show All Items so that you can see all of your image files.

Reviewing and editing metadata

You can quickly see file information in one of several ways: Simply hover the mouse cursor over an image thumbnail in the Thumbnails view, and it will pop up; or switch to the Details view and the same metadata file information appears next to the image thumbnail preview. Or you can use the Metadata palette, which displays more complete metadata. Next, you will compare the two displays of metadata information.

The information in the Metadata palette is nested under headings that you can expand or collapse by clicking the arrow next to a heading. There are three headings for images: File Properties, IPTC, and Camera Data (Exif). Additional headings are available for stock photo images. In Bridge, you can directly edit only some of the IPTC metadata.

1 Make sure you're in Details view, and click to select the thumbnail of one of the five-starred glassware images.

2 If necessary, click the Metadata tab to bring that palette forward in the lower left pane of the browser window. If any of the major headings are collapsed, click the arrows (▶) to expand them so that you can compare the information here to the information listed in the Details view of the thumbnails.

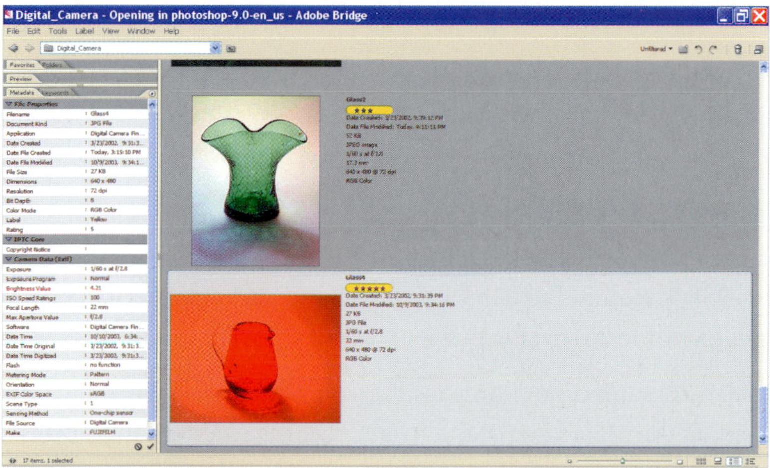

When you work with large amounts of metadata, it helps to enlarge the Metadata palette, even if it reduces or eliminates the Preview, Favorites, and Folders palettes. This can reduce the amount of scrolling needed to review and edit the information.

3 Scroll down the Metadata palette to the IPTC heading so that you can see the items listed under it. The pencil icons (✎) on the left indicate items that you can edit.

4 Click the blank space for Description and type a few words describing the image, such as **red pitcher**.

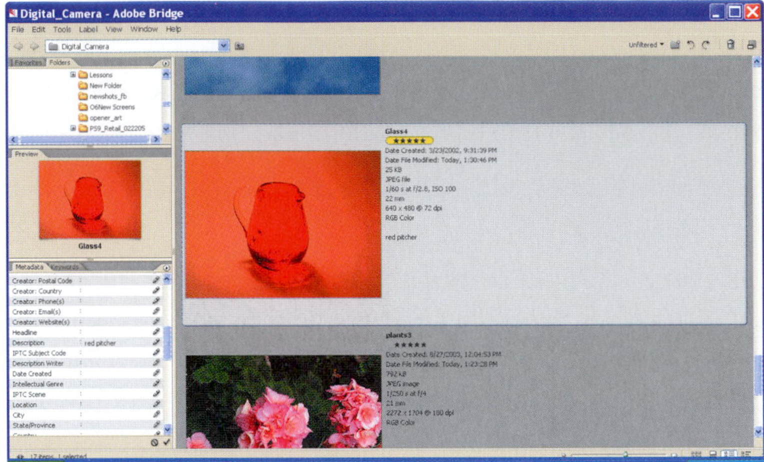

5 At the bottom of the Metadata palette, click the Apply button (✓) to enter the information you typed.

Creating and applying keywords

Keywords can streamline your searches for images. If you have a large collection of images, the few seconds required to enter some well-chosen keywords can save you hours later as you try to locate specific images.

The Keywords palette organizes keywords in categories that you can expand and collapse as you did on the Metadata palette. The Keywords palette standardizes keywords so that you can apply identical terms to specific types of images. This greatly reduces the risks of occasional typographical errors or inconsistencies that can turn keyword searches from a dream come true into a nightmare.

1 Click the Keywords tab to bring that palette forward.

2 Click the Keywords palette menu button (◉), and choose New Keyword Set. Or, click the New Keyword Set button (▭) at the bottom of the Keywords palette.

3 Type **Glass Project** in the new blank to name the keyword set, and press Enter (Windows) or Return (Mac OS). Leave the Glass Project keyword set selected, or reselect it if necessary.

4 Click the New Keyword button (▣) to create a keyword under the Glass Project category, type **Red**, and press Enter (Windows) or Return (Mac OS). Then, select the Glass Project category again and repeat the process until you have created five more new keywords, naming them **Green**, **Blue**, **Orange**, **Purple**, and **Yellow**.

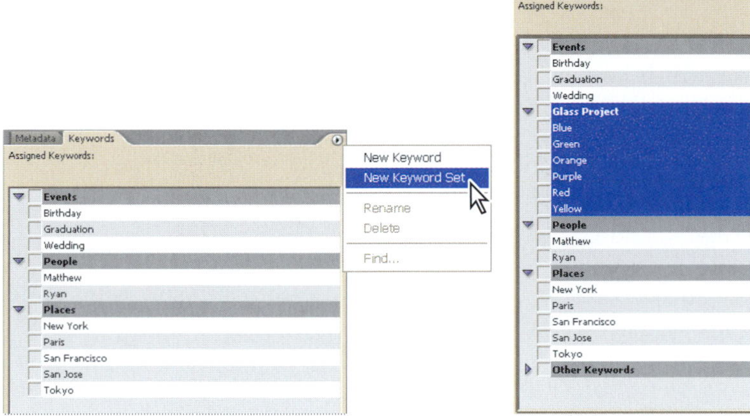

5 Select the thumbnail for the photograph of the green vase and the red pitcher.

6 In the Keywords palette, click the boxes for both the *Red* and *Green* keywords to apply them to the image metadata. Or, double-click each of those keywords.

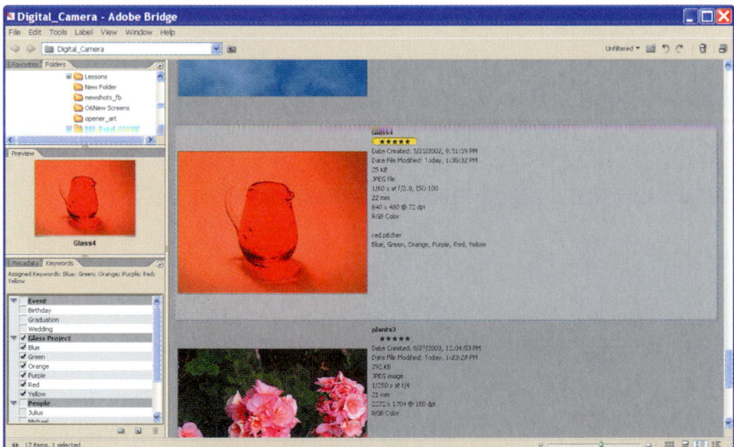

A check mark appears next to the applied keywords. The bold hyphen next to the Glass Project category indicates that some (but not all) of the keywords in that set apply to the selected file.

7 One by one, select each of the other glassware images and apply the appropriate keywords for the glass colors in those photographs. Or, you can select multiple files—such as all the images with blue glassware, if there are several—and simultaneously apply the keyword *Blue* to each of them.

Deleting keywords

The lists on the Keywords palette are application-wide, so the same keyword choices are available regardless of what folder you're browsing. Many of the preset keywords may not be useful to you. Fortunately, you can delete keywords you won't need. Since there is no orange glass in the images, you can delete *Orange*.

You don't have to worry about deleting a keyword that is currently applied to some files. In those cases, the keyword is deleted from the heading but shows up under a new heading named *Other Keywords*. You'll see that in this exercise.

1 In the Keywords palette, select the *Orange* keyword, and then click the Delete Keyword button (🗑) at the bottom of the palette. Click OK to dismiss the warning that appears.

2 Repeat Step 1, but this time delete the *Red* keyword.

3 Select one of the thumbnails showing a red glass item. (You previously assigned *Red* to this file.)

4 In the Keywords palette, find the Other Keywords category and locate the *Red* keyword. Drag the keyword back into the Glass Project category to group it with the other color keywords.

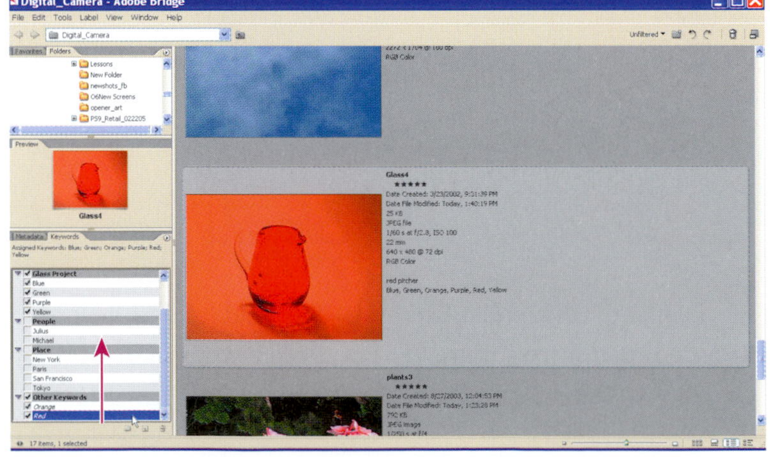

You can also edit keywords. This is easy to do, but there's a little trick to it. Since double-clicking a keyword applies it to any currently selected files, you need to select the keyword and then choose Rename from the Keywords palette menu or context menu. Then, type in your new text.

Searching with Adobe Bridge

Now that you've taken the time to associate information with the images in the Lesson02/Digital_Camera folder, you're ready to see how easy this makes searching.

1 Choose Edit > Find.

2 In the Find dialog box, make sure that the Lesson02/Digital_Camera folder appears in the Look In option, or click Browse and navigate to that folder.

3 Under Criteria, choose Filename > contains, and type **Glass** in the blank field.

4 Click the plus-sign button (⊞) to open another set of criteria menus.

5 In the second row, choose Keywords > contains, and type **Red**.

6 Click the plus-sign button to open a third row, and choose Rating > is equal to, and choose five stars.

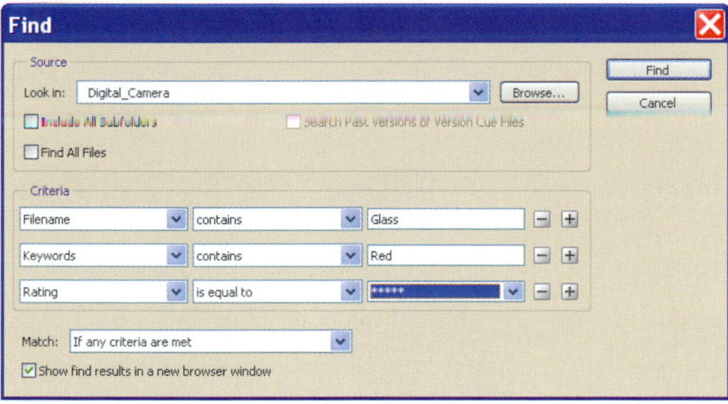

7 Click Find.

Any files that match all three sets of criteria—that is, five-star-quality images of red glassware, if you've completed the previous tasks in this lesson—appear in the thumbnail preview area. Look at the Recent Folders menu, and notice that the current location is a new folder named Find Results.

Julieanne Kost is an official Adobe Photoshop evangelist.

TOOL TIPS FROM THE PHOTOSHOP EVANGELIST

Hi, I'm Julieanne Kost, a Photoshop evangelist for Adobe Systems. That simply means I lecture and teach courses on Adobe Photoshop, as well as use it for my own professional photography. Photoshop is a powerful application, and learning some key shortcuts and tricks not only adds to the functionality of the program but also lets you use it more freely and efficiently. So sprinkled throughout this book are some of my favorite tips and tricks, which I hope that you find useful.

> Keyboard shortcuts with Bridge

Here are some tips to help you get a running start with Adobe Bridge:

- To jump from Photoshop to Bridge using a keyboard shortcut, press Alt-Ctrl-O (Windows) or Option-Command-O (Mac OS).
- In Thumbnails view, quickly navigate image thumbnails in the main preview area using the up, down, right, and left arrow keys.
- Rotate one or more selected images 90 degrees clockwise by pressing Ctrl-] (Windows) or Command-] (Mac OS). Rotate 90 degrees counterclockwise by pressing Ctrl-[(Windows) or Command-[(Mac OS).

Using Favorites and Collections

Favorites and Collections are two organizational features that might help you right about now. *Favorites* are bookmarked locations on your hard drive or network that you can access with the click of a button. *Collections* are groups of images that you can access quickly from the Favorites palette.

Let's start by saving your search results as a collection so that you can easily locate all the five-star red glassware images in the future.

1 Click the Save As Collection button at the top of the browser window (Save As Collection).

2 In the Save Collection dialog box, name your collection **5-star red glassware**, and then click Save.

3 Click the Favorites tab to bring that palette forward if it's behind the Folders palette, and resize to enlarge it if necessary for a better view.

Favorites provide quick links to frequently visited locations. Be default, Bridge provides Favorites for your computer, desktop, and some other folders, such as Pictures and Documents. Another default Favorite is Collections, which can be any group of images or assets that you create, such as the results of your search.

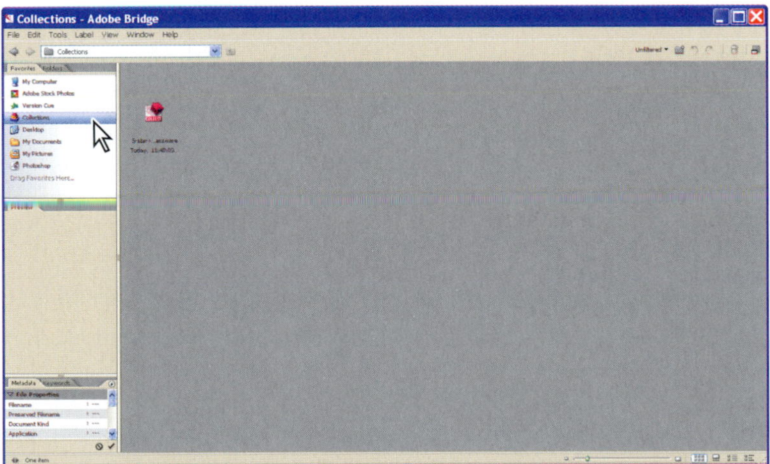

4 Click to select Collections in the Favorites palette, and then double-click the 5-star red glassware collections thumbnail to see thumbnail previews of the images in that collection.

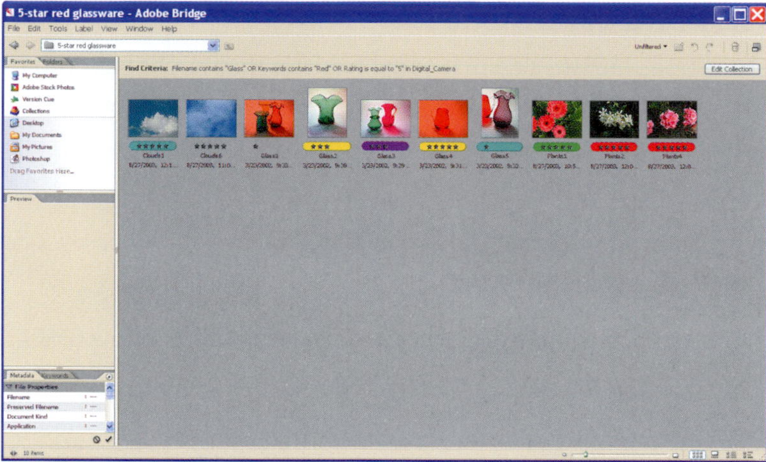

Now let's create a custom favorite that will come in handy for the rest of the lessons of this book.

5 Click the Folders tab to bring that palette forward, and navigate to the Lessons folder that contains all of the individual *Classroom in a Book* lesson folders.

6 Select the Lessons folder (in the Folders palette or preview area) and choose File > Add to Favorites.

Now, when you need to locate files for the other lessons in this book, you can click Lessons in the Favorites palette and double-click to open the folder in the preview area for the particular numbered lesson.

Automating routine tasks

The Adobe Bridge Tools menu includes a number of automated routines that also appear on the File > Automate menu in Photoshop. You'll try out one of these now.

The advantage of the automated commands in Bridge is that you can use them without even opening the files in Photoshop. You can apply these commands to all the files in a selected folder or to individual files in the folder that you select—it's your choice.

Creating a Web photo gallery

The Web Photo Gallery command generates an entire Web site for you, with thumbnails, images, text, and even an area for review feedback that the user fills out on the site and e-mails to the alias you designate. You can choose from a generous assortment of predefined layouts and styles that you can customize.

1 Click the Favorites tab to bring that palette forward, select Lessons, and then navigate to the Lesson02/Presentation folder.

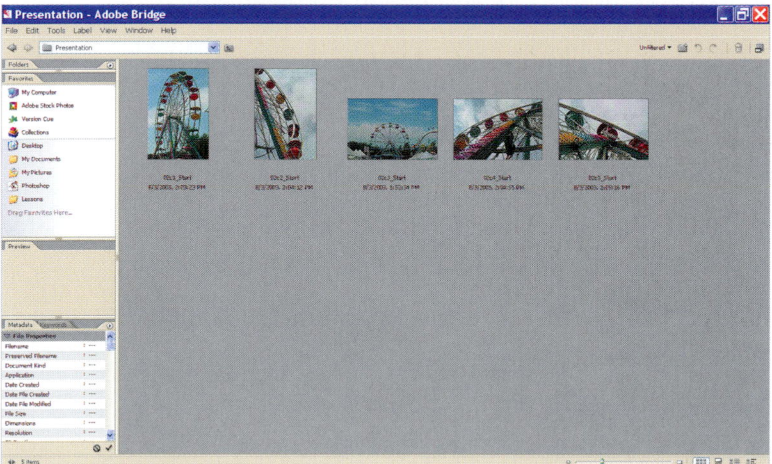

This folder contains five Ferris-wheel photographs; none of them are currently selected.

2 Choose Tools > Photoshop > Web Photo Gallery.

If Photoshop was closed, it will launch now. Otherwise, Bridge simply jumps to the open application. The Web Photo Gallery dialog box opens.

3 In the Web Photo Gallery dialog box, do the following:

- Choose Centered Frame 1- Feedback from the Styles pop-up menu.
- Type your own e-mail address as the address at which you want to receive feedback from reviewers.

4 Under Source Images, do the following, if they are not already done:

- Choose Use > Folder.
- Click the Browse button (Windows) or Choose button (Mac OS), and then verify that the Presentation folder is selected. Or, select it now.
- Create a destination folder for your Web gallery: Click the Destination button, navigate to your desktop, and click the New Folder button. Type **Wheel Web Site** to

name the folder, then click OK (Windows) or Create (Mac OS). You should return to the Web Photo Gallery dialog box.

5 Under Options, use the pop-up menu to toggle through the General, Banner, Large Images, and Thumbnails categories, specifying the following options for each:

- General: Choose .html from the Extension pop-up menu, and deselect all three check boxes.
- Banner: Type **Ferris Wheel Photos** for Site Name, **Adobe Systems** for photographer, and today's date (if necessary) or another date. You can leave the Contact Info option blank or type any phone number or street address.
- Large Images: Select the Resize Images check box (if necessary), choose Large from the pop-up menu, and leave the other options at the default settings.
- Thumbnails: Select Custom from the Size pop-up menu, and type **70** pixels. Leave the other options at the default settings.

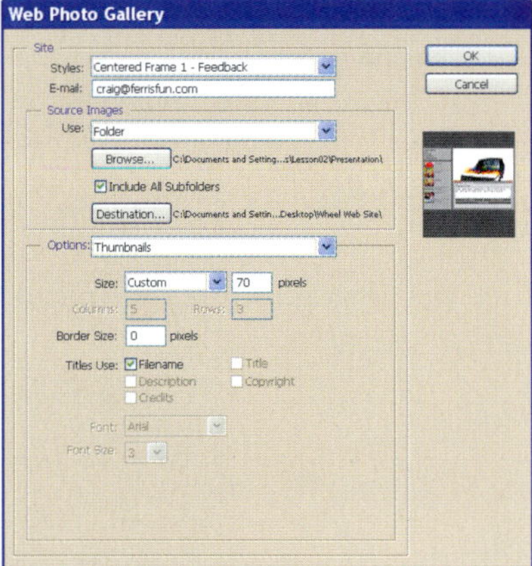

Because you'll accept the default settings for Custom Colors and Security, you don't need to visit those categories.

6 Click OK.

Photoshop automatically opens the files and creates the resources for the Web gallery, and then the gallery opens in your default Web browser application.

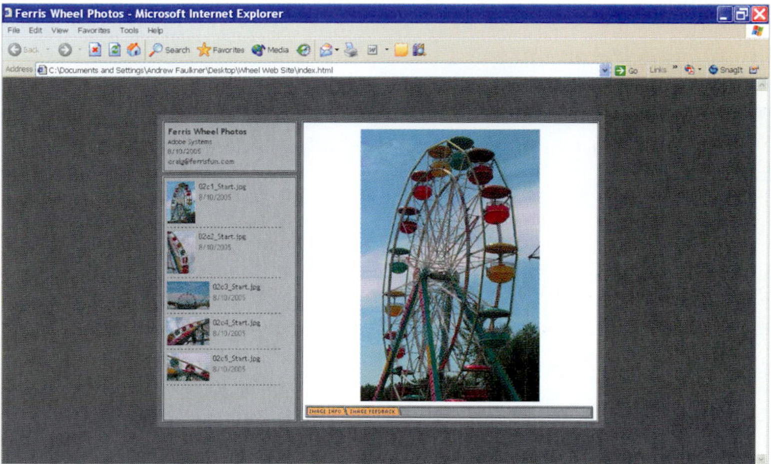

Reviewers can click any thumbnail at left to view a larger preview at right. Clicking the Image Info tab displays information about the selected image. Clicking the Image Feedback tab lets reviewers comment on or approve the image, and e-mail their comments to you.

Web Photo Gallery is just one of several automated tasks you can perform in Adobe Bridge. You can explore the others when you have time.

7 Close your browser and return to Bridge.

Acquiring stock photography

In addition to using Adobe Bridge to organize and locate your own image assets, you can use it to browse and purchase royalty-free stock photography. This is because Adobe Bridge includes a service called Adobe Stock Photos, which provides one-stop shopping for thousands of royalty-free digital images from numerous stock agencies. You can use Adobe Stock Photos to conduct searches, download comps, and purchase images, all from within Adobe Bridge.

Browsing and searching for stock images

As the designer on the Ferris wheel project, let's pretend you've decided to go on a hunt for additional images of Ferris wheels.

1 In the Favorites palette of Adobe Bridge, click Adobe Stock Photos.

The home page for Adobe Stock photos highlights new content and lets you browse and search for royalty-free stock content.

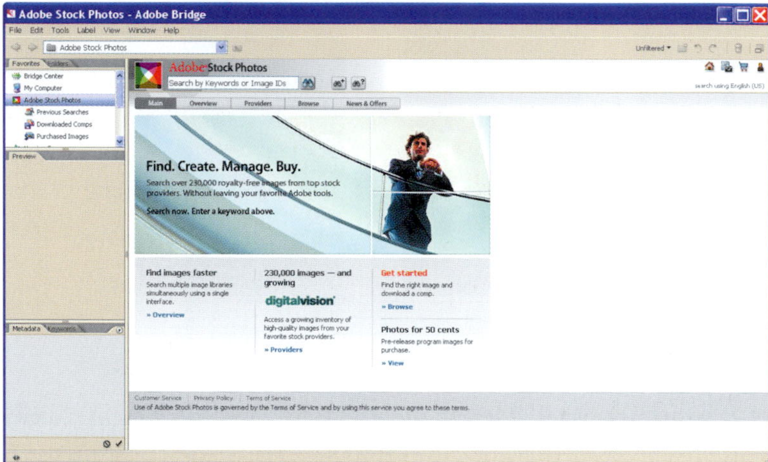

2 In the search box at the top of the page, type the keywords **ferris wheel**, and then press Enter (Windows) or Return (Mac OS), or click the Start Search button.

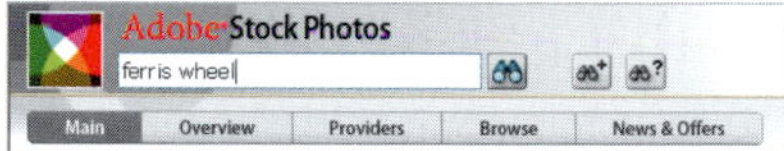

Adobe Stock Photos search results appear in the Bridge browser window, offering all of the same customizable previews controls, including scalable thumbnails, that are available to local image files.

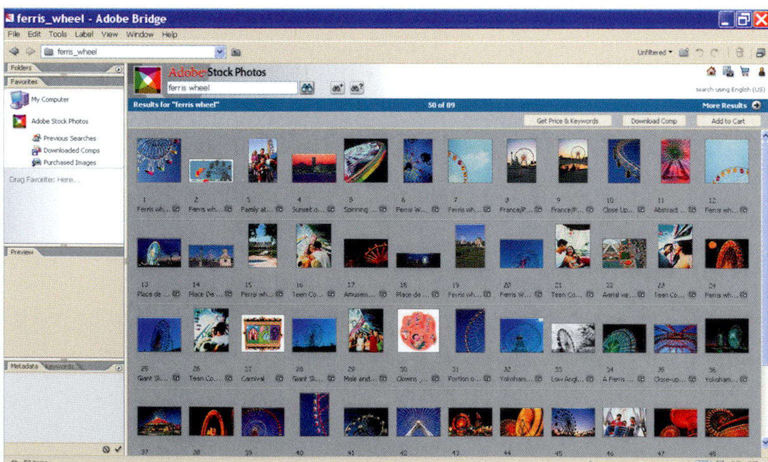

Downloading and purchasing stock photos

Next, download a low-res comp.

1 With an image thumbnail selected (or two or three thumbnails), click the Download Comp button (Download Comp).

Comps may be downloaded for free from Adobe Stock Photos and used without watermarked logos in layouts and proofs. Comps are saved to the Downloaded Comps folder, which is in the My Documents/Adobe Stock Photos folder (Windows) or Documents/Adobe Stock Photos folder (Mac OS).

2 In the Favorites palette, click Downloaded Comps to see your comps.

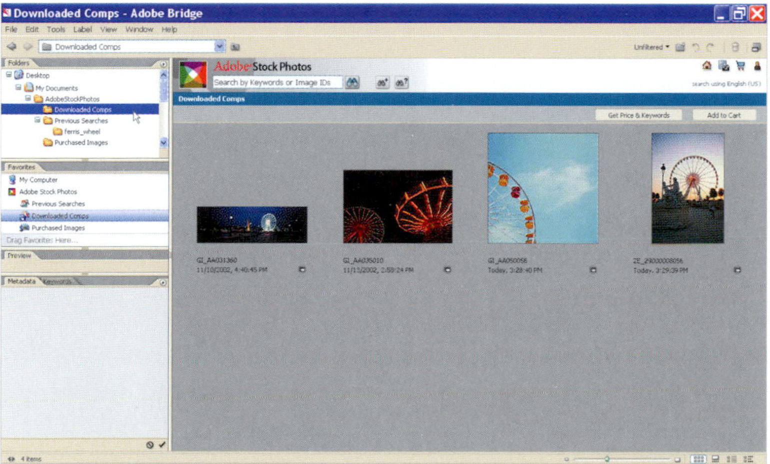

To open these comps in Photoshop, simply double-click on a thumbnail preview as you would any other image file. You can also rename downloaded comps more intuitively, move them to other folders on your hard drive or network, and even place them in page layout files. Adobe Stock Photos preserves the original file information so that when you're ready to purchase an image, you can do it from Bridge.

3 To purchase any image, select its thumbnail preview and click the Add to Cart button (Add to Cart).

***Note:** You will be prompted to choose a country the first time you try to purchase a stock photo. Choose from among the 27 countries in the pop-up menu, then click Continue.*

4 When Adobe Stock Photos tells you that the image has been added to your cart, click the View Shopping Cart button to see what's there.

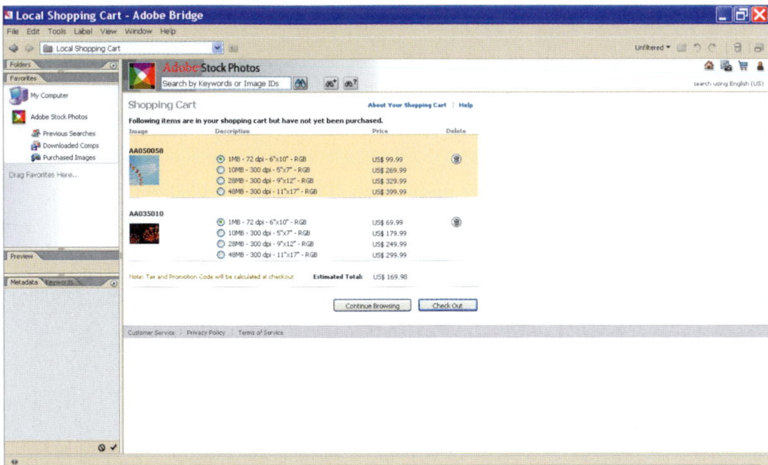

Adobe Stock Photos has added a low-resolution version of the image to your cart.

You can delete images from your shopping cart, choose a different size or resolution, continue shopping, or proceed to checkout from the shopping cart page. Adobe Stock Photos lets you purchase images as a guest, or you can set up an account. Either way, you can purchase images from multiple stock photo libraries in a single transaction. All purchased images are placed in the Purchased Images folder.

Congratulations—you've finished this lesson on Adobe Bridge. As you work through this book, you'll have many more opportunities to use Bridge and to discover what a time-saver it can be.

Review

Review questions

1 Describe three ways to display Adobe Bridge.

2 What are some of the similarities between working with folders and files on the desktop and working with them in Adobe Bridge?

3 How can you customize the browser window and thumbnail previews in Adobe Bridge?

4 What are the advantages of using Adobe Bridge instead of a desktop folder?

Review answers

1 You can display Adobe Bridge in Full mode as a regular application, or toggle to Ultra-Compact or Compact mode. The compact modes display Bridge as a floating palette over other applications.

2 You can use either Adobe Bridge or a desktop folder—such as the Explorer (Windows) or the Finder (Mac OS)—to rename files, move files into the Recycle Bin (Windows) or Trash (Mac OS), move files and folders from one location to another, rename files and folders, and create new folders.

3 You can rearrange the palettes on the left side of the Adobe Bridge browser window by dragging their tabs, and you can resize panes by dragging their edges. You can enlarge and reduce thumbnail previews on the right side of the browser window by dragging the thumbnail slider, and you can choose between Thumbnail, Details, and Filmstrip views, depending on personal preference.

4 Adobe Bridge shows high-resolution, scalable thumbnail previews of image files as well as metadata information about the selected item. You can apply a number of changes to files in Bridge without having to open them in Photoshop; for example, you can rotate them. You can also use Bridge to assign star rankings and colored labels to files, to sort files by various criteria, and to batch-rename files. Finally, you can perform automated functions in Adobe Bridge, such as creating Web photo galleries, and you can browse and purchase royalty-free digital stock photography.

PARIS
Paris is the home of the Rodin Museum.The beautiful surroundings attracted artists including Henri Matisse, and August Rodin rented several rooms in which to store his art. The rooms became his studio where he worked and entertained friends among the wild gardens.The mansion escaped the Reign of Terror unharmed, but during Napoleon's reign, it fell victim to the times. It was sold to the Dames du Sacre-Coeur, a religious group dedicated to the education of young women, who converted the hotel into a boarding school for girls of royal and aristocratic families.
The Church and State separated in 1905 and the school was forced to close. Plans were made to demolish the mansion and replace it by rental apartments. In the meantime, it was divided into several small lodgings. The beautiful surroundings attracted artists including Henri Matisse, and August Rodin rented several rooms in which to store his art. The rooms became his studio where he worked and entertained friends among the wild gardens. Ever since 1919, the sculptures of Auguste Rodin have been housed in a mansion known as the Biron Hotel. The mansion was built by a hairdresser named Abraham Peyrenc in the seventeenth century when Paris Left Bank was still uninhabited.

Adobe Photoshop includes a variety of tools and commands for improving the quality of a photographic image. This lesson steps you through the process of acquiring, resizing, and retouching a photo intended for a print layout. The same basic workflow applies to Web images.

3 Basic Photo Corrections

Lesson overview

In this lesson, you'll learn how to do the following:

- Understand image resolution and size.
- Straighten and crop an image.
- Adjust the tonal range of an image.
- Remove a color cast from an image using Auto Color correction.
- Adjust the saturation and brightness of isolated areas of an image using the Sponge and Dodge tools.
- Apply the Unsharp Mask filter to finish the photo-retouching process.
- Save an image file for use in a page-layout program.

This lesson will take 45 minutes to an hour to complete. If needed, remove the previous lesson folder from your hard drive, and copy the Lesson03 folder onto it. If you need to restore the start files at any time, copy them from the *Adobe Photoshop CS2 Classroom in a Book* CD.

Strategy for retouching

Adobe Photoshop provides a comprehensive set of color-correction tools for adjusting the color and tone of individual images. You can, for example, correct problems in color quality and tonal range created during the original photography or during image scanning, and you can correct problems in composition and sharpen the overall focus of the image.

Organizing an efficient sequence of tasks

Most retouching follows these eight general steps:

- Duplicating the original image or scan. (Always work in a copy of the image file so that you can recover the original later if necessary.)
- Checking the scan quality and making sure that the resolution is appropriate for the way you will use the image.
- Cropping the image to final size and orientation.
- Repairing flaws in scans of damaged photographs (such as rips, dust, or stains).
- Adjusting the overall contrast or tonal range of the image.
- Removing any color casts.
- Adjusting the color and tone in specific parts of the image to bring out highlights, midtones, shadows, and desaturated colors.
- Sharpening the overall focus of the image.

Usually, you should complete these processes in the order listed. Otherwise, the results of one process may cause unintended changes to other aspects of the image, making it necessary for you to redo some of your work.

Note: *Later in this book you'll use adjustment layers, which give you great flexibility to try out different correction settings without risking damage to the original image.*

Adjusting your process for intended uses

The retouching techniques you apply to an image depend in part on how you will use the image. Whether an image is intended for black-and-white publication on newsprint or for full-color Internet distribution affects everything from the resolution of the initial scan to the type of tonal range and color correction that the image requires. Photoshop supports the CMYK color mode for preparing an image to be printed using process colors, as well as RGB and other color modes for Web and mobile authoring.

To illustrate one application of retouching techniques, this lesson takes you through the steps of correcting a photograph intended for four-color print publication.

For more information about CMYK and RGB color modes, see Lesson 16, "Producing and Printing Consistent Color."

Resolution and image size

The first step in retouching a photograph in Photoshop is to make sure that the image is the correct resolution. The term *resolution* refers to the number of small squares known as *pixels* that describe an image and establish its detail. Resolution is determined by *pixel dimensions*, or the number of pixels along the width and height of an image.

Pixels in a photographic image

In computer graphics, there are different types of resolution:

The number of pixels per unit of length in an image is called the *image resolution*, usually measured in pixels per inch (ppi). An image with a high resolution has more pixels (and therefore a larger file size) than an image of the same dimensions with a low resolution. Images in Photoshop can vary from high resolution (300 ppi or higher) to low resolution (72 ppi or 96 ppi).

The number of pixels per unit of length on a monitor is the *monitor resolution*, also usually measured in pixels per inch (ppi). Image pixels are translated directly into monitor pixels. In Photoshop, if the image resolution is higher than the monitor resolution, the image appears larger onscreen than its specified print dimensions. For example, when you display a 1-x-1-inch, 144-ppi image on a 72-ppi monitor, the image fills a 2-x-2-inch area of the screen.

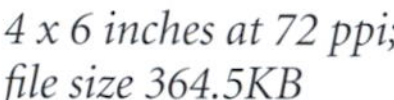

4 x 6 inches at 72 ppi; file size 364.5KB

100% onscreen view

4 x 6 inches at 200 ppi; file size 2.75 MB

100% onscreen view

Note: *It is important to understand what "100% view" means when you work onscreen. At 100%, 1 image pixel = 1 monitor pixel. Unless the resolution of your image is exactly the same as the resolution of the monitor, the image size (in inches, for example) onscreen may be larger or smaller than the image size will be when printed.*

The number of ink dots per inch (dpi) produced by a platesetter or laser printer is the *printer,* or *output, resolution*. Of course, higher-resolution printers combined with higher-resolution images generally produce the best quality. The appropriate resolution for a printed image is determined both by the printer resolution and by the *screen frequency,* or lines per inch (lpi), of the halftone screens used to reproduce images.

Keep in mind that the higher the image resolution, the larger the file size and the longer the file takes to download from the Web.

Note: *To determine the image resolution for the photograph in this lesson, we followed the computer-graphics rule of thumb for color or grayscale images that are intended for print on large commercial printers: Scan at a resolution 1.5 to 2 times the screen frequency used by the printer. Because the magazine in which the image will be printed uses a screen frequency of 133 lpi, the image was scanned at 200 ppi (133 x 1.5).*

For more information on resolution and image size, see Adobe Photoshop Help.

Getting started

The image you'll work on in this lesson is a scanned photograph. You'll prepare the image to be placed in an Adobe InDesign layout for a fictitious magazine. The final image size in the print layout will be 2 x 3 inches.

You'll start the lesson by comparing the original scan to the finished image.

1 Start Photoshop and then immediately hold down Ctrl-Alt-Shift (Windows) or Command-Option-Shift (Mac OS) to restore the default preferences. (See "Restoring default preferences" on page 6.)

2 When prompted, click Yes to confirm that you want to reset preferences, and Close to close the Welcome Screen.

3 Click the Go to Bridge button ( ) on the tool options bar to open Adobe Bridge.

4 In the Favorites palette in the upper left corner of Bridge, click the Lessons favorite, and then double-click the Lesson03 folder in the preview area to see its contents.

5 Make sure your thumbnail previews are large enough for a good look at the images, and compare the 03Start.psd and 03End.psd files.

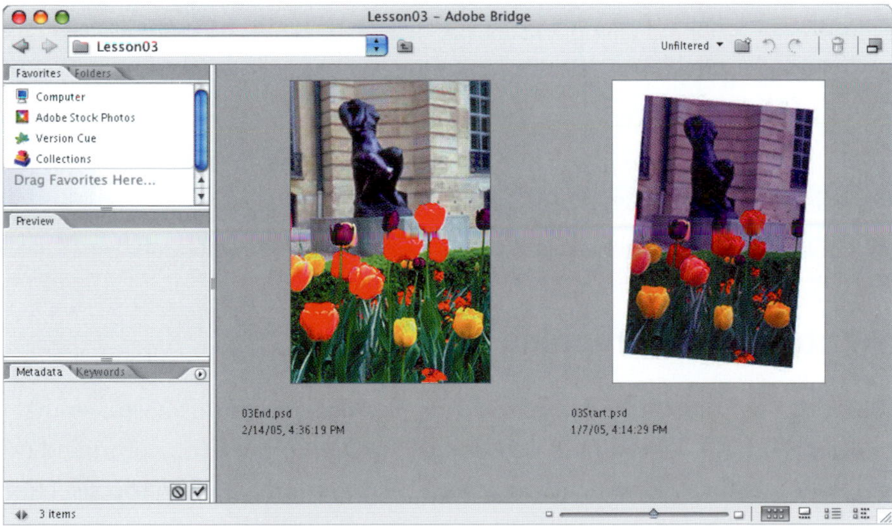

Notice that the scan is crooked, that the colors in the original scanned image are relatively dull, and the image has a red color cast. The dimensions are also larger than needed for the requirements of the magazine. You will fix all of these qualities in this lesson, starting with straightening and cropping the image.

6 Double-click the 03Start.psd thumbnail to open the file in Photoshop.

7 In Photoshop, choose File > Save As, and save the start file in the Lesson03 folder, but rename it 03Work.psd.

Remember, when you're making permanent corrections to an image file, it's always wise to work on a copy rather than on the original. Then, if something goes horribly wrong, at least you'll be able to start over on a fresh copy of the original image.

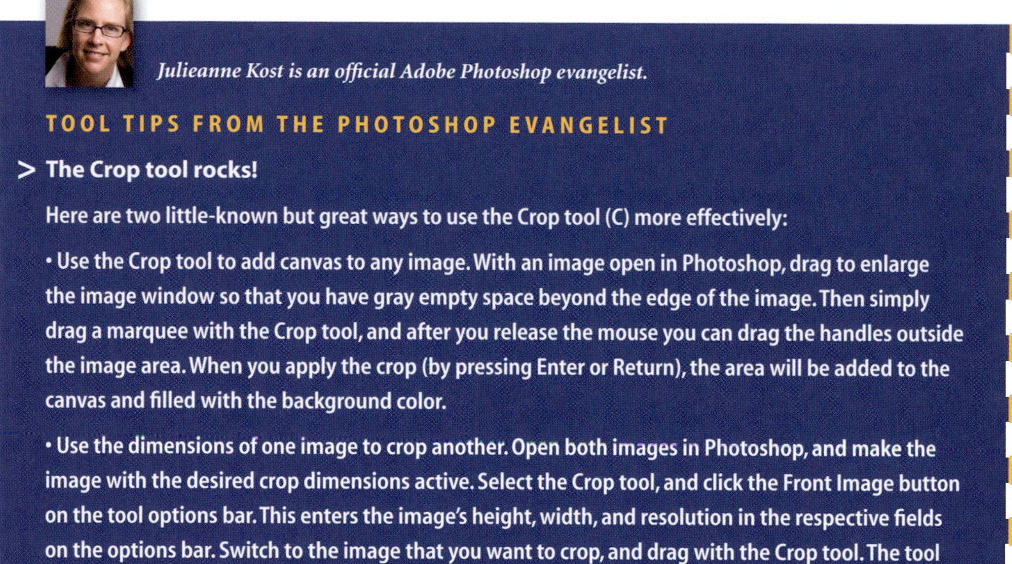

Julieanne Kost is an official Adobe Photoshop evangelist.

TOOL TIPS FROM THE PHOTOSHOP EVANGELIST

> The Crop tool rocks!

Here are two little-known but great ways to use the Crop tool (C) more effectively:

• Use the Crop tool to add canvas to any image. With an image open in Photoshop, drag to enlarge the image window so that you have gray empty space beyond the edge of the image. Then simply drag a marquee with the Crop tool, and after you release the mouse you can drag the handles outside the image area. When you apply the crop (by pressing Enter or Return), the area will be added to the canvas and filled with the background color.

• Use the dimensions of one image to crop another. Open both images in Photoshop, and make the image with the desired crop dimensions active. Select the Crop tool, and click the Front Image button on the tool options bar. This enters the image's height, width, and resolution in the respective fields on the options bar. Switch to the image that you want to crop, and drag with the Crop tool. The tool constrains the aspect ratio as you drag, and when you release and apply the crop, the image will be resized to the desired height, width, and resolution.

Straightening and cropping an image

You'll use the Crop tool to trim and scale the photograph for this lesson so that it fits the space designed for it. You can use either the Crop tool or the Crop command to crop an image. Both methods permanently delete all the pixels outside the crop selection area.

1 In the toolbox, select the Crop tool (⌗). Then, on the tool options bar (at the top of the work area), enter the dimensions (in inches) of the finished image: For Width type **2 in,** and for Height type **3 in**.

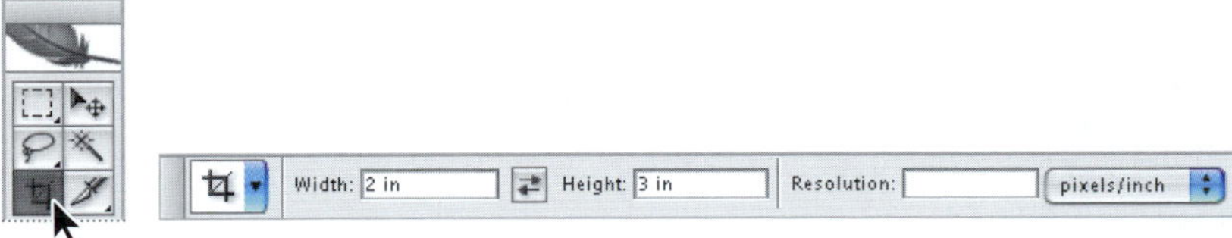

2 Draw a crop marquee around the image. Don't worry about whether the entire image is included, because you'll adjust the marquee in a moment.

As you drag, the marquee retains the same proportion as the dimensions you specified for the target size (2 x 3 inches).

When you release the mouse button, a *cropping shield* covers the area outside the cropping selection, and the tool options bar displays choices about the cropping shield.

3 On the tool options bar, make sure that the Perspective check box is *not* selected.

4 In the image window, move the pointer outside the crop marquee so that it appears as a curved double arrow (↰). Drag clockwise to rotate the marquee until it matches the angle of the picture.

5 Place the pointer inside the crop marquee, and drag the marquee until it contains all the parts of the picture you want shown to produce an artistically pleasing result. If you need to adjust the size of the marquee, drag one of the corner handles.

6 Press Enter (Windows) or Return (Mac OS). The image is now cropped, and the cropped image now fills the image window, straightened, sized, and cropped according to your specifications.

You can use the Image > Trim command to discard a border area around the edge of the image, based on transparency or edge color.

7 Choose File > Save to save your work.

Making automatic adjustments

Photoshop contains a number of highly effective automatic features that fix many pictures with very little effort on your part. These may be all you need for certain types of jobs. However, when you want more control, you can dig down into some of the more technical features and options available in Photoshop.

Just to be a good sport about it, you'll first try the automatic adjustments to brighten the colors in the lesson image file. Then, you'll make adjustments using manual controls on another copy of the image.

1 If you didn't save your work after you cropped the image in the previous exercise, choose File > Save now.

2 Choose File > Save As, rename the cropped file **03Auto.psd**, and click Save.

3 Choose Image > Adjustments > Auto Color.

4 Choose Image > Adjustments > Shadow/Highlight.

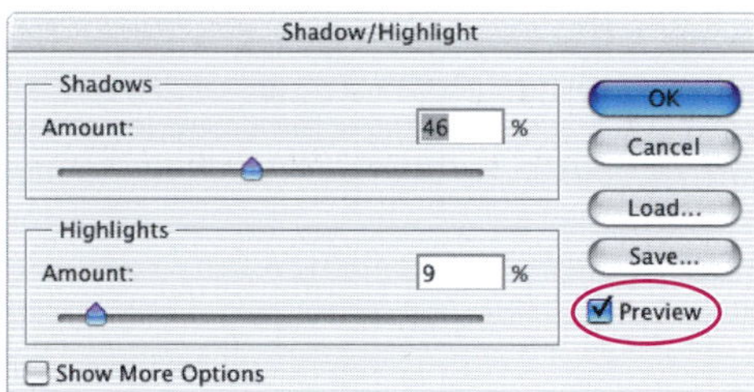

5 In the Shadow/Highlight dialog box, drag the Highlight and Shadow sliders as needed until you think the image looks good. Make sure that Preview is checked so that you can see the changes applied to the image window as you work.

6 Click OK to close the dialog box, and then choose File > Save.

7 Close the 03Auto.psd file. Then choose File > Open Recent > 03Work.psd to open that image file.

Manually adjusting the tonal range

The tonal range of an image represents the amount of *contrast*, or detail, in the image and is determined by the image's distribution of pixels, ranging from the darkest pixels (black) to the lightest pixels (white). You'll now correct the photograph's contrast using the Levels command.

In this task, you'll use a graph in the Levels dialog box that represents the range of values (dark and light) in the image. This graph has controls that adjust the shadows, highlights, and midtones (or gamma) of the image. You'll also refer to the Histogram palette, which displays this information for you. Unless you're aiming for a special effect, the ideal histogram extends across the full width of the graph, and the middle portion has fairly uniform peaks and valleys, representing adequate pixel data in the midtones.

1 Choose Window > Histogram, or click the Histogram tab in the Navigator palette group to make the Histogram palette visible. Then choose Expanded View from the Histogram palette menu.

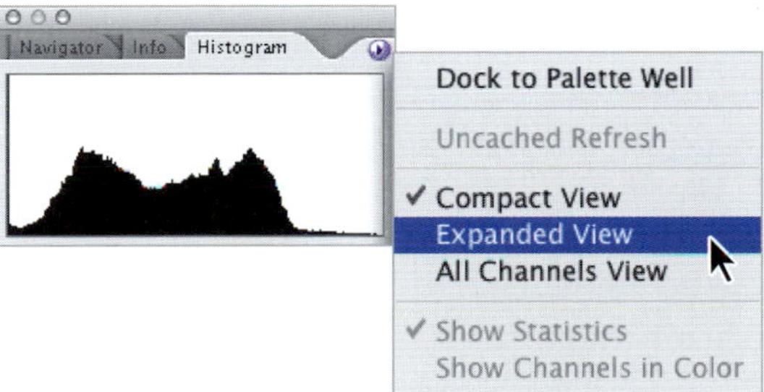

2 Choose Image > Adjustments > Levels to open the Levels dialog box.

3 Make sure that the Preview check box is selected, and then move the dialog box, if necessary, so that you can also see the image window and Histogram palette.

The left (black) triangle below the histogram represents the shadows, the middle (gray) triangle represents the midtones, or *gamma*, and the right (white) triangle represents the highlights. If your image had colors across the entire brightness range, the graph would extend across the full width of the histogram. Notice that at this point, the graphs in the Levels dialog box and the Histogram palette are identical.

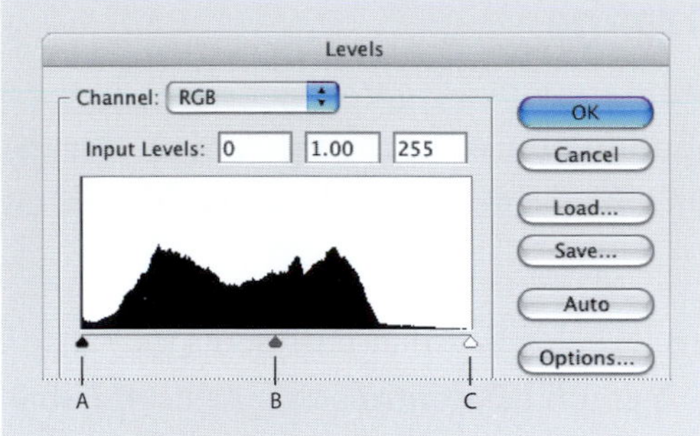

***A.** Shadows **B.** Midtones, or gamma **C.** Highlights*

4 In the Levels dialog box, drag the left triangle to the right to the point where the histogram indicates that the darkest colors begin.

As you drag, the first Input Levels value (above the histogram graph) changes and so does the image itself. In the Histogram palette, the left portion of the graph now stretches to the edge of the frame. This indicates that the darkest shadow values have shifted closer to black.

***Note:** You can also scrub to change the Input Levels value: First click in the text box for the value you want to change, and then drag the pointer over the Input Levels label.*

5 Drag the right triangle to the left to the point where the histogram indicates that the lightest colors begin. Again, notice the changes in the third Input Levels value, in the image itself, and in the Histogram palette graph.

6 Drag the middle triangle a short distance to the left side to lighten the midtones.

Watch the changes in the image window and in the Histogram palette graph to determine how far to drag the middle triangle.

7 When the image looks good to you (we used Input Levels values of 25, 1.20, and 197), click OK to apply the changes. Then save your work.

About the Auto Contrast command

You can also adjust the contrast (highlights and shadows) and the overall mix of colors in an image automatically using the Image > Adjustments > Auto Contrast command. Adjusting the contrast maps the darkest and lightest pixels in the image to black and white. This remapping causes the highlights to appear lighter and the shadows to appear darker and can improve the appearance of many photographic or continuous-tone images. (The Auto Contrast command does not improve flat-color images.)

The Auto Contrast command clips white and black pixels by 0.5%—that is, it ignores the first 0.5% of either extreme when identifying the lightest and darkest pixels in the image. This clipping of color values ensures that white and black values are representative areas of the image content rather than extreme pixel values.

For this project, you won't use the Auto Contrast feature, but it's a feature you should know about so that you can use it in your own projects.

Removing a color cast

Some images contain color casts (imbalanced colors), which may occur during scanning or which may have existed in the original image. This photograph of the window has a red cast. You'll use the Auto Color feature to correct this.

Note: *To see a color cast in an image on your monitor, you need a 24-bit monitor (one that can display millions of colors). On monitors that can display only 256 colors (8 bits), a color cast is difficult, if not impossible, to detect.*

1 Choose Image > Adjustments > Auto Color.

The red color cast goes away.

2 Choose File > Save.

About the Auto Color and Auto Correction commands

The Auto Color command adjusts the contrast and color of an image by searching the actual image rather than the channel histograms for shadows, midtones, and highlights. It neutralizes the midtones and clips the white and black pixels based on the values set in the Auto Correction Options dialog box.

The Auto Correction Options dialog box lets you automatically adjust the overall tonal range of an image, specify clipping percentages, and assign color values to shadows, midtones, and highlights. You can apply the settings during a single use of the Levels or Curves dialog boxes, or you can save the settings for future use with the Levels, Auto Levels, Auto Contrast, Auto Color, and Curves commands.

To open the Auto Correction Options dialog box, click Options in the Levels dialog box or in the Curves dialog box.

Replacing colors in an image

With the Replace Color command, you can create temporary *masks* based on specific colors and then replace these colors. (A mask isolates an area of an image so that changes affect just the selected area and not the rest of the image.) The Replace Color dialog box contains options for adjusting the hue, saturation, and lightness components of the selection: *Hue* is color, *saturation* is the purity of the color, and *lightness* is how much white or black is in the image.

You'll use the Replace Color command to change the color of one of the tulips in the image we've been correcting throughout this lesson.

1 Select the Rectangular Marquee tool (⬚), and draw a selection border around the yellow tulip in the left foreground of the image. Don't worry about making a perfect selection, but be sure to include all of the yellow flower.

2 Choose Image > Adjustments > Replace Color.

The Replace Color dialog box opens, and by default, the Selection area displays a black representation of the current selection.

Notice the three eyedropper tools in the Replace Color dialog box. One selects a color; the second adds a color to the sample; the third removes a color from the sample.

A. *Eyedropper tool*
B. *Add to Sample eyedropper*
C. *Subtract from Sample eyedropper*

3 Using the Eyedropper tool (), click anywhere in the yellow tulip in the image window to sample that color.

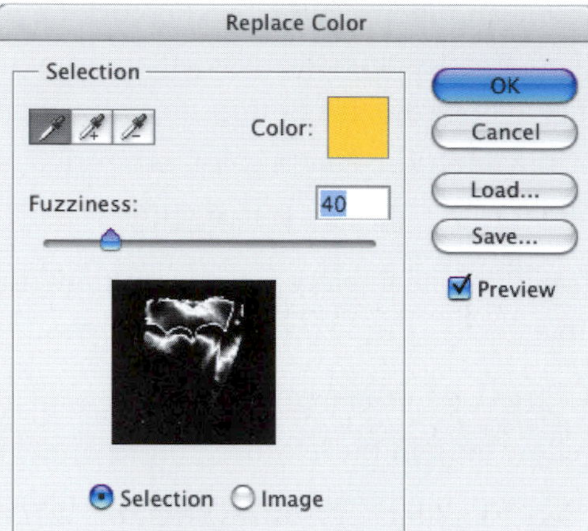

4 Then, use the Add to Sample eyedropper () to sample other areas of the yellow tulip until the entire flower is selected and highlighted in the mask display in the Replace Color dialog box.

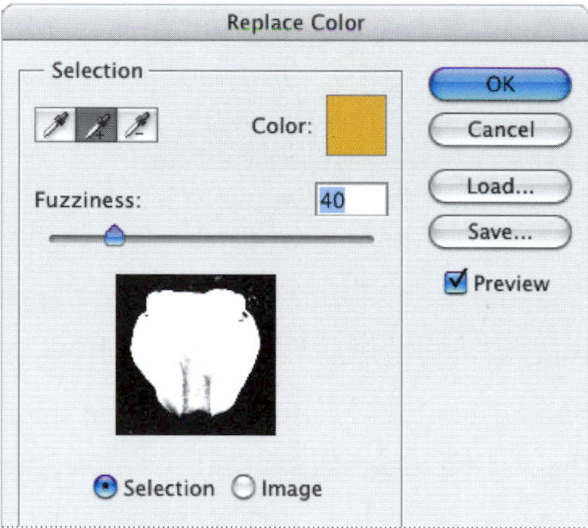

5 Drag the Fuzziness slider up to 45 to increase the tolerance level slightly.

Fuzziness controls the degree to which related colors are included in the mask.

6 If the mask display includes any white areas that are *not* part of the tulip, get rid of those now: Select the Subtract from Sample eyedropper () and click those areas in either the image window or in the Replace Color mask display to remove those stray pixels. (It's OK if a few remain in the selection.)

7 In the Replacement area of the Replace Color dialog box, drag the Hue slider to –40, the Saturation slider to –10, and leave the Lightness slider at 0.

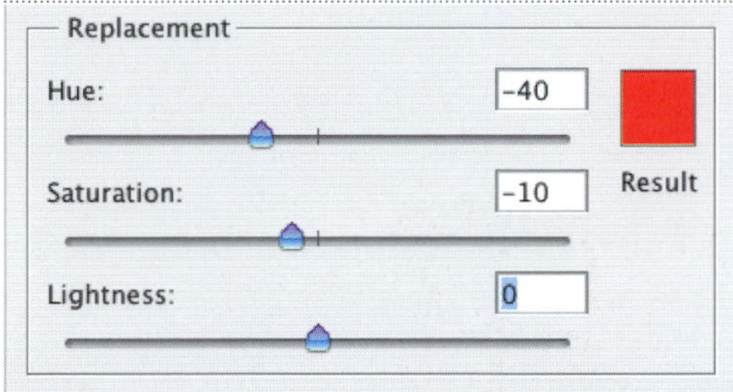

As you change the values, the color of the tulip changes in hue, saturation, and lightness, and the tulip becomes red.

8 Click OK to apply the changes.

9 Choose Select > Deselect, and then choose File > Save.

Adjusting lightness with the Dodge tool

You'll use the Dodge tool next to lighten the highlights and bring out the details of the sculpture in the image. The Dodge tool is based on a traditional photographer's method of holding back light during an exposure to lighten an area of the image.

1 In the toolbox, select the Dodge tool ( ).

2 On the tool options bar, do the following:

- Select a fairly large, feathered brush, such as 27 pixels, from the Brush pop-up palette (click outside the palette to close it).
- Choose Range > Highlights.
- Set Exposure to 15%.

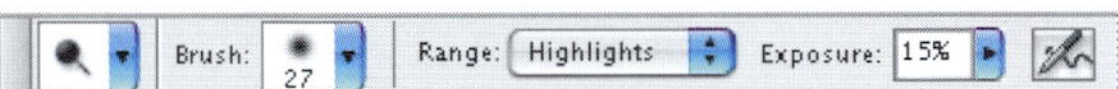

3 Using vertical strokes, drag the Dodge tool over the sculpture to bring out the details and remove the dinginess.

You don't always need to use vertical strokes with the Dodge tool, but they work well with this particular image. If you make a mistake or don't like the results, choose Edit > Undo and try again until you are satisfied.

Original

Result

4 Choose File > Save.

Adjusting saturation with the Sponge tool

Next, you'll use the Sponge tool to saturate the color of the tulips. When you change the saturation of a color, you adjust its strength or purity. The Sponge tool is useful for making subtle saturation changes to specific areas of an image.

1 Select the Sponge tool ( ), hidden under the Dodge tool ( ).

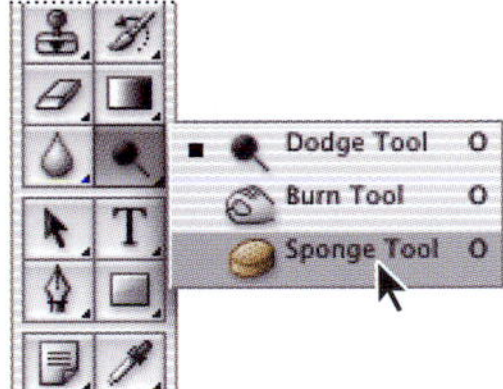

2 On the tool options bar, do the following:

- Again select a large, feathered brush, such as 27 pixels, from the Brush pop-up palette.
- Choose Mode > Saturate.
- For Flow (which sets the intensity of the saturation effect), enter **90%**.

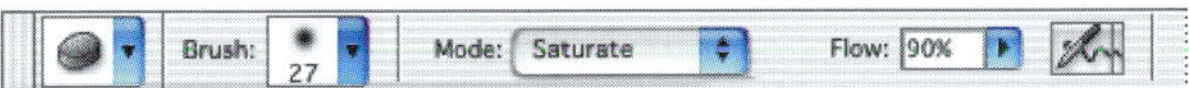

3 Drag the sponge back and forth over the tulips and leaves to increase their saturation. The more you drag over an area, the more saturated the color becomes.

4 Save your work.

Applying the Unsharp Mask filter

The last task you may do when retouching a photo is to apply the Unsharp Mask filter. The Unsharp Mask filter adjusts the contrast of the edge detail and creates the illusion of a more focused image.

1 Choose Filter > Sharpen > Unsharp Mask.

2 In the Unsharp Mask dialog box, make sure that the Preview box is checked so that you can see the results in the image window.

You can drag inside the preview in the dialog box to see different parts of the image, or use the plus (+) and minus (–) buttons below the thumbnail to zoom in and out.

3 Drag the Amount slider to about 62% to sharpen the image.

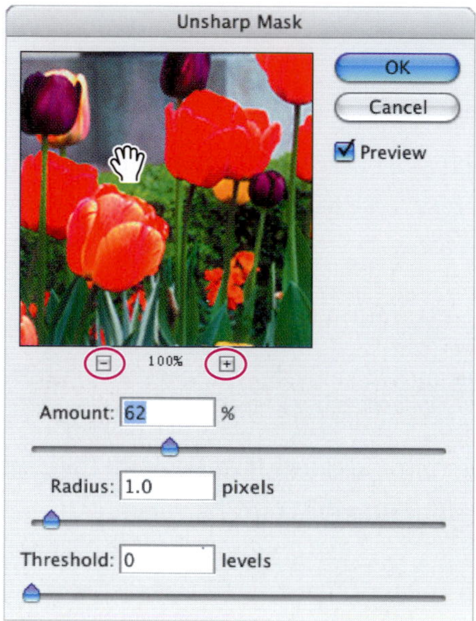

As you try different settings, toggle the Preview check box off and on to see how your changes affect the image. Or, you can click and hold the mouse button on the thumbnail preview in the dialog box to temporarily toggle the filter off. If your image is large, using the thumbnail preview can be more efficient, because only a small area is redrawn.

4 Drag the Radius slider to determine the number of pixels surrounding the edge pixels that will affect the sharpening. The higher the resolution, the higher the Radius setting should be. (We used the default value, 1.0 pixel.)

5 (Optional) Adjust the Threshold slider. This determines how different the sharpened pixels must be from the surrounding area before they are considered edge pixels and subsequently sharpened by the Unsharp Mask filter. The default Threshold value of 0 sharpens all pixels in the image. Try a different value, such as 4 or 5.

6 When you are satisfied with the results, click OK to apply the Unsharp Mask filter.

7 Choose File > Save.

About unsharp masking

Unsharp masking, or USM, is a traditional film-compositing technique used to sharpen edges in an image. The Unsharp Mask filter corrects blurring introduced during photographing, scanning, resampling, or printing. It is useful for images intended for both print and online viewing.

The Unsharp Mask locates pixels that differ from surrounding pixels by the threshold you specify and increases the pixels' contrast by the amount you specify. In addition, you specify the radius of the region to which each pixel is compared.

The effects of the Unsharp Mask filter are far more pronounced onscreen than they are in high-resolution output. If your final destination is print, experiment to determine what settings work best for your image.

Comparing automatic and manual results

Near the beginning of this lesson, you adjusted the lesson image using only automatic color and value controls. For the rest of the lesson, you painstakingly applied manual adjustments to get specific results. Now it's time to compare the two.

1 Choose File > Open Recent > 03Auto.psd, if it is available. Otherwise, choose File > Open, navigate to the Lessons/Lesson03 folder, and open the file.

2 Choose Window > Arrange > Tile Vertically to position the 03Auto.psd and the 03Work.psd image windows side by side.

3 Visually compare the two results.

03Auto.psd

03Work.psd

4 Close the 03Auto.psd file.

For some designers, the automatic commands may be all they'll ever need. For others with more sensitive visual requirements, manual adjustments are the way to go. The best of both worlds is when you understand the trade-offs of the two methods and can choose one or the other according to your requirements for the specific project and image.

Saving the image for four-color printing

Before you save a Photoshop file for use in a four-color publication, you must change the image to CMYK color mode in order to print your publication correctly in four-color process inks. You'll use the Mode command to change the image color mode.

For more information about converting between color modes, see Photoshop Help.

1 Choose Image > Mode > CMYK Color.

- If you use Adobe InDesign to create your publications, you can skip the rest of this process and just choose File > Save. InDesign can import native Photoshop files, so there is no need to convert the image to TIFF format.
- If you are using another layout application, you must save the photo as a TIFF file.

2 Choose File > Save As.

3 In the Save As dialog box, choose TIFF from the Format menu.

4 Click Save.

5 In the TIFF Options dialog box, select the correct Byte Order for your operating system and click OK.

The image is now fully retouched, saved, and ready for placement in a page layout application.

For more information about file formats, see "About file formats," page 229.

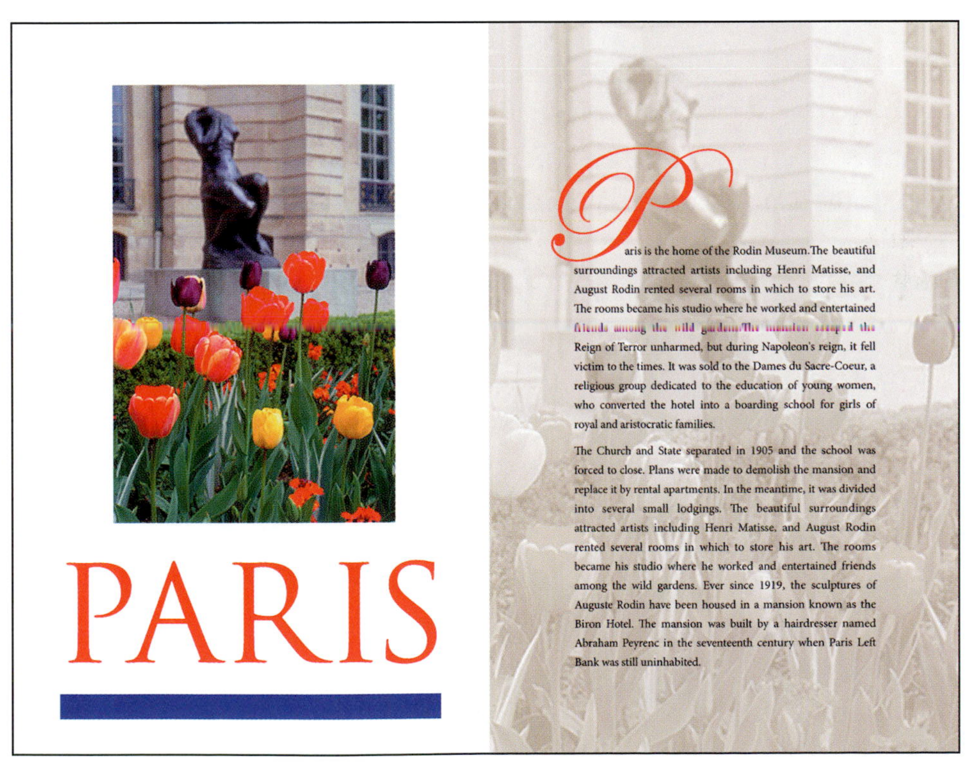
PARIS
Paris is the home of the Rodin Museum.The beautiful surroundings attracted artists including Henri Matisse, and August Rodin rented several rooms in which to store his art. The rooms became his studio where he worked and entertained
Reign of Terror unharmed, but during Napoleon's reign, it fell victim to the times. It was sold to the Dames du Sacre-Coeur, a religious group dedicated to the education of young women, who converted the hotel into a boarding school for girls of royal and aristocratic families.
The Church and State separated in 1905 and the school was forced to close. Plans were made to demolish the mansion and replace it by rental apartments. In the meantime, it was divided into several small lodgings. The beautiful surroundings attracted artists including Henri Matisse, and August Rodin rented several rooms in which to store his art. The rooms became his studio where he worked and entertained friends among the wild gardens. Ever since 1919, the sculptures of Auguste Rodin have been housed in a mansion known as the Biron Hotel. The mansion was built by a hairdresser named Abraham Peyrenc in the seventeenth century when Paris Left Bank was still uninhabited.

Review

Review questions

1 What does *resolution* mean?

2 How can you use the Crop tool when retouching photos?

3 How can you adjust the tonal range of an image?

4 What is saturation, and how can you adjust it?

5 Why would you use the Unsharp Mask filter on a photo?

Review answers

1 The term *resolution* refers to the number of pixels that describe an image and establish its detail. The three different types are *image resolution*, *monitor resolution*—both of which are measured in pixels per inch (ppi)—and *printer,* or *output, resolution,* which is measured in ink dots per inch (dpi).

2 You can use the Crop tool to trim, scale, and straighten an image.

3 You can use the black, white, and gray triangles below the Levels command histogram to control the midpoint and where the darkest and lightest points in the image begin, thus extending its tonal range.

4 Saturation is the strength, or purity, of color in an image. You can use the Sponge tool to increase the saturation in a specific area of an image.

5 The Unsharp Mask filter adjusts the contrast of the edge detail and creates the illusion of a more focused image.

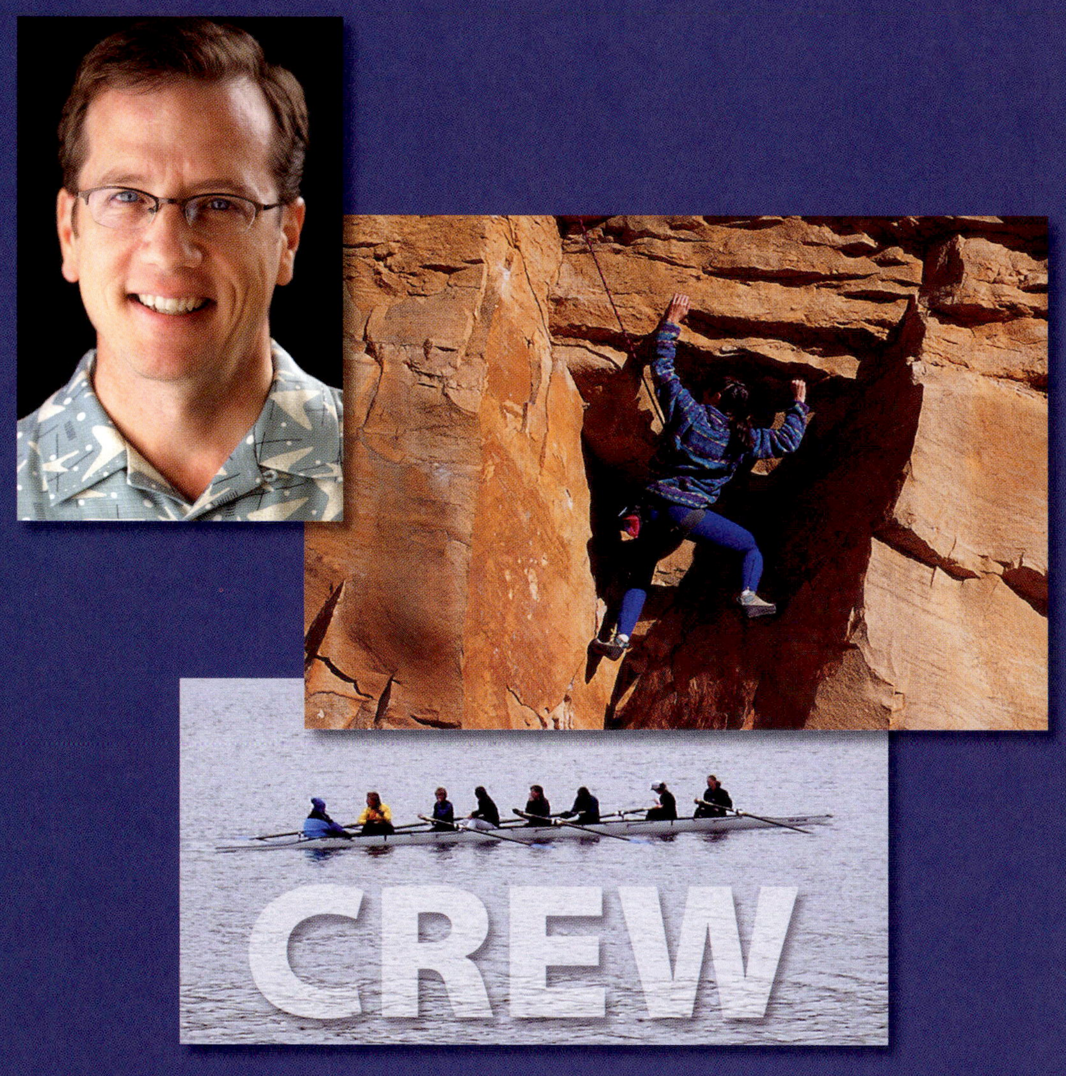

Adobe Photoshop includes a powerful set of cloning tools that make retouching photographs easy and intuitive. Thanks to the underlying technology supporting these features, even touchups of the human face appear so lifelike and natural that it is difficult to detect that a photograph has been altered.

4 Retouching and Repairing

Lesson overview

In this lesson, you'll learn how to do the following:

- Use the Clone Stamp tool to eliminate an unwanted part of an image.
- Use the Spot Healing Brush tool to repair part of an image.
- Use the Healing Brush and Patch tools to blend in corrections.
- Make corrections on a duplicate layer and adjust it for a natural look.
- Backtrack within your work session using the History palette.
- Use the History brush to partially restore an image to a previous state.
- Use snapshots to preserve earlier states of your work and to compare alternative treatments of the image.

This lesson will take about 45 minutes to complete. If needed, remove the previous lesson folder from your hard drive, and copy the Lesson04 folder onto it. As you work on this lesson, you'll overwrite the start files. If you need to restore the start files, copy them from the *Adobe Photoshop CS2 Classroom in a Book* CD.

Getting started

In this lesson, you'll work on three separate projects, editing three different photographs. Each of them employs the different retouching tools in unique ways, so you'll explore the strengths and special uses of the various tools.

You'll start by previewing the three images that you'll retouch in this lesson.

1 Launch Adobe Photoshop, holding down Ctrl-Alt-Shift (Windows) or Command-Option-Shift (Mac OS) to restore the default preferences. (See "Restoring default preferences" on page 6.)

2 When prompted, click Yes to confirm that you want to reset preferences, and Close to close the Welcome Screen.

3 Click the Go to Bridge button ( ) on the tool options bar to open Adobe Bridge.

4 In the Favorites palette, click Lessons, then double-click the Lesson04 folder thumbnail to preview its contents, namely, the Lesson04 A, B, and C start and end files.

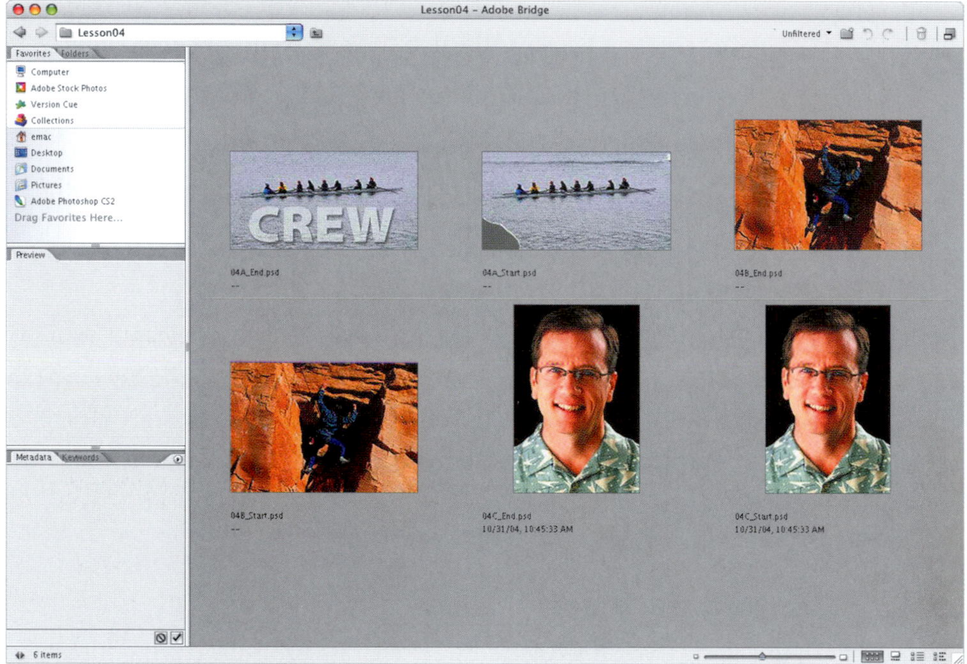

- The first project is a photograph of a women's crew team with semitransparent text superimposed on the foreground. You will repair a torn-off corner of the scanned image and remove some distracting areas where a passing boat and its wake appear in the background.

- The second project shows a rock climber scaling a stone wall. You will clean up the wall beside the climber to remove some graffiti and scars from old bolt holes on the surface of the rock.

• The third project is a portrait of a man. You will retouch the portrait to remove some of the fine lines from the man's forehead and around his eyes.

5 When you have finished previewing the files, double-click the 04A_Start.psd file thumbnail to open the image in Photoshop.

6 If necessary, in Photoshop, zoom in to 100% and resize the image window so that you can see the entire image.

Repairing areas with the Clone Stamp tool

The Clone Stamp tool uses pixels from one area of an image to replace the pixels in another part of the image. Using this tool, you can not only remove unwanted objects from your images, but you can also fill in missing areas in photographs you scan from damaged originals.

You'll start by filling in the torn corner of the photograph with cloned water from another area of the picture.

1 Select the Clone Stamp tool ( ).

2 On the tool options bar, open the Brush pop-up palette and select a medium-sized brush with a soft edge, such as Soft Round 21. Then, make sure that the Aligned option is selected.

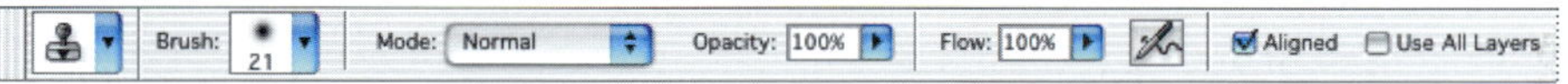

3 Move the Clone Stamp tool pointer to the center of the image so that it is at the same level as the top edge of the torn corner. Then, hold down Alt (Windows) or Option (Mac OS) so that the pointer appears as target crosshairs, and click to start the sampling at that part of the image. Release the Alt or Option key.

4 Starting at the top edge of the torn corner of the photograph, drag the Clone Stamp tool over a small area at the top of the torn area of the image.

Notice the crosshairs that appear to the right of the Clone Stamp tool in the image window. The crosshairs indicate the source area of the image that the Clone Stamp tool is reproducing as you drag.

5 Release the mouse button and move the pointer to another area of the missing corner, and then start dragging again.

Notice that the crosshairs reappear not at the original source spot that you selected in Step 3, but at the same spatial relationship to the Clone Stamp tool pointer that they had when you made the first stroke. This happens because you selected the Aligned option, which resets the crosshairs at that position regardless of the position of the Clone Stamp tool.

Note: *When the Aligned option is not selected and you make multiple brush strokes, the crosshairs and the brush maintain the same spatial relationship (distance and direction) that they had when you started your first brush stroke, regardless of the location of the original sample site.*

6 Continue cloning the water until the entire missing corner of the image is filled in.

If necessary to help make the surface of the water appear to blend in naturally with the rest of the image, you can adjust your cloning by resetting the sample area (as you did in Step 3) and recloning. Or, you can try deselecting the Aligned option and cloning again.

7 When you are satisfied with the appearance of the water, choose File > Save.

Using the Spot Healing Brush tool

The next task to be done is to remove the boat and its wake from the upper area of the image. You could do this with the Clone Stamp tool, but instead you'll use another technique. You'll use the Spot Healing Brush to paint out the wake and boat.

Painting with the Spot Healing Brush

The Spot Healing Brush tool quickly removes blemishes and other imperfections from photos. It works similarly to the Healing Brush: It paints with sampled pixels from an image or pattern and matches the texture, lighting, transparency, and shading of the sampled pixels to the pixels being healed. But unlike the Healing Brush (which you'll use later in this lesson), the Spot Healing Brush doesn't require you to specify a sample spot. It automatically samples from around the retouched area.

The Spot Healing Brush is excellent for retouching blemishes in portraits, but it will also work nicely in this image of the boat on water, because the water has a uniform, muted appearance across the top of the image.

1 In the toolbox, select the Spot Healing Brush tool ( ).

2 On the tool options bar, click the Brush pop-up menu and make the brush larger, about 30 pixels in diameter.

3 Drag with the Spot Healing Brush in the image window across the wake and the small passing motor boat in the background. You can use one stroke or successive strokes; paint until you are satisfied with the results. As you drag, the stroke at first appears dark gray, but when you release the mouse, the painted area is "healed."

You'll add just one final tweak to this retouching project, and then you'll be finished.

4 In the Layers palette, click to place an eye icon (👁) in the CREW layer so that the text is visible in the image window.

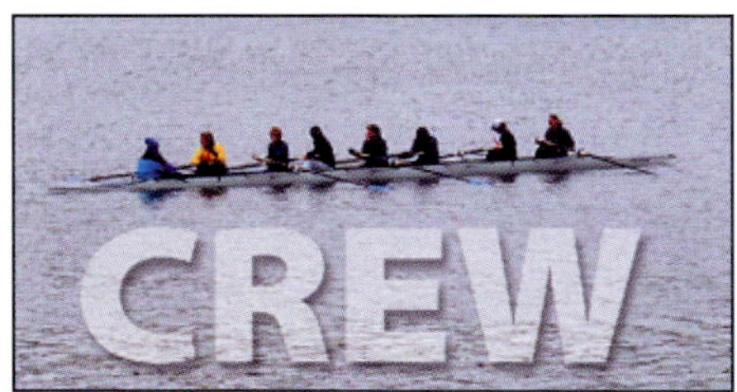

5 Choose File > Save, and then close the 04A_Start.psd file.

Using the Healing Brush and Patch tools

The Healing Brush and Patch tools go one step beyond the capabilities of the Clone Stamp and Spot Healing Brush tools. Using their ability to simultaneously apply and blend pixels from area to area, they open the door to natural-looking touchups in areas that are not uniform in color or texture.

In this project, you'll touch up the stone wall, removing some graffiti and bolt holes left over from obsolete climbing techniques. Because the rock has variations in its colors, textures, and lighting, it would be challenging to successfully use the Clone Stamp tool to touch up the damaged areas. Fortunately, the Healing Brush and Patch tools make this process easy.

If you want to review the "before" and "after" versions of this image, use Adobe Bridge as described in "Getting started" on page 111.

Using the Healing Brush to remove flaws

Your first goal for this image is to remove the initials that mar the natural beauty of the rock wall.

1 Click the Go to Bridge button ( ) on the tool options bar, and in Bridge, double-click the 04B_Start.psd file to open it in Photoshop.

2 In Photoshop, select the Zoom tool ( ) and click the initials "DJ" that have been scratched into the lower left area of the rock so that you see that area of the image at about 200%.

3 In the toolbox, select the Healing Brush tool ( ), hidden under the Spot Healing Brush tool.

4 On the tool options bar, open the Brush pop-up control palette, and change the Diameter value to 10 pixels. Then, close the pop-up palette and make sure that the other settings on the tool options bar are set to the default values: Normal in the Mode option, Sampled in the Source option, and the Aligned check box deselected.

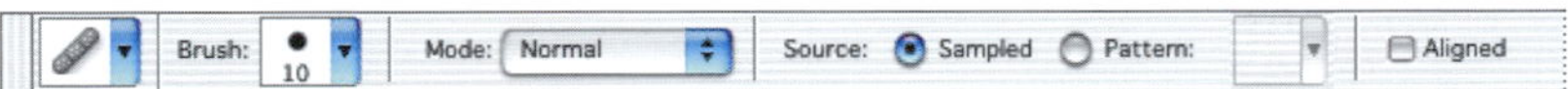

5 Hold down Alt (Windows) or Option (Mac OS) and click just above the scratched-in graffiti in the image to sample that part of the rock. Then release the Alt/Option key.

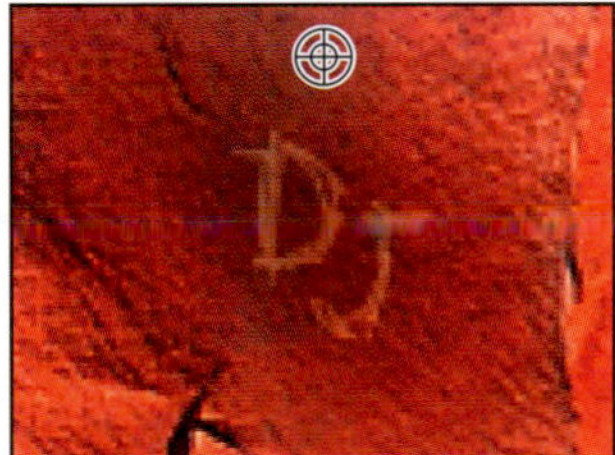

6 Starting above the graffiti "D," paint straight down over the top part of the letter, using a short stroke.

Notice that as you paint, the area the brush covers temporarily looks as if it isn't making a good color match with the underlying image. However, when you release the mouse button, the brush stroke blends in nicely with the rest of the rock surface.

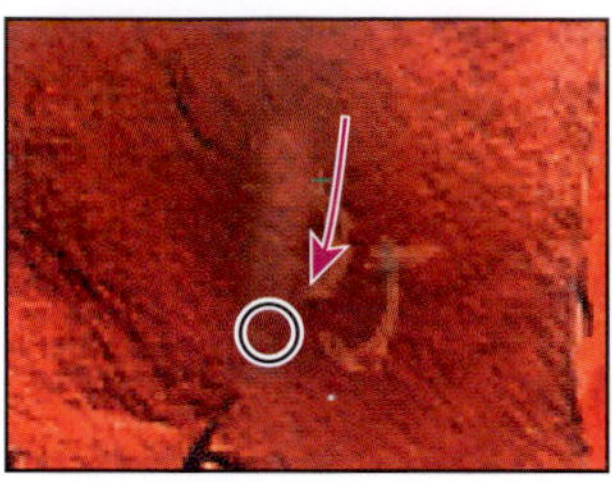

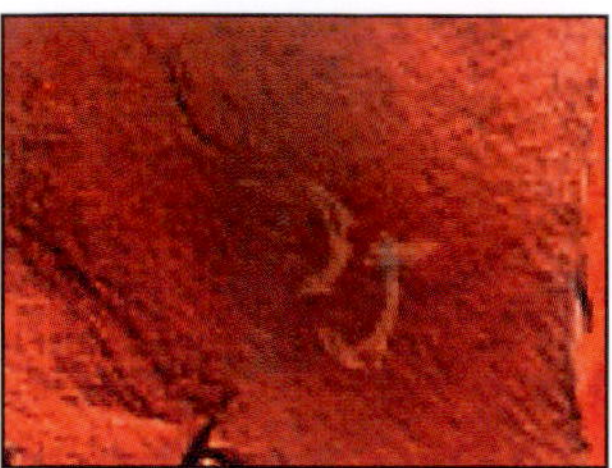

7 Continue using short strokes to paint over the graffiti, starting at the top and moving down until you can no longer detect the graffiti letters.

When you finish removing the graffiti, look closely at the surface of the rock, and notice that even the subtle striations in the stone appear to be fully restored and natural-looking in the image.

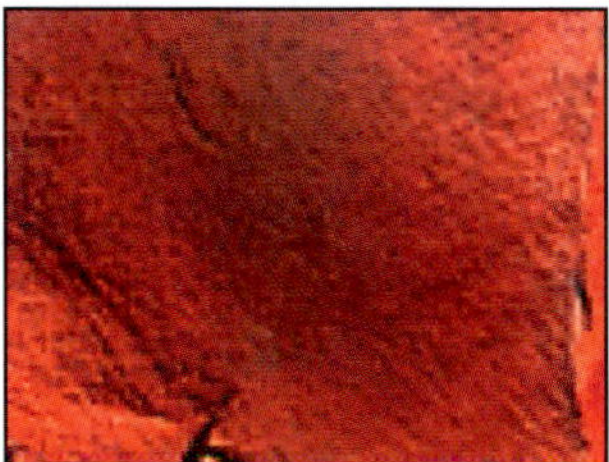

8 Zoom out to 100%, and choose File > Save.

About snapshots and History palette states

When you do retouching work, it can be easy to over-edit images until they no longer look realistic. One of the safeguards you can take to save intermediate stages of your work is to take Photoshop snapshots of the image at various points in your progress.

The History palette automatically records the actions you perform in a Photoshop file. You can use the History palette states like a multiple Undo command to restore the image to previous stages in your work. For example, to undo the most recent six actions, simply click the sixth item above the current state in the History palette. To return to the latest state, scroll back down the History palette and select the state in the lowest position on the list.

The number of items saved in the History palette is determined by a Preferences setting. The default specifies that only the 20 most recent actions are recorded. As you make more changes to the image file, the earliest states are lost as the latest ones are added to the History palette.

When you select an earlier state in the History palette, the image window reverts to the condition it had at that phase. All the subsequent actions are still listed below it in the palette. However, if you select an earlier state in your work and then make a new change, all the states that appeared after the selected state are lost, replaced by the new state.

Note: *The following technique is not recommended when you work with large or complex images, such as images with many layers, because this can slow down performance. Saving many previous states and snapshots is RAM-intensive. If you work frequently with complicated images that require maximum RAM, consider reducing the number of history states saved by changing that setting in your Photoshop preferences.*

Snapshots give you an opportunity to try out different techniques and then choose among them. Typically, you might take a snapshot at a stage of the work that you are confident you want to keep, at least as a base point. Then, you could try out various techniques until you reach a possible completed phase. If you take another snapshot at that phase, it will be saved for the duration of the current work session on that file. Then, you can revert to the first snapshot and try out different techniques and ideas for finishing the image. When that is finalized, you could take a third snapshot, revert to the first snapshot, and try again.

When you finish experimenting, you can scroll to the top of the History palette to where the snapshots are listed. Then, you can select each of the final snapshots in turn and compare the results.

Once you identify the one you like best, you can select it, save your file, and close it. At that time, your snapshots and History palette listings would be permanently lost.

Note: *You can keep an Edit History Log on a Photoshop file. The Edit History Log is a textual history of what has been done to the image file. For more information, see Photoshop Help.*

Taking a snapshot

Because you are satisfied with the results of your healing the graffiti marks, now is a good time to take a snapshot. This will serve as a baseline for any future experimentation during this work session. (Remember that snapshots and history listings are discarded when you close a file.)

1 Close the Navigator, Color, and Layer palette groups—you won't use them in this lesson—and use the space to expand the History palette so that you can see as many items as possible. If necessary, scroll to the bottom of the History palette so that you can see the last change you made to the image.

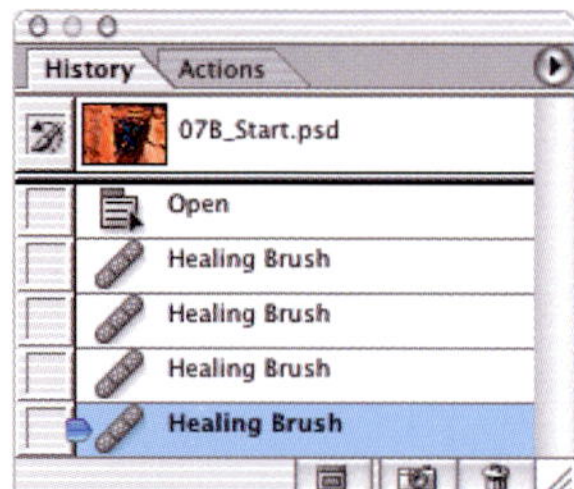

2 With the most recent state in the History palette selected, click the New Snapshot button (📷) at the bottom of the History palette to create a snapshot of the current state.

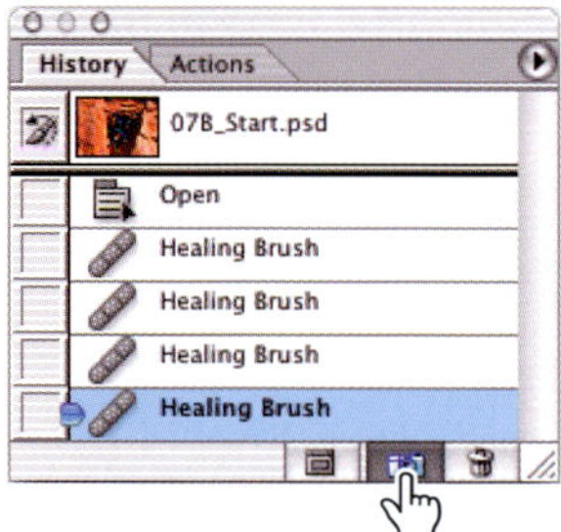

3 Scroll to the top of the History palette. A new snapshot, Snapshot 1, appears at the top of the palette.

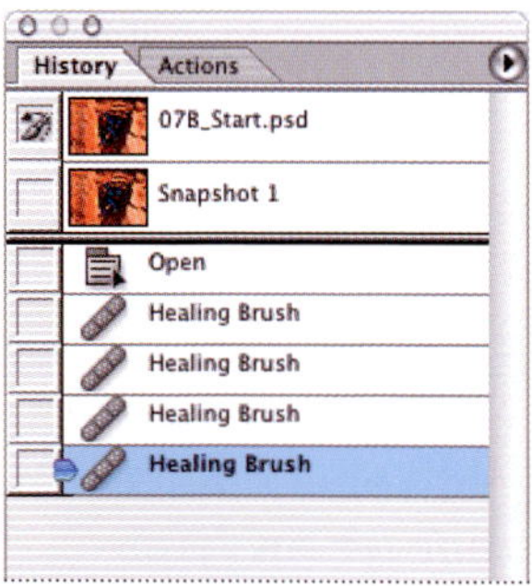

4 Double-click the words *Snapshot 1,* type **Post-graffiti**, and press Enter (Windows) or Return (Mac OS) to rename the snapshot.

Note: You can also take snapshots of earlier phases of your current work session. To do this, scroll to that item in the History palette, select it, and click the New Snapshot button at the bottom of the palette. After you rename the snapshot, reselect the state at which you want to continue working.

5 Make sure that either the Post-graffiti snapshot or the last state in the history list is selected in the History palette. Then, choose File > Save.

Using the Patch tool

The Patch tool combines the selection behavior of the Lasso tool with the color-blending properties of the Healing Brush tool. With the Patch tool, you can select an area that you want to use as the source (area to be fixed) or destination (area used to do the fixing). Then, you drag the Patch tool marquee to another part of the image. When you release the mouse button, the Patch tool does its job. The marquee remains active over the mended area, ready to be dragged again, either to another area that needs patching (if the Destination option is selected) or to another sampling site (if the Source option is selected).

It may be helpful to zoom in before you begin so that you can easily see the details of the image.

1 In the toolbox, select the Patch tool ( ), hidden under the Healing Brush tool ( ).

2 On the tool options bar, make sure that Source is selected.

3 Drag the Patch tool cursor around a few of the bolt holes to the right of the climber, as if you were using the Lasso tool, and then release the mouse.

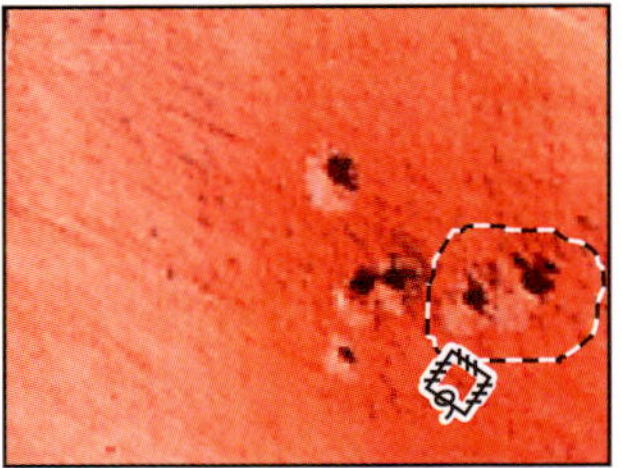

4 Drag the selection to an unblemished area of the rock, preferably—but not necessarily—one that is similar in color to the rock around the bolt holes.

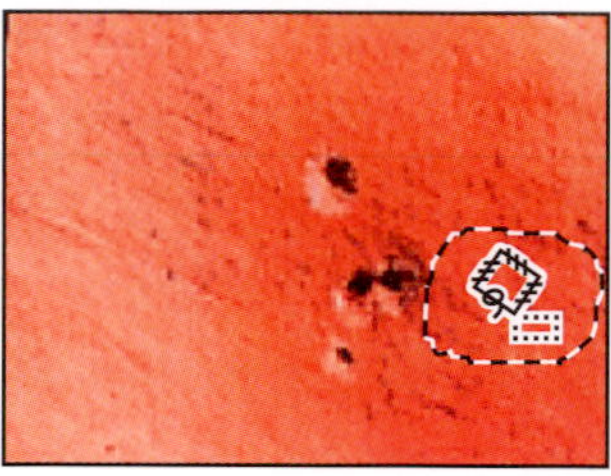
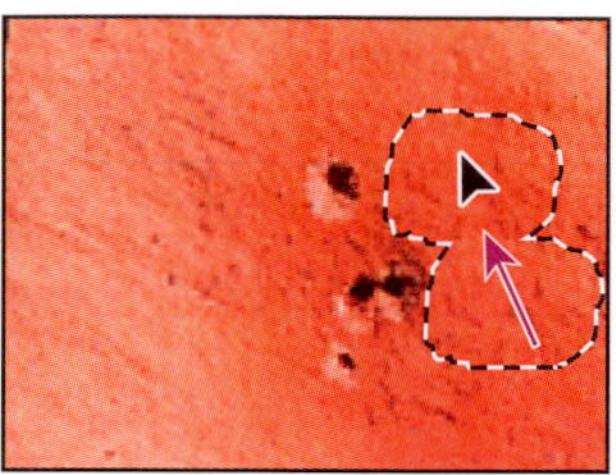
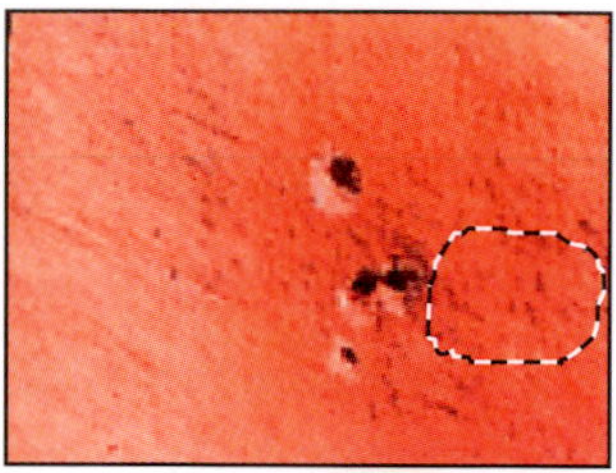

As you drag, the original selected area shows the same pixels as the lassoed selection you are dragging. When you release the mouse, the color—but not the texture—readjust back to the original color scheme of the selection.

5 Drag a new selection around some of the other bolt holes and then drag to an unblemished area of the image. Continue to patch the image until all the scars are repaired to your satisfaction. (Be sure to patch the holes on the left side of the image.)

6 Choose Select > Deselect.

7 Choose File > Save.

Using the History Brush tool to selectively reedit

Even with the best tools, retouching photographs so that they look completely natural is an art and requires some practice. Examine your rock-climber image critically to see if any areas of your work with the Healing Brush or Patch tools are now too uniform or smooth, so the area no longer looks realistic. If so, you can correct that now with another tool.

The History Brush tool is similar to the Clone Stamp tool. The difference is that instead of using a defined area of the image as the source (as the Clone Stamp tool does), the History Brush tool uses a previous History palette state as the source.

The advantage of the History Brush tool is that you can restore limited areas of the image. As a result, you can keep the successful retouching effects you've made to some areas of the image and restore other, less successfully retouched areas to their previous state so that you can make a second attempt.

1 In the toolbox, select the History Brush tool ( ).

2 Scroll to the top of the History palette and click the empty box next to the Post-graffiti snapshot to set the source state that the History Brush tool will use to paint.

3 Drag the History Brush tool over the area where the bolt holes appeared before you edited them, to start restoring that part of the image to its previous condition. The bolt holes reappear as you paint.

4 Using the tool options bar, experiment with the different settings for the History Brush tool, such as Opacity and Mode. Notice how these affect the appearance of the rock as you paint.

If you don't like the results of an experiment, choose Edit > Undo, or click an earlier action at the bottom of the History palette to revert to that state.

5 Continue working with the History Brush and Patch tools until you are satisfied with the final appearance of your image.

6 Choose File > Save, and then choose File > Close.

You've finished your work on this image.

Retouching on a separate layer

In the previous project, you safeguarded your retouching work by using snapshots and the History Brush tool. Another way to protect your original image is to do your retouching work on a duplicate layer of the original image. Then, you can retouch the duplicate layer. When you finish retouching, you can blend the two layers. This technique usually enhances the results, making your touchup work look more natural and realistic.

Using the Healing Brush on a duplicate layer

For this project, you'll work on a portrait photograph.

1 Choose Window > Workspace > Reset Palette Locations to move, reopen, and resize any palette groups that you rearranged in the previous project.

2 Use the Go to Bridge button (button icon) on the tool options bar, and double-click the 04C_Start.psd thumbnail to open the file in Photoshop.

3 In the Layers palette, drag the Background layer onto the New Layer button (button icon) at the bottom of the palette to create a duplicate layer. Double-click the new layer, type **Retouch**, and press Enter (Windows) or Return (Mac OS) to rename it; leave the Retouch layer selected.

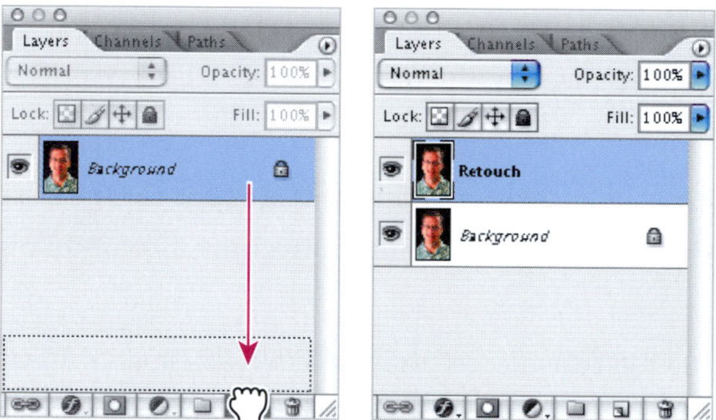

4 In the toolbox, select the Healing Brush tool (tool icon), which may be hidden under the Patch tool (tool icon).

5 On the tool options bar, open the Brush pop-up palette and set the brush diameter to 12 pixels. Close the palette and select the Aligned check box. Leave the other settings at their defaults (Normal selected as the Mode option and Sampled selected for Source).

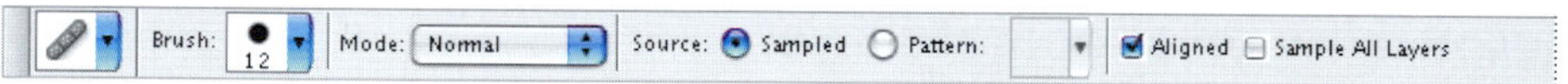

Notice the two wrinkles running horizontally across the man's forehead. (Zoom in if necessary.)

6 Hold down Alt (Windows) or Option (Mac OS) and click a smooth area of the forehead, on the left side of the image, to set the sample point. Then, drag the Healing Brush tool over the lower of the two forehead wrinkles.

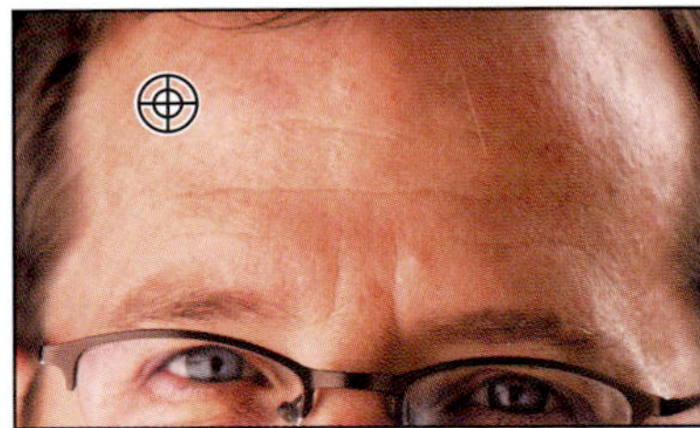

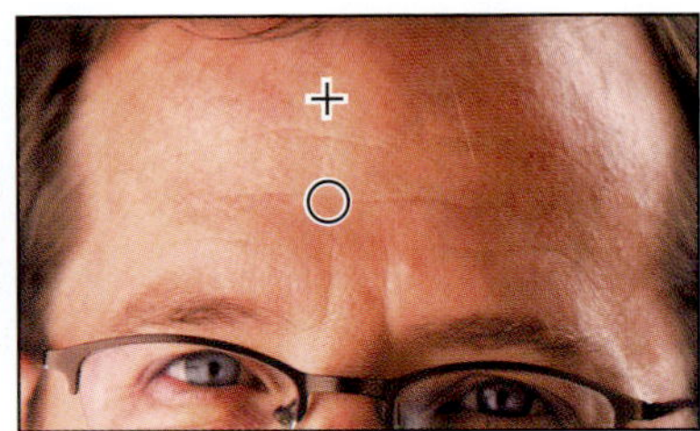

As you drag, the painted pixels don't exactly match the subject's natural skin tones. When you release the mouse button, however, the colors self-correct so that the wrinkle is covered and the skin looks quite natural.

7 Continue painting with the Healing Brush tool to remove the upper forehead wrinkle and the furrow line between the eyebrows.

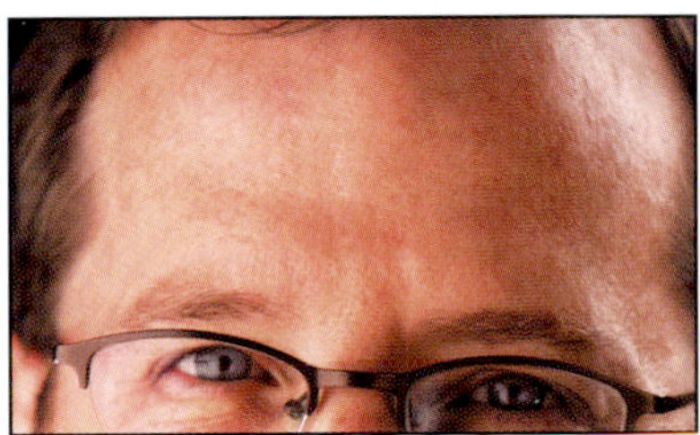

EXTRA CREDIT Try using the Spot Healing Brush on this image and compare the results.

Patching and softening using the separate layer

You'll continue to do cosmetic work on the portrait image using the Patch tool and the duplicate layer (Retouch) you created in the previous exercise. Make sure that the Retouch layer is selected in the Layers palette before you begin.

1 In the toolbox, select the Patch tool ( ), hidden under the Healing Brush tool ( ). Then, drag a marquee around the wrinkles under the subject's right eye, outside the eyeglasses.

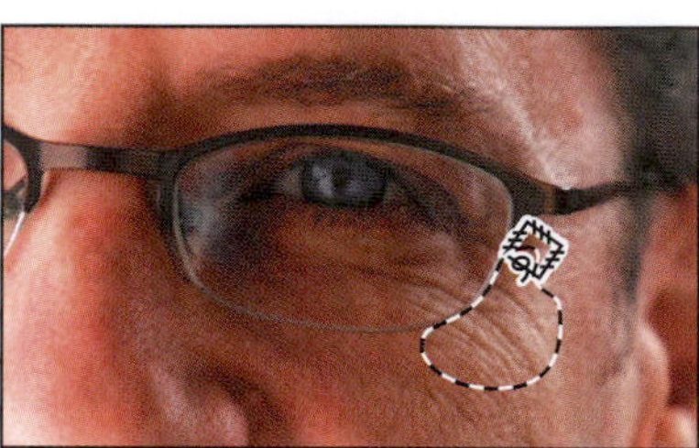

2 Move the Patch tool inside the selected area and drag it to a smooth, similarly toned area on the man's forehead. Then, use the same technique to erase the wrinkles inside the glasses under the right eye, and inside and outside the glasses under the left eye.

3 Continue to touch up the subject's face with the Patch tool until most of the wrinkles are hidden, or at least softened.

It is especially important that cosmetic touchups on the human face look as natural as possible. There's an easy way to make sure that your corrections aren't too smooth or plastic looking. You'll do that now.

4 In the Layers palette, change the Opacity value of the Retouch layer to **65%**. Now, hints of the heaviest skin creases appear in the image, giving the enhanced image a convincing realism.

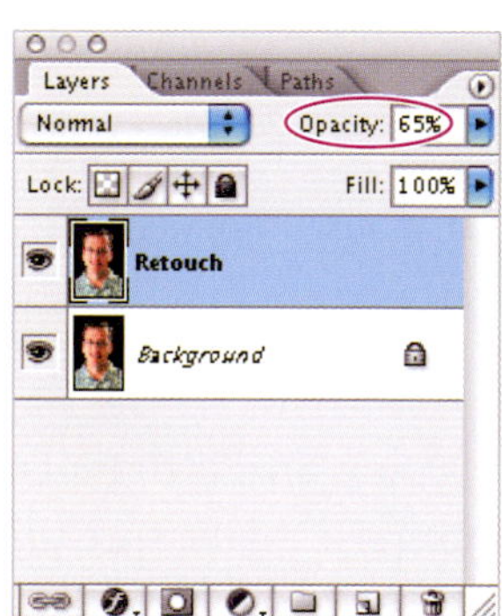

Lee Unkrich

5 Click the eye icon (👁) to toggle the Retouch layer off and on to see the difference between the original image and the corrected one.

Look at the two numbers on the status bar, just to the right of the zoom percentage, at the bottom of the image window. (If you don't see two numbers, click the right-pointing arrow and choose Show > Document Sizes.) The first number (ours is about 6.18 MB) represents the size the file would be if the two layers were flattened into one layer. The second number (ours is about 12.4 MB) shows the current size of the file with its two layers. However, after you flatten the image, you cannot separate the two layers again. When you are sure that you are satisfied with the results of your retouching efforts, it's smart to take advantage of the space-saving of flattening.

6 Choose Layer > Flatten Image, or choose Flatten Image on the Layers palette menu.

7 Choose File > Save.

Now the image has just one layer, combining the unaltered original background and the partly transparent retouched layer.

Congratulations; you've finished your work on this lesson. Close any open files.

Review

Review questions

1 Describe the similarities and differences of the Clone Stamp tool, the Spot Healing Brush tool, the Healing Brush tool, the Patch tool, and the History Brush tool.

2 What is a snapshot and how is it useful?

Review answers

1 As you paint with the Clone Stamp tool, it duplicates the pixels from another area of the image. You set the sample area by holding down Alt (Windows) or Option (Mac OS) and clicking the Clone Stamp tool.

The Spot Healing Brush tool removes blemishes and imperfections from a photograph. It paints with automatically sampled pixels from an image or pattern, matching the texture, lighting, transparency, and shading to the pixels being healed.

The Healing Brush tool works like the Clone Stamp tool except that Photoshop calculates a blending of the sample pixels and the painting area so that the restoration is especially subtle, yet effective.

The Patch tool works like the Healing Brush tool but instead of using brush strokes to paint from a designated area, you drag a marquee around the area to be fixed and then drag the marquee over another area to mend the flawed area.

The History Brush tool works like the Clone Stamp tool except that it paints pixels from a designated previous state or snapshot that you select in the History palette.

2 A snapshot is a temporary record of a specific stage in your work session. The History palette saves only a limited number of actions. After that, each new action you perform removes the earliest item from the History palette list. However, if you select any action listed in the History palette and take a snapshot of that state, you can continue working from that action or another one. Later in your work session, you can revert to the state recorded by the snapshot by selecting it in the History palette, regardless of how many changes you've made in the meantime. You can save as many snapshots as you please.

Learning how to select areas of an image is of primary importance—you must first select what you want to affect. Once you've made a selection, only the area within the selection can be edited. Areas outside the selection are protected from change.

5 Working with Selections

Lesson overview

In this lesson, you'll learn how to do the following:

- Make specific areas of an image active using various tools.
- Reposition a selection marquee.
- Move and duplicate the contents of a selection.
- Use keyboard-mouse combinations that save time and hand motions.
- Deselect a selection.
- Constrain the movement of a selected area.
- Adjust the position of a selected area using the arrow keys.
- Add to and subtract from a selection.
- Rotate a selection.
- Use multiple selection tools to make a complex selection.
- Erase pixels within a selection.

This lesson will take less than an hour to complete. If needed, remove the previous lesson folder from your hard drive, and copy the Lesson05 folder onto it. As you work on this lesson, you'll overwrite the start file. If you need to restore the start file, copy it from the *Adobe Photoshop CS2 Classroom in a Book* CD.

About selecting and selection tools

Selecting and making changes to an area within an image in Photoshop is a two-step process. You first select the part of an image you want to change with one of the selection tools. Then, you can use another tool to make changes, such as moving the selected pixels to another location or erasing pixels within the selection. You can make selections based on size, shape, and color, using four basic sets of tools—the marquee, lasso, Magic Wand, and pen tools. The selection process limits changes to within the selected area. Other areas are unaffected.

Note: *In this lesson, you'll use only the marquee tools, lasso tools, and Magic Wand tool to make your selections. You'll learn about the pen tools in Lesson 10, "Vector Drawing Techniques."*

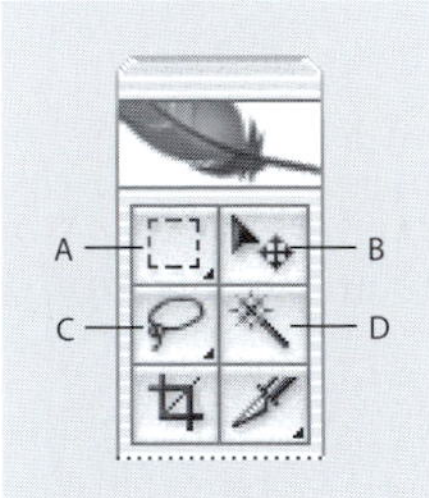

A. *Rectangular Marquee tool*
B. *Move tool*
C. *Lasso tool*
D. *Magic Wand tool*

The best selection tool for a specific area often depends on the characteristics of that area, such as shape or color. There are three types of selections:

Geometric selections You use the Rectangular Marquee tool () to select a rectangular area in an image. The Elliptical Marquee tool (), which is hidden behind the Rectangular Marquee tool, selects elliptical areas. Use the Single Row Marquee tool () and Single Column Marquee tool () to select either a 1-pixel-high row or a 1-pixel-wide column, respectively.

Freehand selections You can drag the Lasso tool () around an area to trace a freehand selection. Using the Polygonal Lasso tool (), you can click to set anchor points in straight-line segments around an area. The Magnetic Lasso tool () works something like a combination of the other two lasso tools, and is best when there is good contrast between the area you want to select and its surroundings.

Color-based selections The Magic Wand tool () selects parts of an image based on the similarity in color of adjacent pixels. It is useful for selecting odd-shaped areas that share a specific range of colors.

Getting started

You'll start the lesson by viewing the finished lesson file to see the image that you'll create as you explore the selection tools in Photoshop.

1 Start Adobe Photoshop and then immediately hold down Ctrl-Alt-Shift (Windows) or Command-Option-Shift (Mac OS) to restore the default preferences. (See "Restoring default preferences" on page 6.)

2 When prompted, click Yes to confirm that you want to reset preferences, and Close to close the Welcome Screen.

3 Click the Go to Bridge button (▣) on the tool options bar to open Adobe Bridge.

4 In the Favorites palette in the upper left corner of Bridge, click the Lessons favorite, and then double-click the Lesson05 folder in the preview area to see its contents.

5 Select the 05End.psd file and study it in the Preview palette.

The project is a collage of objects, including a writing journal, a pen, globes, a number, a flower, and a padlock. The challenge in this lesson is to arrange these elements, each of which is part of a multi-image scan. The "ideal" composition is a judgment call, so this lesson won't describe precise locations. There are no "right" or "wrong" placements of the objects.

6 Double-click the 05Start.psd thumbnail to open the image file in Photoshop.

Selecting with the Magic Wand tool

The Magic Wand tool is one of the easiest ways to make a selection. You simply click a particular colored point in the image to select areas of that color. This method is most successful for selecting an area of closely similar colors that is surrounded by areas of different color. After you make the initial selection, you can add or subtract areas by using specific keyboard combinations with the Magic Wand tool.

The Tolerance option sets the sensitivity of the Magic Wand tool. This limits or extends the range of pixel similarity, so 32—the default tolerance—selects the color you click plus 32 lighter and 32 darker tones of that color. The ideal tolerance level depends on the color ranges and variations in the image.

Using the Magic Wand tool to select a colored area

The large number "5" in the 05Start.psd file (which should be open now) is a good candidate for using the Magic Wand tool because the entire "5" is blue, and the surrounding area is a light gray shadow. For the collage you're creating in this lesson, you'll select and move just the number, not the shadow or background behind it.

1 Select the Magic Wand tool ( ).

2 On the tool options bar, scrub the Tolerance label or type **70** in the Tolerance text box to increase the number of similar tones that will be selected.

3 Using the Magic Wand, click the surface of the large number "5" object. Most of it will be selected.

4 To select the remaining area of the number "5," hold down Shift so that a plus sign appears with the Magic Wand pointer. This indicates that whatever you click will be added to the current selection. Then, click one of the unselected areas of the blue number "5."

Note: When you use other selection tools, such as a marquee tool or a lasso tool, you can also use the Shift key to add to a selection. When you select the water lily in the next exercise, you'll learn how to subtract from a selection.

5 Continue adding to the selection until all the blue areas are selected. If you accidentally select an area outside the blue number, choose Edit > Undo, and try again.

Leave the selection active so that you can use it in the next exercise.

Moving a selected area

Once you've selected an area of an image, any changes you make apply exclusively to the pixels within the selection marquee. The rest of the image is not affected by those changes.

To move the selected image area to another part of the composition, you use the Move tool. On a single-layer image like this one, the moved pixels replace the pixels beneath them. This change is not permanent until you deselect the moved pixels, so you can try different locations for the moved selection before you make a commitment.

1 If the blue "5" is not still selected, repeat the previous exercise to select it.

2 Select the Move tool (▶✥). Notice that the blue "5" remains selected.

3 Drag the selected area (the "5") to the upper left area of the collage so that a small area of the number overlaps the border of the book.

4 Choose Select > Deselect, and then choose File > Save.

In Photoshop, it's not easy to accidentally deselect. Unless a selection tool is active, stray clicks in the image will not deselect the active area. To deliberately deselect, you can use one of three methods: You can choose Select > Deselect, you can press Ctrl-D

(Windows) or Command-D (Mac OS), or you can click outside the selection with one of the selection tools to start a different selection.

Using the Magic Wand with other selection tools

If a multicolored area that you want to select is set against a differently colored background, it can be much easier to select the background than the area itself. In this procedure, you'll try out this neat little technique.

1 Select the Rectangular Marquee tool (⬚).

2 Drag a selection around the water lily. Make sure that your selection marquee is set back from the tips of the flower so that a margin of white appears between the petals and the edges of the marquee.

At this point, the water lily and the white background area are selected. You'll subtract the white area from the selection so that only the water lily remains in the selection.

3 Select the Magic Wand tool; then on the tool options bar, set the Tolerance to **32** to reduce the range of colors the wand will select.

4 Hold down Alt (Windows) or Option (Mac OS) so that a minus sign appears with the Magic Wand pointer, and then click in the white background area within the selection marquee.

Now all the white pixels are deselected, leaving the water lily perfectly selected.

5 Select the Move tool (▸✥) and drag the water lily beside the book, placing it so that a few petals overlap the lower right edge of the book.

6 Choose Select > Deselect, and then save your work.

Julieanne Kost is an official Adobe Photoshop evangelist.

TOOL TIPS FROM THE PHOTOSHOP EVANGELIST

> Move tool tips

If you're moving objects in a multilayer file with the Move tool (V) and you suddenly need to select one of the layers, try this: With the Move tool selected, move the pointer over any area of an image and right-click (Windows) or Control-click (Mac OS). The layers that are under the pointer appear in the contextual menu. Choose the one you'd like to make active.

Working with oval and circular selections

You've already had experience with the Rectangular Marquee tool, which you used to select the area surrounding the water lily image. Now you'll use a different marquee tool.

The best part about this section is the introduction of some more keyboard shortcuts that can save you time and arm motions. The repositioning techniques that you'll try here work equally well with the other marquee shapes.

Repositioning a selection marquee while creating it

Selecting ovals and circles can be tricky. It's not always obvious where you should start dragging, so sometimes the selection will be off-center, or the ratio of width to height won't match what you need. In this exercise, you'll try out techniques for managing those problems, including two important keyboard-mouse combinations that can make your Photoshop work much easier.

As you do this exercise, be very careful to follow the directions about keeping the mouse button or specific keyboard keys pressed. If you accidentally release the mouse button at the wrong time, simply start the exercise again from Step 1.

1 Select the Zoom tool (🔍), and click the black oval on the right side of the image window to zoom in to at least 100% view (use 200% view if the entire oval will fit in the image window on your screen).

2 Select the Elliptical Marquee tool (◯) hidden under the Rectangular Marquee tool.

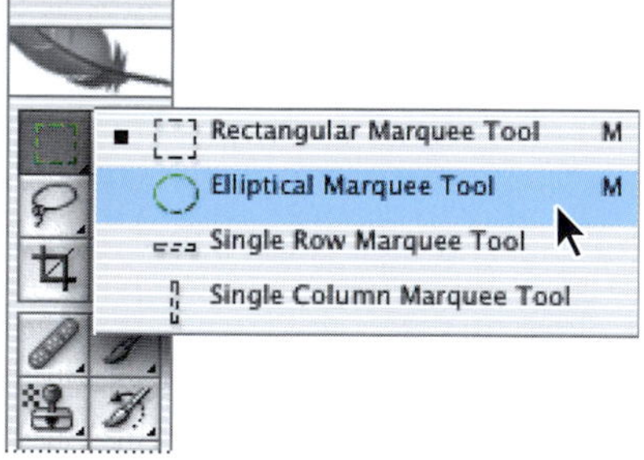

3 Move the pointer over the oval, and drag diagonally across the oval to create a selection, but *do not release the mouse button*. It's OK if your selection does not match the oval shape yet.

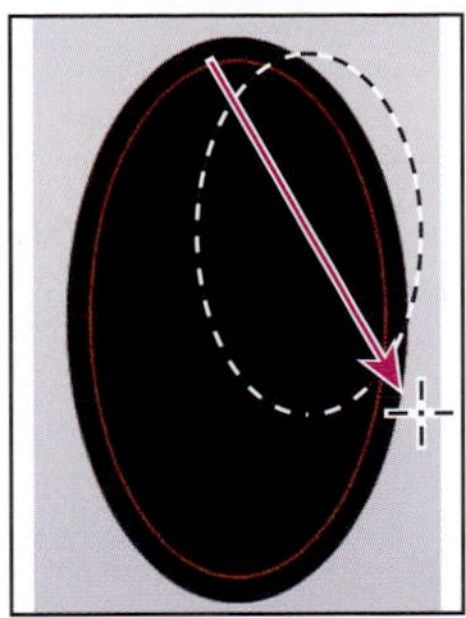

If you accidently release the mouse button, draw the selection again. In most cases—including this one—the new selection replaces the previous one.

4 Still holding down the mouse button, press the spacebar and continue to drag the selection. The border moves as you drag.

5 Carefully release the spacebar (but not the mouse button) and continue to drag, trying to make the size and shape of the selection match the oval as closely as possible. If necessary, hold down the spacebar again and drag to move the selection marquee into position around the black oval.

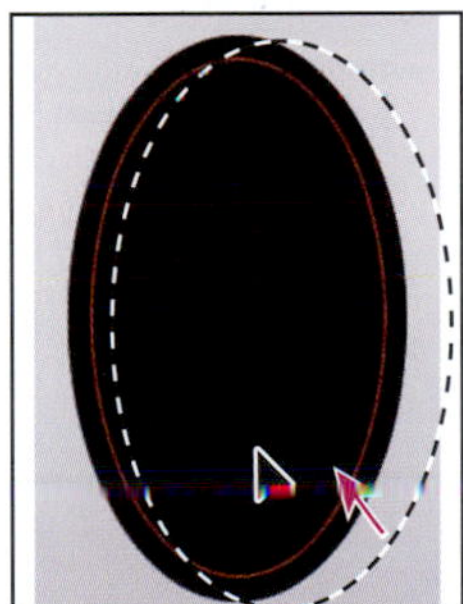

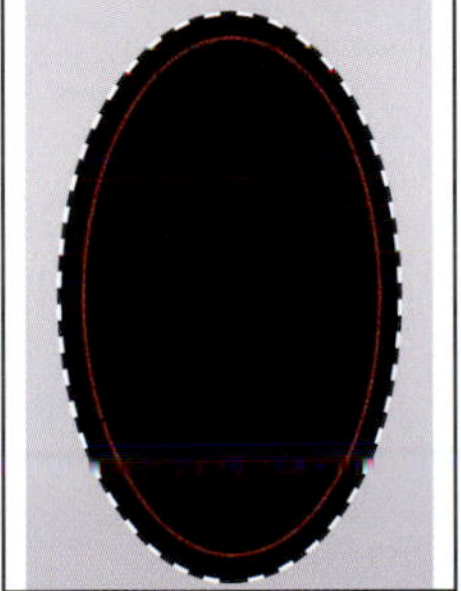

***Note:** You do not have to include absolutely all of the black oval, but make sure that the shape of your selection has the same proportions as the oval and that the thin brown line is contained symmetrically within the selection. As long as the selection marquee is between the brown line and the outer edge, you're fine.*

6 When the selection border is sized and positioned correctly, release the mouse button.

7 Choose View > Zoom Out or use the slider in the Navigator palette to reduce the zoom view so that you can see all of the objects in the image window.

Leave the Elliptical Marquee tool (◌) and the selection active for the next exercise.

Moving selected pixels with a keyboard shortcut

Now, you will move the black oval to the center of the book image using a keyboard shortcut. The shortcut allows you to temporarily access the Move tool instead of selecting it from the toolbox.

1 If the black oval is not still selected, repeat the previous exercise to select it.

Leave the Elliptical Marquee tool (◌) selected in the toolbox.

2 Hold down Ctrl (Windows) or Command (Mac OS), and move the Elliptical Marquee tool pointer within the selection. The pointer icon now includes a pair of scissors (✂) to indicate that the selection will be cut from its current location.

Note: *When you use the Ctrl (Windows) or Command (Mac OS) keyboard shortcut to temporarily switch to the Move tool, you can release the keyboard key after you start to drag. The Move tool remains active even after you release the mouse button. Photoshop reverts to the previously selected tool when you deselect, either by clicking outside the selection or using the Deselect command.*

3 Drag the oval onto the book so that it is roughly centered. (You'll use another technique to nudge the oval into the exact position in a minute.) Release the mouse button but do not deselect the black oval.

Moving with the arrow keys

You can make minor adjustments to the position of selected pixels using the arrow keys to nudge the oval in increments of either 1 pixel or 10 pixels.

When a selection tool is active in the toolbox, the arrow keys nudge the selection border, but not the contents. When the Move tool is active, the arrow keys move the selection border and its contents.

Before you begin, make sure that the black oval shape is still selected in the image window.

1 In the toolbox, select the Move tool (▸✥) and press the Up Arrow key (↑) on your keyboard a few times to move the oval upward.

Notice that each time you press the arrow key, the oval moves 1 pixel. Experiment by pressing the other arrow keys to see how they affect the selection.

2 Hold down Shift, and press an arrow key.

Notice that the selection now moves in a 10-pixel increment.

Sometimes the border around a selected area can distract you as you make adjustments. You can hide the edges of a selection temporarily without actually deselecting and then display the selection border once you've completed the adjustments.

3 Choose View > Show > Selection Edges or View > Extras.

Either command makes the selection border around the oval disappear.

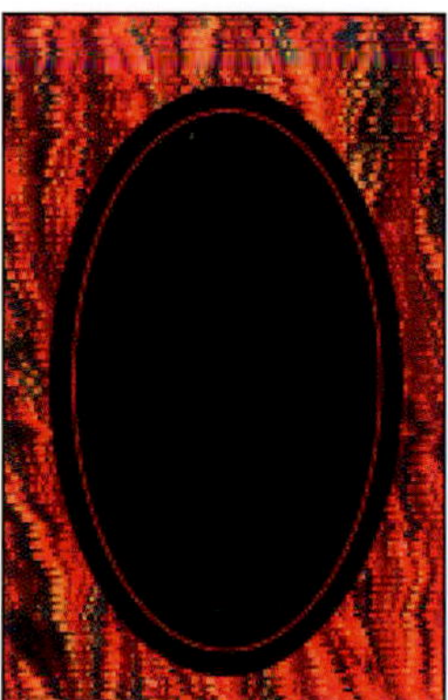

4 Use the arrow keys to nudge the oval until it is positioned where you want it. Then choose View > Show > Selection Edges to toggle visibility of the selection border back on.

5 Choose Select > Deselect, or press Ctrl-D (Windows) or Command-D (Mac OS).

Selecting from a center point

In some cases it's easier to make elliptical or rectangular selections by drawing a selection from the center point. You'll use this technique to select the globe.

1 If necessary, scroll to the lower left area of the image where the globe appears.

2 Select the Zoom tool (🔍) and click the globe as needed to increase the magnification to about 300%. Make sure that you can see the entire globe in your image window.

3 In the toolbox, select the Elliptical Marquee tool (◌).

4 Move the pointer to the approximate center of the globe. You can use the equator and the top of the metal arms that hold the globe as visual guides to help you locate the center.

5 Click and begin dragging. Then, without releasing the mouse button, hold down Alt (Windows) or Option (Mac OS) and continue dragging the selection to the outer edge of the globe.

Notice that the selection is centered over its starting point.

To ensure that your selection is a perfect circle, you can also hold down Shift as you drag. If you held down Shift while using the Rectangular Marquee tool, you would constrain the marquee shape to a perfect square.

6 When you have the entire globe selected, release the mouse button first and then release Alt or Option (and the Shift key if you used it). Do not deselect, because you'll use this selection in the next topic.

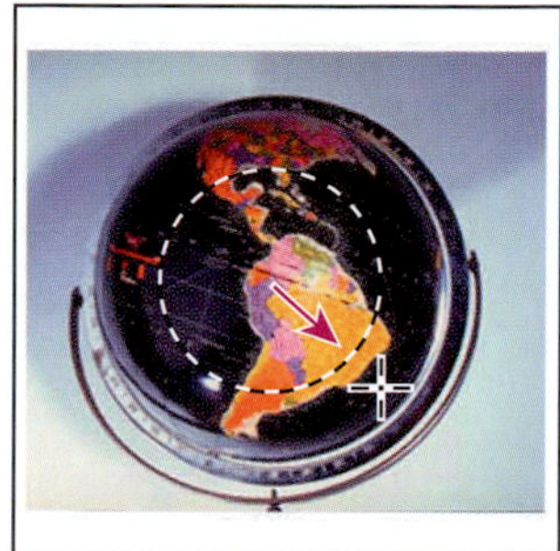

7 If necessary, adjust the selection border using one of the methods you learned earlier. If you accidentally released the Alt or Option key before you released the mouse button, try selecting the globe again.

Moving and changing the pixels in a selection

Now you'll move the globe to the upper right area of the book image. Then, you'll change the its color for a dramatic effect.

Before you begin, make sure that the globe is still selected. If it is not, reselect it by completing the previous exercise.

1 Choose View > Fit on Screen to adjust the magnification so that the entire image fits within the image window.

2 In the toolbox, select the Move tool (▸✥).

3 Position the pointer within the globe selection. The pointer becomes an arrow with a pair of scissors (▸✂), which indicates that dragging the selection will cut it from its current location and move it to the new location.

4 Drag the globe over the book image to the right of center. If you want to adjust the position after you stop dragging, simply start dragging again. The globe remains selected throughout the process.

5 Choose Image > Adjustments > Invert.

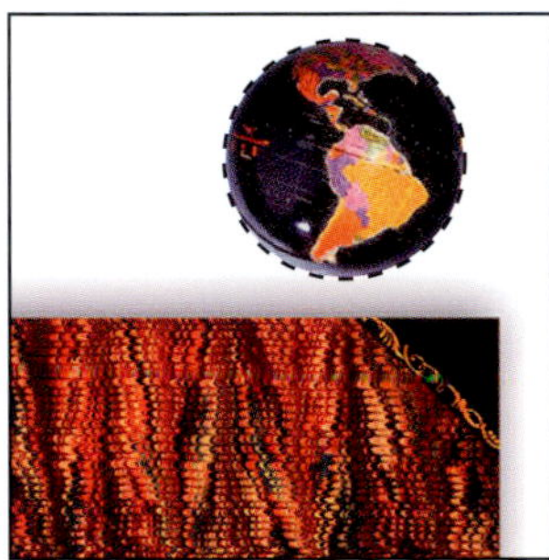

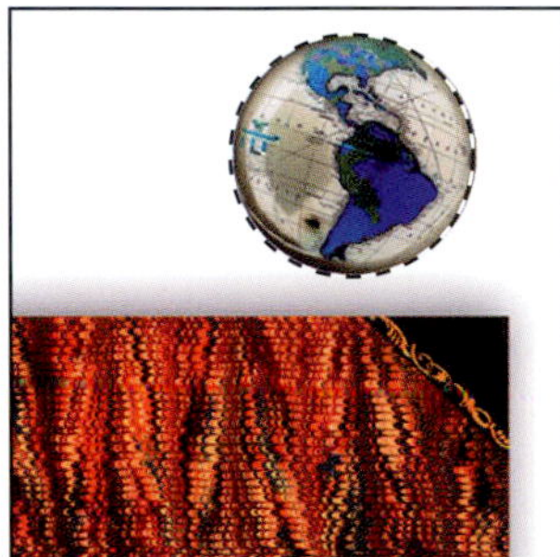

The colors making up the globe are inverted so that now it is effectively a color negative of itself.

6 Leaving the globe selected, choose File > Save to save your work.

Moving and duplicating simultaneously

Next, you'll simultaneously move and duplicate a selection. If your globe image is no longer selected, reselect it now, using the techniques you learned earlier.

1 With the Move tool (▸✥) selected, hold down Alt (Windows) or Option (Mac OS) as you position the pointer inside the globe selection. The pointer becomes a double arrow, which indicates that a duplicate will be made when you move the selection.

2 Continue holding down Alt or Option, and drag a duplicate of the globe down and to the right, so that it is near the upper right corner of the book image. You can allow the

duplicate globe to partially overlap the original one. Release the mouse button and the Alt or Option key, but do not deselect the duplicate globe.

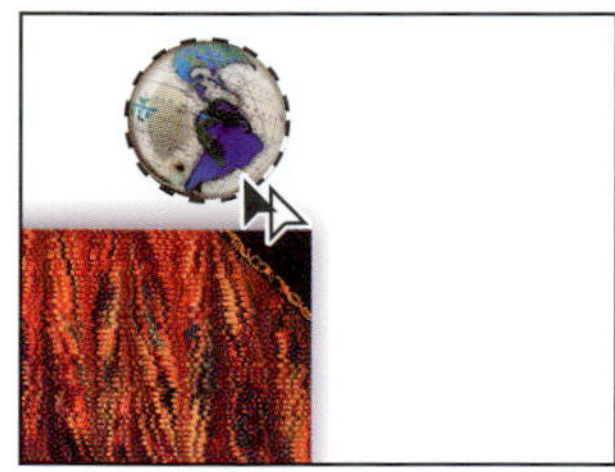

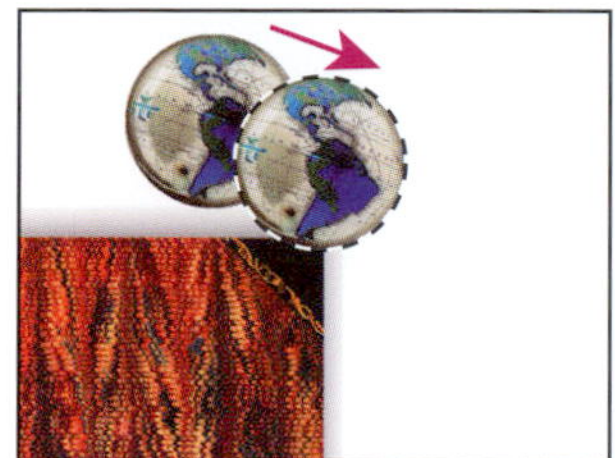

3 Choose Edit > Transform > Scale. A bounding box appears around the selection.

4 Hold down Shift and drag one of the corner points to enlarge the globe so that it becomes about 50% larger than the original. Then, press Enter (Windows) or Return (Mac OS) to commit the change and remove the transformation bounding box.

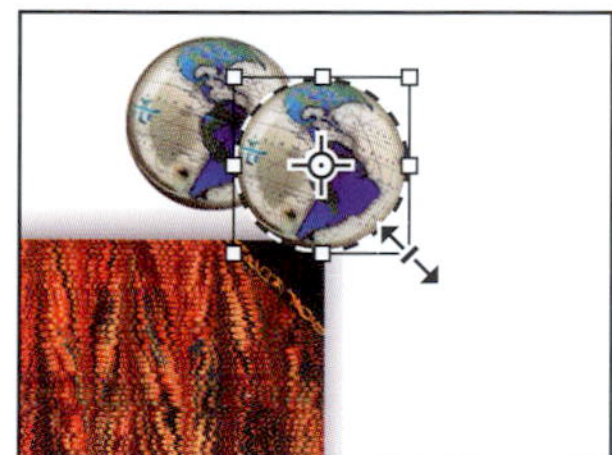

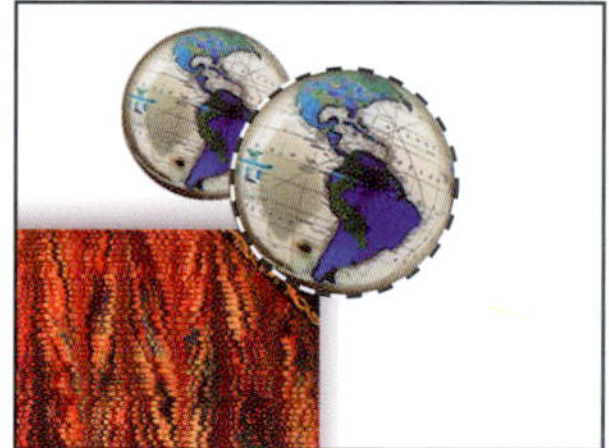

Notice that the selection marquee also resizes, and that the resized, copied globe remains selected. The Shift key constrains the proportions so that the enlarged globe is not distorted.

5 Hold down Shift-Alt (Windows) or Shift-Option (Mac OS), and drag a new copy of the second globe down and to the right.

Holding down Shift when you move a selection constrains the movement horizontally or vertically in 45-degree increments.

6 Repeat Steps 3 and 4 for the third globe, making it about twice the size of the first one.

7 When you are satisfied with the size and position of the third globe, choose Select > Deselect, and then choose File > Save.

For information on working with the center point in a transformation, see "To set or move the reference point for a transformation" in Photoshop Help.

Copying selections or layers

You can use the Move tool to copy selections as you drag them within or between images, or you can copy and move selections using the Copy, Copy Merged, Cut, and Paste commands. Dragging with the Move tool saves memory because the Clipboard is not used as it is with the Copy, Copy Merged, Cut, and Paste commands.

Photoshop has several copy and paste commands:

- *Copy* copies the selected area on the active layer.
- *Copy Merged* makes a merged copy of all the visible layers in the selected area.
- *Paste* pastes a cut or copied selection into another part of the image or into another image as a new layer.
- *Paste Into* pastes a cut or copied selection inside another selection in the same or a different image. The source selection is pasted onto a new layer, and the destination selection border is converted into a layer mask.

Keep in mind that when a selection or layer is pasted between images with different resolutions, the pasted data retains its pixel dimensions. This can make the pasted portion appear out of proportion to the new image. Use the Image Size command to make the source and destination images the same resolution before copying and pasting.

Selecting with the lasso tools

You can use the lasso tools to make selections that require both freehand and straight lines. You'll select the fountain pen for the collage using the lasso tools in this way. It takes a bit of practice to use the lasso tools to alternate between straight-line and freehand selections—if you make a mistake while you're selecting the fountain pen, simply deselect and start again.

1 Select the Zoom tool (), and click the fountain-pen object as needed until the view enlarges to 100%. Make sure that you can see the entire pen in the window.

2 Select the Lasso tool (). Starting at the lower left of the image, drag around the rounded end of the fountain pen, tracing the shape as accurately as possible. *Do not release the mouse button.*

3 Hold down Alt (Windows) or Option (Mac OS), and then release the mouse button so that the lasso pointer changes to the polygonal lasso shape (). *Do not release the Alt or Option key.*

4 Begin clicking along the top side of the cap and barrel of the pen to place anchor points, following the contours of the fountain pen. Be sure to keep the Alt or Option key held down throughout this process.

The selection border automatically stretches like a rubber band between anchor points.

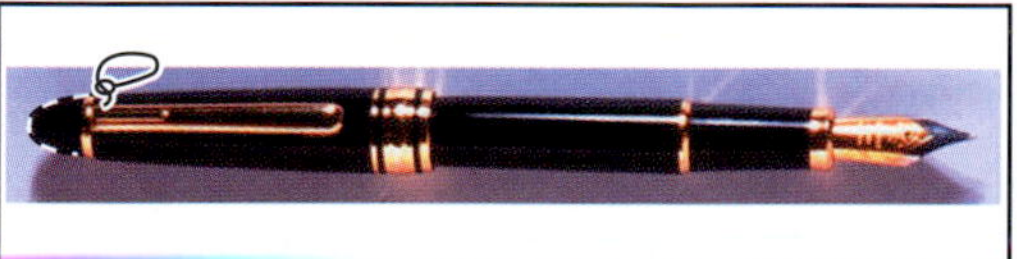

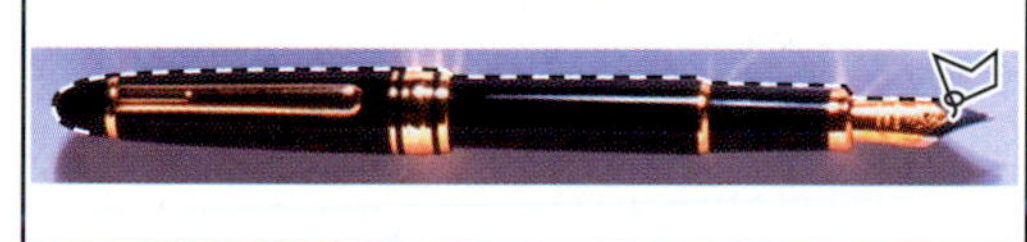

5 When you reach the curved edge of the nib, keep the mouse button held down and then release the Alt or Option key. The pointer again appears as the lasso icon.

6 Carefully drag around the nib of the pen, keeping the mouse button down.

7 When you finish tracing the nib and reach the lower side of the barrel, first hold down Alt or Option again, and then release the mouse button and start clicking along the lower side of the pen. Continue to trace the pen until you arrive back at the starting point of your selection near the left end of the image.

8 Make sure that the click with the mouse crosses the start of the selection, and then release Alt or Option. The pen is now entirely selected. Leave the pen selected for the next exercise.

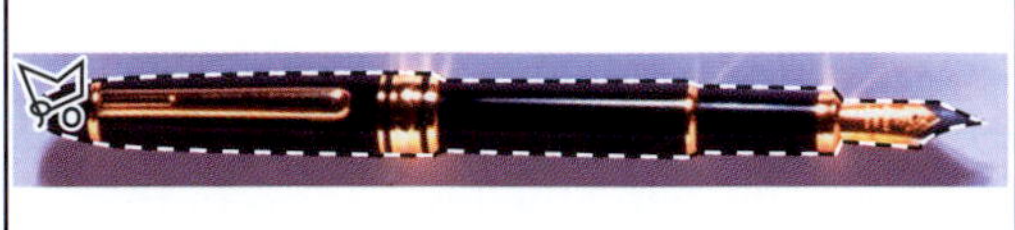

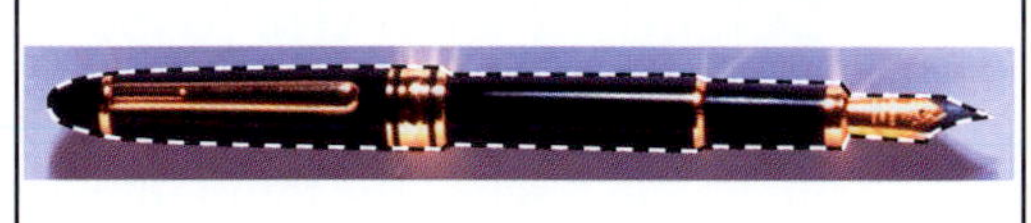

Rotating a selection

So far, you've moved selected images and inverted the color of a selected area. But there are many more things that you can do with a selection. In this exercise, you'll see how easy it is to rotate a selected object.

Before you begin, make sure that the fountain pen is still selected.

1 Choose View > Fit on Screen to resize the image window to fit on your screen.

2 Hold down Ctrl (Windows) or Command (Mac OS), and drag the fountain-pen selection to the area just below and off-center to the left of the book.

3 Choose Edit > Transform > Rotate. The pen and selection marquee are enclosed in a bounding box and the pointer appears as a curved double-headed arrow (↰).

4 Move the pointer outside the bounding box and drag to rotate the pen to a jaunty angle. Then, press Enter (Windows) or Return (Mac OS) to commit the transformation changes.

5 If necessary, select the Move tool (▸✥) and drag to reposition the pen. When you're satisfied, choose Select > Deselect.

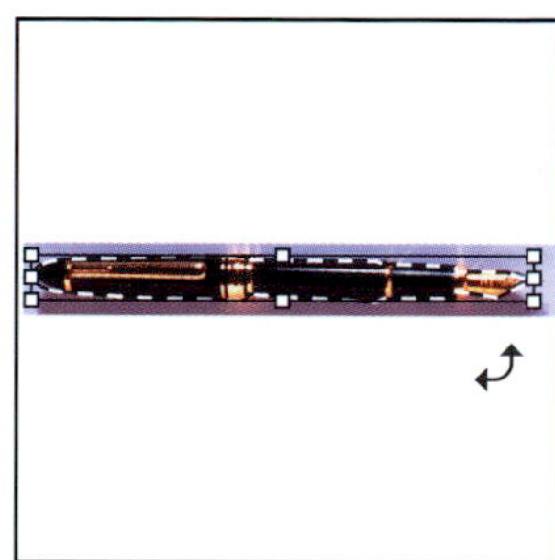

6 Choose File > Save.

Selecting with the Magnetic Lasso tool

You can use the Magnetic Lasso tool to make freehand selections of areas with high-contrast edges. When you draw with the Magnetic Lasso tool, the border automatically snaps to the borders between areas of contrast. You can also control the selection path by occasionally clicking the mouse to place anchor points in the selection border.

You'll now move the padlock to the center of the black oval you placed on the book cover earlier in this lesson, using the Magnetic Lasso tool to select the padlock.

1 Select the Zoom tool (), and click the padlock to zoom in to a 300% view.

2 Select the Magnetic Lasso tool (), hidden under the Lasso tool ().

3 Click once along the left edge of the padlock, and begin tracing the outline of the padlock by moving the magnetic lasso pointer around the outline of the padlock, staying fairly close to the edge of the padlock as you move.

Even though you're not holding down the mouse button, the tool snaps to the edge of the padlock and automatically adds fastening points.

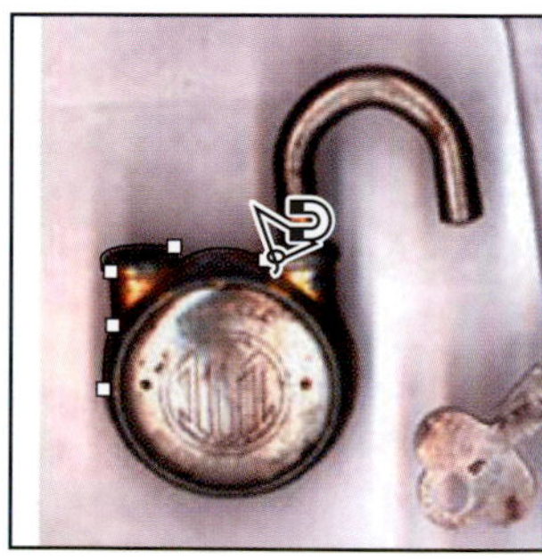

If you think that the tool is not following the edge closely enough (such as in low-contrast areas), you can place your own fastening points in the border by clicking the mouse button. You can add as many fastening points as you feel are necessary. You can also remove the most recent fastening points by pressing Delete for each anchor point you want to remove. Then, move the mouse back to the last remaining fastening point and continue selecting.

4 When you reach the left side of the padlock again, double-click the mouse button to make the Magnetic Lasso tool return to the starting point, closing the selection. Or, move the Magnetic Lasso over the starting point and click once.

5 Double-click the Hand tool ( ) to fit the image onscreen.

6 Select the Move tool ( ), and drag the padlock to the middle of the black oval in the center of the notebook.

7 Choose Select > Deselect, and then choose File > Save.

Softening the edges of a selection

You can smooth the hard edges of a selection by anti-aliasing and by feathering.

Anti-aliasing smooths the jagged edges of a selection by softening the color transition between edge pixels and background pixels. Since only the edge pixels change, no detail is lost. Anti-aliasing is useful when cutting, copying, and pasting selections to create composite images.

Anti-aliasing is available for the Lasso, Polygonal Lasso, Magnetic Lasso, Elliptical Marquee, and Magic Wand tools. (Select the tool to display its tool options bar.) You must specify the anti-aliasing option before using these tools. Once a selection is made, you cannot add anti-aliasing.

Feathering blurs edges by building a transition boundary between the selection and its surrounding pixels. This blurring can cause some loss of detail at the edge of the selection.

You can define feathering for the marquee, Lasso, Polygonal Lasso, and Magnetic Lasso tools as you use them, or you can add feathering to an existing selection. Feathering effects become apparent when you move, cut, or copy the selection.

- To use anti-aliasing, select the Lasso, Polygonal Lasso, Magnetic Lasso, Elliptical Marquee, or Magic Wand tool, and select Anti-alias on the tool options bar.
- To define a feathered edge for a selection tool, select any of the lasso or marquee tools. Enter a Feather value on the options bar. This value defines the width of the feathered edge and can range from 1 to 250 pixels.
- To define a feathered edge for an existing selection, choose Select > Feather. Enter a value for the Feather Radius, and click OK.

Cropping an image and erasing within a selection

To complete the composition, you'll crop the image to a final size and clean up some of the background scraps left behind when you moved selections. You can use either the Crop tool or the Crop command to crop an image.

1 Select the Crop tool (⌗), or press C to switch from the current tool to the Crop tool. Then, drag diagonally across the collage composition to prepare for cropping.

2 Adjust the crop area, as necessary:

- If you need to reposition the crop border, position the pointer anywhere inside the cropping area and drag.
- If you want to resize the crop area, drag a handle.

3 When you are satisfied with the position of the crop area, press Enter (Windows) or Return (Mac OS) to crop the image.

The cropped image may include some scraps of the gray background from which you selected and removed shapes. You'll fix that next.

4 Use a marquee selection tool or the Lasso tool (ℒ) to drag a selection marquee around a scrap of unwanted gray background. Be careful not to include any of the image that you want to keep.

5 In the toolbox, select the Eraser tool (◊), and then make sure that the foreground and background color swatches in the toolbox are set to the defaults: black in the foreground and white in the background.

If the default colors are not black and white, click the Default Foreground and Background Colors icon (■).

6 Drag the eraser over the gray in the selection area. The gray pixels are erased and replaced by the background color, white. If your erasing strays outside the selection border, nothing happens because the unselected area is protected from being changed.

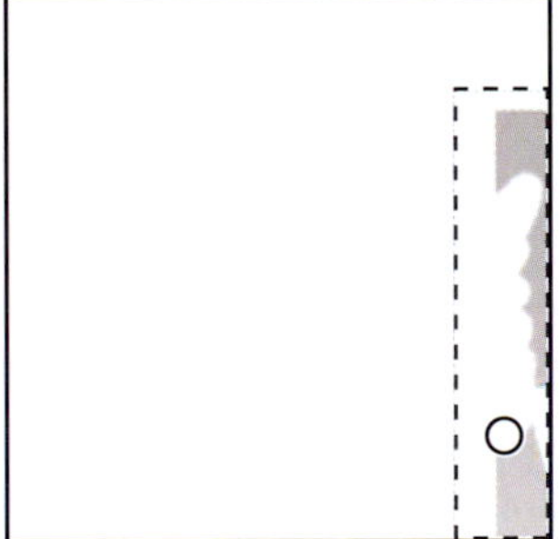

To erase in large strokes, select a larger brush size on the tool options bar.

7 Select another area with only unwanted pixels, and then press Delete.

Continue selecting and erasing or deleting until you finish removing all the unwanted scraps of background. When you finish, choose File > Save to save your work.

Note: *You don't have to select an area in order to erase. However, it's often a good idea, especially when the area that you want to erase is close to another area that you want to protect.*

Good job. The collage is complete.

To quickly create multiple images from one scan, use the Crop and Straighten Photos command. Images with a clearly delineated outline and a uniform background—such as the 05Start.psd file—work best. Try it by opening the original Lesson05 start file and choosing File > Automate > Crop and Straighten Photos. Photoshop automatically crops each image in the start file and creates individual Photoshop files for each. Once you've tried this, simply close each file without saving.

Original image

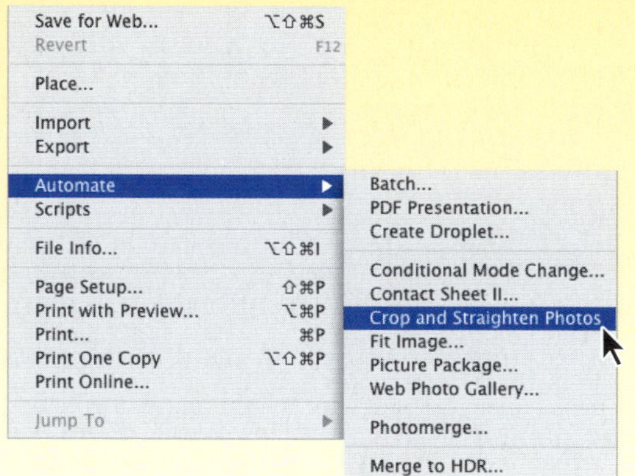

Choose File > Automate > Crop and Straighten Photos

Result

Review

Review questions

1 Once you've made a selection, what area of the image can be edited?

2 How do you add to and subtract from a selection?

3 How can you move a selection while you're drawing it?

4 When drawing a selection with the Lasso tool, how should you finish drawing the selection to ensure that it is the shape you want?

5 How does the Magic Wand tool determine which areas of an image to select? What is tolerance, and how does it affect a selection?

Review answers

1 Only the area within the selection can be edited.

2 To add to a selection, hold down Shift and then drag or click the active selection tool on the area you want to add to the selection. To subtract from a selection, hold down Alt (Windows) or Option (Mac OS) and drag or click the active selection tool on the area you want to remove from the selection.

3 Without releasing the mouse button, hold down the spacebar and drag to reposition the selection.

4 To make sure that the selection is the shape you want, end the selection by dragging across the starting point of the selection. If you start and stop the selection at different points, Photoshop draws a straight line between the start point of the selection and the end point of the selection.

5 The Magic Wand tool selects adjacent pixels based on their similarity in color. The Tolerance setting determines how many color tones the Magic Wand tool will select. The higher the tolerance setting, the more tones the Magic Wand selects.

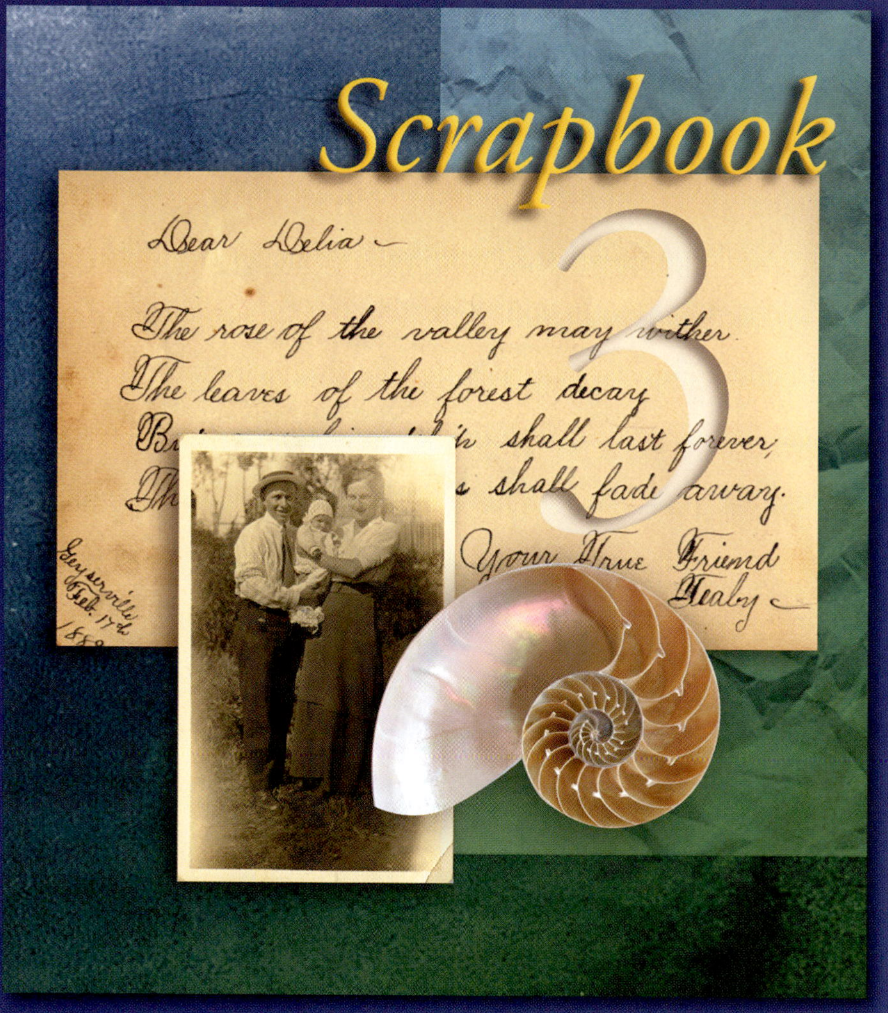

Scrapbook
3
Dear Delia ~
The rose of the valley may wither
The leaves of the forest decay
shall last forever,
shall fade away.
Your True Friend

Adobe Photoshop lets you isolate different parts of an image on layers. Each layer can then be edited as discrete artwork, allowing tremendous flexibility in composing and revising an image.

6 Layer Basics

Lesson overview

In this lesson, you'll learn how to do the following:

- Organize artwork on layers.
- Create, view, hide, and select layers.
- Rearrange layers to change the stacking order of artwork in the image.
- Apply blending modes to layers.
- Link layers to work on them simultaneously.
- Apply a gradient to a layer.
- Add text and layer effects to a layer.
- Save a copy of the file with the layers flattened.

This lesson will take about an hour to complete. If needed, remove the previous lesson folder from your hard drive, and copy the Lesson06 folder onto it. As you work on this lesson, you'll overwrite the start files. If you need to restore the start files, copy them from the *Adobe Photoshop CS2 Classroom in a Book* CD.

About layers

Every Photoshop file contains one or more *layers*. New files are generally created with a *background layer,* which contains a color or an image that shows through the transparent areas of subsequent layers. All new layers in an image are transparent until you add text or artwork (pixel values).

Working with layers is analogous to placing portions of a drawing on sheets of acetate: Individual sheets of acetate may be edited, repositioned, and deleted without affecting the other sheets. When the sheets are stacked, the entire composition is visible.

Getting started

You'll start the lesson by viewing an image of the final composition.

1 Start Photoshop and then immediately hold down Ctrl-Alt-Shift (Windows) or Command-Option-Shift (Mac OS) to restore the default preferences. (See "Restoring default preferences" on page 6.)

2 When prompted, click Yes to confirm that you want to reset preferences, and Close to close the Welcome Screen.

3 Click the Go to Bridge button ( ) on the tool options bar to open Adobe Bridge.

4 In the Favorites palette, click Lessons, then double-click to open the Lesson06 folder, and select the 06End.psd file to preview it.

This layered composite represents the cover of a scrapbook. You will create it now, and in doing so, learn how to create, edit, and manage layers.

5 Select the 06Start.psd file and double-click it to open it in Photoshop.

Using the Layers palette

The Layers palette displays all layers with the layer names and thumbnails of the images on each layer. You can use the Layers palette to hide, view, reposition, delete, rename, and merge layers. The palette thumbnails are automatically updated as you edit the layers.

1 If the Layers palette is not visible in the work area, choose Window > Layers.

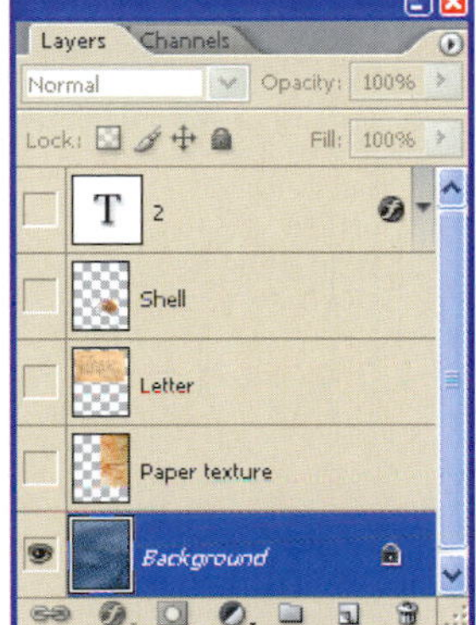

There are five layers listed in the Layers palette for the 06Start.psd file (from top to bottom): a text layer called 2, Shell, Letter, Paper texture, and Background.

2 Click to select the Background layer to make it active (if it is not already selected). Notice the layer thumbnail and the icons on the Background layer level:

- The lock icon (🔒) indicates that the layer is protected.
- The eye icon (👁) indicates that the layer is visible in the image window. If you click the eye, the image window no longer displays that layer.

Use the context menu to hide or resize the layer thumbnail. Right-click (Windows) or Control-click (Mac OS) on a thumbnail in the Layers palette to open the context menu, and then select No Thumbnails, Small Thumbnails, Medium Thumbnails, or Large Thumbnails.

The first task for this project is to add a sepia-toned photo to the scrapbook montage. You will retrieve it now.

3 Click the Go to Bridge button ( ) on the tool options bar, and in the Lesson06 folder, double-click the Photo.psd file to open it in Photoshop.

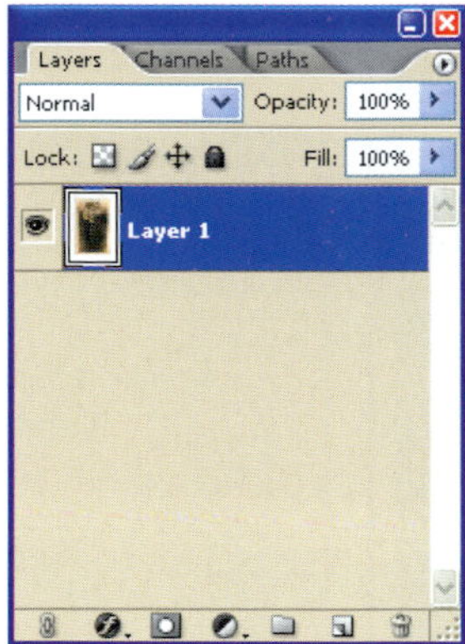

The Layers palette changes to display the layer information and a thumbnail for the active Photo.psd file. Notice that here is only one layer in the Photo.psd image: Layer 1, not Background. (For more information, see "About the Background layer" on the following page.)

About the Background layer

When you create a new image with a white or colored background, the bottom layer in the Layers palette is named Background. An image can have only one background. You cannot change the stacking order of a background, its blending mode, or its opacity. You can, however, convert a background to a regular layer.

When you create a new image with transparent content, the image does not have a Background layer. The bottom layer is not constrained like the Background layer; you can move it anywhere in the Layers palette, and change its opacity and blending mode.

To convert a background into a layer:

1 Double-click *Background* in the Layers palette, or choose Layer > New > Layer From Background.

2 Set layer options as desired, including renaming the layer.

3 Click OK.

To convert a layer into a background:

1 Select a layer in the Layers palette.

2 Choose Layer > New > Background From Layer.

Note: You cannot create a background by renaming a regular layer Background. You must use the Layer From Background command.

Renaming and copying a layer

Creating a new layer can be as simple as dragging from one file into the image window of another file. Whether you drag from the image window of the original file or from its Layers palette, only the active layer is reproduced in the destination file. Before you begin, make sure that both the 06Start.psd and Photo.psd files are open, and that the Photo.psd file is active.

First, you will give Layer 1 a more descriptive name.

1 In the Layers palette, double-click the name *Layer 1*, type **Photo**, and then press Enter (Windows) or Return (Mac OS). Keep it selected.

2 If necessary, drag the Photo.psd and 06Start.psd image windows so that you can see at least part of both images onscreen. Then, select the Photo.psd image so that it is the active file.

3 In the toolbox, select the Move tool (⊹) and position it over the Photo.psd image window.

4 Drag the photo image and drop it into your 06Start.psd image window.

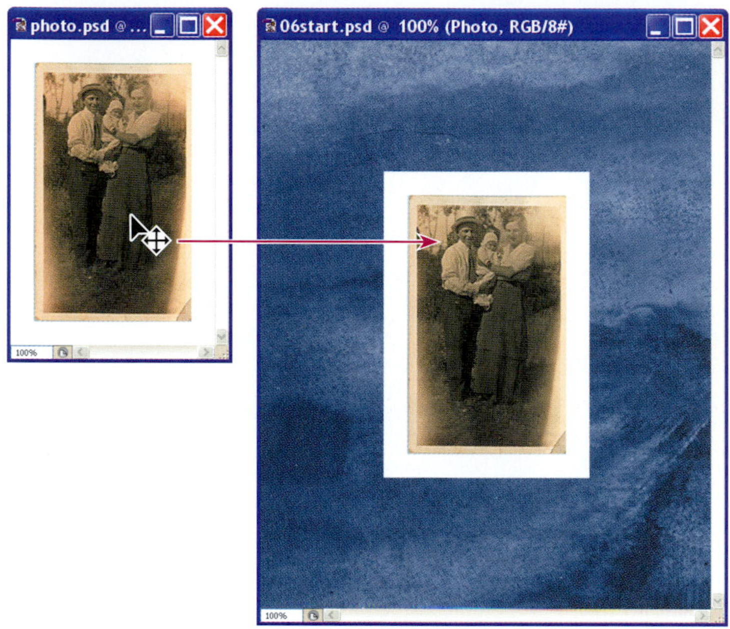

The Photo layer now appears in the 06Start.psd file image window and its Layers palette, between the Paper texture and Background layers.

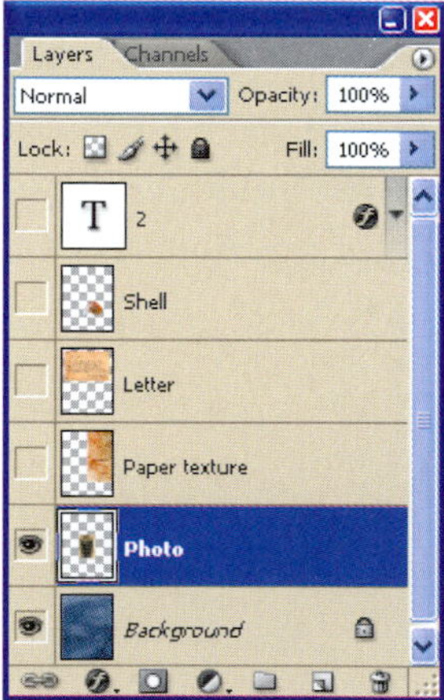

5 Close the Photo.psd file, and do not save your changes to that file.

If you hold down Shift when you drag an image from one file into another, the dragged image automatically centers itself in the target image window.

Viewing individual layers

The Layers palette shows that the 06Start.psd file now contains six layers, some of which are visible and some of which are hidden. The eye icon (👁) to the far left of a layer name in the palette indicates that that layer is visible. You can hide or show a layer by clicking this icon.

1 Click the eye icon (👁) for the Photo layer to hide the photo.

2 Click again to reveal it.

Selecting and removing some pixels from a layer

Notice that when you moved the photo image onto the start file, you also moved the white area around the photo. This opaque area obscures part of the blue background, since the photo layer sits on top of the blue Background layer.

Now, you'll use an Eraser tool to remove the white area around the photo.

1 Make sure that the Photo layer is selected. (To select the layer, click the layer name in the Layers palette.)

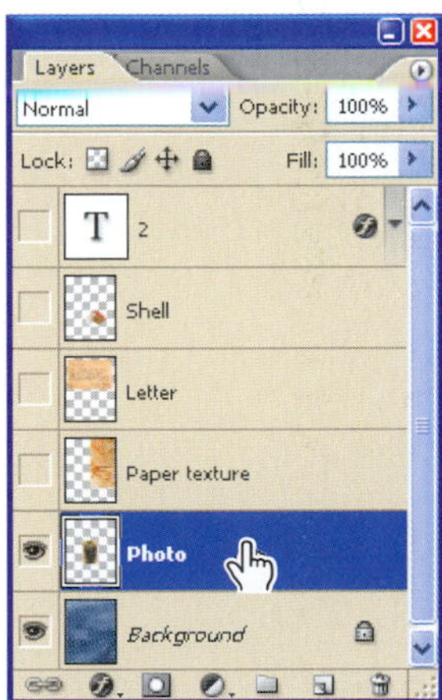

The layer is highlighted, indicating that it is active.

2 To make the opaque areas on this layer more obvious, hide all layers except the Photo layer by holding down Alt (Windows) or Option (Mac OS) and clicking the eye icon (👁) for the Photo layer.

The blue background and other objects in the start image disappear, and the photo appears against a checkerboard backdrop. The checkerboard indicates transparent areas of the active layer.

3 Select the Magic Eraser tool (), hidden under the Eraser tool ().

Now you will set the tolerance for the Magic Eraser tool. If the tolerance is too low, the Magic Eraser tool leaves some white remaining around the photo. If the tolerance setting is too high, the Magic Eraser tool removes some of the photo image.

4 On the tool options bar, set the Tolerance value either by scrubbing the Tolerance label or by typing **22** in the Tolerance text box.

5 Click the white area around the photo in the image window.

The white area is replaced by the checkerboard, indicating that this area is now transparent.

6 Turn the background back on by clicking the eye-icon box next to its name. The blue scrapbook background now shows through where the white area on the Photo layer has become transparent.

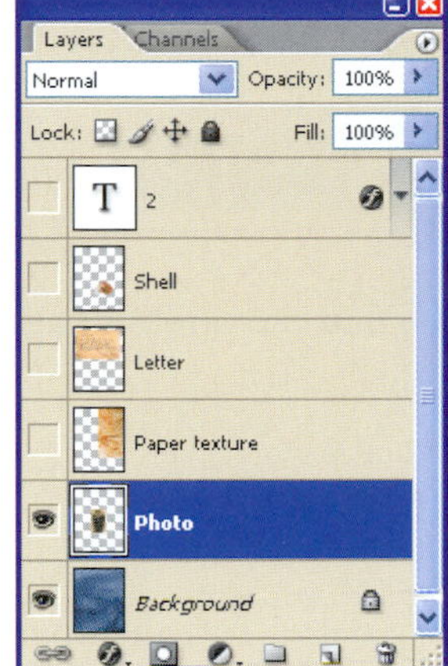

Rearranging layers

The order in which the layers of an image are organized is called the *stacking order*. The stacking order of layers determines how the image is viewed—you can change the order to make certain parts of the image appear in front of or behind other layers.

Now, you'll rearrange layers so that the photo image is in front of another image that is currently hidden in the file.

1 Make the Shell, Letter, and Paper texture layers visible by clicking the eye-icon boxes next to their layer names.

Now you can see that the photo image is partially blocked by these other images on other layers.

Note: *The Photo layer is also below the 2 text layer, which is at the top of the stack, but we'll leave that layer hidden for the moment. We'll get to it later in this lesson.*

2 In the Layers palette, drag the Photo layer up so that it is positioned between the Shell and Letter layers—look for a thick line between the layers in the stack—and then release the mouse button.

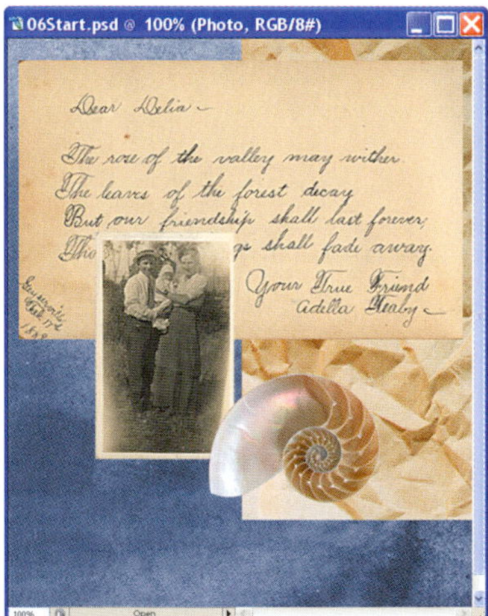

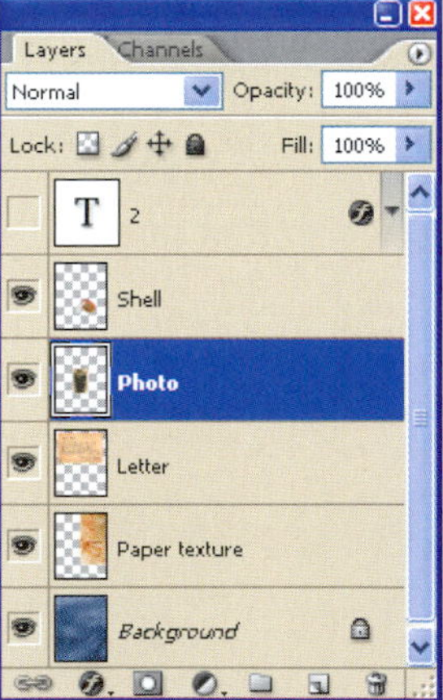

The Photo layer moves up two levels in the stacking order, and the photo image appears on top of the letter and paper texture images, but under the shell and the "2."

You can also control the stacking order of layered images by selecting them in the Layers palette and using the Layer > Arrange subcommands: Bring to Front, Bring Forward, Send to Back, and Send Backward.

Changing the opacity and mode of a layer

Notice how the crinkled piece of paper is opaque, blocking the blue background in the layer below it. You can reduce the opacity of any layer to allow other layers to show through it. You can also apply different *blending modes* to a layer, which affect how the color pixels in the opaque image blend with pixels in the layers underneath. (Currently, the blending mode is Normal.) Let's edit the Paper texture layer to allow the background to show through.

1 Select the Paper texture layer, and then click the arrow next to the Opacity box in the Layers palette and drag the slider to **50%**. Or, type the value into the Opacity box, or scrub the Opacity label.

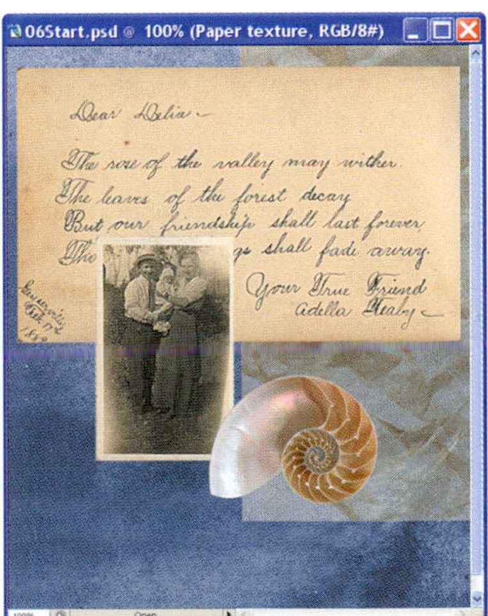

The Paper texture becomes partially transparent, and you can see the background underneath. Notice that the change in opacity affects only the image area of the Paper texture layer. The letter, photo, and shell images remain opaque.

2 To the left of the Opacity option in the Layers palette, open the Blending Mode pop-up menu, and choose Luminosity.

3 Increase the Opacity to **75%**.

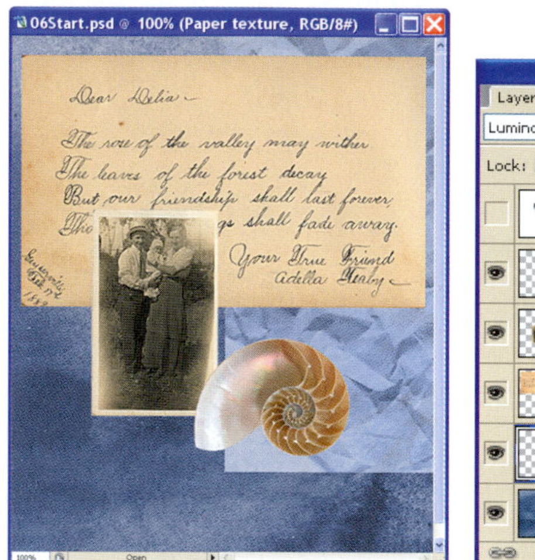

4 Choose File > Save to save your work.

For more about blending modes, including definitions and visual examples, see Photoshop Help.

Linking layers

Sometimes an efficient way to work with layers is to link two or more related layers. By linking layers together, you can move and transform them simultaneously, thereby maintaining their relative alignment.

You'll now link the Photo and Letter layers, then transform and move them as a unit.

1 Select the Photo layer in the Layers palette, and then press Shift and click to select the Letter layer.

2 Choose Link Layers from the Layers palette pop-up menu, or click the Link Layers button at the bottom of the palette.

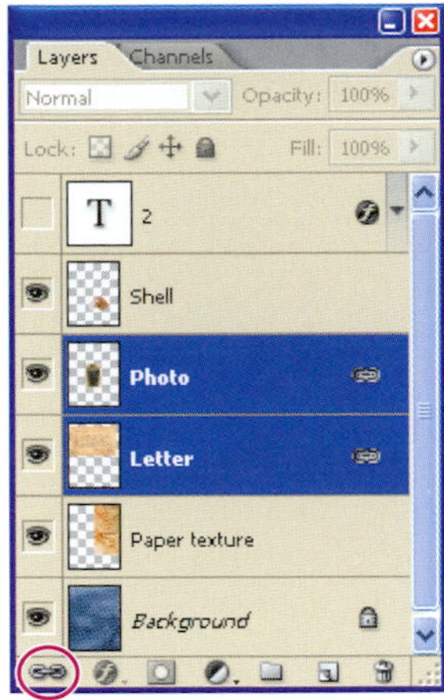

A link icon (⊜) appears next to both of the layer names in the Layers palette, indicating that they are linked.

Now, you'll resize the linked layers.

3 With the linked layers still selected in the Layers palette, choose Edit > Free Transform. A transform bounding box appears around the images in the linked layers.

4 Hold down Shift and drag a corner handle inward, scaling the photo and the letter down by about 20%.

5 Then, with the pointer inside the bounding box, drag the photo and the letter images to reposition them down and to the left in the image window so that the montage resembles the following image.

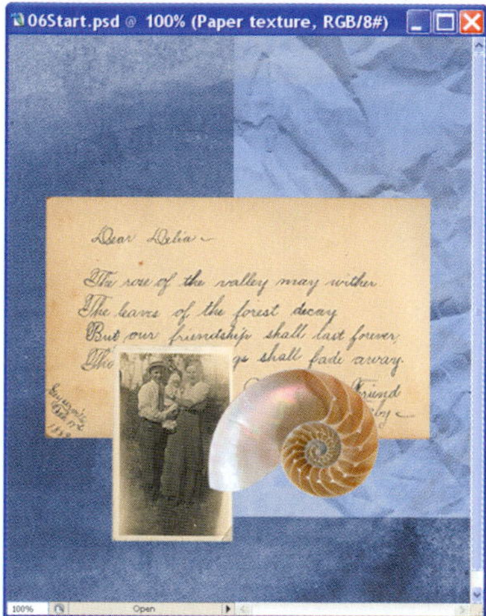

6 Press Enter (Windows) or Return (Mac OS) to apply the transformation changes.

7 Choose File > Save.

Adding a gradient layer

Next, you'll create a new layer with no artwork on it. (Adding empty layers to a file is comparable to adding blank sheets of acetate to a stack of images.) You'll use this layer to add a semi-transparent gradient effect that influences the layers stacked below it.

1 In the Layers palette, select the Paper texture layer to make it active, and then click the New Layer button (▣) at the bottom of the Layers palette.

A new layer, named Layer 1, appears between the Paper texture and the Letter layer.

Note: *You can also create a new layer by choosing New Layer from the Layers palette menu or Layer > New > Layer on the Photoshop menu bar.*

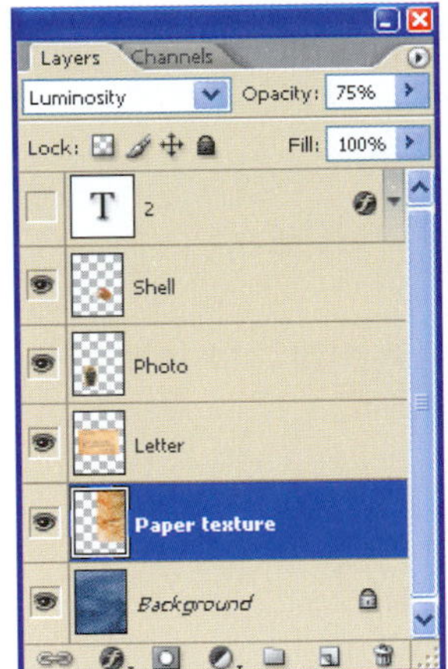

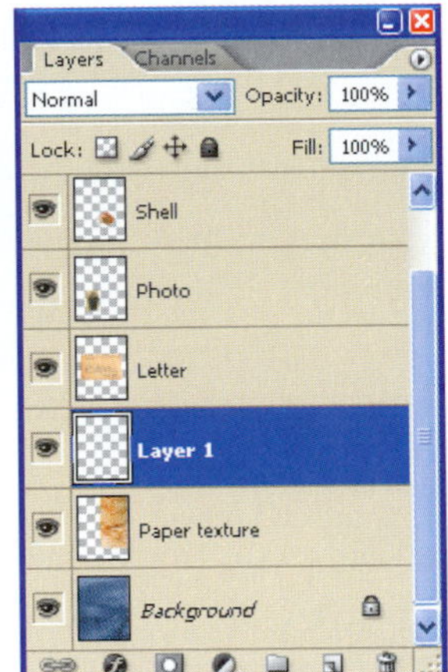

2 Double-click the name Layer 1, type **Gradient**, and press Enter (Windows) or Return (Mac OS) to rename the layer.

3 In the toolbox, select the Gradient tool (▣).

4 On the tool options bar, make sure that the Linear Gradient button (▣) is selected, and then click the small downward arrow to expand the gradient picker.

5 Select the Foreground to Transparent swatch, and then click anywhere outside the gradient picker to close it.

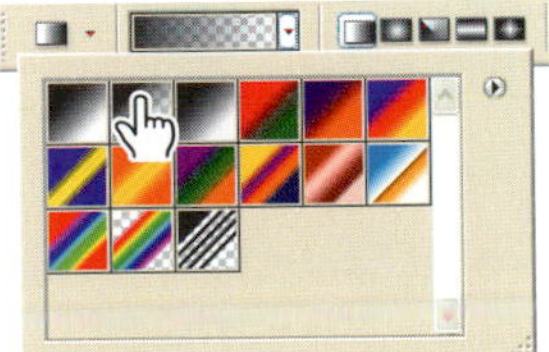

You can list the gradient options by name rather than by sample. Just click the right-pointing palette menu button (◉) on the gradient picker and choose either Small List or Large List. Or, hover the pointer over a thumbnail until a tooltip appears, showing the gradient name.

6 Click the Swatches tab to bring that palette to the front of its group, and select a shade of green that appeals to you.

7 With the Gradient layer still active in the Layers palette, drag the Gradient tool from the lower right corner of the image to the upper left corner.

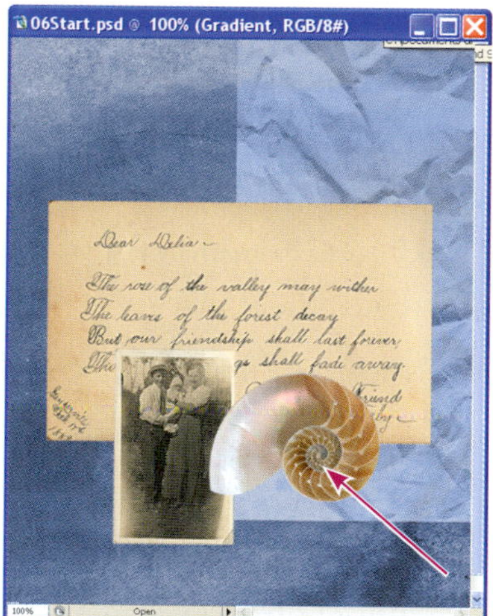

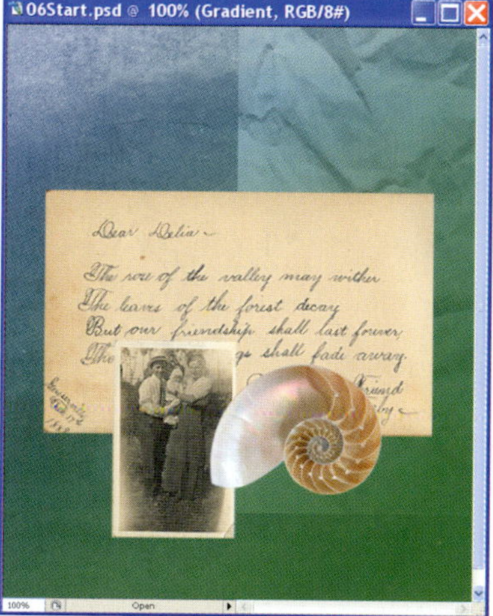

The gradient extends across the layer, starting with green on the lower right and gradually blending to transparent on the upper left. The gradient partially obscures the paper texture and background below it, so you'll change its blending mode and reduce its opacity to partially reveal those images.

8 With the Gradient layer still active, in the Layers palette choose Multiply from the Blending Mode pop-up menu and change the Opacity to **75%**. Now, the Paper texture and Background layers show through the gradient.

Adding text

Now, you're ready to create some type using the Horizontal Type tool, which places the text on its own type layer. You'll then edit the text and apply a special effect to that layer.

1 Deselect all layers in the Layers palette by clicking outside the layer names (drag to enlarge the palette to create a blank area, if necessary).

2 Set the foreground color to black by clicking the small Default Foreground and Background Colors icon (■) near the swatches in the toolbox.

3 In the toolbox, select the Horizontal Type tool (T). Then, on the tool options bar, do the following:

- Select a serif font from the Font pop-up menu (we used Adobe Garamond).
- Select a font style (we used Italic).
- Enter a large point size in the Size text box (we used **76** points), and press Enter (Windows) or Return (Mac OS).
- Select Crisp from the Anti-aliasing pop-up menu (aa).
- Select the Right align text (≡) option.

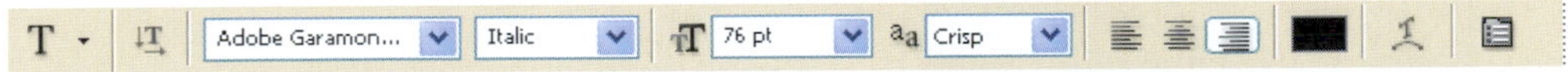

4 Click in the upper *right* corner of the letter area in the image window and type **Scrapbook**. Then, click the Commit Any Current Edits button (✓).

The Layers palette now includes a layer named Scrapbook with a "T" thumbnail icon, indicating that it is a type layer. This layer is at the top of the layer stack.

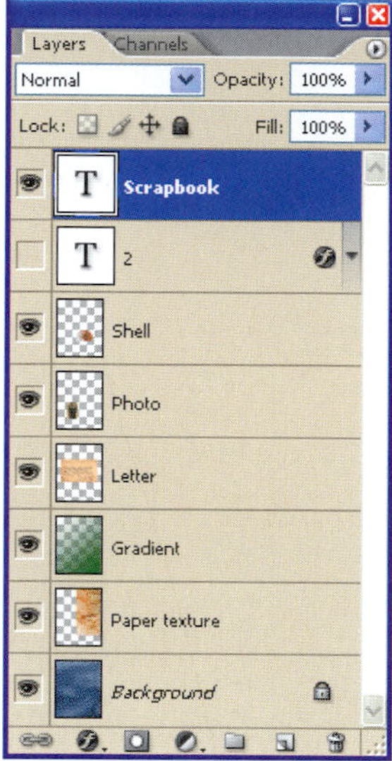

The text appears in the area of the image where you clicked, which probably isn't exactly where you want it to be positioned.

5 Select the Move tool (), and drag the "Scrapbook" text so that the baseline aligns with the top right edge of the letter.

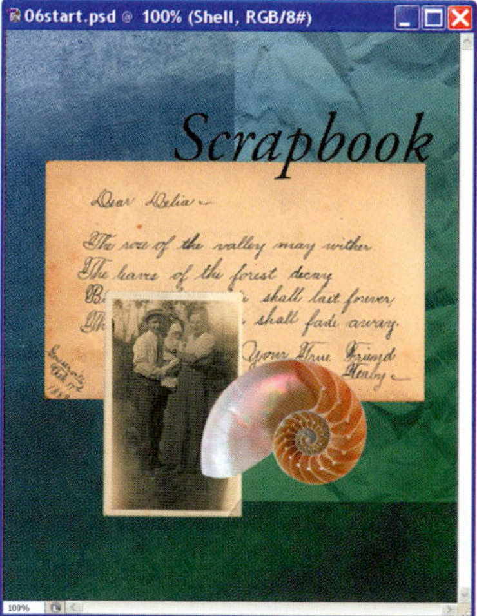

Applying a layer style

You can enhance a layer by adding a shadow, glow, bevel, emboss, or other special effect from a collection of automated and editable layer styles. These styles are easy to apply and link directly to the layer you specify.

Like layers, layer styles can be hidden by clicking eye icons (👁) in the Layers palette. You can apply a copy of a layer style to a different layer by dragging the effect onto the destination layer.

Now, you'll make the text stand out by adding a bevel and drop shadow around the type, and coloring the text yellow.

1 With the Scrapbook type layer active, choose Layer > Layer Style > Bevel and Emboss. (There may be a slight pause as the Layer Style dialog box opens.)

You can also open the Layer Style dialog box by clicking the Add a Layer Style button (⊘) at the bottom of the Layers palette and then choosing a layer style, such as Bevel and Emboss, from the pop-up menu.

2 In the Layer Style dialog box, make sure that the Preview option is selected, and then move the dialog box aside as needed so that you can see the Scrapbook text in the image window.

3 In the Structure area, make sure Style is Inner Bevel and Technique is Smooth. Then, set Depth at **50%**, Size to **5** pixels, and Soften to **0** pixels. Choose Up for your Direction.

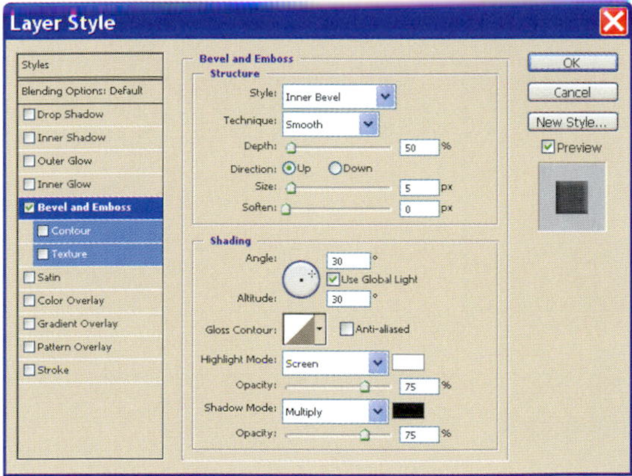

4 In the left pane of the Layer Style dialog box, click the name *Drop Shadow* at the top of the Styles list. Photoshop automatically checks the Drop Shadow box and displays the Drop Shadow layer style options. The preview at right now includes the bevel and the default drop shadow.

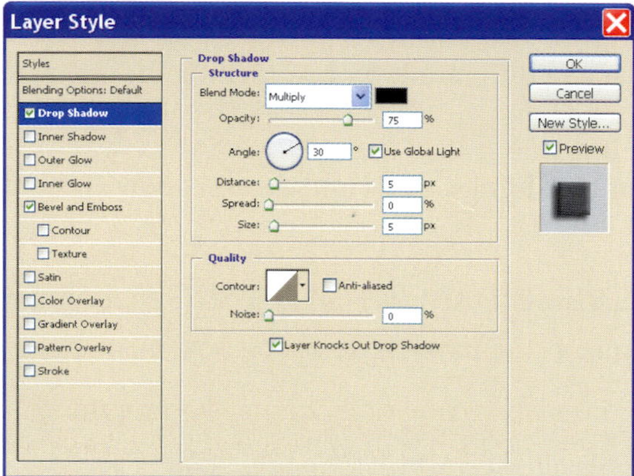

5 The default Drop Shadow options are fine, so click Color Overlay in the Styles list.

6 In the Color Overlay area, click the color swatch to open the Color Picker, and then choose a shade of yellow (we used R=**255**, G=**218**, and B=**47**). Click OK to close the Color Picker and return to the Layer Style dialog box.

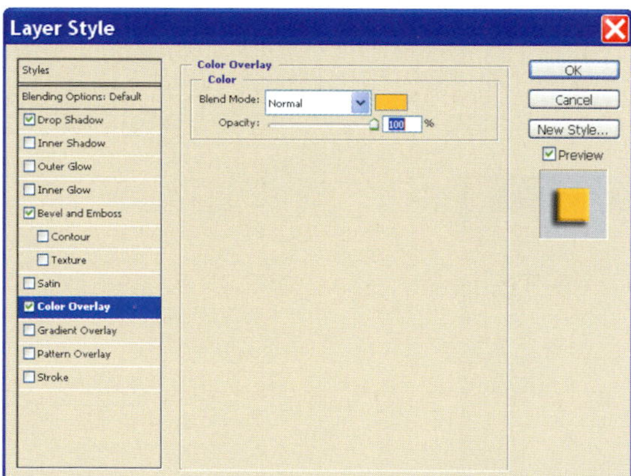

7 Examine the Scrapbook text in the image window. Then click OK to accept the settings and close the Layer Style dialog box.

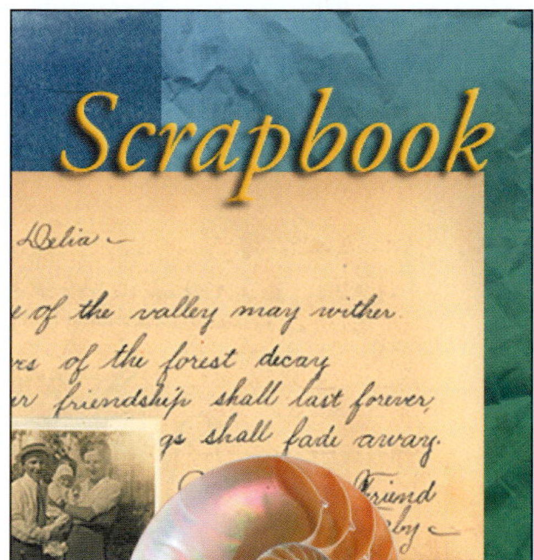

8 In the Layers palette, click the Reveal Layer Effects arrow for the Scrapbook text layer.

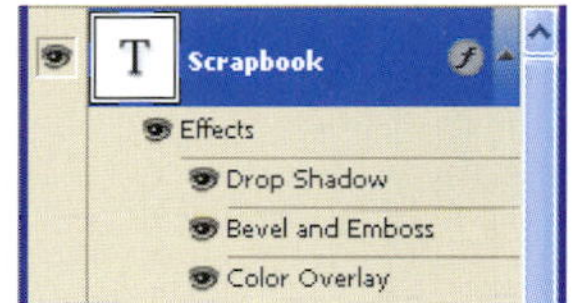

You should find four rows of information nested in the Scrapbook text layer. The top row identifies them as Effects. The other three rows are the three styles that you applied to the layer: Drop Shadow, Bevel and Emboss, and Color Overlay. There is also a visibility eye icon ( ) next to each of the three effects. You can turn off any effect by clicking its eye icon to make it disappear. Clicking this visibility box again restores both the icon and the effect. You can hide all three layer styles by clicking the eye icon for Effects. Before you continue, make sure that eye icons appear for all four items nested under the Scrapbook layer.

9 To hide the layer styles listings, click the reveal arrow again to collapse the effects list.

Updating the layer effect

Layer effects are automatically updated when you make changes to a layer. You can edit the text and watch how the layer effect tracks the change.

1 In the Layers palette, turn on visibility for the 2 text layer and select it to make it active.

2 In the toolbox, select the Horizontal Type tool (T) but do not click in the image window yet.

3 On the tool options bar, set the font size to **225** points and press Enter (Window) or Return (Mac OS).

Although you didn't select the text by dragging the Type tool (as you would have to do in a word-processing program), the "2" now appears in 225-point type.

4 Using the Horizontal Type tool, select the "2" and change it to **3**.

Notice that the text formatting and layer styles remain applied to all the text.

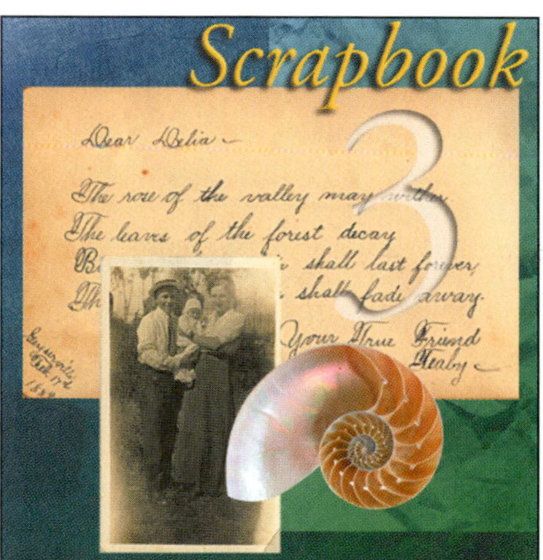

5 Select the Move tool (▸✥) and drag the "3" to center it vertically between the "Scrapbook" text and the shell object.

Note: *You don't have to click the Commit Any Current Edits button after typing 3, because choosing the Move tool has the same effect.*

6 Choose File > Save.

Adding depth with a drop shadow

The scrapbook cover is almost done; the elements are arranged correctly in the composition. You'll finish up by adding a bit of depth to the Letter, Photo, and Shell layers using simple drop shadow effects.

1 Select the Letter layer in the Layers palette, click the Add a Layer Style button ( ) at the bottom of the palette, and choose Drop Shadow from the pop-up menu.

2 In the Drop Shadow pane of the Layer Styles dialog box, set the Opacity to **50%**, Distance to **5** pixels, Spread to **5%**, and Size to **10** pixels. Then click OK to close the dialog box and apply the effect.

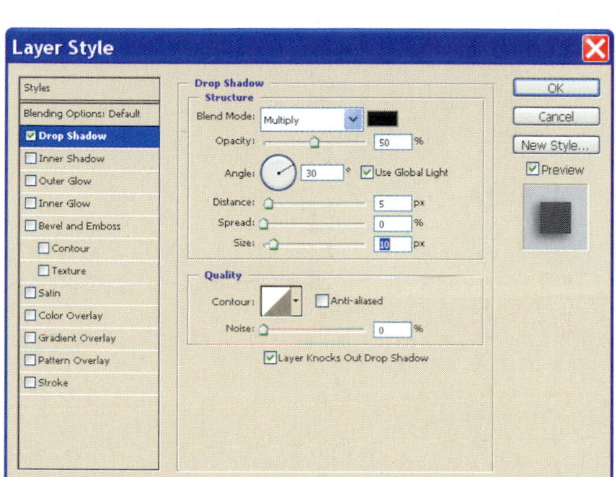

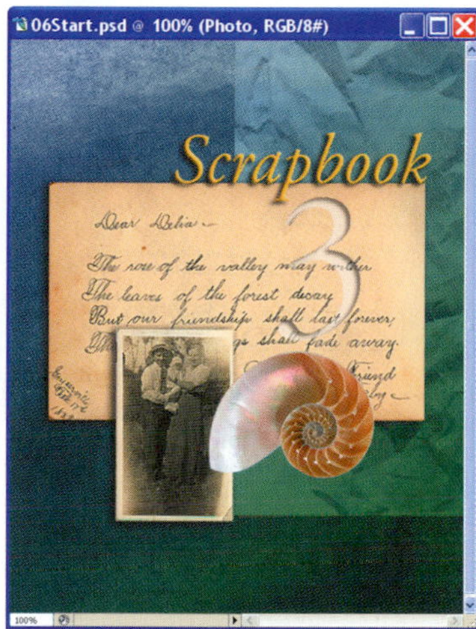

Instead of creating another drop shadow for the photo and shell images from scratch, we'll copy this one.

3 Press Alt (Windows) or Option (Mac OS) and drag the Drop Shadow layer style icon (👁) from the Letters layer onto the Photos layer.

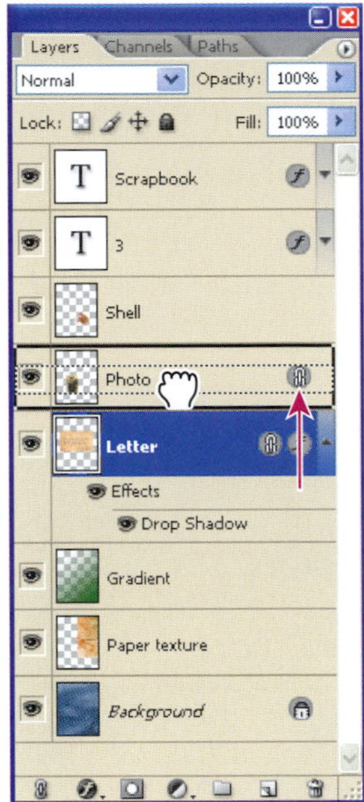

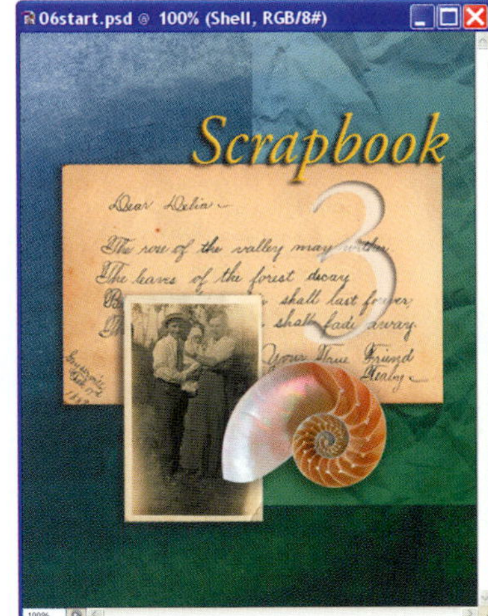

4 Repeat Step 3 to add a drop shadow to the Shell layer.

5 Finally, to give just a bit more depth below the Shell layer, double-click its layer style icon to open the Layer Styles dialog box. Select Drop Shadow from the Styles list and change the Size to **25** pixels. Click OK to accept the change and close the dialog box.

Your final image and Layers palette should resemble the figure on the opposite page.

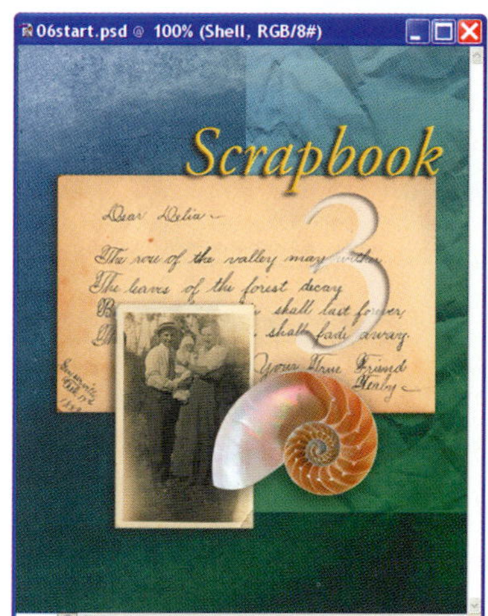

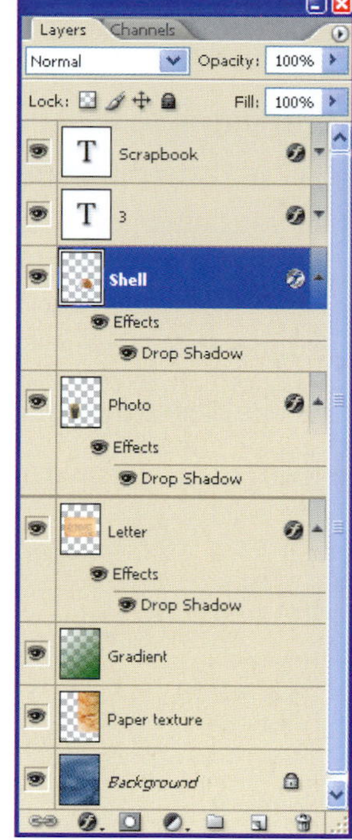

Flattening and saving files

When you finish editing all the layers in your image, you can merge or flatten layers to reduce the file size. Flattening combines all the layers into a single background. However, you shouldn't flatten an image until you are certain that you're satisfied with all your design decisions. Rather than flattening your original .psd files, it's a good idea to save a copy of the file with its layers intact, in case you need to edit a layer later.

To appreciate what flattening does, notice the two numbers for the file size in the status bar at the bottom of the image window.

***Note:** Click the status bar pop-up menu arrow and choose Show > Document Sizes if the sizes do not appear in the status bar.*

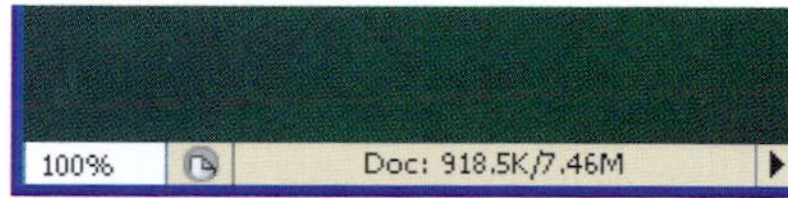

The first number represents what the file size would be if you flattened the image. The second number represents the file size without flattening. This lesson file, if flattened, would be about 918.5 KB, but the current file is actually much larger—about 7.5 MB. So flattening is well worth it in this case.

1 If the Type tool (T) is currently selected in the toolbox, select any other tool, to be sure that you're no longer in text-editing mode. Then choose File > Save (if it is available) to be sure that all your changes have been saved in the file.

2 Choose Image > Duplicate.

3 In the Duplicate Image dialog box, name the file **06Flat.psd** and click OK.

4 Close the 06Start.psd file, but leave the 06Flat.psd file open.

5 Choose Flatten Image from the Layers palette menu.

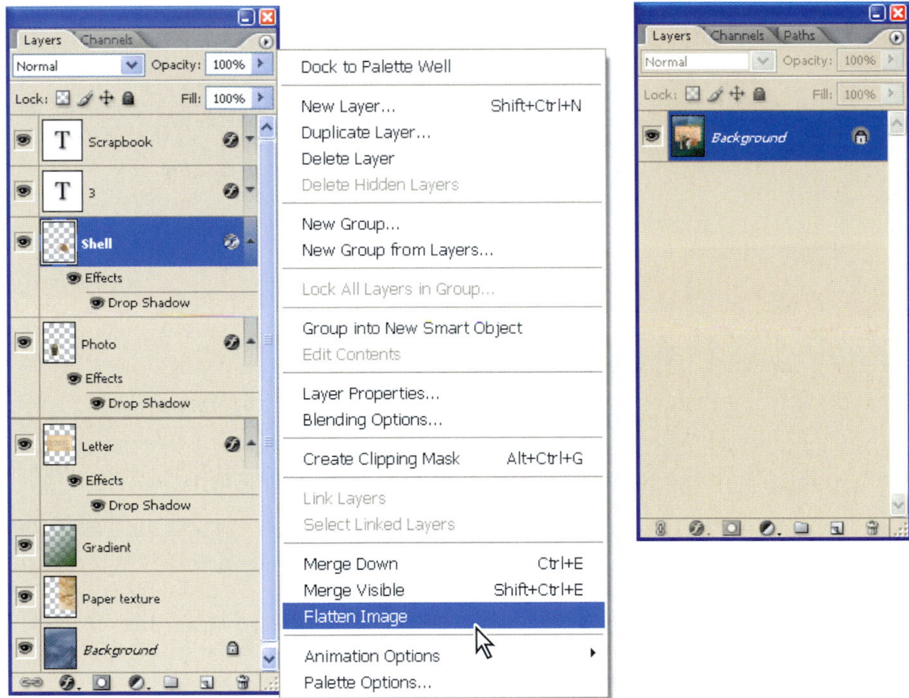

6 Choose File > Save. Even though you chose Save rather than Save As, the Save As dialog box appears.

7 Make sure that the location is the Lessons/Lesson06 folder, and then click Save to accept the default settings and save the flattened file.

You have saved two versions of the file: a one-layer, flattened copy as well as the original file, in which all the layers remain intact.

If you want to flatten only some of the layers in a file, click the eye icons to hide the layers you don't want to flatten, and then choose Merge Visible from the Layers palette menu.

About layer comps

Layer comps provide one-click flexibility in switching between different views of a multilayered image file. A layer comp is simply a definition of the settings in the Layers palette. Once you've defined a layer comp, you can change as many settings as you please in the Layers palette and then create another layer comp to preserve that configuration of layer properties. Then, by switching from one layer comp to another, you can quickly review the two designs. The beauty of layer comps becomes apparent when you want to demonstrate a number of possible design arrangements, for example. When you've created a few layer comps, you can review the design variations without having to tediously select and deselect eye icons or change settings in the Layers palette.

Say, for example, that you are designing a brochure, and you're producing a version in English as well as in French. You might have the French text on one layer, and the English text on another in the same image file. To create two different layer comps, you would simply turn on visibility for the French layer and turn off visibility for the English layer, and then click the Create New Layer Comp button on the Layer Comps palette. Then, you'd do the inverse—turn on visibility for the English layer and turn off visibility for the French layer, and click the create New Layer Comp button—to create an English layer comp.

To view the different layer comps, you click the Apply Layer comp box ( ) for each comp to view them in turn. With a little imagination you can appreciate how much of a time-saver this would be for more complex variations. Layer comps can be an especially valuable feature when the design is in flux or when you need to create multiple versions of the same image file.

Congratulations! Your work on the scrapbook-cover montage is now complete. This lesson only begins to explore the vast possibilities and the flexibility you gain when you master the art of using Photoshop layers. You'll get more experience and try out different techniques for layers in almost every chapter as you progress forward in the book, and especially in Lesson 11, "Advanced Layer Techniques."

Photoshop for Kids*

** An excerpt from Russell Brown's Wonderfully Wacky Wardrobe*

Russell before . . .

Russell after . . .

Simple enough for a kid—fun enough for everyone!

Hey, Photoshop enthusiasts!

Russell Brown here, the official Photoshop Nutty Professor. Back at my lab, I've concocted a fun Photoshop tutorial that will appeal to the whole family. Any kids in the house should pull up a chair.

Welcome to Russell's Wonderfully Wacky Wardrobe, where we will learn some of the ins and outs of moving and transforming layers in Photoshop, all while making a profound fashion statement. Hold on to your hat while we explore my digital closet and create a new me!

—Russell Brown

The image files used in this exercise are located in the Movies/RussellBrown/PS_ForKids_Files_Wardrobe folder on the *Photoshop CS2 Classroom in a Book* CD.

Watch the movie! See the detailed steps of this tutorial on the QuickTime movie included in the Movies folder on the ***Photoshop CS2 Classroom in a Book*** CD.

Step 1: Open project files

In Bridge, navigate to and select my "before" photo—Russell.psd. Then Command-click (Mac OS) or Ctrl-click (Windows) to also select one jacket, one pair of glasses, one crown, and one tie. Double-click any one of those thumbnails to open all of the image files in Photoshop. Choose Window > Arrange > Tile Horizontally. Select my image to make it active, position the cursor on the title bar, and press Command (Mac OS) or Ctrl (Windows) and the – or + key until you see the whole image next to the wardrobe items.

Step 2: Drag it, drop it, close it

Select the jacket image to make it active and, using the Move tool, drag the jacket onto my photo. Don't worry about exact placement or sizing. Repeat for the glasses, crown, and tie. Then, close each of those image files so that only my photo is open. Double-click the Hand tool to fill the screen with the photo image. If necessary, drag the crown layer in the Layers palette so that it's under the glasses layer. That's better. Just drag and drop to reorder the layers stack.

Step 3: Transform the layers

Next, resize and position the wardrobe items. Select the Move tool, and on the tool options bar, check the Auto Select Layer and Show Transform Control boxes. Click the glasses in the image window to select them, press Shift Option (Mac OS) or Shift-Alt (Windows), and drag a corner handle of the transform box to scale them proportionally from their center point. Move the cursor inside the box and drag to position the glasses correctly on my face. Press Enter or Return to commit the transform. Repeat for the other wardrobe items.

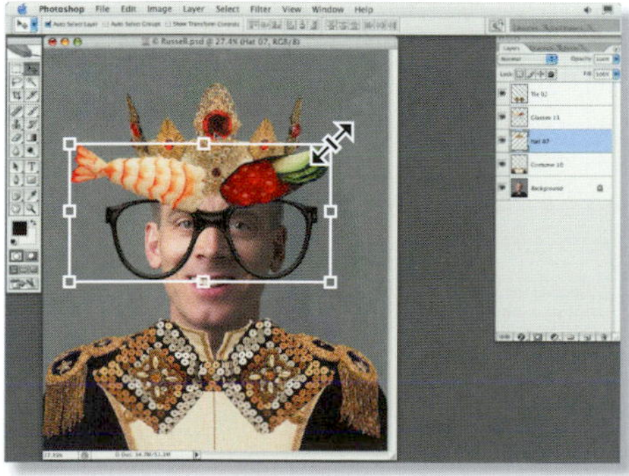

Step 4: Warp and drop shadow

To make the jacket fit better, select it in the Layers palette and choose Edit > Transform > Warp. Drag the control handles to adjust the fit around my neck and shoulders, and then click the Commit Transform button. Then select the tie in the Layers palette, click the Add a Layer Style button, and choose Drop Shadow from the pop-up menu. Drag the cursor over the tie in the image window to interactively adjust the angle and distance. Adjust other settings in the dialog box, and click OK when you're done.

Review

Review questions

1 What is the advantage of using layers?

2 When you create a new layer, where does it appear in the Layers palette stack?

3 How can you make artwork on one layer appear in front of artwork on another layer?

4 How can you manipulate multiple layers simultaneously?

5 When you've completed your artwork, what can you do to minimize the file size without changing the quality or dimensions?

Review answers

1 Layers let you move and edit different parts of an image as discrete objects. You can also hide individual layers as you work on other layers by clicking to remove the eye icons (👁) for the layers you don't need to see.

2 The new layer always appears immediately above the active layer.

3 You can make artwork on one layer appear in front of artwork on another layer by dragging layers up or down the stacking order in the Layers palette, or by using the Layer > Arrange subcommands—Bring to Front, Bring Forward, Send to Back, and Send Backward. However, you cannot change the layer position of a Background layer.

4 You can link the layers by first selecting one of the layers in the Layers palette. Then you click the box to the left of the Layer name of the layer to which you want to link it. Once linked, both layers can be moved, rotated, and resized together.

5 You can flatten the image, which merges all the layers onto a single background. It's a good idea to duplicate image files with layers intact before you flatten them, in case you have to make changes to a layer later.

Adobe Photoshop uses masks to isolate and manipulate specific parts of an image. A mask is like a stencil. The cutout portion of the mask can be altered, but the area surrounding the cutout is protected from change. You can create a temporary mask for one-time use, or you can save masks for repeated use.

7 Masks and Channels

Lesson overview

In this lesson, you'll learn how to do the following:

- Refine a selection using a quick mask.
- Save a selection as a channel mask.
- View a mask using the Channels palette.
- Load a saved mask and apply effects.
- Paint in a mask to modify a selection.
- Make an intricate selection using the Extract command.
- Create and use a gradient mask.

This lesson will take about an hour to complete. If needed, remove the previous lesson folder from your hard drive, and copy the Lesson07 folder onto it. As you work on this lesson, you'll overwrite the start files. If you need to restore the start files, copy them from the *Adobe Photoshop CS2 Classroom in a Book* CD.

Working with masks and channels

Photoshop masks isolate and protect parts of an image, just like masking tape prevents a house painter from getting paint on the window glass or trim. When you create a mask based on a selection, the area not selected is *masked,* or protected from editing. With masks, you can create and save time-consuming selections and then use them again. In addition, you can use masks for other complex editing tasks—for example, to apply color changes or filter effects to an image.

In Adobe Photoshop, you can make temporary masks, called *quick masks*, or you can create permanent masks and store them as special grayscale channels called *alpha channels*. Photoshop also uses channels to store an image's color information and information about spot color. Unlike layers, channels do not print. You use the Channels palette to view and work with alpha channels.

Getting started

You'll start the lesson by viewing the finished image that you'll create using masks and channels.

1 Start Photoshop and then immediately hold down Ctrl-Alt-Shift (Windows) or Command-Option-Shift (Mac OS) to restore the default preferences. (See "Restoring default preferences" on page 6.)

2 When prompted, click Yes to confirm that you want to reset preferences, and Close to close the Welcome Screen.

3 Click the Go to Bridge button (▣) on the tool options bar to open Adobe Bridge.

4 In the Favorites palette in the upper left corner of Bridge, click the Lessons favorite, and then double-click the Lesson07 folder in the preview area to see its contents.

5 Select the 07End.psd file and study it in the Preview palette.

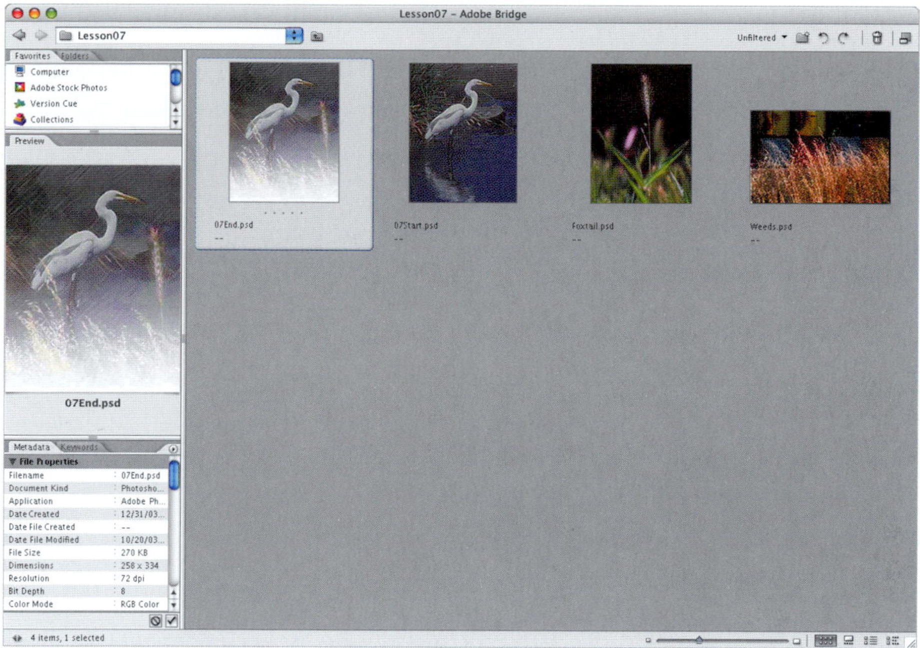

Your primary goal in this lesson is to take an ordinary photograph of an egret in the wild and make the landscape around the bird look as if it were hand-drawn in colored-pencil strokes. You'll also make intricate selections of the grasses from other photographs and place them in the foreground of the egret image. Your final touch will be to add a gradient to soften the image.

6 Double-click the 07Start.psd thumbnail to open it in Photoshop.

Creating a quick mask

You'll begin the lesson by using Quick Mask mode to convert a selection border into a temporary mask. Later, you will convert this temporary quick mask back into a selection border. Unless you save a quick mask as a more permanent alpha-channel mask, the temporary mask will be discarded once it is converted to a selection.

You'll start by making a partial selection of the egret in the 07Start file, using the Magic Wand tool, and then you'll edit the selection using a quick mask.

1 Select the Magic Wand tool (✲).

2 On the tool options bar, enter **12** in the Tolerance text box.

3 Click anywhere in the white area of the egret to begin the selection process.

4 Hold down Shift so that a plus sign appears next to the Magic Wand pointer, and click one of the unselected white areas of the egret to add to the selection.

5 Click a few more times with the Shift key down to add more areas to the selection, but don't try to make the selection perfect.

Magic Wand selection

Selection extended

6 Click the Quick Mask mode button (◘) in the toolbox. (By default, you have been working in Standard mode.)

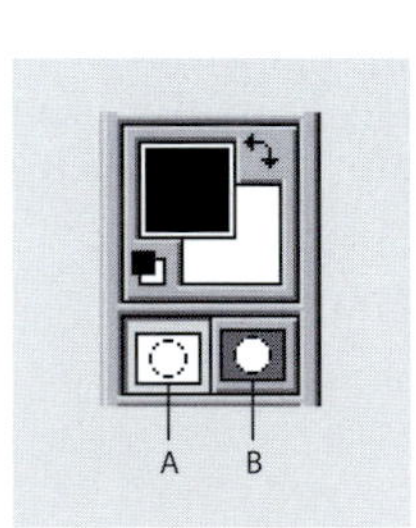

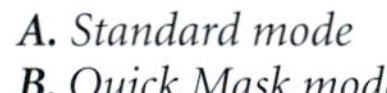

A. *Standard mode*
B. *Quick Mask mode*

Quick mask selection showing red overlay

In Quick Mask mode, a red overlay appears, masking and protecting the area outside the selection the way *rubylith*, or red acetate, masked images in traditional print shops. You can apply changes only to the unprotected area that is visible and selected.

Note: *A partial selection must exist to see the overlay in Quick Mask mode.*

Editing a quick mask

Next, you will refine the selection of the egret by adding to or erasing parts of the masked area. You'll use the Brush tool to make changes to your quick mask. The advantage of editing your selection as a mask is that you can use almost any tool or filter to modify the mask. (You can even use selection tools.) In Quick Mask mode, you do all of your editing in the image window.

In Quick Mask mode, Photoshop automatically defaults to Grayscale mode. The foreground color defaults to black, and the background color defaults to white. When using a painting or editing tool in Quick Mask mode, keep these principles in mind:

- Painting with white erases the mask (the red overlay) and increases the selected area.
- Painting with black adds to the mask (the red overlay) and decreases the selected area.

Adding to a selection by erasing masked areas

You'll begin by painting with white to increase the selected area within the egret. This erases some of the mask.

1 To make the foreground color white, click the Switch Foreground and Background Colors icon (↰) above the foreground and background color-selection boxes.

2 Select the Zoom tool( ) and magnify your view of the image, if needed.

Julieanne Kost is an official Adobe Photoshop evangelist.

TOOL TIPS FROM THE PHOTOSHOP EVANGELIST

> Zoom tool shortcuts

Often when you are editing an image, you'll need to zoom in to work on a detail and then zoom out again to see the changes in context. Here are several keyboard shortcuts that make the zooming even faster and easier to do.

- Press Ctrl-spacebar (Windows) or Command-spacebar (Mac OS) to temporarily select the Zoom In tool from the keyboard. When you finish zooming, release the keys to return to the tool you were previously using.
- Press Alt-spacebar (Windows) or Option-spacebar (Mac OS) to temporarily select the Zoom Out tool from the keyboard. When you finish zooming, release the keys to return to the tool you were using.
- In the toolbox, double-click the Zoom tool to return the image to 100% view.
- Hold down Alt (Windows) or Option (Mac OS) to change the Zoom In tool to the Zoom Out tool, and click the area of the image you want to reduce. Each Alt/Option-click reduces the image by the next preset increment.
- With any tool selected, press Ctrl-+ (Windows) or Command-+ (Mac OS) to zoom in, or press Ctrl-- or Command-- to zoom out.

3 Select the Brush tool ( ).

4 On the tool options bar, make sure that the mode is Normal. Then, click the arrow to display the Brushes pop-up palette, and select a medium-sized brush, such as one with a diameter of 13 pixels. Click off the palette to close it.

Note: *You'll switch brushes several times during this lesson. For convenience, you can drag the Brushes palette from the palette well (on the right side of the tool options bar) so that it stays open, making your brush choices readily available.*

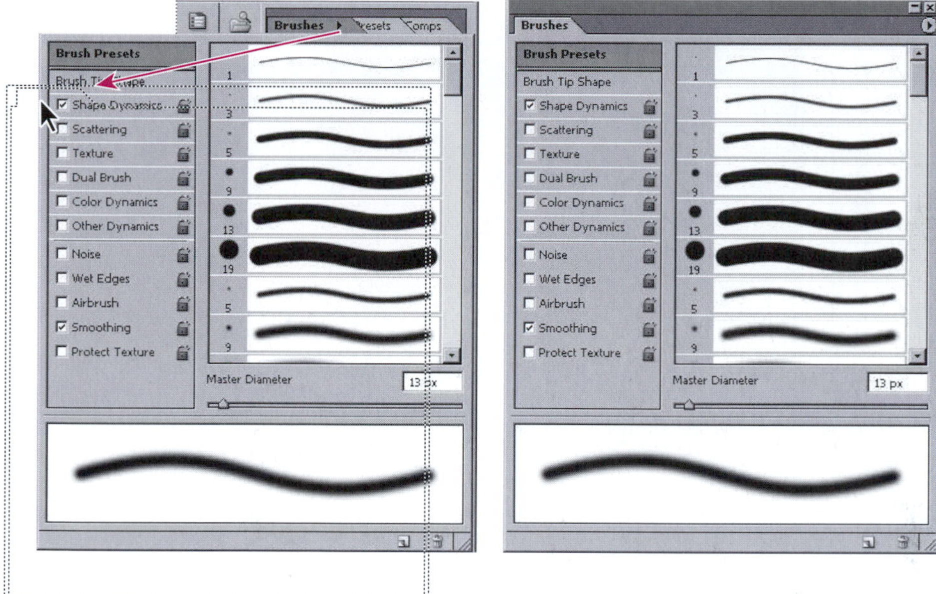

5 Using the Brush tool, begin painting over the red areas within the egret's body.

Although you are painting with white, what you see in the image window is the erasure of the red mask areas.

Don't worry if you paint outside the outline of the egret's body. You'll have a chance to make adjustments later by masking areas of the image as needed.

Unedited mask

Painting with white

Result

6 Continue painting with white to erase all of the mask (red) in the egret, including its beak and legs. As you work, you can easily switch between Quick Mask mode and Standard mode to see how painting in the mask alters the selected area. In Standard mode, notice that the selection border increases to encompass more of the egret's body.

Standard mode

Edited mask in Standard mode

Quick Mask selection

If any areas within the body of the egret still appear to be selected, it means that you haven't erased all of the mask.

Selection in Standard mode

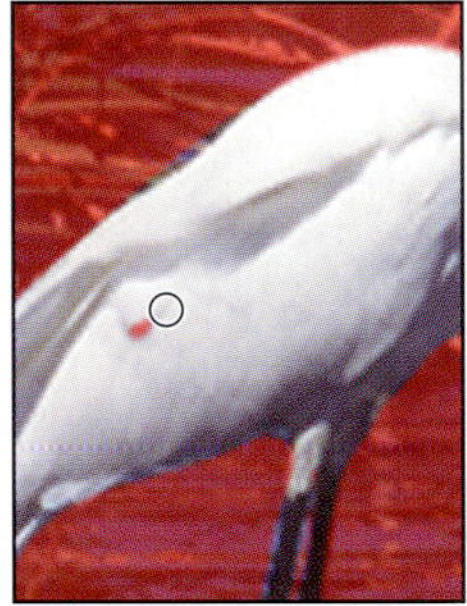

Erasing in Quick Mask mode

7 Once you've erased all of the red areas within the egret, click the Standard Mode button (◙) again to view the quick mask as a selection.

Subtracting from a selection by adding masked areas

You may have erased the mask beyond the edges of the egret. This means that part of the background is included in the selection. You'll fix these flaws by returning to Quick Mask mode and restoring the mask to those edge areas by painting with black.

1 Click the Quick Mask Mode button (◙) to return to Quick Mask mode.

2 To make the foreground color black, click the Switch Foreground and Background Colors icon (↰) in the toolbox so that the black color swatch appears on top. Remember that in the image window, painting with black will add to the red overlay.

3 Choose a small brush, such as 1, 3, or 5 pixels, from the Brushes pop-up palette.

4 Paint with black to restore the mask (the red overlay) to any of the background area that is still unprotected. Continue working until only the area inside the egret remains unmasked and you are completely satisfied with your mask selection.

Remember that you can zoom in and out as you work. You can also switch back and forth between Standard mode and Quick Mask mode.

Note: In Quick Mask mode, you can also use the Eraser tool to remove any excess selection.

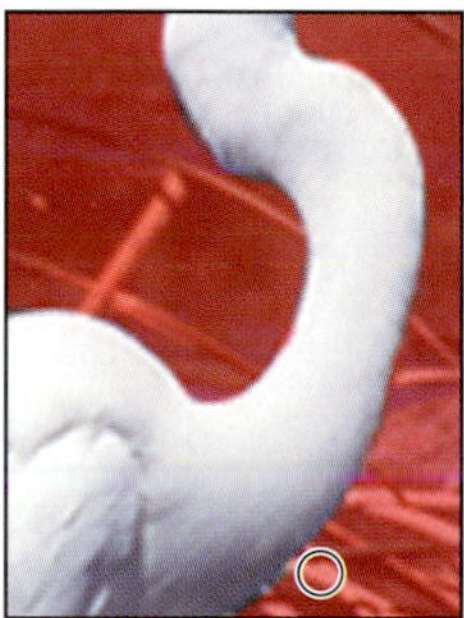

Painting with black to restore mask

5 In the toolbox, switch to Standard mode to view your final egret selection.

6 Double-click the Hand tool (✋) to make the egret image fit in the window.

Saving a selection as a mask

Quick masks are temporary. They disappear as soon as you deselect. However, you can save a selection as an alpha-channel mask so that your time-consuming work won't be lost and you can reuse the selection in this work session or a later one. You can even use alpha channels in other Photoshop image files.

To avoid confusing channels and layers, think of channels as containing an image's color and selection information; think of layers as containing painting and effects.

Note: If you save and close a file while in Quick Mask mode, the quick mask will show in its own channel the next time you open the file. If, however, you save and close your file while in Standard mode, the quick mask will be gone the next time you open your file.

1 In the Layers palette group, click the Channels tab to bring that palette forward, or choose Window > Channels.

In the Channels palette, the default color-information channels are listed—a full-color preview channel for the RGB image and separate channels for red, green, and blue.

Note: You can click eye icons (👁) in the Channels palette to hide and display individual color channels. When the RGB channel is visible, eye icons also appear for all three individual channels, and vice versa. If you hide one of the individual channels, the eye icon for the composite (the RGB channel) also disappears.

2 With the (Standard mode) egret selection still active in the image window, click the Save Selection as Channel button (◙) at the bottom of the Channels palette.

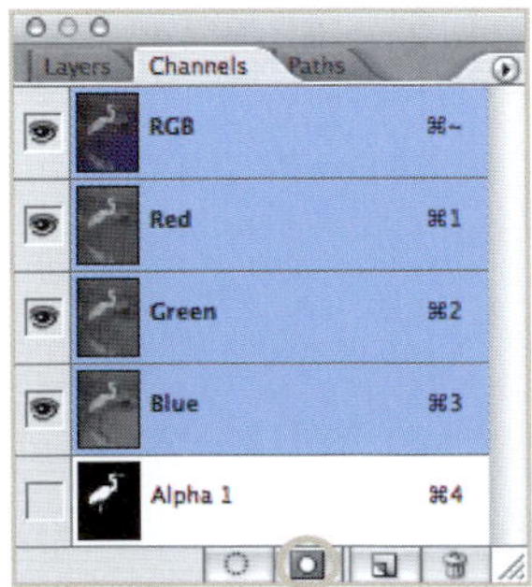

A new channel, Alpha 1, appears at the bottom of the Channels palette.

3 Double-click the Alpha 1 channel, type **Egret** to rename it, and press Enter (Windows) or Return (Mac OS).

When you select the channel, Photoshop displays a black-and-white of the egret selection in the image window, and it hides all the color channels.

4 Choose Select > Deselect to deselect the egret.

Using alpha channels

Here are some useful facts about alpha channels:

- An image can contain up to 56 channels, including all color and alpha channels.
- All channels are 8-bit grayscale images, capable of displaying 256 levels of gray.
- You can specify a name, color, mask option, and opacity for each channel. (The opacity affects the preview of the channel, not the image.)
- All new channels have the same dimensions and number of pixels as the original image.
- You can edit the mask in an alpha channel using the painting tools, editing tools, and filters.
- You can convert alpha channels to spot-color channels.

Editing a mask

Your next job is to touch up your selection of the egret by editing the mask. It's easy to miss tiny areas when making a selection. You may not even see these imperfections until you view the saved selection as a channel mask.

You can use most painting and editing tools to edit a channel mask. This time, you will display and edit the mask as a grayscale image.

1 Make sure that the Egret channel is selected and that the RGB channels are all hidden, or hide them now, as appropriate.

(If you left all of the channels selected, the colored egret image would appear with a red overlay.)

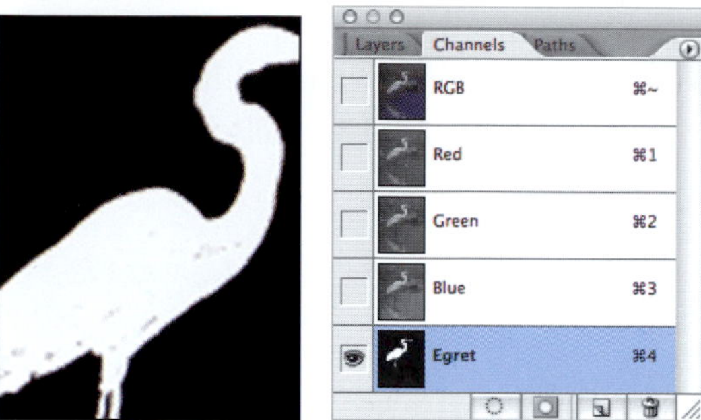

Look for any black or gray flecks within the body of the egret. You'll erase them by painting with white to increase the selected area. Remember these guidelines on editing a channel with a painting or editing tool:

- Painting with white erases the mask and increases the selected area.
- Painting with black adds to the mask and decreases the selected area.
- Painting with gray values adds to or subtracts from the mask in varying opacity, in proportion to the level of gray used to paint: The darker the gray, the greater the opacity of the mask and the fewer number of pixels included in the selection.

2 Zoom in if necessary to see the white egret area clearly.

3 In the toolbox, select the Brush tool ( ), and make sure that white appears in the Foreground Color swatch. If it doesn't, click the Switch Foreground and Background Colors icon ( ).

4 In the Brushes palette, select a small brush size, such as 3 or 5 pixels, and use it to paint out any black or gray flecks in the white egret.

Selection in channel

Painting out black or gray

5 If any white or gray specks appear in the black area of the channel, switch to black as the foreground color and paint those spots. Remember that when you paint with black, you increase the masked area, which will decrease the selection.

6 Dock the Brushes palette by dragging the tab into the palette well.

7 Choose File > Save.

Loading a mask as a selection and applying an adjustment

Next, you'll load the Egret channel mask as a selection. The channel mask remains stored in the Channels palette even after you've loaded it as a selection. This means that you can reuse the mask whenever you want.

1 In the Channels palette, click the RGB preview channel to display the entire image, and then click the eye icon (👁) for the Egret channel to hide it.

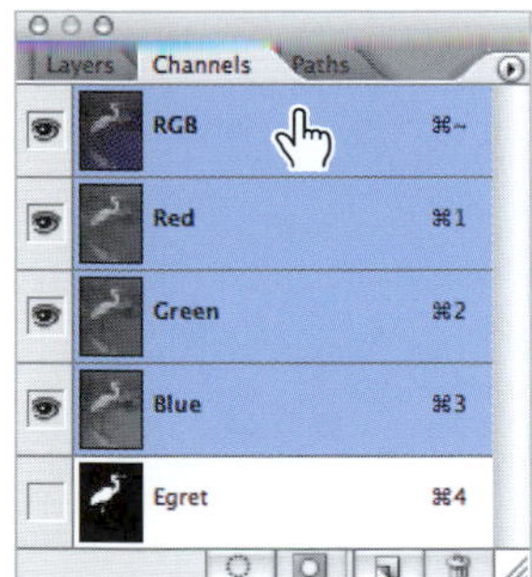

2 Choose Select > Load Selection. Click OK to accept the default options in the Load Selection dialog box.

Load Selection
Source
Document: 07Start.psd
Channel: Egret
Invert
OK
Cancel
Operation
New Selection
Add to Selection
Subtract from Selection
Intersect with Selection

The egret selection appears in the image window.

3 Click the Layers tab to bring it forward again in the palette group, and make sure that the Background layer is selected.

Now that you've corrected any flaws in the selection by painting in the channel, you'll adjust the tonal balance of the egret.

Loading a selection into an image using shortcuts

You can reuse a previously saved selection by loading it into an image. To load a saved selection using shortcuts, do one of the following in the Channels palette:

- Select the alpha channel, click the Load Channel as Selection button at the bottom of the palette, and then click the composite color channel near the top of the palette.
- Drag the channel that contains the selection you want to load onto the Load Channel as Selection button.
- Ctrl-click (Windows) or Command-click (Mac OS) the channel containing the selection you want to load.
- To add the mask to an existing selection, press Ctrl-Shift (Windows) or Command-Shift (Mac OS), and click the channel.
- To subtract the mask from an existing selection, press Ctrl-Alt (Windows) or Command-Option (Mac OS), and click the channel.
- To load the intersection of the saved selection and an existing selection, press Ctrl-Alt-Shift (Windows) or Command-Option-Shift (Mac OS), and select the channel.

4 Choose Image > Adjustments > Auto Levels. This automatically adjusts the tonal balance of the colors within the selection.

Auto Levels defines the lightest and darkest pixels in each channel as white and black, and then redistributes the intermediate pixel values proportionately.

5 Choose Edit > Undo to compare the adjustment you just made. Then choose Edit > Redo to reapply the adjustment.

6 Choose Select > Deselect.

7 Choose File > Save.

Extracting an image

The next task involves another masking and selection tool, the Extract command. This command can make some difficult selections—in this case, some feathery marsh grasses and a spear of a foxtail plant.

The Extract command provides a sophisticated way to isolate a foreground object from its background. Even objects with wispy, intricate, or undefinable edges can be clipped from their backgrounds with a minimum of effort.

You'll start with an image that consists of only one layer. You must be working in a layer to use the Extract command. If your original image has no layers (that is, it has only a Background), you can duplicate the image to a new layer.

***Note:** The foxtail grass image has the same resolution as the egret image, 72 ppi. To avoid unexpected results when combining elements from multiple files, you must either use files with the same image resolution, or compensate for differing resolutions. For example, if your original image is 72 ppi and you add an element from a 144-ppi image, the additional element will appear twice as large. For information on resolutions, see "Pixel dimensions and image resolution" in Photoshop Help.*

Extracting an object from its background

Applying an extraction erases the background area to transparency, leaving just the extracted object. You'll use the Extract command on a foxtail grass image, which is set against a dark background. This command opens the Extract dialog box, where you'll highlight the edges of the object, define the object's interior, and preview the extraction. You can refine and preview the extraction as many times as you wish.

1 Click the Go to Bridge button (▣) to jump to Adobe Bridge, locate the Foxtail.psd image file in the Lessons/Lesson07 folder, and double-click its thumbnail preview to open it in Photoshop.

2 Choose Filter > Extract.

The Extract dialog box appears with the Edge Highlighter tool (✎) selected in the upper left area of the dialog box.

If needed, you can resize the dialog box by dragging its bottom right corner.

3 On the right side of the dialog box, locate the Brush Size option, and then type or drag the slider to **20** pixels, if necessary.

You can select a brush smaller than 20 pixels, but it's not necessary. The beauty of the Extract function is that it distinguishes between the light-colored stem and the dark background, so a few extra background pixels won't affect the results.

4 Using the Edge Highlighter tool, do both of the following:

• Drag to highlight the stem of the foxtail grass and the single leaf. (The highlighting will extend beyond the edges of the stem and leaf.)

• Drag all the way around the tip of the foxtail, covering the entire area around the fuzzy edges of the grass. Make sure that the outline forms a closed shape around the entire tip area.

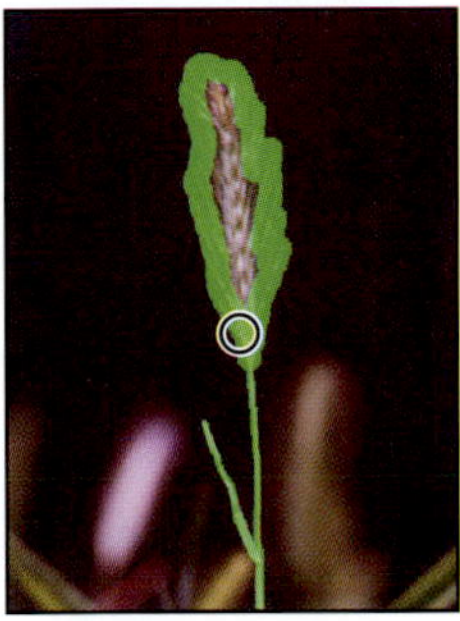

Note: *It's OK if the highlight overlaps the edge. The Extract command makes its selection by finding the difference in contrast between pixels. You do not need to highlight areas where the object touches the image boundaries.*

If you make a mistake and highlight more than desired, select the Eraser tool () in the dialog box and drag over the highlight in the preview.

5 Select the Fill tool (), under the Edge Highlighter tool, and click inside the outlined foxtail tip to fill its interior. (You must define the object's interior before you can preview the extraction.)

The default fill color (bright blue) contrasts well with the edge highlight color (green). You can change either color if you need more contrast with the image colors using the Highlight and Fill pop-up menus in the Extract dialog box.

6 Click the Preview button to view the extraction, and do one of the following:

- If you are satisfied with the results, click OK to apply the extraction.

- If you want to refine the extraction, select Original in the Show menu, and check both the Show Highlight and Show Fill boxes. Continue to work with the tools in the Extract dialog box to add to or erase areas of the selection until you create a satisfactory result. (You may need to preview the results after you adjust the highlighting.) Then click OK.

The Extract dialog box closes and the image window displays the extracted area. (This may be difficult to see because the color is pale and does not stand out well against the checkerboard pattern that indicates transparency.)

Refining a selection in the Extract dialog box

To refine your selection, edit the extraction boundaries using these techniques:

- Switch between the Original and Extracted views using the Show menu.
- Click a filled area with the Fill tool to remove the fill.
- Select the Eraser tool (🖉) and drag to remove any undesired highlighting.
- Select the Show Highlight and Show Fill options to view the highlight and fill colors; deselect the options to hide them.
- Zoom in on your selection using the Zoom tool. Then, use a smaller brush size as you edit, switching between the Edge Highlighter tool and the Eraser tool as needed for more precise work.
- Toggle quickly between the Edge Highlighter and Eraser tools when one of them is selected by pressing B (Edge Highlighter) or E (Eraser).
- Switch to a smaller brush by entering a different size in the Brush Size option, and continue to refine the selection border using the Edge Highlighter tool or to erase using the Eraser tool.

Adding the extracted image as a layer

It's time to add the extracted image to the egret image.

1 With the foxtail image window active, use the Move tool (▸✥) to drag the image to the right side of the egret image. The foxtail is added as a new layer to the egret image.

2 Close Foxtail.psd without saving changes. The 07Start.psd file is now the active file, and the new layer with the foxtail, Layer 1, is selected.

3 Zoom out so that the egret image covers only about half of the height of the image window.

4 Choose Edit > Transform > Scale. Then, drag a resize corner handle, holding down Shift to constrain the proportions, until the foxtail is about two-thirds its original size. Position the cursor inside the box and drag to move it in the image window, if necessary. Press Enter (Windows) or Return (Mac OS) to apply the scaling.

5 With Layer 1 still selected, decrease its Opacity in the Layers palette to **70%**.

6 Choose File > Save.

Extracting by forcing the foreground

The Force Foreground option lets you make intricate selections when an object lacks a clear interior.

1 Use Adobe Bridge or the File > Open command to locate the Weeds.psd image in the Lessons/Lesson07 folder and open it in Photoshop.

2 Choose Filter > Extract.

3 On the right side of the dialog box, under Extraction, select the Force Foreground check box.

You'll start by selecting the color on which to base your selection. The Force Foreground technique works best with objects that are monochromatic or fairly uniform in color.

4 Select the Eyedropper tool ( ), and then click a light area of the weeds to sample the color to be treated as the foreground.

5 Select the Edge Highlighter tool ( ) and set the brush size to **20** or **30**, either by typing or dragging the slider for Brush Size on the right side of the dialog box.

6 Drag to highlight the wispy tops of the weeds where they overlap the dark background. When the weeds' edges are completely highlighted, highlight the top third of the weeds fully. The highlight should be solid.

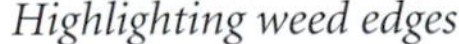
Highlighting weed edges

Selecting top third of weeds

7 At the right side of the dialog box, choose Display > Black Matte.

A black matte provides good contrast for a light-colored selection. For a dark selection, try the Gray or White Matte option. None previews a selection against a transparent background.

8 Click the Preview button to preview the extracted weeds.

9 Refine the extraction if necessary using the techniques described on page 207, and preview the results using the Show pop-up menu and the Show Highlight and Show Fill options.

10 When you are satisfied with the selection, click OK to apply the extraction. All pixels on the layer outside the extracted object are erased to transparency.

Once you've extracted an image, you can also use the Background Eraser and History Brush tools to clean up any stray edges in the image.

An alternative method for making intricate selections is to select areas by color. To do so, choose Select > Color Range. Then, use the eyedropper tools from the Color Range dialog box to sample the colors for your selection. You can sample from your image window or from the preview window.

Adding the forced-foreground extraction as another layer

You can now add the extracted weeds to the egret image.

1 With the Weeds.psd file active, use the Move tool (▸✥) to drag the extracted selection to the egret image. Position the weeds so that they fill the bottom third of the egret image.

The selection is added to the egret image as a new layer.

2 In the Layers palette, decrease the opacity of the new layer to **70%**.

3 Choose File > Save.

4 Close the Weeds.psd file without saving changes.

Applying a filter effect to a masked selection

To complete the composite of the marsh grasses and egret image, you'll isolate the egret as you apply a filter effect to the image background.

1 In the Layers palette, select the Background layer.

2 In the Channels palette, drag the Egret channel to the Load Channel as Selection button (◌) at the bottom of the palette. *Before continuing to the next step, make sure that the RGB channel is selected, not the Egret channel.*

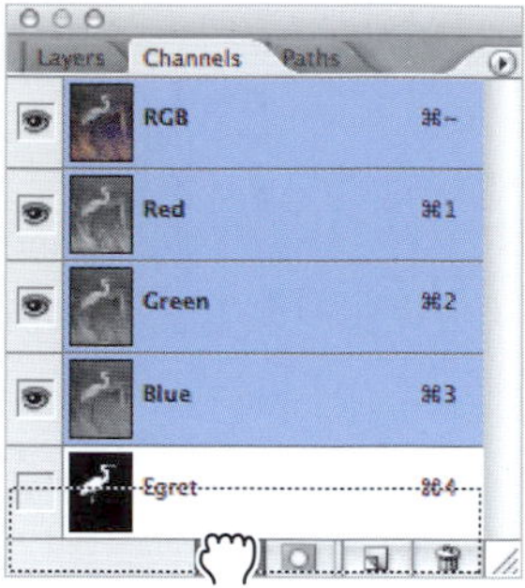

3 Choose Select > Inverse.

The previous selection (the egret) is protected, and the background is selected. You can now apply changes to the background without affecting the egret.

4 Click the Layers palette tab and make sure that the Background layer is selected. Then choose Filter > Artistic > Colored Pencil. Experiment with the Pencil Width, Stroke Pressure, and Paper Brightness sliders to create an effect you like.

Note: *If the Filter menu is not available (dimmed), you may have accidentally selected the Egret channel when you dragged it to the Load Channel as Selection button. To try again, choose Select > Deselect now and make sure that the RGB channel remains selected when you load the Egret channel.*

5 Click OK when you're satisfied with the Colored Pencil settings. The filter is applied to the background selection.

You can experiment with other filter effects for the background. Choose Edit > Undo to undo your last-performed operation.

6 Choose Select > Deselect to deselect everything.

Before you save your file, you'll flatten your image to reduce the file size. Make sure that you are satisfied with the image before you go on to the next step, because you won't be able to make corrections to the separate layers after the image is flattened.

7 Choose Layer > Flatten Image, and then choose File > Save.

Creating a gradient mask

In addition to using black to indicate what's hidden and white to indicate what's selected, you can paint with shades of gray to indicate partial transparency. For example, if you paint in a channel with a shade of gray that is at least halfway between white and black, the underlying image becomes partially (50% or more) visible.

You'll experiment by adding a gradient (which makes a transition from black to gray to white) to a channel and then filling the selection with a color to see how the transparency levels of the black, gray, and white in the gradient affect the image.

1 In the Channels palette, click the New Channel button (◘) at the bottom of the palette to create a new channel.

The new channel, Alpha 1, appears at the bottom of the palette, and the other channels are hidden in the image window.

2 Double-click the Alpha 1 channel and type **Gradient**, then press Enter (Windows) or Return (Mac OS) to rename it.

3 Select the Gradient tool (▣).

4 On the tool options bar, click the arrow to display the gradient picker and select the Black, White gradient if it is not already selected. (Use tooltips or another view option in the gradient picker palette menu if you are unsure which thumbnail represents this option.) Then click outside the picker to close it.

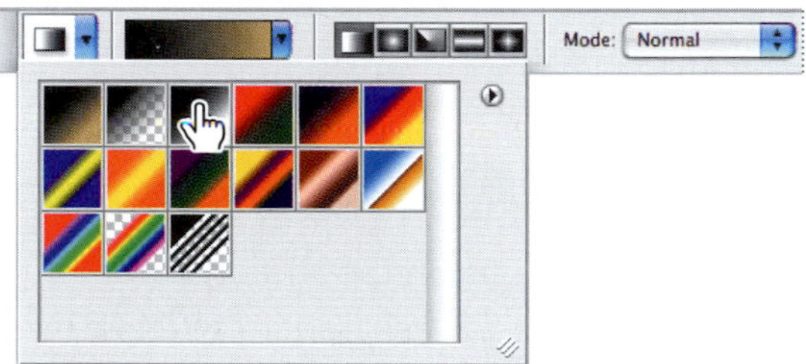

5 Hold down Shift to keep the gradient vertical, and drag the Gradient tool from the top of the image window to the bottom of the window.

The gradient is applied to the channel.

Applying effects using a gradient mask

When you load a gradient as a selection and then fill the selection with a color, the opacity of the fill color varies over the length of the gradient. Where the gradient is black, no fill color is present; where the gradient is gray, the fill color is partially visible; and where the gradient is white, the fill color is completely visible.

1 In the Channels palette, click the RGB channel to display the full-color preview, and then click the Gradient channel eye icon (👁) to hide that channel.

Next, you'll load the Gradient channel as a selection.

2 With the RGB channel selected, drag the Gradient channel to the Load Channel as Selection button (◌) at the bottom of the palette to load the gradient as a selection.

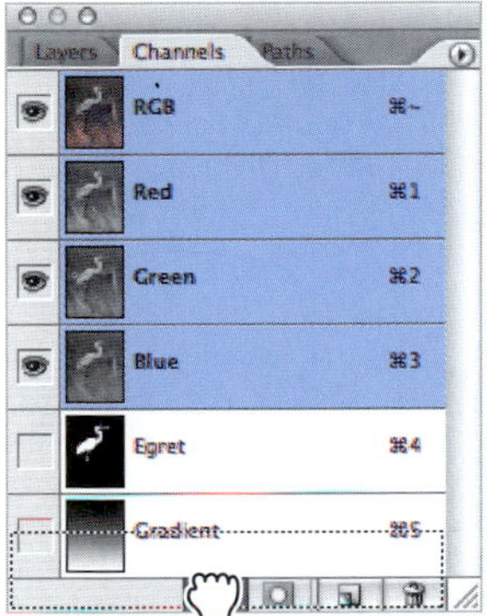

A selection border appears in the image window. Although the selection border appears over only about half the image, it is correct.

3 Make sure that the background color is set to white and the foreground color is set to black. If necessary, click the Default Foreground and Background Colors icon (◪) at the lower left corner of the color-selection boxes.

4 Press Delete to fill the gradient selection with the background color (white).

5 Choose Select > Deselect to deselect everything.

6 Choose File > Save.

You have completed this lesson. Although it takes some practice to become comfortable using channels, you've learned all the fundamental concepts and skills you need to get started using masks and channels.

Review

Review questions

1 What is the benefit of using a quick mask?

2 What happens to a quick mask when you deselect it?

3 When you save a selection as a mask, where is the mask stored?

4 How can you edit a mask in a channel once you've saved it?

5 How do channels differ from layers?

6 How do you use the Extract command to isolate an object with intricate borders from an image?

Review answers

1 Quick masks are helpful for creating quick, onetime selections. In addition, using a quick mask is an easy way to edit a selection using the painting tools.

2 The quick mask disappears when you deselect it.

3 Masks are saved in channels, which can be thought of as storage areas for color and selection information in an image.

4 You can paint on a mask in a channel using black, white, and shades of gray.

5 Channels are used as storage areas for saved selections. Unless you explicitly display a channel, it does not appear in the image or print. Layers can be used to isolate various parts of an image so that they can be edited as discrete objects with the painting or editing tools or other effects.

6 You use the Extract command to extract an object, and the Extract dialog box to highlight the edges of the object. Then, you define the object's interior and preview the extraction. Applying the extraction erases the background to transparency, leaving just the extracted object. You can also use the Force Foreground option to extract a monochromatic or uniform-colored object based on its predominant color.

Digital photography isn't just for professionals anymore. Whether you have a collection of digital images amassed for various clients or projects, or a personal collection that you want to refine, archive, and preserve for posterity, Photoshop has an array of tools for importing, editing, and archiving digital photographs.

8 Correcting and Enhancing Digital Photographs

Lesson overview

In this lesson, you'll learn how to do the following:

- Process a proprietary camera raw image and save it as an industry-standard digital negative.
- Make typical corrections to a digital photograph, including removing red eye and noise and bringing out shadow and highlights detail.
- Adjust the visual perspective of objects in an image using the Vanishing Point filter.
- Apply optical lens correction to an image.
- Prepare a PDF presentation of your corrected images.

This lesson will take 1½ to 2 hours to complete. If needed, remove the previous lesson folder from your hard drive, and copy the Lessons/Lesson08 folder onto it. As you work on this lesson, you'll overwrite the start files. If you need to restore the start files, copy them again from the *Adobe Photoshop CS2 Classroom in a Book* CD.

Getting started

In this lesson, you will work with several images to learn about Photoshop's support for camera raw image processing and editing, as well as to explore many features that let you enhance and clean up your digital photographs. You will save each edited image in a Portfolio folder when you're finished, and at the end of the lesson, you will prepare a PDF slide show of your corrected images. You will start by viewing the before and after images in Adobe Bridge.

1 Start Photoshop and then immediately hold down Ctrl-Alt-Shift (Windows) or Command-Option-Shift (Mac OS) to restore the default preferences. (See "Restoring default preferences" on page 6.)

2 When prompted, click Yes to confirm that you want to reset preferences, and Close to close the Welcome Screen.

3 Click the Go to Bridge button (▣) on the tool options bar to open Adobe Bridge.

4 In the Favorites palette in the upper left corner of Bridge, click the Lessons favorite, and then double-click the Lesson08 folder in the preview area to see its contents.

5 Make sure your thumbnail previews are large enough for a good look at the images, and locate the 08A_Start.crw and 08A_End.psd files.

Before

After

The original photograph of a Spanish-style church is a camera raw file, so it doesn't have the usual .psd file extension you've worked with so far in this book. It was shot with a Canon Digital Rebel camera and has the Canon proprietary .crw raw file extension instead. You will process this proprietary camera raw image to make it brighter, sharper, and clearer, and then save it as an industry-standard DNG digital negative.

6 Locate the 08B_Start.psd and 08B_End.psd files and study their thumbnail previews.

Before

After

You are going to make several corrections to this portrait of mother and son, including bringing out shadow and highlight detail, removing red eye, and sharpening the image.

7 Locate the 08C_Start.psd and 08C_End.psd files and study their thumbnail previews.

Before

After

You are going to edit the image of this red clapboard farmhouse to add a window and remove the seasonal wreath, preserving the vanishing-point perspective as you make corrections.

8 Locate the 08D_Start.psd and 08D_End.psd files and study their thumbnail previews.

Before

After

You are going to correct the lens barrel distortion in this image.

About camera raw

A *camera raw* file contains unprocessed picture data from a digital camera's image sensor. Many digital cameras can save images as camera raw format files. The advantage of camera raw files are that they give the photographer control over interpreting the image data, rather than letting the camera make the adjustments and conversions. Because the camera doesn't do any of the image processing, you can set the white balance, tonal range, contrast, color saturation, and sharpening in Photoshop. Think of camera raw files as your photo negative. You can go back and reprocess the file anytime you like to achieve the results you want.

To create camera raw files, you need to set your digital camera to save files in its own raw file format, which may be a proprietary format. When you download a camera raw file from the camera, it will have a file extension such as .nef (from Nikon) or .crw (from Canon). In Bridge or Photoshop, you can process camera raw files from an extensive list of supported digital cameras from Canon, Kodak, Leica, Nikon, and other manufacturers—and can even process multiple images simultaneously. Then you can export the proprietary camera raw files to the Digital Negative (DNG) file format, Adobe's nonproprietary format for standardizing camera raw files, or to such other formats as JPEG, TIFF, and PSD.

For a complete list of cameras supported by Adobe Camera Raw, go to www.adobe.com/products/photoshop/cameraraw.html.

Processing camera raw files

When you make adjustments to a camera raw image, such as straightening or cropping the image, Photoshop and Bridge preserve the original camera raw file data. This way, you can edit the image as you desire, export the edited image, and keep the original intact for future use or other adjustments.

Opening camera raw images

Both Adobe Bridge and Photoshop CS2 let you open and process multiple camera raw images simultaneously. They feature an identical Camera Raw dialog box, which provides extensive controls for adjusting white balance, exposure, contrast, sharpness, tone curves, and much more. If you have multiple exposures of the same shot, you can use the Camera Raw dialog box to process one of the images, and then apply the settings to all of the other shots. You will do that in this exercise.

1 In Bridge, navigate to the Lessons/Lesson08/Mission folder, which contains three shots of the Spanish church you previewed in the previous exercise.

2 Press Shift and click to select all of the images—Mission01.crw, Mission02.crw, and Mission03.crw, and then choose File > Open in Camera Raw.

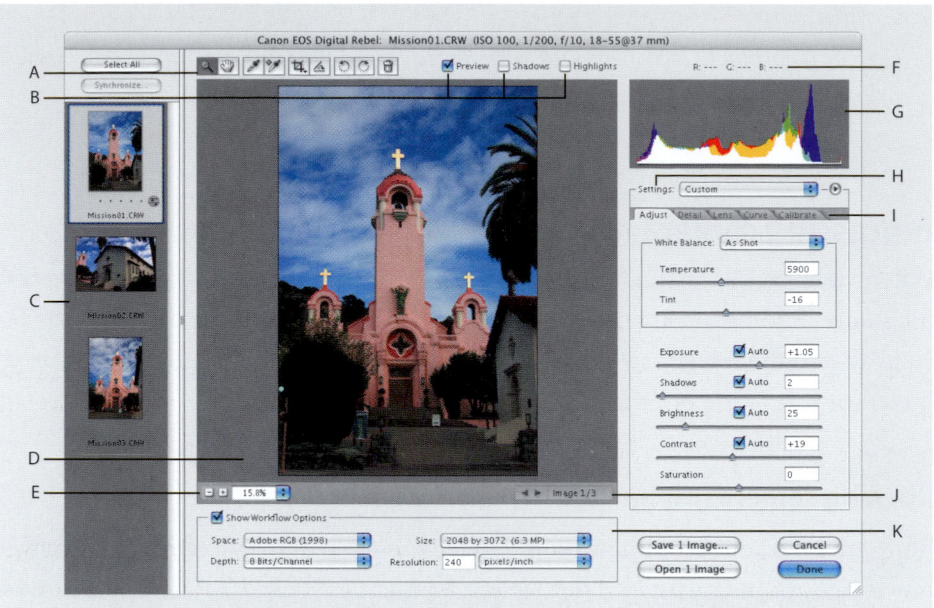

*A. Tools **B.** Preview controls **C.** Filmstrip thumbnail **D.** Image preview **E.** Zoom controls **F.** RGB values* *G. Histogram **H.** Settings menu **I.** Tonal and color-correction palettes **J.** Multi-image navigation controls* ***K.** Workflow options*

The Camera Raw dialog box displays a large preview of the first raw image, and a filmstrip down the left side of the dialog box of all of the open camera raw images. The histogram at right shows the tonal range of the first image, and the workflow options at the bottom of the dialog box show the first image's color space, bit-depth, size, and resolution. An array of tools at the top of the dialog box let you zoom and pan the image, select colors, crop, rotate, and more. Tabbed palettes along the right side of the dialog box allow you to adjust the image's white balance, color, tone, and detail. You will explore these controls now, editing the first image file.

3 Click the forward arrow button under the main preview area—or scroll down the filmstrip and select each thumbnail in turn—to cycle through the images, and return to Mission 01.crw.

4 Make sure the Preview box is checked at the top of the dialog box so that you can interactively see the adjustments you're about to make. For now, leave the Shadows and Highlights boxes unchecked.

Adjusting white balance and exposure

An image's white balance reflects the lighting conditions under which the photo was captured. A digital camera records the white balance at the time of exposure, and this is what initially appears in the Camera Raw dialog box image preview.

White balance comprises two components. The first is temperature, which is measured in kelvins and determines the level of "coolness" or "warmness" of the image—that is, its cool blue-green tones or warm yellow-red tones. The second component is tint, which compensates for magenta or green color casts in the image.

A camera's white balance usually comes close to being optimal, but you can adjust it if it's not quite right. Adjusting an image's white balance is a good way to start your corrections.

1 Click the Adjust tab to bring that palette forward (if it's not already open) and choose Cloudy from the White Balance pop-up menu.

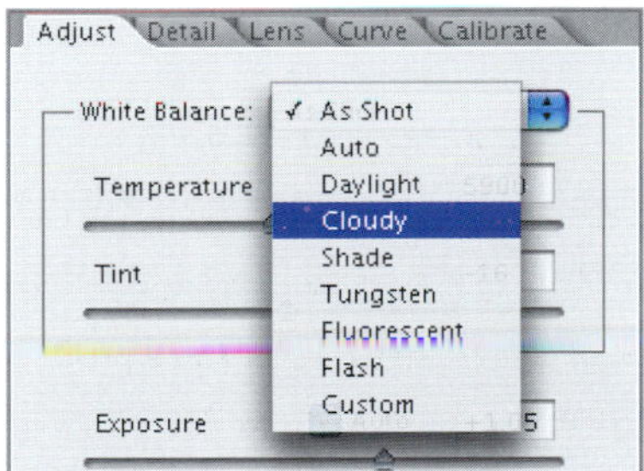

The Cloudy White Balance temperature is a little warmer than the Daylight setting and nicely suits this image, which was taken on a cloudy day.

2 Change the other sliders in the Adjust palette as follows:

- Set the Exposure to +1.20.
- Set Shadows to 0.
- Set Brightness to 50.
- Set Contrast to +29.
- Set Saturation to –5.

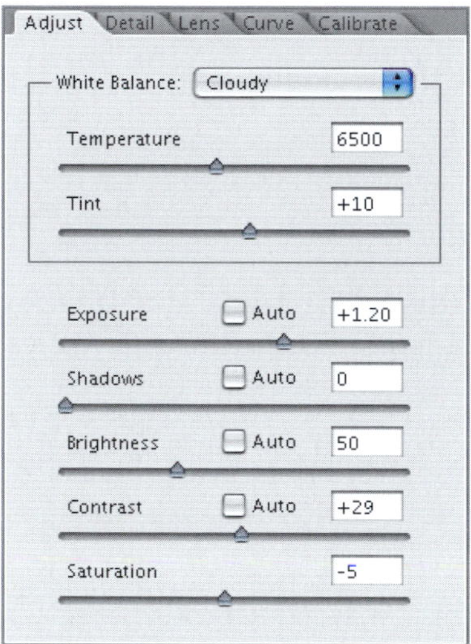

These settings help pump up the midtones of this image and make the image look bolder and more dimensional without being oversaturated.

About the camera raw histogram

The histogram in the upper right corner of the Camera Raw dialog box simultaneously shows the Red, Green, and Blue channels of the previewed image, and it updates interactively as you adjust any settings. Also, as you move any tool over the preview image, the RGB values for the area under the cursor appear above the histogram.

Applying sharpening

Next, you will sharpen the image to bring out more detail.

1 Click the Detail tab to bring that palette forward, and zoom in to the top of the mission tower so that you can see the detail (to at least 100%).

2 Drag the Sharpness slider to about 35.

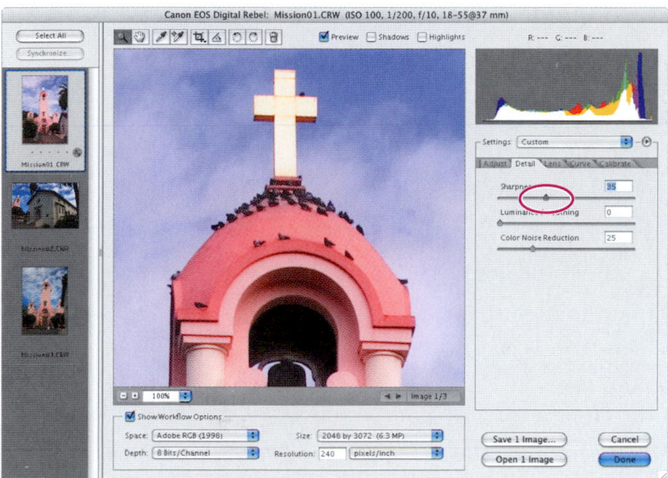

The higher sharpness value gives stronger definition to the details and edges in this mission image.

Synchronizing settings across images

Now that you've made this one mission image look stunning, you can automatically apply these camera raw settings to the other two mission images, which were shot at the same time under the same lighting conditions. You do this using the Synchronize command.

1 In the upper left corner of the Camera Raw dialog box, click the Select All button to select all of the thumbnails in the filmstrip.

2 Click the Synchronize button.

The Synchronize dialog box that appears lets you choose which settings you want to synchronize across the selected images. By default, all options (except Crop) are checked. That's OK for our project, even though we didn't change all of the settings.

3 Click OK.

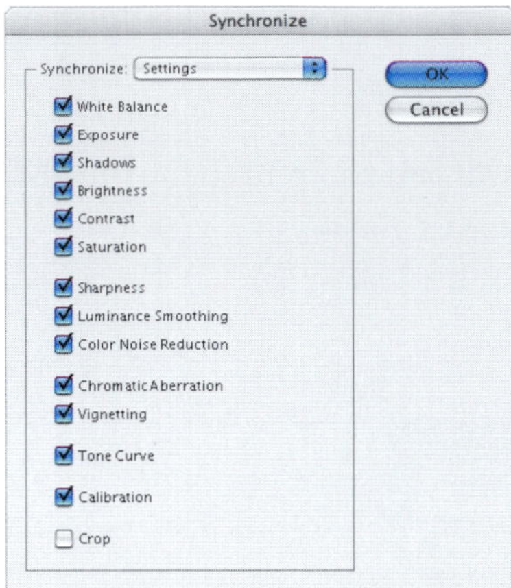

When you synchronize the settings across all of the selected camera raw images, the thumbnails update to reflect the changes you made. If you'd like, you can click the navigational arrows to cycle through a large preview of each image to see the adjustments.

Note: *If you'd like, check the Highlights and Shadows boxes at the top of the dialog box now. Portions of the images that are in danger of being clipped because they are either too light or too dark will appear red or blue, respectively, in the image preview. It's important to try to minimize the risk of clipping by adjusting an image's tonal levels, but these images don't have a significant amount of blown-out highlights or shadows to adjust.*

Saving camera raw changes

Saving your changes so far involves two tasks: first, saving the synchronized changes to all three images and then saving one image, Mission01, for the PDF portfolio you will create later in this lesson.

1 Make sure all three images are still selected in the Camera Raw filmstrip, and then click the Save 3 Images button.

2 In the Save Options dialog box that appears, do the following:

- Choose the same location (the Lessons/Lesson08/Mission folder).
- Under File Naming, leave *Document Name* in the first blank field.
- Choose Format > JPEG at the bottom of the dialog box.
- Click Save.

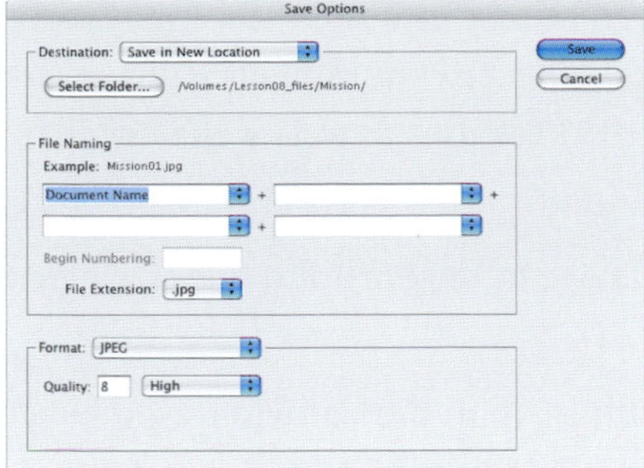

This will save your corrected images as downsampled 72-dpi JPEGs, which can be shared with colleagues and viewed on the Web. Your files will be named Mission01.jpg, Mission02.jpg, and Mission03.jpg.

Note: *Before sharing these images on the Web, you would probably want to open them in Photoshop and resize them to 640 x 480 pixels. They are currently much larger, and the full-size images would not be visible on most monitors without requiring the viewer to scroll.*

About file formats

The camera raw Save Options dialog box provides four file-format options: DNG, JPEG, TIFF, and PSD. All of these formats can be used to save RGB and CMYK continuous-tone, bitmapped images, and all of them (except DNG) are also available in the Photoshop Save and Save As dialog boxes.

The Adobe Digital Negative (DNG) format contains raw image data from a digital camera as well as metadata that defines what the image data means. DNG is meant to be an industry-wide standard format for camera raw image data, helping photographers manage the variety of proprietary camera raw formats and providing a compatible archival format.

The Joint Photographic Experts Group (JPEG) file format is commonly used to display photographs and other continuous-tone RGB images on the World Wide Web. JPEG format retains all color information in an image but compresses file size by selectively discarding data. The greater the compression, the lower the image quality, and vice versa.

The Tagged Image File Format (TIFF) is used to exchange files between applications and computer platforms. TIFF is a flexible format supported by virtually all paint, image-editing, and page-layout applications. Also, virtually all desktop scanners can produce TIFF images.

The Photoshop format (PSD) is the default file format. Because of the tight integration between Adobe products, other Adobe applications such as Adobe Illustrator, Adobe InDesign, and Adobe GoLive can directly import PSD files and preserve many Photoshop features.

Bridge returns you to the Camera Raw dialog box and indicates how many images have been processed until all images are saved. The .crw thumbnails still appear in the Camera Raw dialog box—you now have JPG versions as well as the original, unedited .crw image files, which you can continue to edit or leave for another time.

Now, you will save a copy of the Mission01 image to the Portfolio folder, where all of your portfolio images will be saved.

3 With only Mission01.crw selected in the filmstrip in the Camera Raw dialog box, click the Open 1 Image button to open the (edited) raw image in Photoshop.

4 Choose File > Save As. In the Save As dialog box, choose Photoshop as your Format, and save this image with the name mission_final.psd in the Lesson08/Portfolio folder. Then close it.

Now that you know how to process a camera raw image, you will learn how to make some common corrections to a different digital photograph.

Correcting digital photographs

Photoshop contains a number of features that let you easily improve the quality of digital photographs. These include the ability to automatically bring out details in shadow and highlight areas of an image, easily remove red eye, reduce unwanted noise in an image, and sharpen an image. To explore these capabilities, you will edit a different digital image now: a portrait of a mother and a child.

Making shadow /highlight adjustments

The Shadow/Highlight command is suitable for correcting 8- or 16-bit RGB, CMYK, or Lab photos whose subjects are silhouetted against strong backlighting or are washed out from being too close to the camera flash. The adjustment is also useful for brightening areas of shadow in an otherwise well-lit image.

1 Click the Go to Bridge button ( ). In Bridge, click the Lessons folder favorite (if it is not already selected), and then double-click the Lesson08 folder. Locate the 08B_Start.psd image, and double-click to open it in Photoshop.

2 Choose Image > Adjustments > Shadow/Highlight. Photoshop automatically applies default settings to the image, lightening the background, but you will customize them next to bring out more detail in both the shadows and the highlights, and enhance the red sunset in the sky. (Make sure the Preview box in the Shadow/Highlight dialog box is checked so that you can see the effect in the image window.)

3 In the Shadow/Highlight dialog box, check the Show More Options box, and do the following:

- In the Shadows area, set Amount to **80%** and Tonal Width to **65%**. Leave Radius at 30 pixels.
- In the Highlights area, set Amount to **5%**. Leave Tonal Width at 50% and Radius at 30 pixels.
- In the Adjustments area, drag the Color Correction slider to +45.

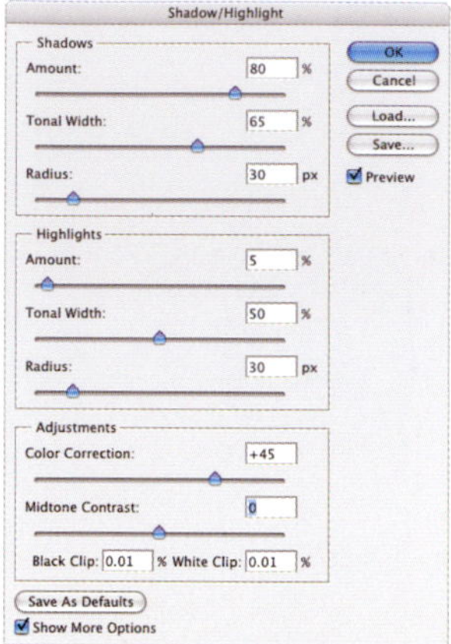

4 Click OK to accept your changes.

5 Choose File > Save to save your work so far.

Correcting red eye

Red eye occurs when the retinas of a subject's eyes are reflected by the camera flash. It commonly occurs in photographs of a subject in a darkened room, because the subject's irises are wide open. Red eye is easy to fix in Photoshop. Next, you will remove the red eye from the boy's eyes in the portrait.

1 Using the Zoom tool, drag a marquee around the boy's eyes to zoom into them.

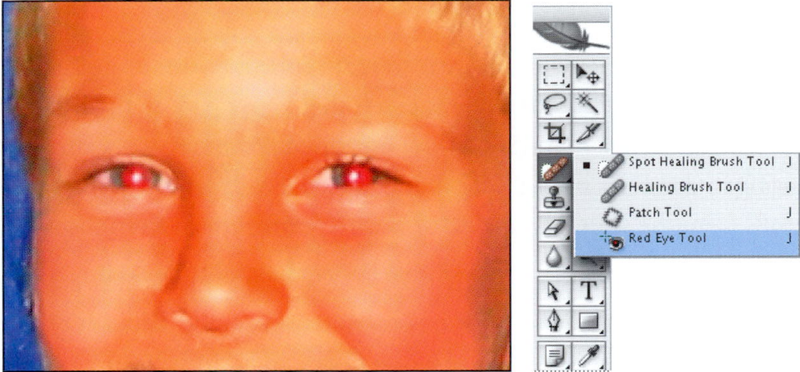

2 Select the Red Eye tool (), hidden under the Spot Healing Brush tool.

3 On the tool options bar, leave Pupil Size set to 50%, but change Darken Amount to 10%. Darken specifies how dark the pupil should be. Because this child's eyes are blue, we want the Darken Amount setting to be lighter than the default.

4 Click on the red area in the boy's left eye, then click the red area in his right eye. The red retinal reflection disappears.

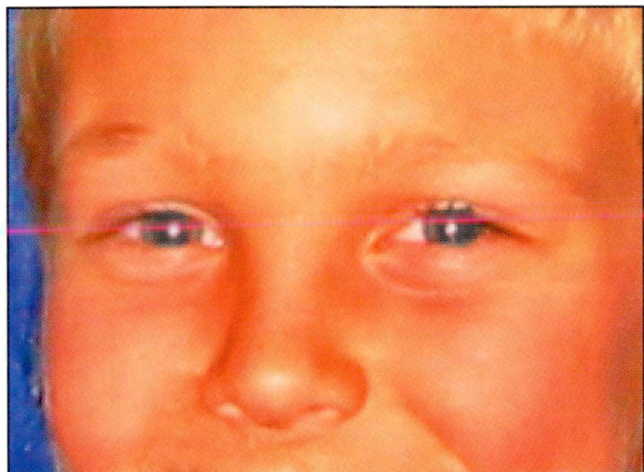

5 Zoom back out to 100% by pressing Alt (Windows) or Option (Mac OS) and clicking on the image window with the Zoom tool.

6 Choose File > Save to save your work so far.

Reducing noise

The next correction to make on this image is to reduce the amount of noise that it contains. *Image noise* is random, extraneous pixels that aren't part of the image detail. Noise can result from using a high ISO setting on a digital camera, from underexposure, or from shooting in darkness with a long shutter speed. Scanned images may contain noise that results from the scanning sensor, or from a grain pattern from the scanned film.

There are two types of image noise: luminance noise, which is grayscale data that makes an image look grainy or patchy, and color noise, which is usually visible as colored artifacts in the image. Photoshop's Reduce Noise filter can address both types of noise in individual color channels while preserving edge detail, as well as correct JPEG compression artifacts.

You will start by zooming in to the sky to get a good look at the noise in this image.

1 Using the Zoom tool, click in the center of the sky above the woman's head and zoom in to about 300%.

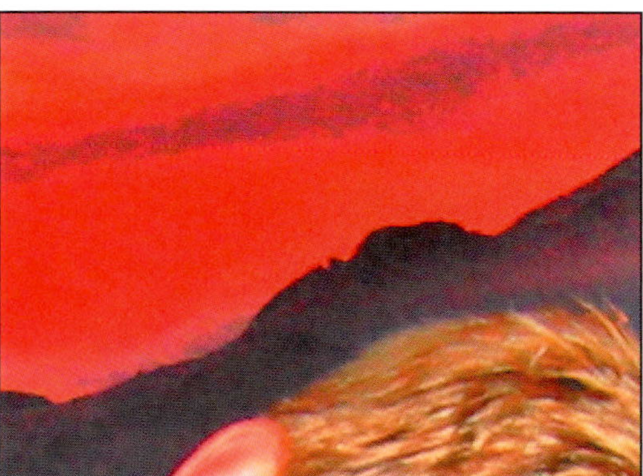

The noise in this image appears as speckled and rough with uneven graininess in the sky. Using the Reduce Noise filter, we can soften and smooth out this area and give the sky more depth.

2 Choose Filter > Noise > Reduce Noise.

3 In the Reduce Noise dialog box, do the following:

- Decrease Strength to 5. (The Strength option controls the amount of luminance noise.)
- Increase Preserve Details to 70%.

- Leave the Reduce Color Noise slider at 45%.
- Increase Sharpen Details to 35%.

You don't need to check the Remove JPEG Artifact box, because this image is not a JPEG and has no JPEG artifacts.

***Note:** To correct noise in individual channels of the image, you can click the Advanced button and adjust these same settings in each channel.*

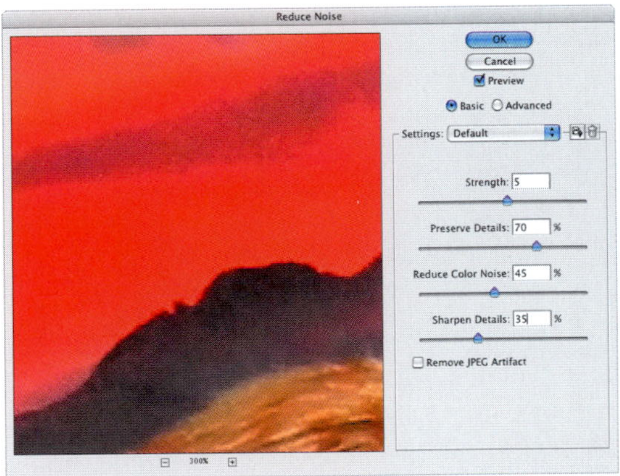

4 To clearly see the results of your changes, click the plus button at the bottom of the dialog box to zoom in to about 300%, and then drag to position the sky in the preview area. Click and hold the mouse button down in the preview area to see the "before" image, and release the mouse button to see the corrected result. Or, make sure the Preview box is checked and watch the results in the main image window.

5 Click OK to apply your changes and to close the Reduce Noise dialog box, and then double-click the Zoom tool to return the image to 100%.

6 Choose File > Save to save your work so far.

Sharpening edges

Reducing noise can soften an image, so, as a final correction to this photograph, you will sharpen it to improve its clarity.

Photoshop has several Sharpen filters, including Sharpen, Unsharp Mask, Sharpen Edges, and Smart Sharpen. All of them focus blurry images by increasing the contrast of adjacent pixels, but some are better than others, depending on, among other things, whether all or part of an image needs to be sharpened. Smart Sharpen sharpens an image while also reducing noise and lets you specify whether the filter is applied to the overall image, to its shadows, or to its highlights.

 *For more on the other Sharpen filters, see Photoshop Help.*

1 Choose Filter > Sharpen > Smart Sharpen.

2 In the Smart Sharpen dialog box, do the following:

- Reduce the Amount to 40%.
- Set the Radius to 5 pixels.
- Choose Remove > Lens Blur.
- Select the More Accurate check box.

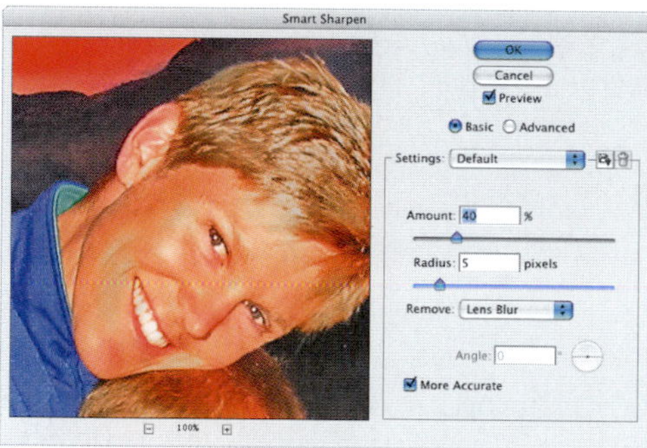

The Remove option determines the algorithm used to sharpen the image. The Unsharp Mask filter uses Gaussian Blur. Lens Blur detects the edges and detail in an image and provides finer detail sharpening and results in fewer sharpening "halos."

Choosing More Accurate yields more accurate sharpening, but takes longer to process.

3 To examine the results of Smart Sharpen, click and hold the mouse button in the preview area, then release. Or, toggle the Preview check box and watch the results in the main image window.

4 Click OK to apply your changes and close the Smart Sharpen dialog box.

5 Choose File > Save As. In the Save As dialog box, name the file portrait_final.psd, navigate to the Lesson08/Portfolio folder, and save the file. Then, close the image window.

Congratulations. You have made several typical corrections to a digital photograph. Next, you will try something a little more unusual—editing an image while preserving its perspective.

Editing images with a vanishing-point perspective

The Vanishing Point filter lets you define the perspective planes in an image and then paint, clone, and transform images according to that perspective. You can even create multiple planes that are related to each other by tearing off perpendicular planes from the plane you define. Then you can paint, clone, and transform across the different planes, and Photoshop will automatically scale and orient your edits in the proper perspective throughout the image.

The Vanishing Point filter works with 8-bit-per-channel images, but not with vector data. To use it, you first create a grid that defines your perspective; then you edit your image normally. Vanishing Point adjusts your editing to the defined perspective.

Defining a grid

In this exercise, you'll work with an image of a snow-covered house. You will use the Vanishing Point filter to add a window to the wall and to remove the seasonal holiday wreath, all while maintaining perspective.

1 Click the Go to Bridge button (). In Bridge, click the Lessons folder favorite (if it is not already selected), and then double-click on the Lesson08 folder. Locate the 08C_Start.psd image, and double-click it to open it in Photoshop.

You will start by defining the perspective grid. Then you will create a fourth window and remove the seasonal wreath.

2 Choose Filter > Vanishing Point. An image preview appears in the Vanishing Point dialog box, which provides a variety of tools and options for creating a perspective grid.

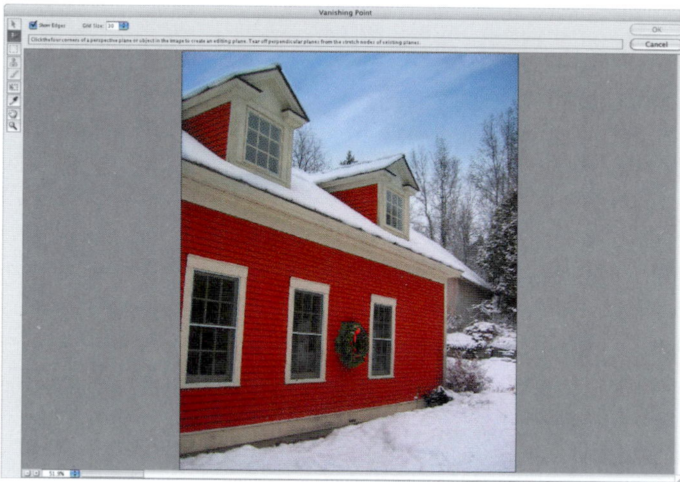

3 Using the Create Plane tool (), define the size and shape of the perspective plane by successively clicking each of the four corner points of the main wall of the house. A blue outline appears as you click. Try to click the four corners where the red siding meets the white trim, clicking over the plant in the lower right corner. When you finish, Photoshop displays a blue grid over the plane that you just defined.

Note: *If you make a mistake—for example, if a red border appears and the perspective grid doesn't—either press Delete and try again, or drag the handles to adjust the grid.*

4 If necessary, drag a corner or a side handle to adjust the grid.

Editing objects in the image

Now that the perspective grid is created, you can select and move the window.

1 Select the Marquee tool () from the Vanishing Point dialog box's tool palette. Notice that the detailed grid disappears from the preview window, replaced by a less-distracting blue outline of the perspective grid.

2 To slightly blur the edge of the selection you're about to make, set the Feather option to 3 at the top of the dialog box. Leave Opacity set at 100 and Heal set to Off. Move Mode, which is set to Destination, should be dimmed.

Note: *The Heal option determines how the selection, cloning, or paint stroke blends with the color, lighting, and shading of the surrounding pixels. Off doesn't blend the selection or stroke with the color, lighting, and shading of the surrounding pixels. Move Mode determines the behavior when moving a selection. Destination lets you move the selection marquee anywhere in the image. For more on these options, see Photoshop Help.*

3 Drag a selection marquee around and a little larger than the center window. Then, press Alt (Windows) or Option (Mac OS) and drag the selected area to the right. Release the mouse when the copied window is positioned between the right window and the far end of the wall. As you drag, Photoshop scales the selection according to the perspective of the wall.

4 To prepare to remove the wreath from the wall, select the Zoom tool and drag it over the three left-most windows to get a closer view of them.

5 Switch back to the Marquee tool () and drag to select the empty wall between the two left windows.

6 Once again, hold down Alt (Windows) or Option (Mac OS) and drag the wall selection between the center and right windows, on top of the wreath.

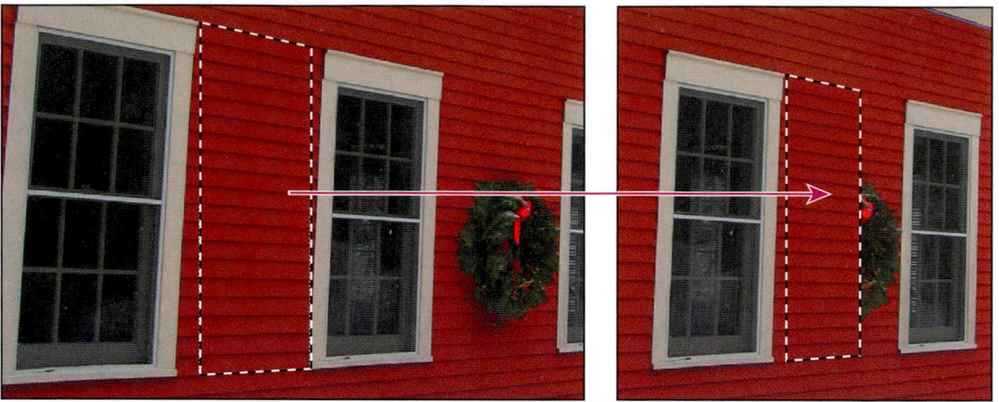

Although the copied selection keeps perspective in its new location, it doesn't cover the whole wreath. Some of the wreath still shows in the image. You will fix this next.

7 Select the Transform tool (). Notice that Photoshop now displays handles on the selection.

8 Drag the transform handles to expand the selection and cover the wreath. If necessary, use the up, down, right, and left arrow keys to nudge the selection and align the cloned clapboards.

9 Deselect the Show Edges box and zoom back out to see the results of your work. Then, then click OK to apply the vanishing-point filter effect.

10 Choose File > Save As. In the Save As dialog box, name the file farmhouse_final.psd and save it in the Lesson08/Portfolio folder. Then, close the image window.

Note: *Images with the Vanishing Point filter applied must be saved as PSD, TIFF, or JPEG in order for the perspective plane information in the image to be preserved.*

Next, you will correct an image that contains camera lens distortion.

Correcting image distortion

The Lens Correction filter fixes common camera lens flaws, such as barrel and pincushion distortion, vignetting, and chromatic aberration. *Barrel distortion* is a lens defect that causes straight lines to bow out toward the edges of the image. *Pincushion distortion* is the opposite effect, where straight lines bend inward. *Vignetting* occurs when the edges of an image, especially the corners, are darker than the center. Finally, *chromatic aberration* appears as a color fringe along the edges of image objects.

Some lenses exhibit these defects depending on the focal length or the f-stop used. You can have the Lens Correction filter use settings based on the camera, lens, and focal length used to make the image. You can also use the filter to rotate an image or fix image perspective caused by vertical or horizontal camera tilt. The filter's image grid makes these adjustments easier and more accurate than using the Transform command.

In this exercise, you will adjust the lens distortion in an image of a Greek temple.

1 Click the Go to Bridge button ( ). In Bridge, click the Lessons folder favorite (if it is not already selected), and then double-click on the Lesson08 folder. Locate the 08D_Start.psd image, and double-click to open it in Photoshop.

Notice how the columns bend toward the camera and appear warped. This distortion was caused because the photo was shot at too close range with a wide-angle lens.

2 Choose Filter > Distort > Lens Correction. The image appears in the Lens Correction dialog box with a large interactive preview, an alignment grid overlay, and options at right for removing distortion, correcting chromatic aberration, removing vignettes, and transforming perspective.

3 In the Lens Correction dialog box, do the following:

• Drag the Remove Distortion slider to about +52.00 to remove the barrel distortion in the image. Or, select the Remove Distortion tool ( ) and drag in the image preview area to accomplish this, watching the Remove Distortion slider to see when you reach +52.00.

Watch the alignment grid as you make these changes so that you can see when the vertical columns are straightened in the image.

- Choose Edge > Transparency if it is not already chosen.
- Drag the Scale slider to 146%.

4 Click OK to apply your changes and close the Lens Correction dialog box. The curving distortion caused by the wide-angle lens and low shooting angle are eliminated.

5 (Optional) To see the effect of your change in the main image window, press Ctrl-Z (Windows) or Command-Z (Mac OS) twice to undo and redo the filter.

Now you'll save the image for your PDF portfolio.

6 Choose File > Save As. In the Save As dialog box, name the file columns_final.psd and save it in the Lesson08/Portfolio folder. Then, close the image window.

Creating a PDF portfolio

You can create an Adobe PDF slide show or a multipage PDF document from a set of Photoshop files by applying the PDF Presentation command in Photoshop or Bridge and setting the options you want. You can select which files within a folder you want to include, or simply select a folder to include all the files stored inside it. Now that you've created a portfolio of images (in the Portfolio folder), you can easily turn it into a PDF slide show to share with clients and colleagues.

1 Click the Go to Bridge button (). In Bridge, click the Lessons folder favorite (if it is not already selected from the previous exercise), and navigate to the Lesson08/Portfolio folder. The Portfolio folder should contain the following image files: mission_final.psd, portrait_final.psd, farmhouse_final.psd, and columns_final.psd.

2 Choose Tools > Photoshop > PDF Presentation.

The Photoshop PDF Presentation dialog box opens. Notice that the four files from the Portfolio folder already appear in the Source Files area.

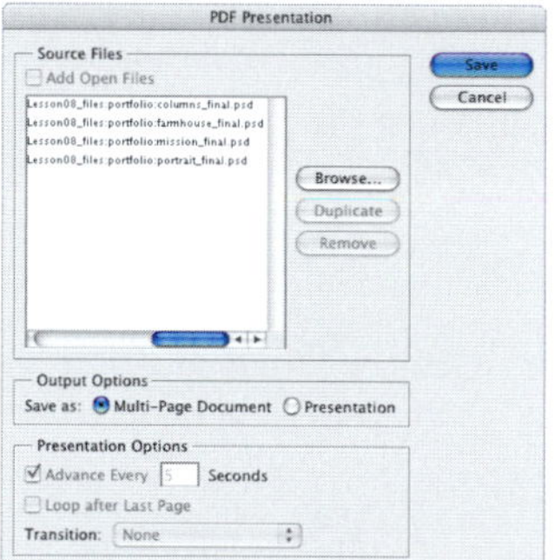

3 In the PDF Presentation dialog box, do the following:

- Under Output Options, select Presentation.
- Under Presentation Options, check the Advance Every box, and accept the default to advance every 5 seconds.
- Check the Loop after Last Page box.
- Choose Wipe Right from the Transition pop-up menu.
- Click Save.

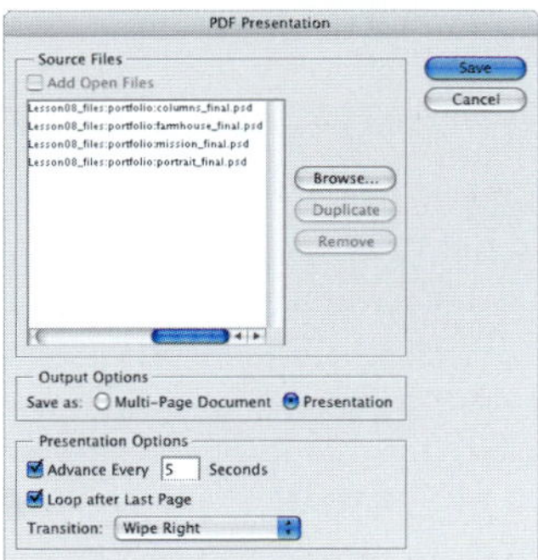

4 In the Save dialog box that appears, type **Photography_portfolio.pdf** as the filename, and specify the location as the Lesson08 folder. (Do *not* select the Portfolio folder.) Then click Save.

5 In the Save Adobe PDF dialog box, do the following:

- Choose Adobe PDF Preset > Smallest File Size to create a PDF document that is suitable for onscreen display.
- Under Options, check View PDF After Saving.
- Click Save PDF.

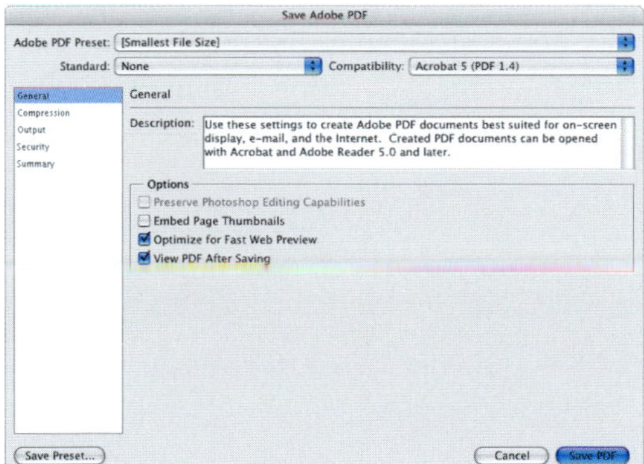

If you have a version of Adobe Acrobat or Adobe Reader installed on your computer, it launches automatically and starts the PDF slide-show presentation.

6 When the slide show finishes, press Esc to return to the standard Acrobat window. Then quit your Acrobat application and return to Photoshop.

Review

Review questions

1 What happens to camera raw images when you edit them in Photoshop or Bridge?

2 What is the advantage of the Adobe Digital Negative file format?

3 How do you correct red eye in Photoshop?

Review answers

1 A camera raw file contains unprocessed picture data from a digital camera's image sensor. Camera raw files give photographers control over interpreting the image data, rather than letting the camera make the adjustments and conversions. When you make adjustments to a camera raw image, Photoshop and Bridge preserve the original camera raw file data. This way, you can edit the image as you desire, export it, and keep the original intact for future use or other adjustments.

2 The Adobe Digital Negative (DNG) file format contains the raw image data from a digital camera as well as metadata that defines what the image data means. DNG is an industry-wide standard for camera raw image data that helps photographers manage proprietary camera raw file formats and provides a compatible archival format.

3 *Red eye* occurs when the retinas of a subject's eyes are reflected by the camera flash. To correct red eye in Adobe Photoshop, zoom in to the subject's eyes, select the Red Eye tool, and then click the red eyes. The red reflection disappears.

Pictures may speak a thousand words, but sometimes you need to put at least a few words in your image compositions. Luckily, Photoshop has powerful text tools that let you add type to your images with great flexibility and control.

OLIO
EXTRA VIRGIN
Olive Oil
Like fine wine, each variety of olive is unique, and therefore olive oil made from different varieties of olives tastes, smells, and looks different. Even the same varieties grown in different regions can have a different taste and aroma.
PRODUCT OF ITALY
16 FL Ounces

9 Typographic Design

Lesson overview

In this lesson, you'll learn how to do the following:

- Use guides to position text in a composition.
- Make a clipping mask from type.
- Merge type with other layers.
- Use layer styles with text.
- Preview typefaces interactively to choose them for a composition.
- Control type and positioning using advanced type palette features.
- Warp a layer around a 3D object.

This lesson will take about an hour to complete. If needed, remove the previous lesson folder from your hard drive, and copy the Lesson09 folder onto it. As you work on this lesson, you'll overwrite the start files. If you need to restore the start files, copy them from the *Adobe Photoshop CS2 Classroom in a Book* CD.

About type

Type in Photoshop consists of mathematically defined shapes that describe the letters, numbers, and symbols of a typeface. Many typefaces are available in more than one format, the most common formats being Type 1 or PostScript fonts, TrueType, and OpenType (for more on OpenType, see page 268).

When you add type to an image in Photoshop, the characters are composed of pixels and have the same resolution as the image file—zooming in on characters shows jagged edges. However, Photoshop preserves the vector-based type outlines and uses them when you scale or resize type, save a PDF or EPS file, or print the image to a PostScript printer. As a result, you can produce type with crisp, resolution-independent edges, apply effects and styles to type, and transform its shape and size.

Getting started

In this lesson, you'll work on the layout for the label of a bottle of olive oil. You will start from an illustration of a bottle, created in Adobe Illustrator, and then add and stylize type in Photoshop, including wrapping the text to conform to the 3D shape. You will start with a blank label on a layer above the bottle background.

You'll start the lesson by viewing an image of the final composition.

1 Start Photoshop and then immediately hold down Ctrl-Alt-Shift (Windows) or Command-Option-Shift (Mac OS) to restore the default preferences. (See "Restoring default preferences" on page 6.)

2 When prompted, click Yes to confirm that you want to reset preferences, and Close to close the Welcome Screen.

3 Click the Go to Bridge button (icon) on the tool options bar to open Adobe Bridge.

4 In the Favorites palette in the upper left corner of Bridge, click the Lessons favorite, and then double-click the Lesson09 folder in the thumbnail preview area.

5 Select the 09End.psd file so that it appears in the Preview palette at left. Enlarge the palette if necessary to get a good close-up view.

This layered composite represents a comp of packaging for a new brand of olive oil. For this lesson, you are a designer creating the comp for the product. The bottle shape was created by another designer in Adobe Illustrator. Your job is to apply the type treatment in Photoshop in preparation to present it to a client for review. All of the type controls you need are available in Photoshop, and you don't have to switch to another application to complete the project.

6 Select the 09Start.psd file and double-click it to open it in Photoshop.

Creating a clipping mask from type

A *clipping mask* is an object or a group of objects whose shape masks other artwork so that only areas that lie within the shape of the masking object are visible. In effect, you are clipping the artwork to conform to the shape of the object (or mask). In Photoshop, you can create a clipping mask from shapes or letters. In this exercise, you will use letters as a clipping mask to allow an image in another layer to show through the letters.

Adding guides to position type

The 09Start.psd file contains a background layer, which is the bottle, and a Blank Label layer, which will be the foundation for your typography. The Blank Label is the active layer on which you will begin your work. You'll start by zooming in on your work area and using ruler guides to help position your type.

1 Select the Zoom tool (🔍) and drag over the black and white portion of the blank label to zoom in to the area and center it in the image window. Repeat until you have a nice close-up view of the area, and enlarge the image window if necessary.

2 Choose View > Rulers to turn on guide rulers along the left and top borders of the image window. Then, drag a vertical guide from the left ruler to the center of the label (3½ inches) and release.

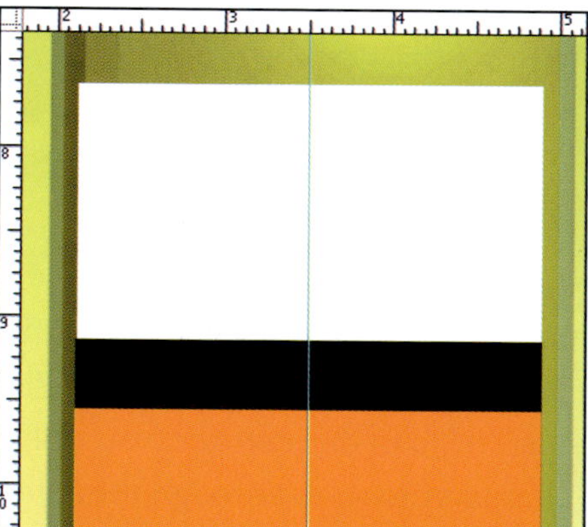

Adding point type

Now you're ready to actually add type to the composition. Photoshop lets you create horizontal or vertical type anywhere in an image. You can enter *point type* (a single letter, word, or line) or *paragraph type*. You will do both in this lesson, starting with point type.

1 Make sure the Blank Layer is selected in the Layers palette. Then, select the Horizontal Type tool (T), and on the tool options bar, do the following:

- Choose a sans serif typeface, such as Myriad, from the Font Family pop-up menu, and choose Bold from the Font Style pop-up menu.
- Type **79 pt** into the Size field and press Enter (Windows) or Return (Mac OS).
- Click the Center text alignment button.

2 Click on the center guide in the white area of the label to set an insertion point, and type **OLIO** in all caps. Then click the Commit Any Current Edits button (✓) on the tool options bar.

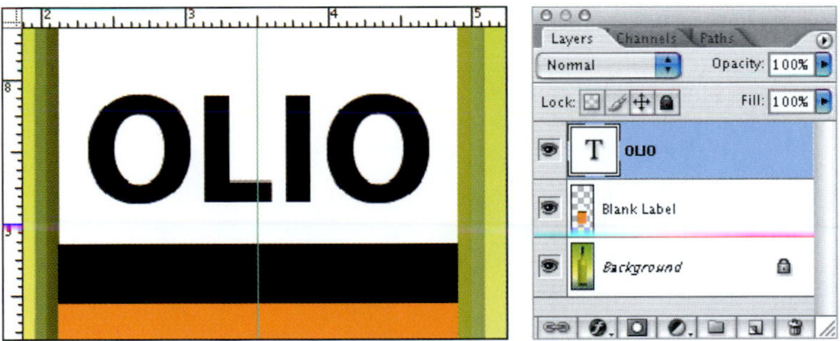

The word "Olio" is added to your label, and it appears in the Layers palette as a new text layer, OLIO. You can edit and manage the text layer as you would any other layer. You can add or change the text, change the orientation of the type, apply anti-aliasing, apply layer styles and transformations, and create masks. You can move, restack, copy, and edit layer options of a type layer as you would for any other layer.

3 Press Ctrl (Windows) or Command (Mac OS), and drag the OLIO type to visually center it vertically in the white box.

Making a clipping mask and applying a drop shadow

Photoshop wrote the letters in black, the default text color. You want the letters to appear to be filled with an image of olives, so next you will use the letters to make a clipping mask that will allow another image layer to show through.

1 Click the Go to Bridge button (icon) or use File > Open to open the Olives.psd file (located in the Lesson09 folder) in Photoshop. In Photoshop, arrange the image windows onscreen so that you can see both of them at once, and make sure that Olives.psd is the active image window.

2 In Layers palette for the Olives.psd image, hold down Shift and drag the Background layer to the center of the 09Start.psd file, and then release the mouse. Pressing Shift as you drag centers the Olives.psd image in the composition.

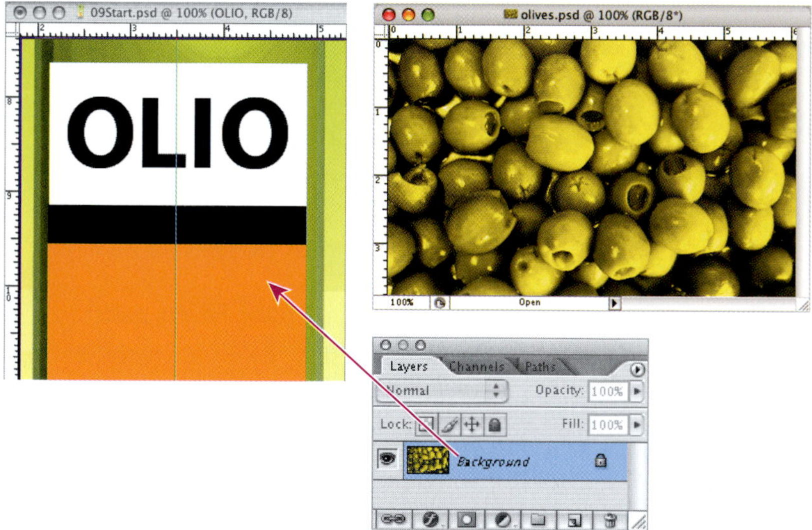

A new layer appears in the 09Start.psd Layers palette, Layer 1. This new layer contains the olives image, which you will use to show through the type. But before you make the clipping mask for it, you need make the olives image smaller, as it is too large for the composition.

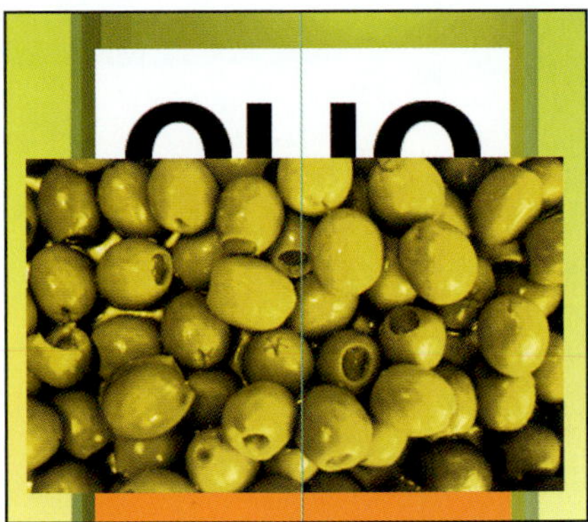

3 With Layer 1 selected, choose Edit > Transform > Scale.

4 Grab a corner handle on the bounding box for the olives, and Shift-drag to make it smaller. You may need to move the cursor inside the box and drag to reposition the olives so that the image remains centered on the label. Resize the olives image so that it is approximately the same width as the white label.

5 Press Enter (Windows) or Return (Mac OS) to apply the transformation.

6 Double-click the Layer 1 name and change it to **olives**. Then, press Enter or Return, or click away from the name in the Layers palette, to apply the change.

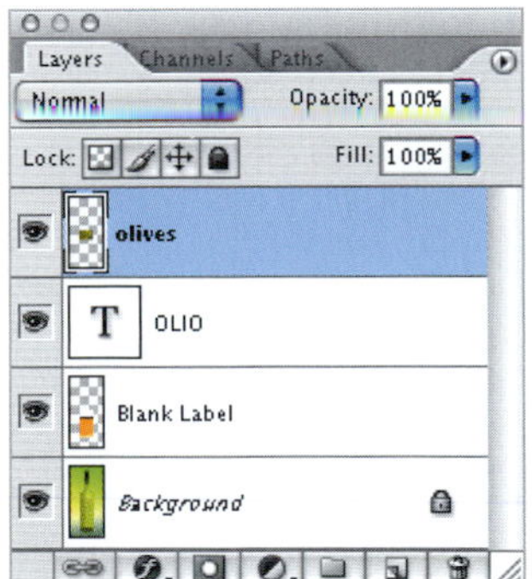

7 With the olives layer still selected, choose Create Clipping Mask from the Layers palette menu.

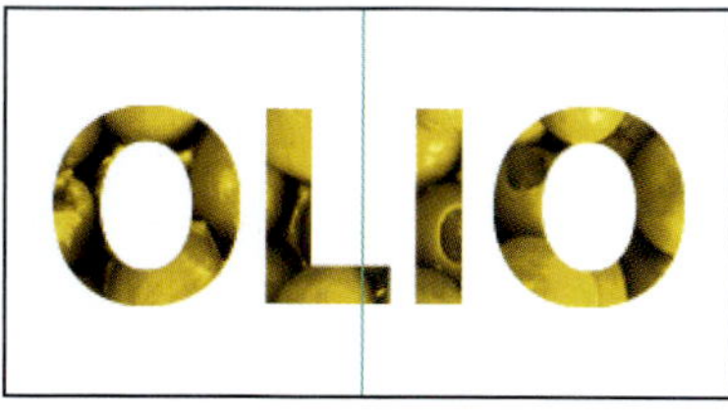

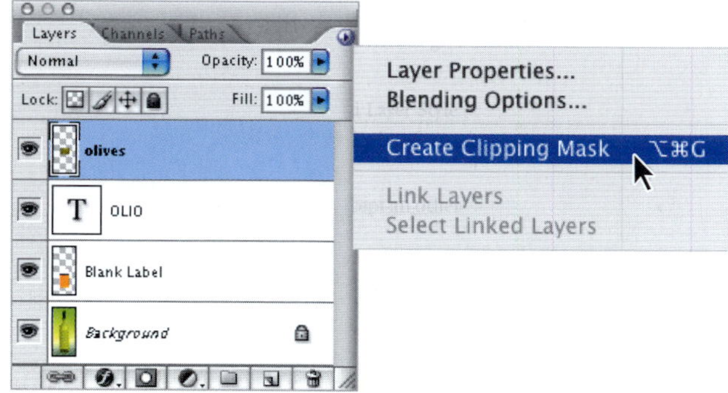

You can also make a clipping mask by holding down the Alt (Windows) or Option (Mac OS) key and clicking between the olives and OLIO type layers.

The olives now show through the OLIO letters. A small arrow in the olives layer indicates the clipping mask. Next, you will add a drop shadow to give the letters depth.

8 Select the OLIO type layer to make it active, and then click the Add a Layer Style button (ƒ) at the bottom of the Layers palette and choose Drop Shadow from the pop-up menu.

9 In the Layer Style dialog box, change the Opacity to **35%**, accept all other default settings, and then click OK.

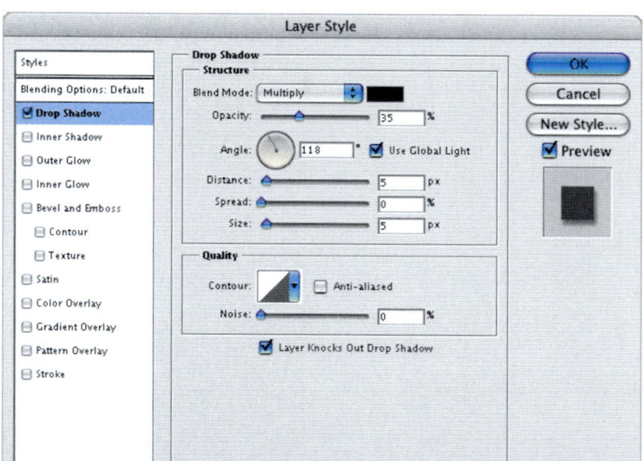

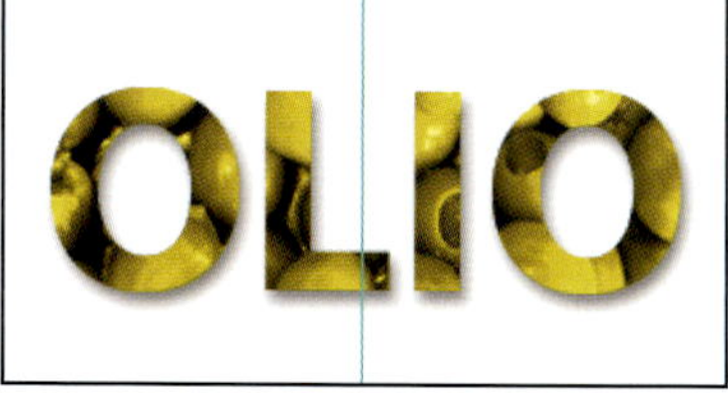

10 Choose File > Save to save your work so far, and close the Olives.psd image file without saving any changes.

Creating a design element from type

Next, you will add the vertical lines that appear at the top of the label using a type trick. These vertical lines need to be perfectly aligned, so you will use the capital "I" of a sans serif font instead of creating, copying, and moving individual lines. You will also easily adjust the size and spacing of the "lines" using the Character palette.

1 Make sure no layers are selected in the Layers palette, then select the Horizontal Type tool (T). On the tool options bar, do the following:

- Choose a sans serif typeface, preferably a narrow one such as Myriad Condensed.
- Set the size to **36 pt** and press Enter (Windows) or Return (Mac OS).
- Leave the Anti-aliasing pop-up menu set to Sharp.
- Choose Left alignment.
- Click the color swatch to open the Color Picker, and then move the mouse over the olives showing through the OLIO letters to select a dark green from the photo, then click OK.

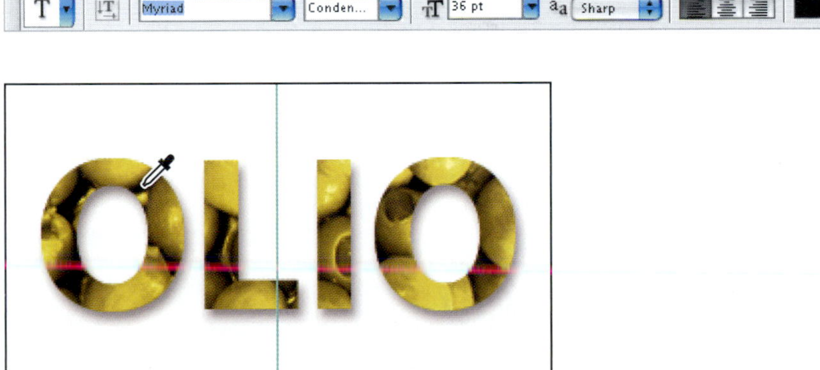

2 Click the cursor in the upper left corner of the white box and, holding down the Shift key, type **I** 12 times.

This creates a new type layer in the Layers palette.

3 Select the Move tool (▸✣), position it inside the box, and drag the letters so that their tops touch the top edge of the white box.

Note: When you enter type in a Photoshop image window, you put the Type tool in edit mode. *Before you can perform other actions or use other tools, you must commit your editing in the layer—as you did with the OLIO type using the Commit Any Current Edits button. Selecting another tool or layer has the same effect as clicking the Commit Any Current Edits button on the tool options bar. You cannot commit to current edits by pressing Enter or Return, as this action merely creates a new line for typing.*

Now, you will adjust the tracking to space the "lines" a bit wider apart.

4 Toggle open the Character palette by choosing Window > Character.

5 Type **40** in the Tracking box, or scrub the Tracking label to set the value.

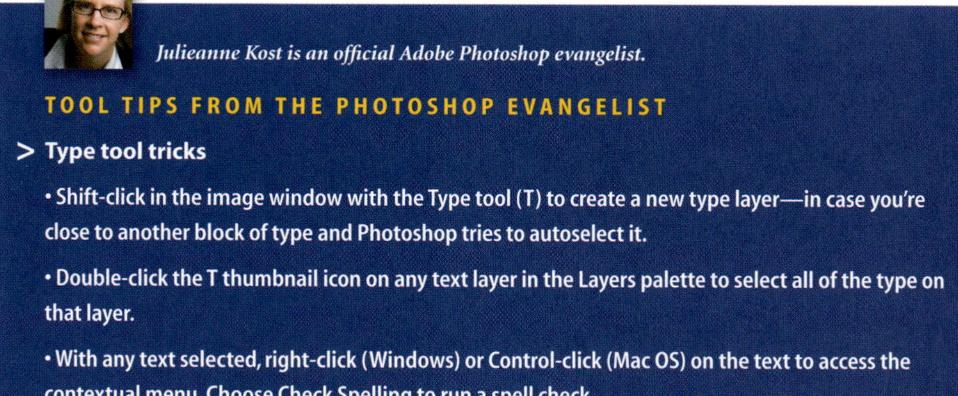

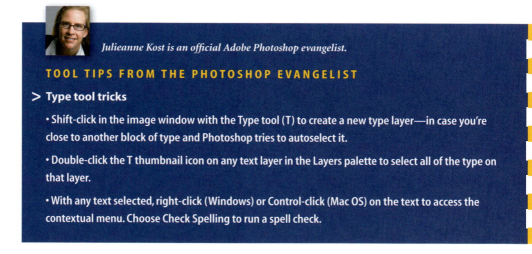

Julieanne Kost is an official Adobe Photoshop evangelist.

TOOL TIPS FROM THE PHOTOSHOP EVANGELIST

> Type tool tricks

• Shift-click in the image window with the Type tool (T) to create a new type layer—in case you're close to another block of type and Photoshop tries to autoselect it.

• Double-click the T thumbnail icon on any text layer in the Layers palette to select all of the type on that layer.

• With any text selected, right-click (Windows) or Control-click (Mac OS) on the text to access the contextual menu. Choose Check Spelling to run a spell check.

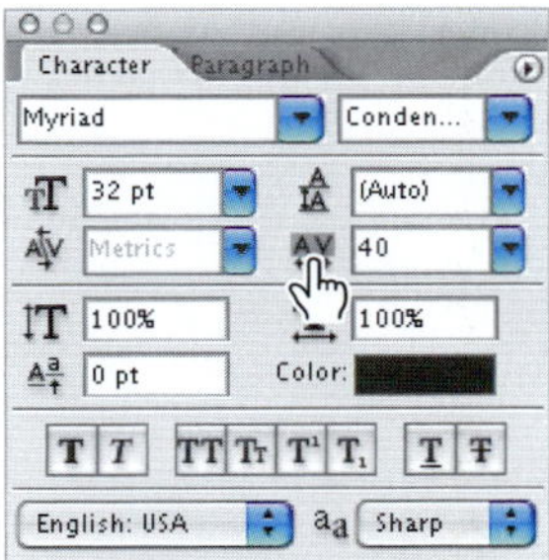

Now it is time to adjust the positioning of the OLIO letters so that they're not too close to the vertical lines. To do that, you need to link the OLIO type layer and the olive image mask layer and move them as a unit.

6 Click to select the olives layer and then press Shift to also select the OLIO type layer. Then choose Link Layers from the Layers palette pop-up menu. A link icon appears next to the names of both layers.

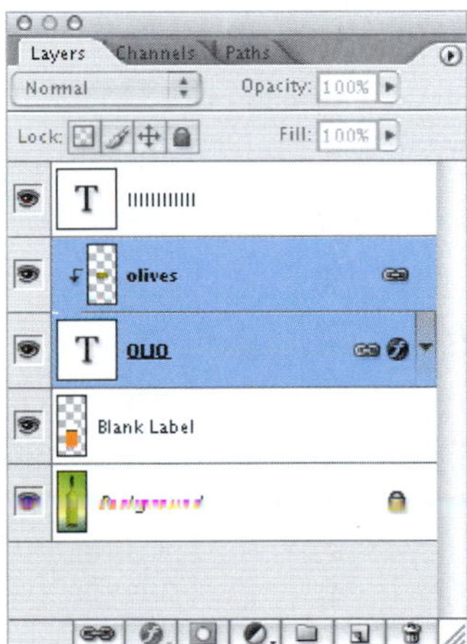

7 Select the Move tool (▸✥) and drag the type down as desired.

8 Choose File > Save to save your work so far.

Using interactive formatting controls

The Character palette in Photoshop contains many options to help you set beautiful type, but not all of the choices and controls are obvious—as in the trick of scrubbing the Tracking icon to choose a tracking value. In this exercise, you will make a type selection using another advanced trick for previewing type in the Character palette.

1 Make sure no layers are selected in the Layers palette, then select the Horizontal Type tool (T). On the tool options bar, click the Center text alignment button, and then click the color box and choose a bright red color. Click OK to close the Color Picker. For the moment, don't worry about which typeface or size you're using.

2 Click the cursor on the center guide in the black stripe in the label. To be sure that you don't accidentally start editing the OLIO text, make sure the cursor has a thin dotted line around it ( ) when you click. This means you'll create a new text layer when you type.

3 Type **EXTRA VIRGIN** in all caps.

Photoshop writes the text in whatever typeface (and size) was previously specified. But what if you want to use a different typeface? What if you're not sure which typeface you want to use?

4 Select the EXTRA VIRGIN text in the image window, and then, in the Character palette, click on the name in the Font Family pop-up menu. The name becomes highlighted.

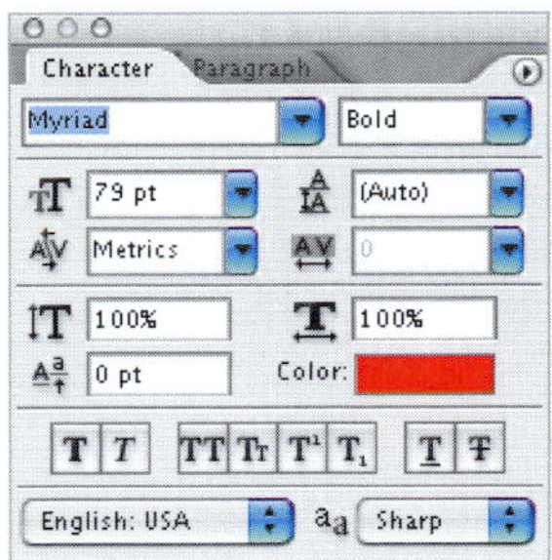

5 Press the up or down arrow key to cycle through the available fonts, and watch as Photoshop interactively previews each font in the highlighted EXTRA VIRGIN letters onscreen.

6 After experimenting, choose the sans serif typeface that you used for the OLIO letters —Myriad, in our example—and then use the Tab key to jump to the Font Style box.

7 Again, use the up and down arrow keys to cycle through available styles (if available) to choose one (we chose Bold), and watch as the styles preview interactively in the image window.

8 Tab to the Size box, and use the up or down arrow keys to set the type at **11** points.

Press Shift as you use the up and down arrow keys to change the Size increment by 10 points.

9 Tab to the Tracking field, and set the Tracking to 280: Type the value, use the up arrow key (press Shift as you tap the key to increase the increment by 100), or scrub to set it.

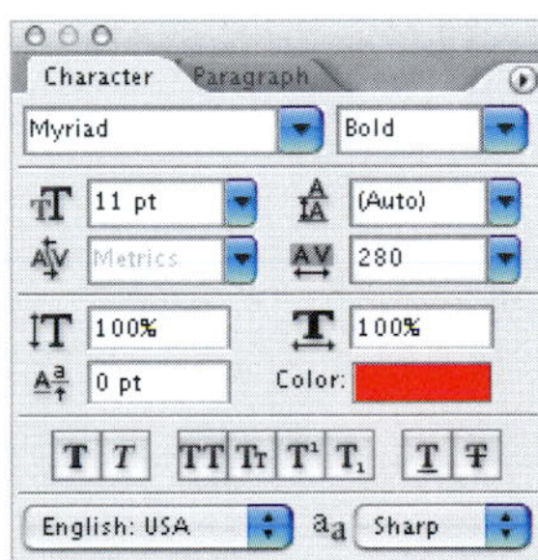

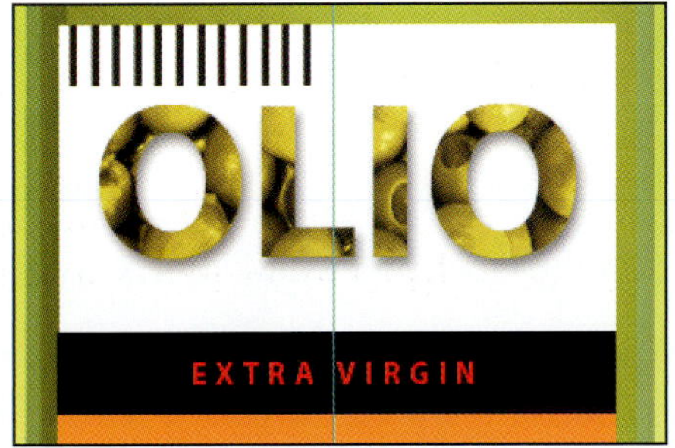

10 Select the Move tool (![move tool]) and drag the EXTRA VIRGIN text so that it is centered in the black bar of the label.

11 Choose File > Save to save your work so far.

Warping point type

Now you will add the words "Olive Oil" to the label, and then warp them to make them more playful. *Warping* lets you distort type to conform to a variety of shapes, such as an arc or a wave. The warp style you select is an attribute of the type layer—you can change a layer's warp style at any time to change the overall shape of the warp. Warping options give you precise control over the orientation and perspective of the warp effect.

1 Scroll or use the Hand tool (![hand tool]) to move the visible area of the image window so that the orange part of the label, below the black bar, is in the center of the screen. Enlarge the image window by dragging the lower right corner, if necessary.

2 Deselect all layers in the Layers palette. Then select the Horizontal Type tool (T), and in the Character palette, choose a traditional serif typeface, such as Adobe Garamond. Set it to 40 points, make the Color white, and set Tracking to 0.

3 Click and drag a text box in the upper area of the orange box, and then type **Olive Oil**. Then click the Commit Any Current Edits button (✓) on the tool options bar.

The words appear on the label, and a new layer, Olive Oil, appears in the Layers palette.

4 Right-click (Windows) or Control-click (Mac OS) on the Olive Oil layer in the Layers palette, and choose Warp Text from the contextual menu.

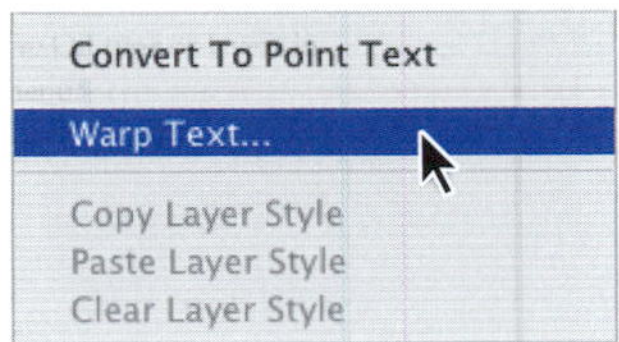

5 In the Warp Text dialog box, choose Style > Wave and click the Horizontal radio button. For Bend, specify +77%, Horizontal Distribution **–7%**, and Vertical Distribution **–24%**. Then click OK.

The words "Olive Oil" appear to float like a wave on the label.

Designing a paragraph of type

All of the text you've written on this label so far has been a few discrete words or lines—point type. Often, however, many designs call for full paragraphs of text. You can design complete paragraphs of type in Photoshop; you don't have to switch to a dedicated page-layout program for sophisticated paragraph type controls.

Using guides for positioning

Next, you will add a paragraph of descriptive content to the label in Photoshop. You will start by adding some guides to the work area to help you position the paragraph.

1 Drag two guides from the left vertical ruler, placing the first one at 2½ inches and the second at 4½ inches.

2 Drag two guides down from the top horizontal ruler, placing the first one at 10¾ inches and the second at 13 inches.

Adding paragraph type from a sticky note

Now you're ready to add the text. In a real design environment, it might be provided to you in the form of a word processing document, or perhaps in the body of an e-mail, which you could copy and paste into Photoshop. Or you might have to type it in. Another easy way to add a bit of text is for the copy writer to attach it to the image file in a sticky note.

1 Double-click the yellow sticky note annotation in the lower right corner of the image window to open it.

Note: *You may need to change the view or scroll to see the open note onscreen.*

2 Drag with the cursor to select all of the text in the note, and then press Ctrl-C (Windows) or Command-C (Mac OS) to copy it to the Clipboard. Then click the Close button to close the sticky note window.

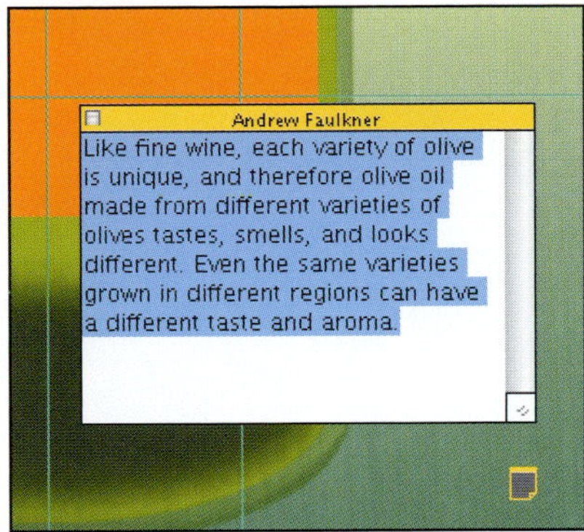
Andrew Faulkner
Like fine wine, each variety of olive is unique, and therefore olive oil made from different varieties of olives tastes, smells, and looks different. Even the same varieties grown in different regions can have a different taste and aroma.

Before you paste it in, specify your type options.

3 Make sure no layers are selected in the Layers palette. Then select the Horizontal Type tool (T), and in the Character palette, choose a sans serif typeface such as Myriad Roman, set the Size to 10 points, Leading to 24 points, Tracking to 5, and Color to black.

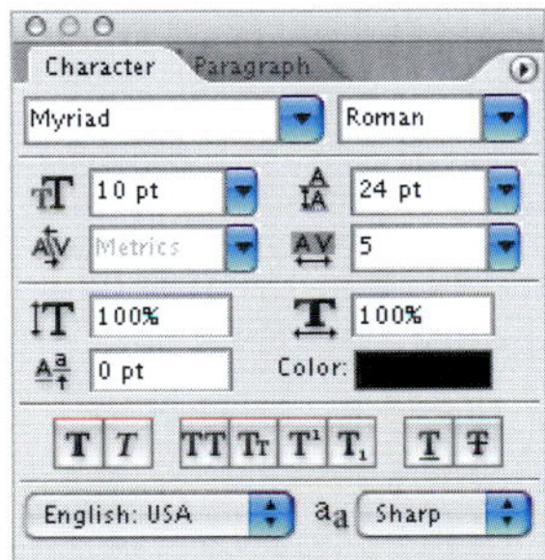
Character
Paragraph
Myriad
Roman
10 pt
24 pt
Metrics
5
100%
100%
0 pt
Color:
English: USA
Sharp

4 Click the Paragraph tab to bring the Paragraph palette forward, and click the Justify All button ( ).

5 Drag with the Type tool to create a text box that matches the guides you positioned in the previous exercise, and then press Ctrl-V (Windows) or Command-V (Mac OS) to paste the text from the Clipboard into the text box.

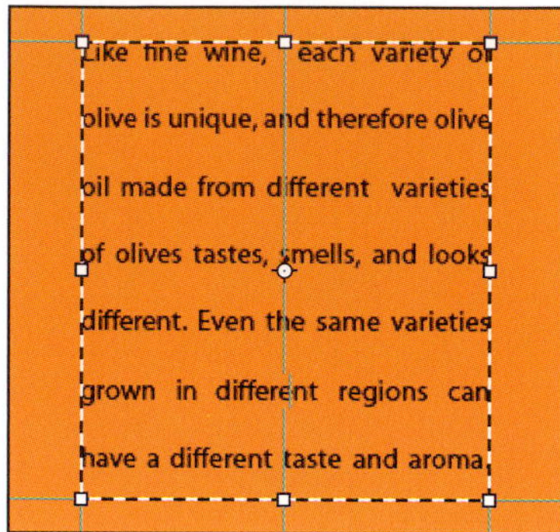
Like fine wine, each variety of
olive is unique, and therefore olive
oil made from different varieties
of olives tastes, smells, and looks
different. Even the same varieties
grown in different regions can
have a different taste and aroma.

The text appears in the image window with the styles you specified, and it wraps to the dimensions of the bounding box. In our example, the second-to-last line had some unsightly gaps, so as a fine-tuning measure, we will fix that now.

If you resize the bounding box, the type will reflow within the adjusted rectangle.

6 Drag with the Horizontal Type tool (T) to select all of the text in the second-to-last line of the paragraph, and in the Character palette, set Tracking to 60.

7 Click the Commit Any Current Edits button (✓) on the tool options bar. Your paragraph text now appears as the layer named, "Like fine wine. . . ."

8 Choose File > Save to save your work so far.

Adding the last two lines

You're almost done adding text to the label. You just have to add two more lines.

1 With the Like fine wine. . . layer selected, click inside the paragraph of text, and then drag the handle in the middle of the lower edge of the text box down to the bottom of the edge of the label.

2 Place the text cursor at the end of the paragraph of text and press Enter (Windows) or Return (Mac OS).

3 Type **16 FL Ounces**.

4 Drag to select "16 FL Ounces," and in the Character palette, set the words to 13 points and make them white. Set the Baseline Shift to –10.

5 In the Paragraph palette, click the Center text button (☰). Then, click the Commit Any Current Edits button (✓) on the tool options bar.

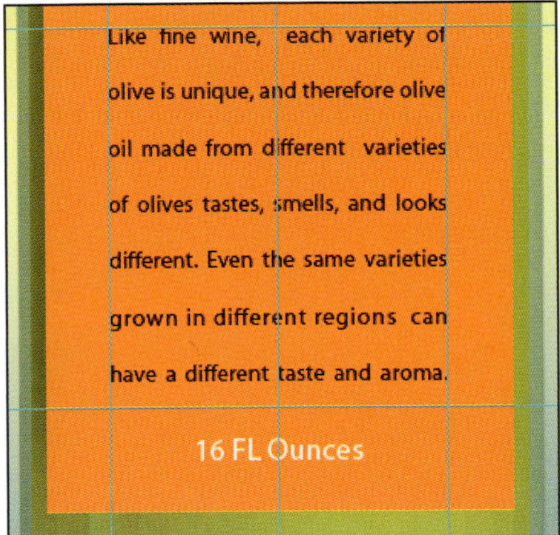

Adding vertical type

The last line will be vertical.

1 Deselect all layers in the Layers palette. Then, click and hold on the Horizontal Type tool to select the Vertical Type tool (↓T), which is hidden under the Horizontal Type tool.

2 Drag in the orange area of the label to the right of the descriptive text to create a long, narrow text box. Start from the lower- or upper-right corner so that you don't accidentally select the paragraph text.

3 Type **PRODUCT OF ITALY**, all caps.

4 Select the letters, and then, in the Character palette, choose a serif typeface such as Adobe Garamond, set it to 8 points, set Tracking to 300, and make the color red.

OpenType in Photoshop: More fun with bottles

OpenType is a cross-platform font file format developed jointly by Adobe and Microsoft. It allows the same font to work on both Macintosh and Windows computers, and it supports widely expanded character sets and layout features. This, in turn, provides richer linguistic support and advanced typography control. Photoshop CS2 supports OpenType, and the *Adobe Photoshop CS2 Classroom in a Book* CD contains a QuickTime movie that explores how to use OpenType in Photoshop in greater depth. Here are some of the highlights.

The OpenType menu The Character palette pop-up menu includes an OpenType submenu that displays all available features for a selected OpenType font, including ligatures, alternates, and fractions. Features that are grayed out are unavailable for that typeface; features that are checked have been applied.

Discretionary ligatures To add a discretionary ligature to two OpenType letters, such as to a "th" in the Bickham Script Standard typeface, select them in the image window, and choose OpenType > Discretionary Ligatures from the Character palette pop-up menu.

If you'd like to preview your OpenType choices before committing to them, work with the Adobe Illustrator CS or CS2 Glyphs palette: Copy your text in Photoshop and paste it into an Illustrator document. Then, open the Glyphs palette by choosing Window > Type > Glyphs. Select the text you want to change, and choose Show > Alternates for Current Selection. Double-click a glyph to apply it, and when you're done, copy and paste the new type into your Photoshop file.

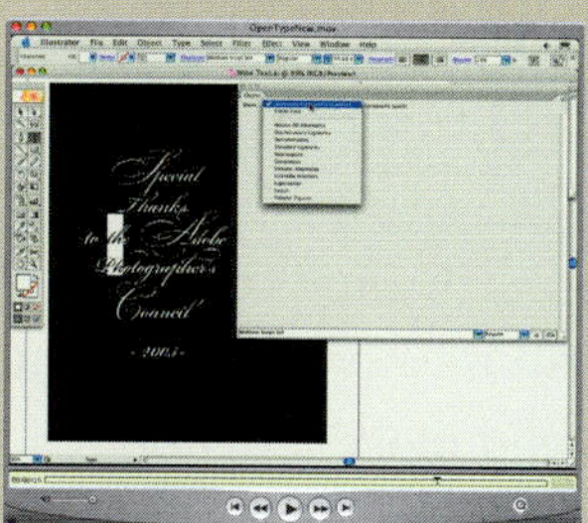

Swashes Adding swashes or alternate characters works the same way: Select the letter, such as a capital "T" in Bickham Script, and choose OpenType > Swash to change the ordinary capital into a dramatically ornate swash T.

Creating true fractions Type fractions as usual—for example, 1-slash-2—then select the characters, and from the Character palette menu, choose OpenType > Fractions. Photoshop applies the true fraction.

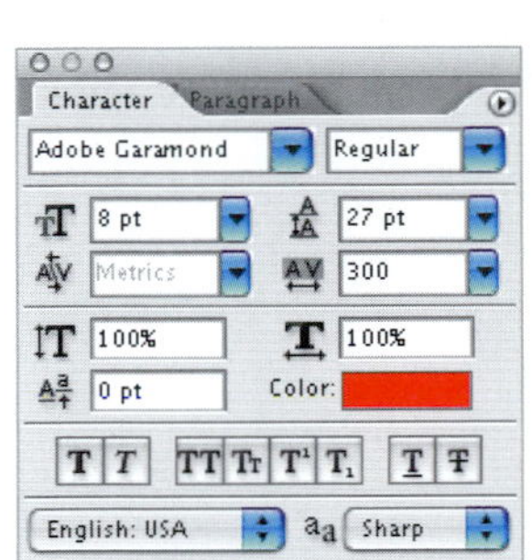

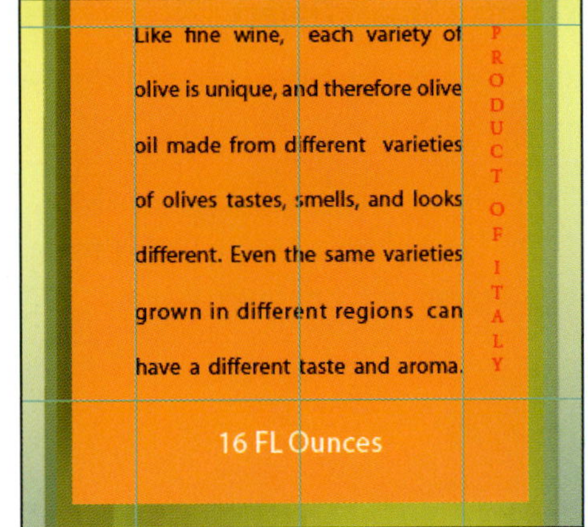

Like fine wine, each variety of
olive is unique, and therefore olive
oil made from different varieties
of olives tastes, smells, and looks
different. Even the same varieties
grown in different regions can
have a different taste and aroma.
PRODUCT OF ITALY
16 FL Ounces

5 Click the Commit Any Current Edits button (✔) on the tool options bar. Your vertical text now appears as the layer named PRODUCT OF ITALY. Use the Move tool (▸✥) and drag to center it if necessary.

Now, you'll do a bit of clean up.

6 Click to select the annotation, and then right-click (Windows) or Control-click (Mac OS) and choose Delete Note from the contextual menu to delete the annotation.

7 Hide the guides by choosing the Hand tool (✋) and then pressing Ctrl-; (Windows) or Command-; (Mac OS). Then, zoom out to get a nice look at your handiwork.

8 Choose File > Save to save your work so far.

Warping a layer

All of the text is now on the label, but there's one problem: The bottle looks three-dimensional, while the label looks unrealistically flat on its surface. So your final effect will be to warp the label and its contents to look like they realistically conform to the bottle shape.

Earlier in this lesson, you warped the words "Olive Oil" so that the letters appeared wavy. For this exercise, however, you will apply the warp transformation to a layer, rather than to individual letters. To do this, you will group the label and type layers, and then transform the new, grouped layer using the Smart Objects feature. Using Smart Objects allows you to continue to edit both the contents of the layer (the type) and to edit the warp after you apply the transformation.

Grouping layers into a Smart Object

Creating the Smart Object is a two-step process. First you have to merge the OLIO text layer and its clipping mask, then you will group all of the label's layers into the Smart Object.

1 Click to select the OLIO layer in the Layers palette, then press Shift and click to also select the olives layer. Then choose Merge Layers from the Layers palette pop-up menu. Photoshop combines them into one layer, olives.

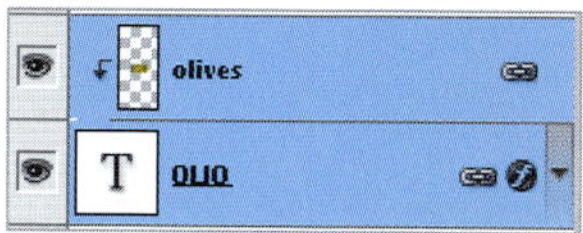

2 Click to select the Blank Label layer in the Layers palette and then press Shift and click on the topmost layer in the stack, PRODUCT OF ITALY. Photoshop selects the two layers and all of the layers in between. Then, choose Group into New Smart Object from the Layers palette pop-up menu.

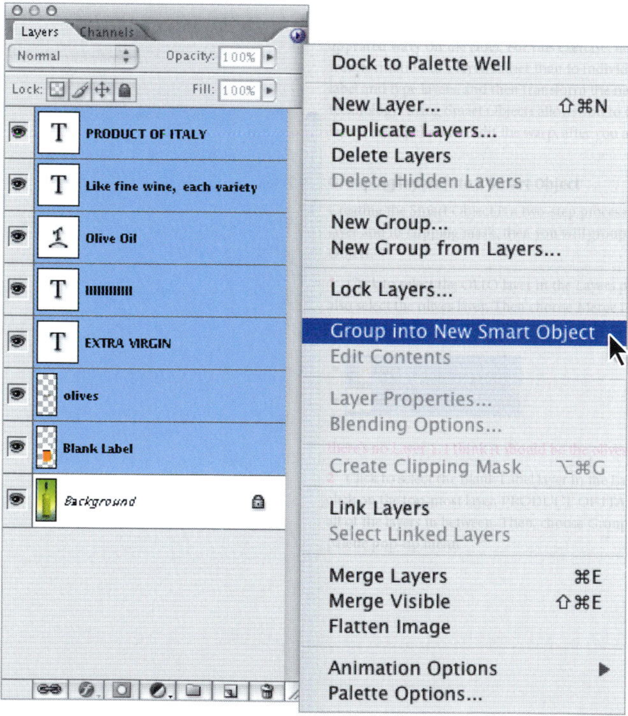

Photoshop groups the selected layers into one Smart Object layer. The name for this new layer is the name of the top layer of the old stack, PRODUCT OF ITALY.

Warping with Smart Objects

Now you will warp the Smart Object layer to match the contour of the bottle. To do this, it helps to have your guides visible.

1 Choose View > Show > Guides. Then, zoom in to the label.

2 With the PRODUCT OF ITALY layer selected, choose Edit > Transform > Warp.

Photoshop lays a 3-x-3 grid over the layer in the image window, with handles and lines that you can drag to warp the layer as desired.

Drag four horizontal guides out now to help you as you apply the warp in the following steps. Place one guide at the top of the label, and one guide along the bottom of the label. Then, place two more guides one-quarter inch below each of those guides.

3 One at a time, click the center of each horizontal line of the grid and drag the line down one-quarter inch to create the curved label.

OLIO
EXTRA VIRGIN
Olive Oil
Like fine wine, each variety of olive is unique, and therefore olive oil made from different varieties of olives tastes, smells, and looks different. Even the same varieties grown in different regions can have a different taste and aroma.
PRODUCT OF ITALY
12 FL Ounces

OLIO
EXTRA VIRGIN

4 When you're done, press Enter (Windows) or Return (Mac OS) to apply the warp transformation.

5 Hide the visible guides by choosing the Hand tool (✋) and pressing Ctrl-; (Windows) or Command-; (Mac OS). Then, double-click the Hand tool to see the whole bottle composition onscreen.

OLIO
EXTRA VIRGIN
Olive Oil
Like fine wine, each variety of olive is unique, and therefore olive oil made from different varieties of olives tastes, smells, and looks different. Even the same varieties grown in different regions can have a different taste and aroma.
16 FL Ounces

Congratulations! You've added and stylized all of the type on the Olio olive oil bottle. If you'd like to experiment further with the capabilities of Smart Objects, go on to the Extra Credit sidebar on page 274. Otherwise, in the real world, you would flatten and save this image file for printing.

6 Choose Layer > Flatten Image.

7 Choose File > Save, and then close the image window.

EXTRA CREDIT You can take full advantage of your Smart Object now by editing the label's content and letting Photoshop automatically update the bottle composition.

1 Double-click the PRODUCT OF ITALY Smart Object thumbnail in the Layers palette. (If you get a Smart Object alert dialog box, just click OK.) Photoshop opens the Smart Object in its own window.

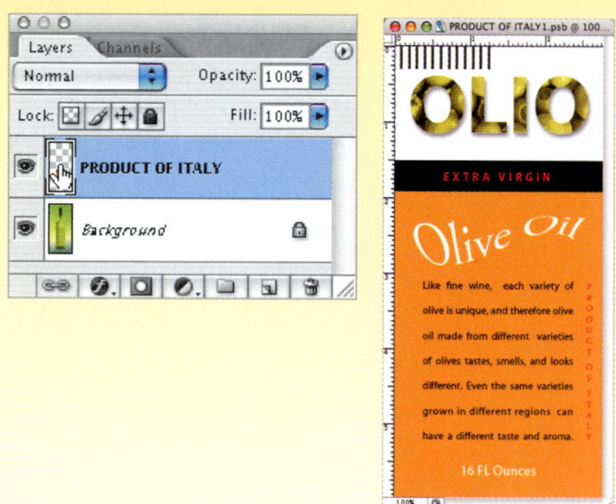

2 Select the Horizontal type tool (T), and in the Smart Object image window, change the "16 FL Ounces" text and to **32 fl. ounces**. Then click the Commit Any Current Edits button (✓).

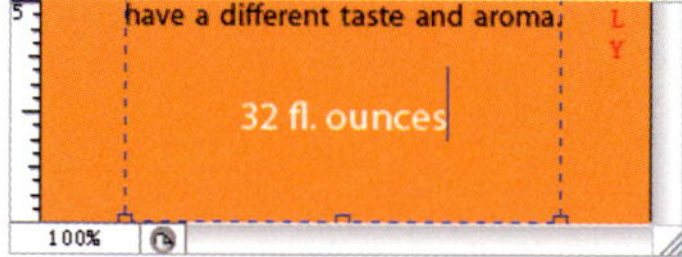

3 Click the red Close button, and when prompted, click Yes to save your changes.

Photoshop returns to the 09Start.psd image file, and the Smart Object updates are applied to the label. You can repeat this process to make more edits as frequently as you'd like without compromising the quality of the image or the transformation. To edit the warp effect at any time, simply choose Edit > Transform > Warp in the 09Start.psd image file, and you can continue to nondestructively edit the warp transformation.

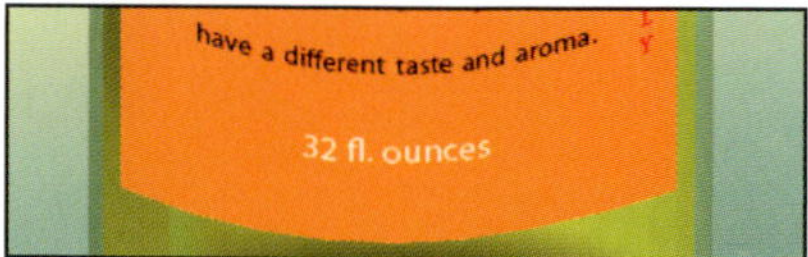

Review

Review questions

1 How does Photoshop treat type?

2 How is a text layer the same or different from other layers in Photoshop?

3 What is a clipping mask and how do you make one from type?

4 Describe two little-known ways to control type formatting in Photoshop.

Review answers

1 Type in Photoshop consists of mathematically defined shapes that describe the letters, numbers, and symbols of a typeface. When you add type to an image in Photoshop, the characters are composed of pixels and have the same resolution as the image file. However, Photoshop preserves the vector-based type outlines and uses them when you scale or resize type, save a PDF or EPS file, or print the image to a PostScript printer.

2 Type that is added to an image appears in the Layers palette as a text layer that can be edited and managed in the same way as any other kind of layer. You can add and edit the text, change the orientation of the type, and apply anti-aliasing as well as move, restack, copy, and edit layer options.

3 A *clipping mask* is an object or group whose shape masks other artwork so that only areas that lie within the shape are visible. The letters on any text layer can be converted to a clipping mask by selecting both the text layer and the layer you want to show through the letters, and then choosing Create Clipping Mask from the Layers palette pop-up menu.

4 Select text in the image window, and in the Character palette or on the Type tool options bar you can do the following:

- Scrub the Size, Leading, Tracking, Kerning, Scaling, and Baseline Shift values.

- Select some type in the image window, click the font displayed in the Font Family pop-up menu, and press the up and down arrow keys to cycle through the available fonts and watch them preview interactively in the image window.

Dancing with Type*

* *An excerpt from Russell Brown's Power Hour: Adobe Photoshop Tips and Techniques*

Russell Brown

Dancer before

Dancer with type

Applying text to a complex path

In this fine sidebar, I'm going to demonstrate how to place text on a path. We will start with an image of a dancer. We will create a selection around the contours of her body, which we will then convert to a path. Then, we will apply the text to the path, finesse it, and voilà—you will apply text to a complex path. As you read the steps, follow along with the QuickTime movie of this tutorial that comes on the *Adobe Photoshop CS2 Classroom in a Book* CD.

—Russell Brown

Watch the movie
See the detailed steps of this tutorial on the QuickTime movie that is included on the *Photoshop CS2 Classroom in a Book* CD.

Step 1: Select the dancer

The evenly colored, flat background makes the Magic Wand a good selection tool to use with this image. With the Dancer layer active, click with the Magic Wand in the background to select similarly colored pixels, and then press Shift and continue clicking until everything but the dancer is selected. Then simply invert the selection by pressing Ctrl-Shift-I (Windows) or Command-Shift-I (Mac OS).

Step 2: Convert to a path

Convert the selection to a path by choosing Make Work Path from the Paths palette pop-up menu. In the Make Work Path dialog box, set Tolerance to 1.0 and click OK. The lower the tolerance, the greater detail and more control points you'll have on the path. Because this is a complex path, we want to be sure we have enough detail.

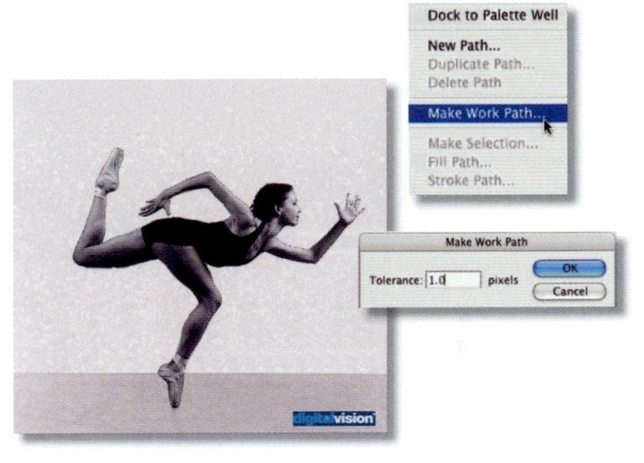

Step 3: Place text on the path

The text is waiting in a text layer, Dancing with Type. Select that layer and, using the Type tool, select and copy the text to the Clipboard. Then hide the text layer, select the Dancer layer, click on the path, and press Ctrl-V (Windows) or Command-V multiple times to paste the text all around the dancer path.

Step 4: Hide inside descenders

To finish up, we will hide the descenders that obscure the dancer. In the Paths palette, press Ctrl (Windows) or Command (Mac OS) and click on the Dancer path icon to convert the path to a selection. In the Layers palette, select the type-on-a-path layer and press Alt (Windows) or Option (Mac OS) and click the Add a Layer Mask button. Ta da—the descenders are hidden!

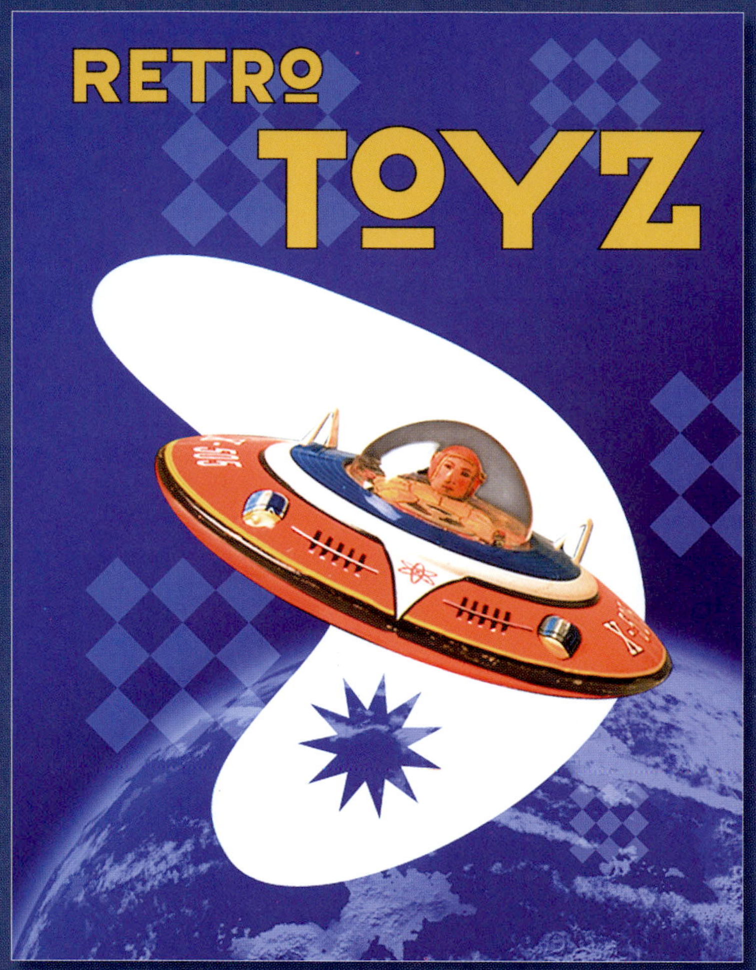

Unlike bitmap images, vector images retain their crisp edges at any enlargement. You can draw vector shapes and paths in your Photoshop images and add vector masks to control what is shown in an image. This lesson will introduce you to advanced uses of vector shapes and vector masks.

10 Vector Drawing Techniques

Lesson overview

In this lesson, you'll learn how to do the following:

- Differentiate between bitmap and vector graphics.
- Draw straight and curved paths using the Pen tool.
- Convert a path to a selection, and convert a selection to a path.
- Save paths.
- Draw and edit layer shapes.
- Draw custom layer shapes.
- Import and edit a Smart Object from Adobe Illustrator.

This lesson will take about 90 minutes to complete. If needed, remove the previous lesson folder from your hard drive, and copy the Lesson10 folder onto it from the *Adobe Photoshop CS2 Classroom in a Book* CD.

About bitmap images and vector graphics

Before working with vector shapes and vector paths, it's important to understand the basic differences between the two main categories of computer graphics: *bitmap images* and *vector graphics*. You can use Photoshop to work with either type of graphic; in fact, you can combine both bitmap and vector data in an individual Photoshop image file.

Bitmap images, technically called *raster images*, are based on a grid of colors known as pixels. Each pixel is assigned a specific location and color value. In working with bitmap images, you edit groups of pixels rather than objects or shapes. Because bitmap graphics can represent subtle gradations of shade and color, they are appropriate for continuous-tone images such as photographs or artwork created in painting programs. A disadvantage of bitmap graphics is that they contain a fixed number of pixels. As a result, they can lose detail and appear jagged when scaled up onscreen or if they are printed at a lower resolution than that for which they were created.

Vector graphics are made up of lines and curves defined by mathematical objects called *vectors*. These graphics retain their crispness whether they are moved, resized, or have their color changed. Vector graphics are appropriate for illustrations, type, and graphics such as logos that may be scaled to different sizes.

Logo drawn as vector art

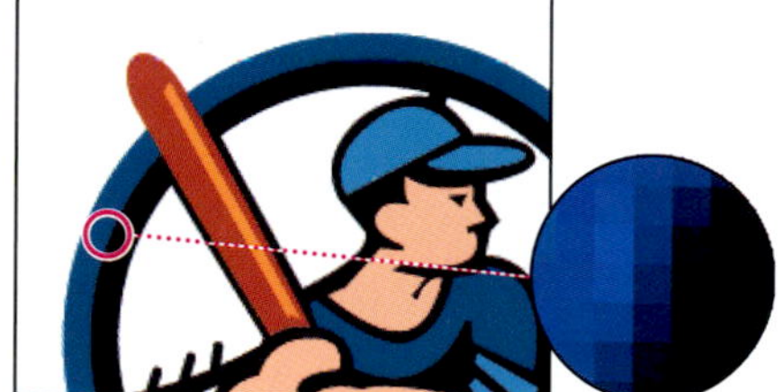

Logo rasterized as bitmap art

About paths and the Pen tool

In Photoshop, the outline of a vector shape is a *path*. A path is a curved or straight line segment you draw using the Pen tool, Magnetic Pen tool, or Freeform Pen tool. Of these tools, the Pen tool draws paths with the greatest precision; the Magnetic Pen tool and Freeform Pen tool draw paths as if you were drawing with a pencil on paper.

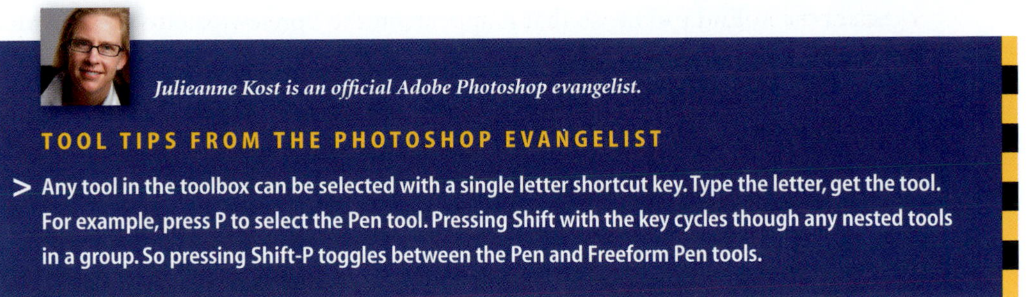

Julieanne Kost is an official Adobe Photoshop evangelist.
TOOL TIPS FROM THE PHOTOSHOP EVANGELIST
> Any tool in the toolbox can be selected with a single letter shortcut key. Type the letter, get the tool. For example, press P to select the Pen tool. Pressing Shift with the key cycles though any nested tools in a group. So pressing Shift-P toggles between the Pen and Freeform Pen tools.

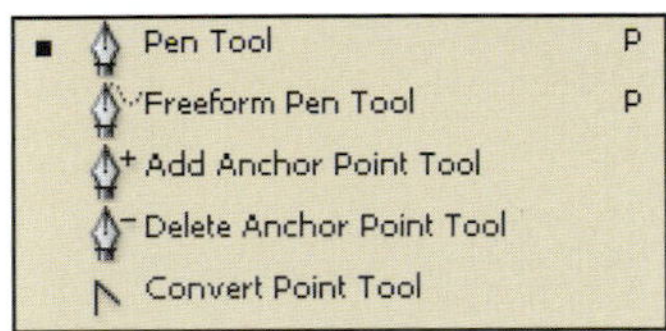

Paths can be open or closed. Open paths (such as a wavy line) have two distinct endpoints. Closed paths (such as a circle) are continuous. The type of path you draw affects how it can be selected and adjusted.

Paths that have not been filled or stroked do not print when you print your artwork. This is because paths are vector objects that contain no pixels, unlike the bitmap shapes drawn by the Pencil tool and other painting tools.

Getting started

You'll start the lesson by viewing a copy of the finished image that you'll create—a poster for a fictitious toy company.

1 Start Adobe Photoshop, holding down Ctrl-Alt-Shift (Windows) or Command-Option-Shift (Mac OS) to restore the default preferences. (See "Restoring default preferences" on page 6.)

2 When prompted, click Yes to confirm that you want to reset preferences, and Close to close the Welcome Screen.

3 Click the Go to Bridge button (▣) on the tool options bar to open Adobe Bridge.

4 In the Favorites palette in the upper left corner of Bridge, click the Lessons favorite, and then double-click the Lesson10 folder in the thumbnail preview area.

5 Select the 10End.psd file so that it appears in the Preview palette at left. Enlarge the palette if necessary to get a good close-up view.

To create this poster, you'll open the image of the toy space ship and practice making paths and selections using the Pen tool. Along the way, you'll learn advanced uses of path and vector masks, and ways to use Smart Objects, as you create the background shapes and type.

Note: *If you open the 10End.psd file in Photoshop, you might be prompted to update text layers. If so, click Update. This notice sometimes appears when files are transferred between computers, especially between Windows and Mac OS.*

6 When you're done looking at 10End.psd, double-click the Saucer.psd file to open it in Photoshop.

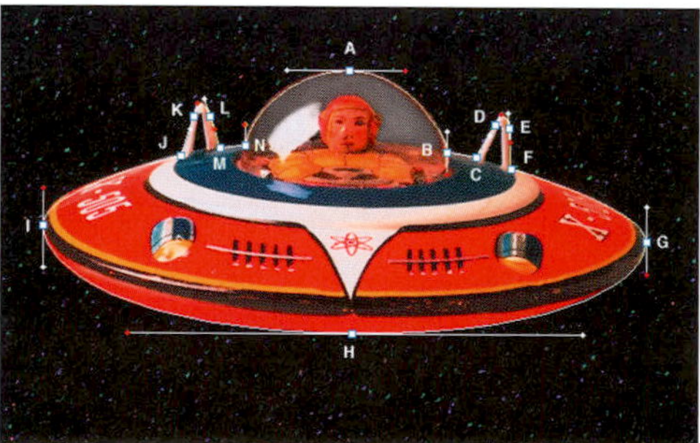

Using paths with artwork

You'll start by using the Pen tool to make selections in the fanciful image of the flying saucer. The saucer has long, smooth, curved edges that would be difficult to select using other methods.

You'll draw a path around the saucer and create two paths inside it. After you've drawn the paths, you'll convert them to selections. Then you'll subtract one selection from the other so that only the saucer and none of the starry sky is selected. Finally, you'll make a new layer from the saucer image and change the image that appears behind it.

When drawing a freehand path using the Pen tool, use as few points as possible to create the shape you want. The fewer points you use, the smoother the curves are and the more efficient your file is.

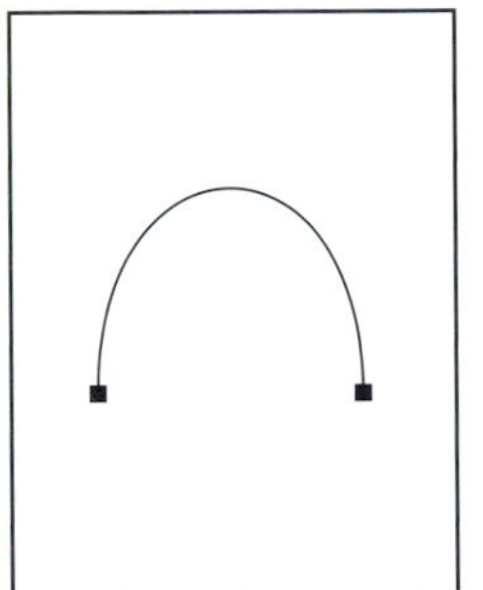

Correct number of points

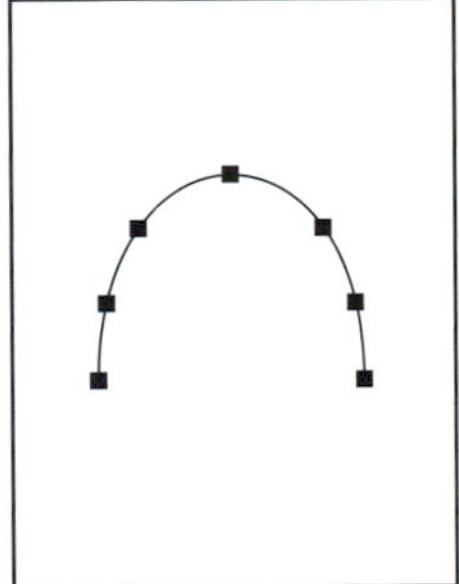

Too many points

Drawing the outline of a shape

In this exercise, you're going to use the Pen tool to connect the dots from point A to point N, and then back to point A. You'll set some straight segments, some smooth curve points, and some corner points.

You'll begin by configuring the Pen tool options and your work area, and then you'll trace the outline of a flying saucer using a template.

Note: *If you need practice creating and editing paths in Photoshop, read "Creating paths with the Pen tool" on page 285 before starting this exercise.*

1 In the toolbox, select the Pen tool (✒).

2 On the tool options bar, select or verify the following settings:

- Select the Paths (▣) option.
- Click the arrow for Geometry Options and make sure that the Rubber Band check box is *not* selected in the Pen Options pop-up palette.
- Make sure that the Auto Add/Delete option is selected.
- Select the Add to Path Area option (▣).

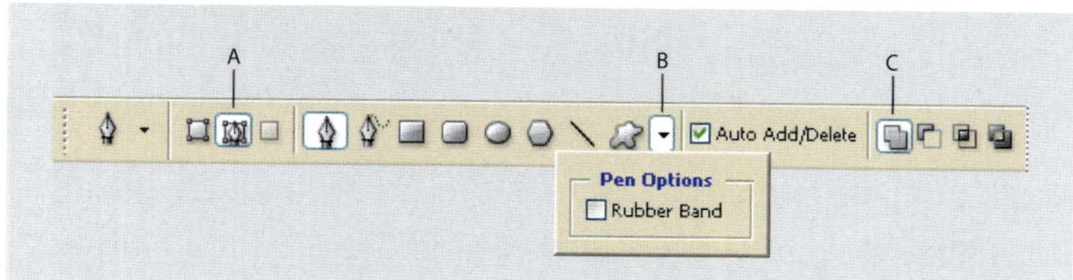

A. *Paths option* ***B.*** *Geometry Options menu* ***C.*** *Add to Path Area option*

3 Click the Paths tab to bring that palette to the front of the Layers palette group.

The Paths palette displays thumbnail previews of the paths you draw. Currently, the palette is empty because you haven't started drawing.

4 If necessary, zoom in so that you can easily see the lettered points and red dots on the shape template that has been created for you. Make sure you can see the whole template in the image window, and be sure to reselect the Pen tool after you zoom.

5 Position the pointer on point A. Click the point and drag to its red dot to set the first anchor point and the direction of the first curve. Do the same thing at point B.

At the corner of the cockpit (point B), you'll need to make a corner point to create a sharp transition between the curved segment and the straight one.

6 Alt-click (Windows) or Option-click (Mac OS) point B to convert the smooth point into a corner point and remove one of the direction lines.

Creating paths with the Pen tool

You can use the Pen tool to create paths that are straight or curved, open or closed. If you're unfamiliar with the Pen tool, it can be confusing to use at first. Understanding the elements of a path and how to create them with the Pen tool makes paths much easier to draw.

To create a straight path, click the mouse button. The first time you click, you set the starting point. Each time that you click thereafter, a straight line is drawn between the previous point and the current point. To draw complex straight-segment paths with the Pen tool, simply continue to add points.

To create a curved path, click to place an anchor point, drag to create a direction line for that point, and then click to place the next anchor point. Each direction line ends in two direction points; the positions of direction lines and points determine the size and shape of the curved segment. Moving the direction lines and points reshapes the curves in a path.

Smooth curves are connected by anchor points called *smooth points*. Sharply curved paths are connected by *corner points*. When you move a direction line on a smooth point, the curved segments on both sides of the point adjust simultaneously, but when you move a direction line on a corner point, only the curve on the same side of the point as the direction line is adjusted.

Path segments and anchor points can be moved after they're drawn, either individually or as a group. When a path contains more than one segment, you can drag individual anchor points to adjust individual segments of the path, or select all of the anchor points in a path to edit the entire path. Use the Direct Selection tool (↖) to select and adjust an anchor point, a path segment, or an entire path.

Creating a closed path differs from creating an open path in the way that you end the path. To end an open path, click the Pen tool (✒) in the toolbox. To create a closed path, position the Pen tool pointer over the starting point and click. Closing a path automatically ends the path. After the path closes, the Pen tool pointer appears with a small x, indicating that your next click will start a new path.

As you draw paths, a temporary storage area named *Work Path* appears in the Paths palette. It's a good idea to save work paths, and it's essential if you use multiple discrete paths in the same image file. If you deselect an existing Work Path in the Paths palette and then start drawing again, a new work path will replace the original one, which will be lost. To save a work path, double-click it in the Paths palette, type a name in the Save Path dialog box, and click OK to rename and save the path. The path remains selected in the Paths palette.

Setting a smooth point at B

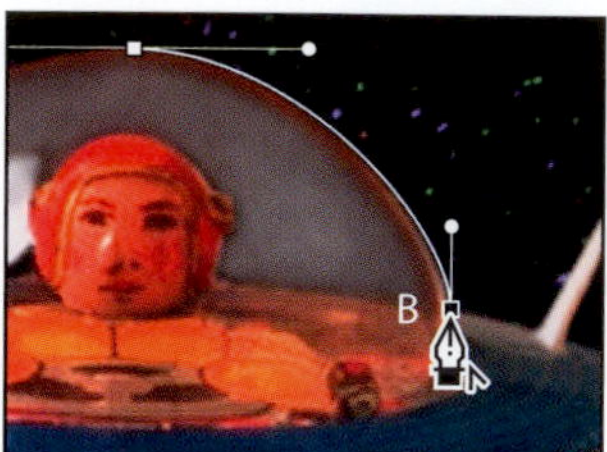

Converting the smooth point to a corner point

7 Click point C to set a straight segment (don't drag).

If you make a mistake while you're drawing, choose Edit > Undo to undo the step. Then resume drawing.

8 Click point D and drag up from point D to its red dot. Then, click point E and drag down from point E to its red dot.

9 Click point F.

10 Set curve points at G, H, and I by clicking each point and dragging from the point to its red dot, each in turn.

11 Click point J.

12 Set curve points at K and L by clicking each point and dragging from each one to its respective red dot.

13 Click point M.

14 Click point N and don't release the mouse button. Press Alt (Windows) or Option (Mac OS) and drag from point N to the red dot to add one direction line to the anchor point at N. Then, release the mouse button and the Alt or Option key.

15 Move the pointer over point A so that a small circle appears in the pointer icon, and click to close the path. (The small circle may be difficult to see because the image is dark and the circle is faint.)

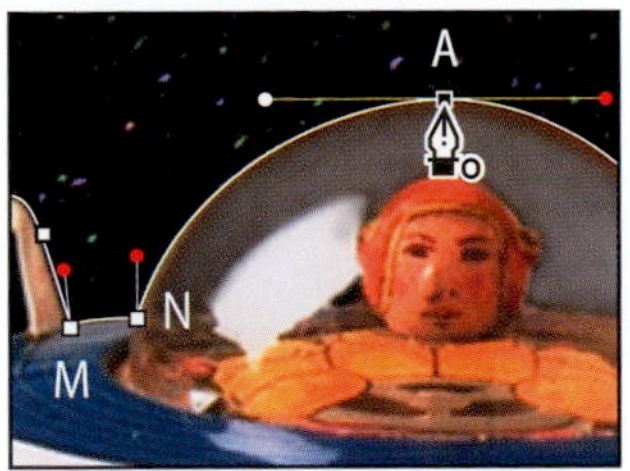

16 In the Paths palette, double-click the Work Path, type **Saucer** in the Save Path dialog box, and click OK to save it.

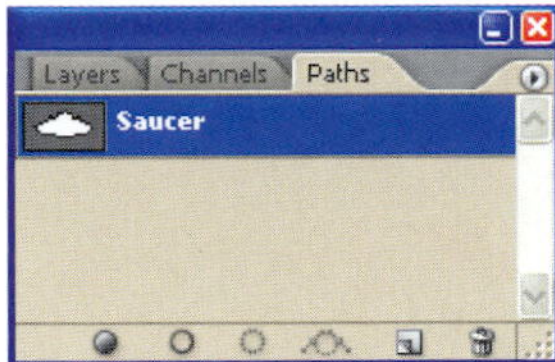

17 Choose File > Save to save your work.

Converting selections to paths

Now, you'll create a second path using a different method. First, you'll use a selection tool to select a similarly colored area, and then you'll convert the selection to a path. (You can convert any selection made with a selection tool into a path.)

1 Click the Layers tab to display the Layers palette, and then drag the Template layer to the Trash button at the bottom of the palette. You no longer need this layer.

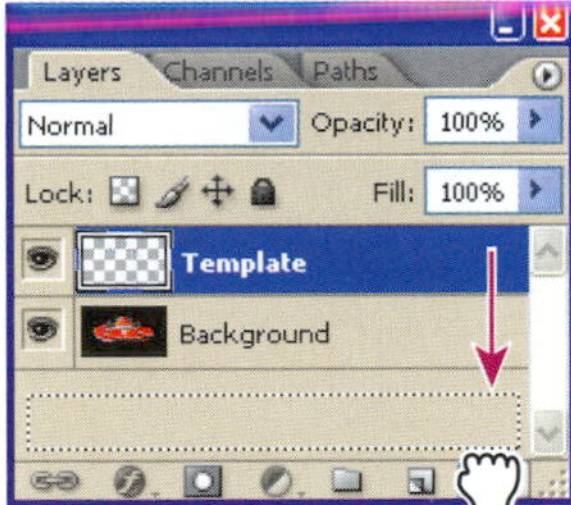

2 Select the Magic Wand tool ( ).

3 On the Magic Wand tool options bar, make sure that the Tolerance value is **32**.

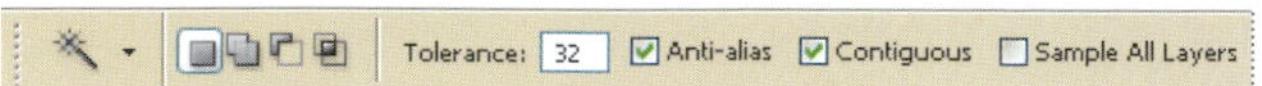

4 Carefully click the black area inside one of the saucer's vertical fins.

5 Shift-click inside the other fin to add that black area to the selection.

6 Click the Paths tab to bring the Paths palette forward. Then, click the Make Work Path From Selection button (⌂) at the bottom of the palette.

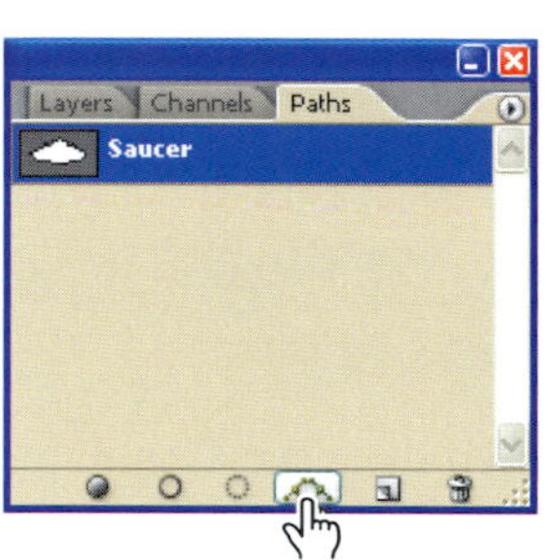

The selections are converted to paths, and a new Work Path is created.

7 Double-click the Work Path, name it **Fins**, and then click OK to save the path.

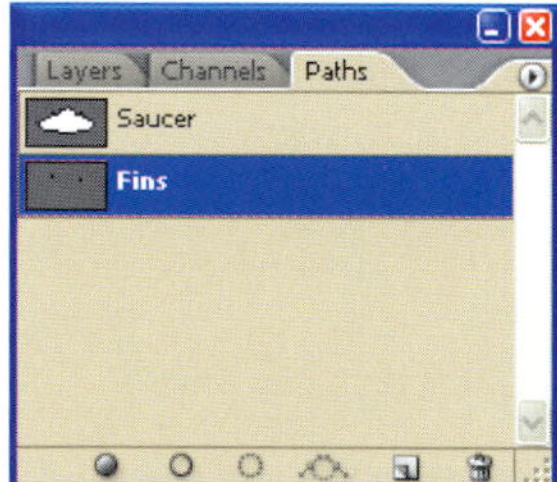

8 Choose File > Save to save your work.

Converting paths to selections

Just as you can convert selection borders to paths, so you can convert paths to selections. With their smooth outlines, paths let you make precise selections. Now that you've drawn paths for the spaceship and its fins, you'll convert those paths to a selection and apply a filter to the selection.

1 In the Paths palette, click the Saucer path to make it active.

2 Convert the Saucer path to a selection by doing one of the following:

• From the Paths palette menu, choose Make Selection, and then click OK to close the dialog box that appears.

• Drag the Saucer path to the Load Path as a Selection button (◌) at the bottom of the Paths palette.

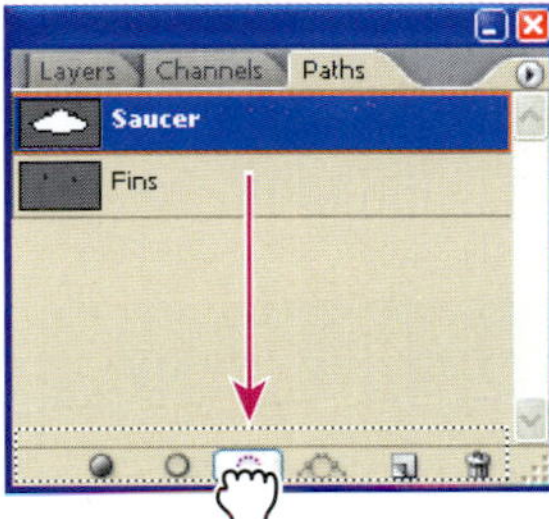

Next, you'll subtract the Fins selection from the Saucer selection so that you can see the background through the vacant areas in the fins.

3 In the Paths palette, click the Fins path. Then, from the Paths palette menu, choose Make Selection.

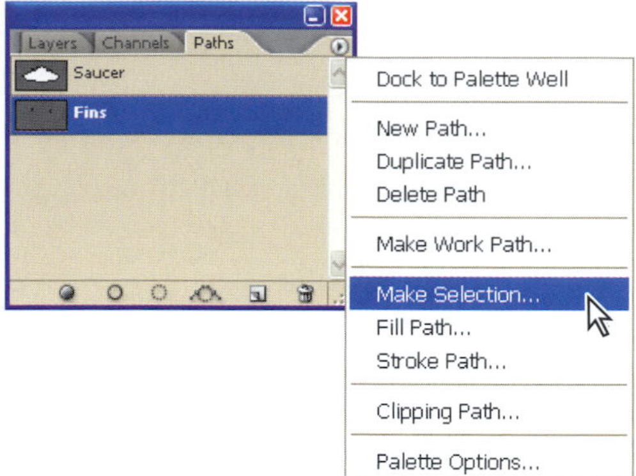

4 In the Operation area of the Make Selection dialog box, select Subtract from Selection, and click OK.

The Fins path is simultaneously converted to a selection and subtracted from the Saucer selection.

Leave the paths selected, because you're going to use the selection in the next procedure.

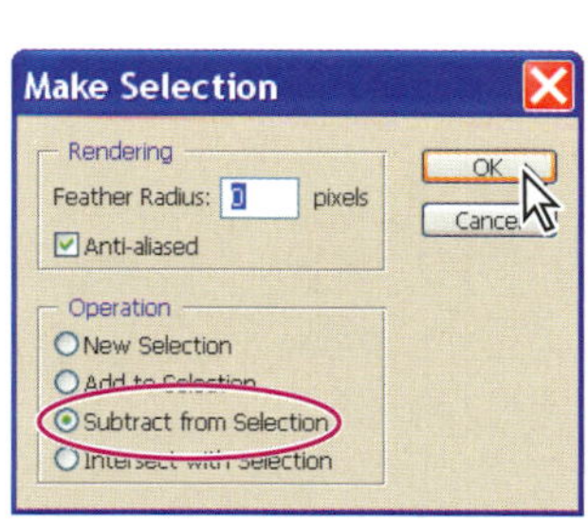

Subtracting the Fins selection from the Saucer selection

Result

Converting the selection to a layer

Now, you'll see how creating the selection with the Pen tool can help you achieve interesting effects. Because you've isolated the saucer, you can create a duplicate of it on a new layer. Then, you can copy it to another image file—specifically, to the image that is the background for the toy store poster.

1 In the Layers palette, make sure that the Background layer is selected. You should still see the selection outline in the image window. If you deselected it, you need to repeat the preceding exercise, "Converting paths to selections."

2 Choose Layer > New > Layer Via Copy.

A new layer appears in the Layers palette, Layer 1. The Layer 1 thumbnail shows that the layer contains only the image of the flying saucer, not the sky areas of the original layer.

3 In the Layers palette, double-click Layer 1, type **Saucer** to rename it, and press Enter (Windows) or Return (Mac OS).

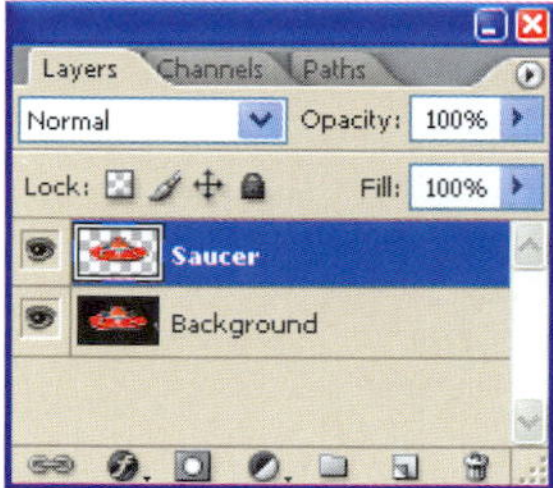

4 Use Adobe Bridge or the File > Open command to open the 10Start.psd file, which is located in the Lessons/Lesson10 folder.

This is a Photoshop image of a graduated blue background with a planet in the lower portion of the image.

5 If necessary, move the image windows so that you can see at least part of both the Saucer.psd window and the 10Start.psd window onscreen. Make sure that no layers

are selected in the 10Start.psd file Layers palette, then make the Saucer.psd image window active, and select the Saucer layer in the Layers palette.

6 In the toolbox, select the Move tool (▶✥), and drag from the Saucer.psd image window to the 10Start.psd image window so that the saucer appears in the sky.

7 Close the Saucer.psd image without saving changes, leaving the 10Start.psd file open and active.

Now you'll position the flying saucer more precisely in the poster background.

8 Select the Saucer layer in the Layers palette and choose Edit > Free Transform.

A bounding box appears around the saucer.

9 Position the cursor near any corner control handle until it turns into rotate cursor (↰), then drag to rotate the saucer until it's at about a 20-degree angle. When you're satisfied, press Enter (Windows) or Return (Mac OS).

***Note:** If you accidentally distort the saucer instead of rotating it, press Command-. (Mac OS) or Ctrl-. (Windows) and start over.*

10 To finesse the positioning of the saucer, make sure the Saucer layer is still selected and use the Move tool to drag the saucer so that it grazes the top of the planet, as in the following image.

11 Choose File > Save.

Creating vector objects for the background

Many posters are designed to be scalable, either up or down, while retaining a crisp appearance. This is a good use for vector shapes. Next, you'll create vector shapes with paths and use masks to control what appears in the poster. Because they're vector, the shapes can be scaled in future design revisions without a loss of quality or detail.

Drawing a scalable shape

You'll begin by creating a white kidney-shaped object for the backdrop of the poster.

1 Choose View > Rulers to display the horizontal and vertical rulers.

2 Drag the tab for the Paths palette out of the Layers palette group so that it floats independently. Since you'll be using the Layers and Paths palettes frequently in this exercise, it's convenient to have them separated.

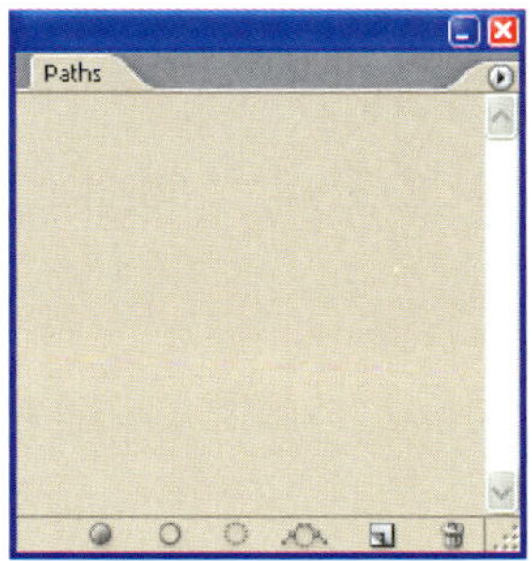

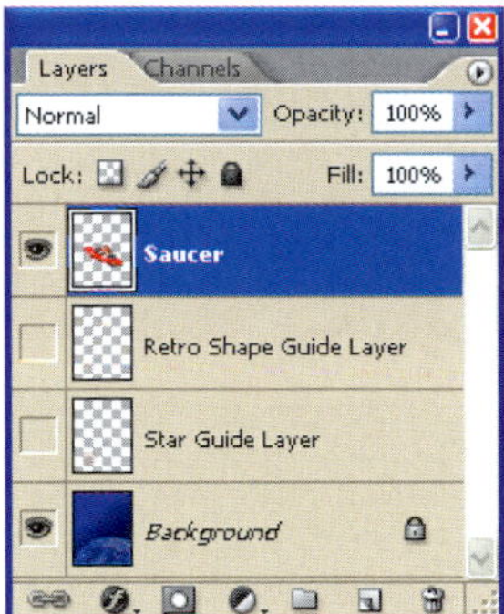

3 Hide all of the layers except the Retro Shape Guide layer and the Background layer by clicking the appropriate eye icons in the Layers palette, and then select the Background layer to make it active.

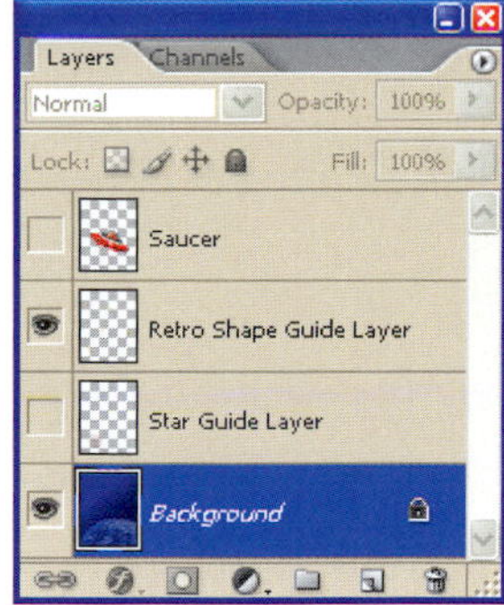

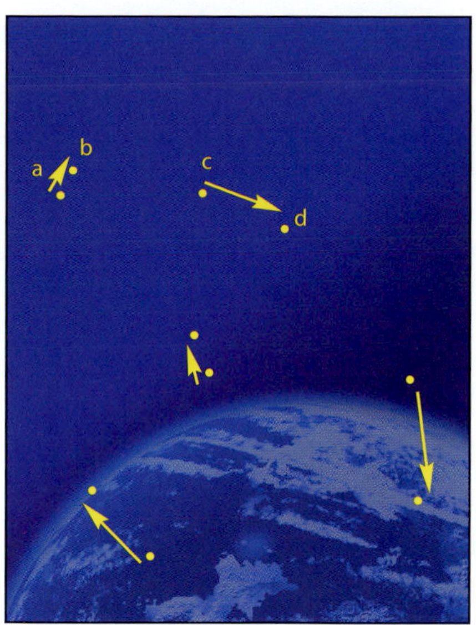

The guide layer will serve as a template as you draw the kidney shape.

4 Set the foreground and background colors to their defaults (black and white, respectively) by clicking the Default Foreground and Background Colors button (■) in the toolbox (or type the keyboard shortcut D), then swap the foreground and background colors by clicking the Switch Foreground and Background Colors button (↰) (or type X). Now the foreground color is white.

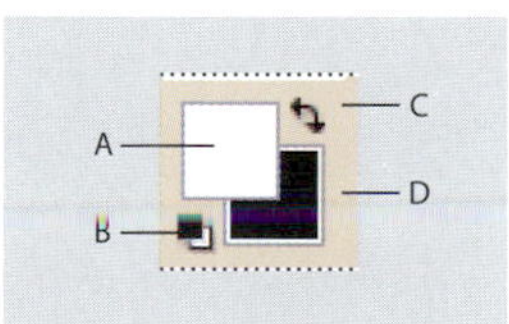

***A.** Foreground Color button*
***B.** Default Foreground and Background Colors button*
***C.** Switch Foreground and Background Colors button*
***D.** Background Color button*

5 In the toolbox, select the Pen tool (). Then, on the tool options bar, make sure that the Shape Layers option is selected.

6 Create the shape by clicking and dragging as follows:

- Click point A and drag a direction line up and to the left of point B, and then release.
- Click point B and drag a direction line toward and slightly above point C, and then release.
- Click point C and drag a direction line toward and above point D, and then release.
- Continue to draw curved segments in this way around the shape until you return to point A, and then click on A to close the path.

***Note:** If you have trouble, open the saucer image again and practice drawing the path around the saucer shape until you get more comfortable with drawing curved path segments. Also, be sure to read the sidebar, "Creating paths with the Pen tool," on page 285.*

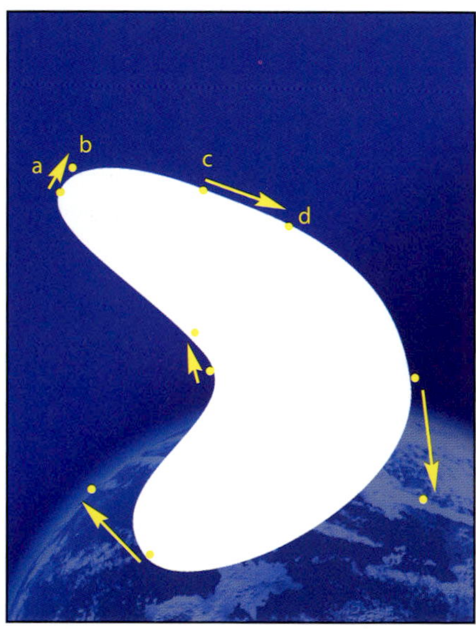

Notice as you drew that Photoshop automatically created a new layer, Shape 1, in the Layers palette.

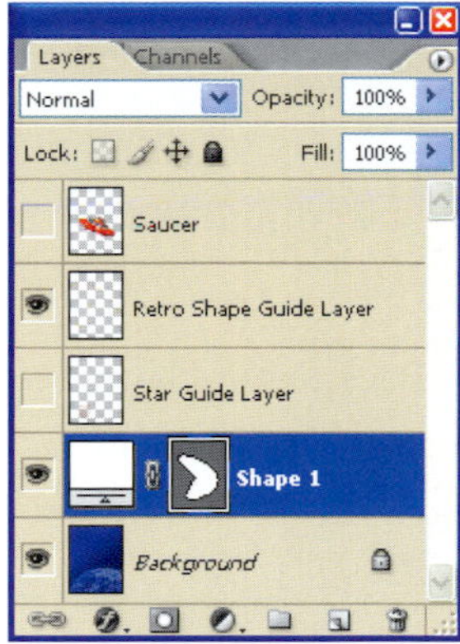

7 Double-click the Shape 1 shape layer, rename it **Retro Shape**, and press Enter (Windows) or Return (Mac OS).

8 Hide the Retro Shape Guide layer by clicking its eye icon in the Layers palette.

Deselecting paths

Deselecting paths is sometimes necessary to see the appropriate tool options bar when you select a vector tool. Deselecting paths can also help you view certain effects that might be obscured if a path is highlighted. Before proceeding to the next exercise, you'll make sure that all paths are deselected.

1 Select the Path Selection tool (), which may be hidden under the Direct Selection tool ().

2 On the tool options bar, click the Dismiss Target Path button (✓).

Note: *You can also deselect paths by clicking in the blank area below the paths in the Paths palette.*

Notice that the border between the white kidney shape and the blue background has a grainy quality. What you see is actually the path itself, which is a nonprinting item. This is a visual clue that the Retro Shape layer is still selected.

About shape layers

A shape layer has two components: a fill and a shape. The fill properties determine the color (or colors), pattern, and transparency of the layer. The shape is a layer mask that defines the areas in which the fill can be seen and those areas in which the fill is hidden.

In the layer you've just created, the fill is white. The fill color is visible within the shape you drew and is not visible in the rest of the image, so the background sky can be seen around it.

In the Layers palette, your Retro Shape layer sits above the Background layer because the Background was selected when you started to draw. There are three items in the shape layer along with the layer name: two thumbnail images and a link icon between them.

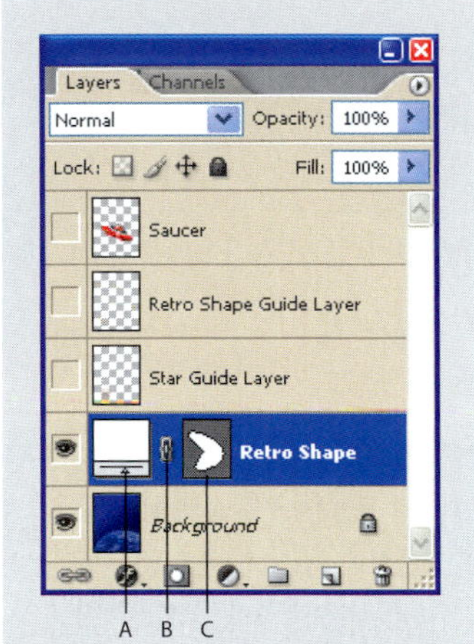

A. Fill thumbnail B. Layer mask link icon C. Mask thumbnail

The left thumbnail shows that the entire layer is filled with the white foreground color. The small slider underneath the thumbnail is not functional, but symbolizes that the layer is editable.

The Mask thumbnail on the right shows the vector mask for the layer. In this thumbnail, white indicates the area where the image is exposed, and gray indicates the areas where the image is blocked.

The icon between the two thumbnails indicates that the layer and the vector mask are linked.

Subtracting shapes from a shape layer

After you create a shape layer (vector graphic), you can set options to subtract new shapes from the vector graphic. You can also use the Path Selection tool and the Direct Selection tool to move, resize, and edit shapes. You'll add some interest to the retro shape by subtracting a star shape from it, allowing the outer space background to show through. To help you position the star, you'll refer to the Star Guide layer, which has been created for you. Currently, that layer is hidden.

1 In the Layers palette, click the box to the far left of the Star Guide layer to display the eye icon (👁) for that layer (but leave the Retro Shape layer selected). The Star Guide layer is now visible in the image window.

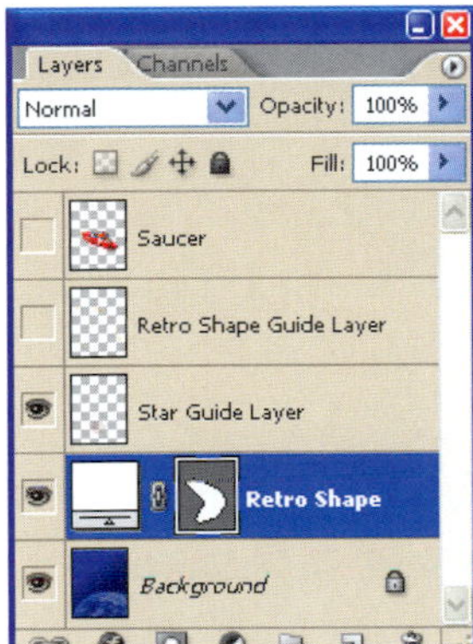

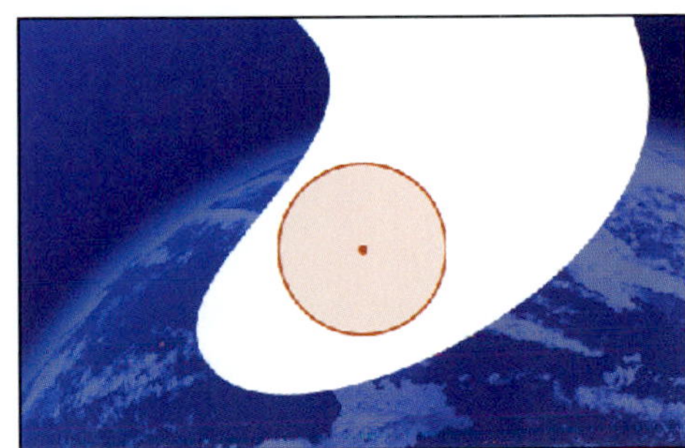

2 In the Paths palette, make sure that the Retro Shape Vector Mask is selected.

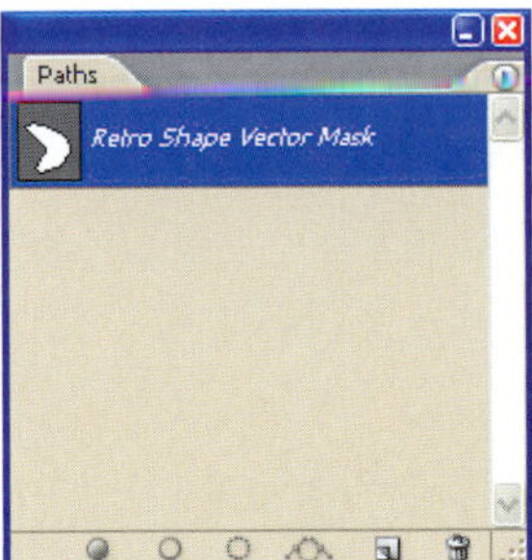

3 In the toolbox, select the Polygon tool (⬡), hidden under the Rectangle tool (▭).

4 On the tool options bar, do the following:

- For Sides, type **11**.
- Click the Geometry Options arrow (immediately to the left of the Sides option) to open the Polygon Options. Select the Star check box, and type **50%** in the Indent Sides By option. Then click anywhere outside the Polygon Options to close it.

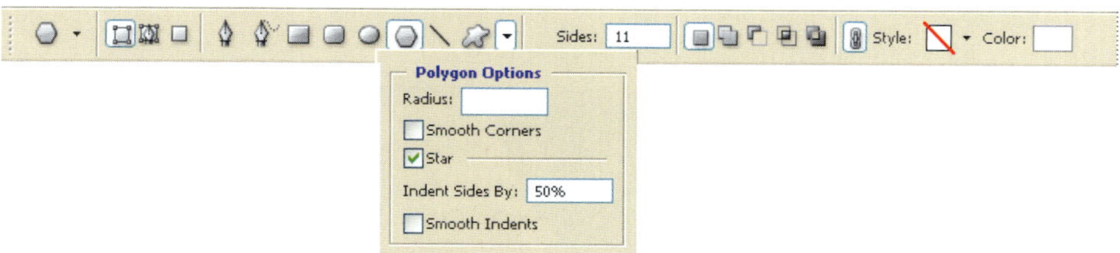

- Select the Subtract From Shape Area option (⧉), or press either hyphen or minus to select it with a keyboard shortcut. The pointer now appears as crosshairs with a small minus sign (+-).

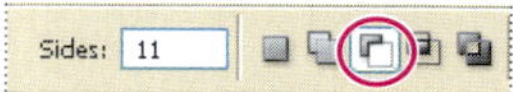

5 Move the crosshairs pointer over the orange dot in the center of the orange circle in the image window, and click and drag outward until the tips of the star rays touch the circle's perimeter.

***Note:** As you drag, you can rotate the star by dragging the pointer to the side.*

When you release the mouse, the star shape becomes a cutout, allowing the planet to show through. If the background layer were another image, pattern, or color, you would see it inside the star shape.

Notice that all the star has a grainy outline, reminding you that the shape is selected. Another indication that the shape is selected is that the Retro Shape vector mask thumbnail is highlighted (outlined in white) in the Layers palette.

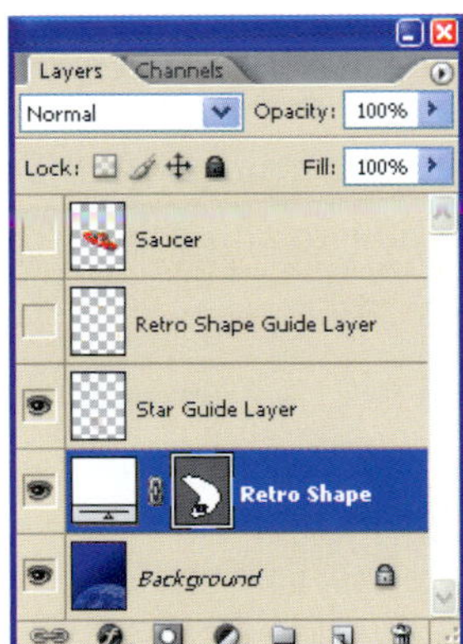

6 In the Layers palette, click the eye icon for the Star Guide layer to hide it.

Notice how the thumbnails have changed in the palettes. In the Layers palette, the left thumbnail for the Retro Shape layer is unchanged, but the mask thumbnails in both the Layers palette and Paths palette show the retro shape with the star-shaped cutout.

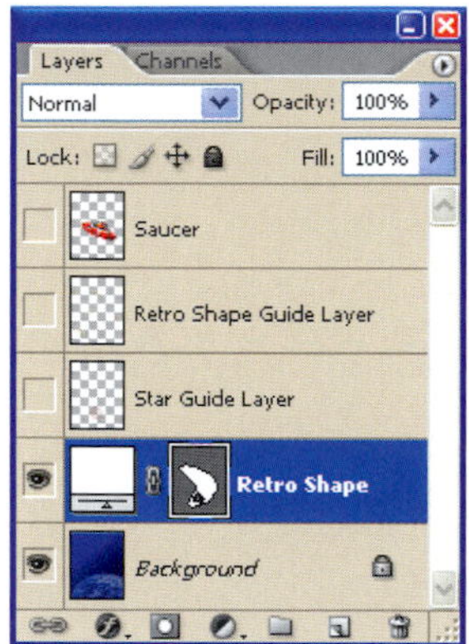

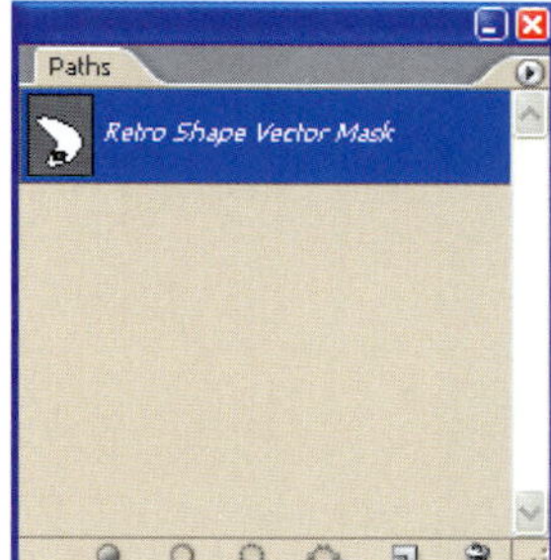

7 Deselect the star and retro shape paths by selecting the Path Selection tool (↖) and clicking the Dismiss Target Path button (✓) on the tool options bar.

Your paths are now deselected, and the grainy path lines have disappeared, leaving a sharp edge between the blue and white areas. Also, the Retro Shape Vector Mask is no longer highlighted in the Paths palette.

Working with defined custom shapes

Another way to use shapes in your artwork is to draw a custom or preset shape. Doing so is as easy as selecting the Custom Shape tool, picking a shape from the Custom Shape picker, and drawing in your image window. You will do so now to add checkerboard patterns to the background of your poster for the toy store.

1 Make sure the Retro Shape layer is selected in the Layers palette, then click the New Layer button (▣) to add a layer above it. Double-click the default Layer 1 name and rename it **Pattern**, and then press Enter (Windows) or Return (Mac OS).

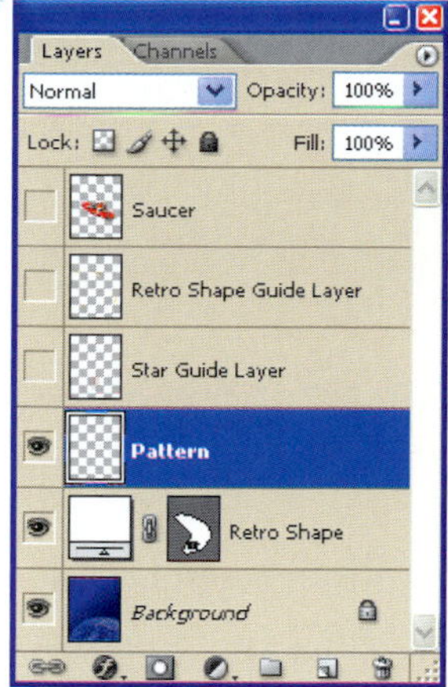

2 In the toolbox, select the Custom Shape tool (), which is hidden under the Polygon tool ().

3 On the tool options bar, click the pop-up arrow for the Shape option to open the custom shape picker.

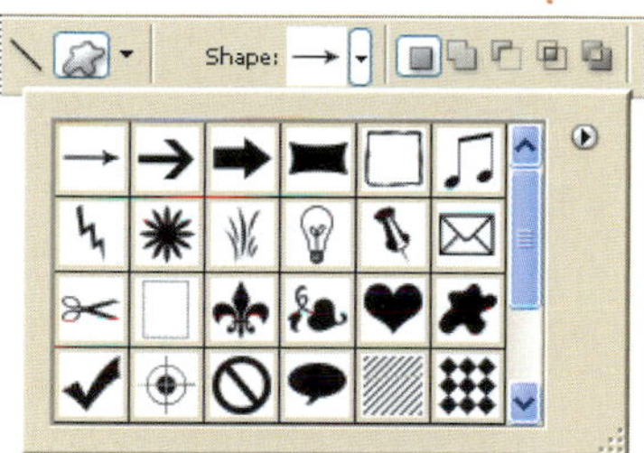

4 Locate the checkerboard preset at the bottom of the custom shape picker (you may need to scroll or drag the corner of the picker to see it), and double-click to select it and simultaneously close the picker.

5 On the tool options bar, select the Fill Pixels option.

6 Make sure that the foreground color is white (or select white now), and then press Shift and drag diagonally in the image window to draw and size the shape. (Pressing Shift constrains the shape to its original proportions.)

7 Add five more checkerboards of various sizes until your poster resembles the following figure.

8 On the Layers palette, reduce the opacity of the Pattern layer to **20%**.

Your poster background is now complete.

9 Turn on visibility for the Saucer layer to see the whole composition.

10 Choose File > Save to save your work.

Importing a Smart Object

Photoshop offers support for Smart Objects, which allows you to import vector objects from Adobe Illustrator and edit them in Photoshop without a loss of quality. Regardless of how often you scale, rotate, skew, or otherwise transform a Smart Object, it retains its sharp, precise edges. In addition, you can edit the original object in Illustrator, and the changes will be reflected in the placed Smart Object in your Photoshop image file. You learned a bit about Smart Objects in Lesson 9. You will explore them more now by placing text created in Illustrator into the toy store poster.

Adding the title

We created the toy store name for you in Illustrator. Let's add it to the poster.

1 Make sure the Saucer layer is selected and choose File > Place. Navigate to the Lessons/Lesson10 folder, select the title.ai file, and click Place. Click OK in the Place PDF dialog box that appears.

The Retro Toys text is added to the middle of your composition, inside a bounding box with adjustable handles. A new layer, title, appears in the Layers palette.

2 Drag the Retro Toys object to the upper right corner of the poster, and then press Shift and drag a corner to make the text object proportionally larger—so that it fills the top portion of the poster, as in the following figure. When you're done, press Enter (Windows) or Return (Mac OS), or click the Commit Transform button (✓) on the tool options bar.

When you commit to the transform, the layer thumbnail icon changes to reflect that the title layer is a Smart Object.

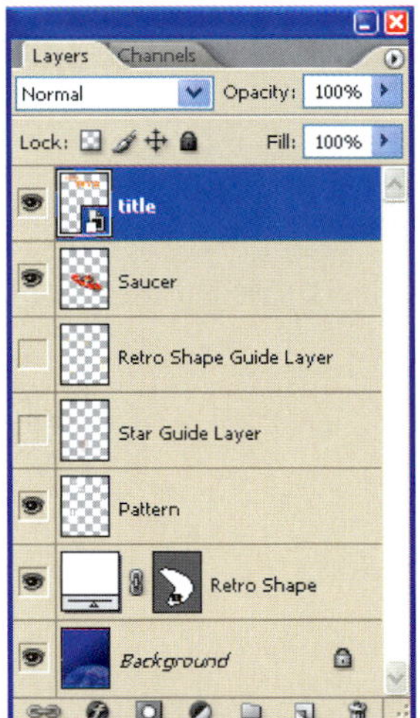

Because the Retro Toys title is a Smart Object, you can continue to edit its size and shape, if you'd like. Simply select its layer and choose Edit > Free Transform to access the control handles, and drag to adjust them. Or, select the Move tool (▸✥), and check Show Transform Controls on the tool options bar. Then adjust the handles.

Finishing up

As a final step, let's clean up the Layers palette by deleting your guide template layers.

1 Make sure that the title, Saucer, Pattern, Retro Shape, and Background layers are the only visible layers in the Layers palette.

2 Choose Delete Hidden Layers from the Layers palette pop-up menu, and then click Yes to confirm the delete action.

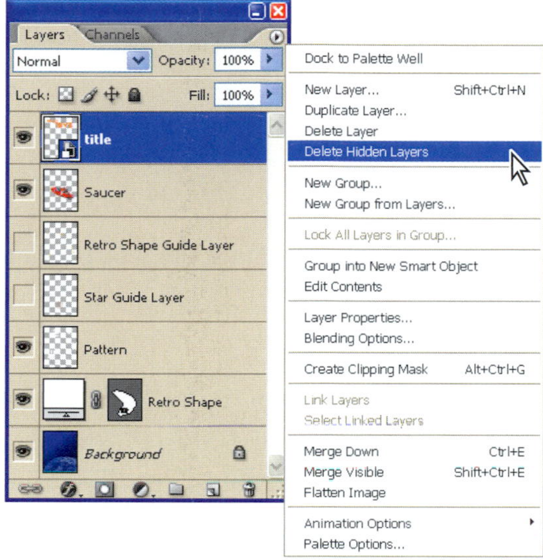

3 Choose File > Save to save your work.

Congratulations! You've finished the poster. It should look like the following image (the title text will only be stroked if you complete the Extra Credit task).

EXTRA CREDIT If you have Adobe Illustrator CS or CS2, you can go even further with the Retro Toys text Smart Object—you can edit it in Illustrator, and it will update automatically in Photoshop. Try this:

1 Double-click the Smart Object thumbnail in the title layer. If an alert dialog box appears, click OK. Illustrator opens and displays the Retro Toys Smart Object in a document window.

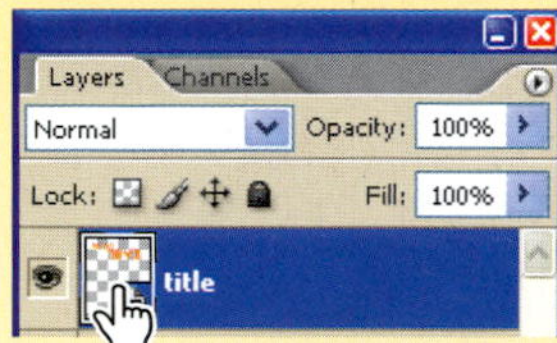

2 Using the Direct Selection tool (), drag a marquee around the type to select all of the letters.

3 Select the Stroke icon () in the toolbox.

4 Move the mouse over the Color palette (choose Window > Color if the palette isn't already open onscreen). Notice that the cursor changes to an eyedropper. Use the eyedropper to choose black in the Color palette, and then, in the Stroke palette, specify a 0.5-point width.

A 0.5-point black stroke appears around the Retro Toys type.

5 Click the Close button to close the Vector Smart Object document, and click Save when prompted.

6 Switch back to Photoshop. The Retro Toys poster image window updates to reflect the stroked type.

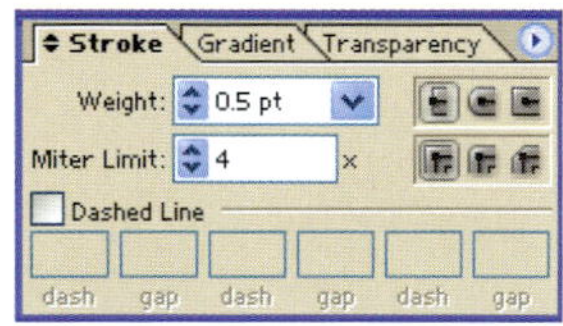

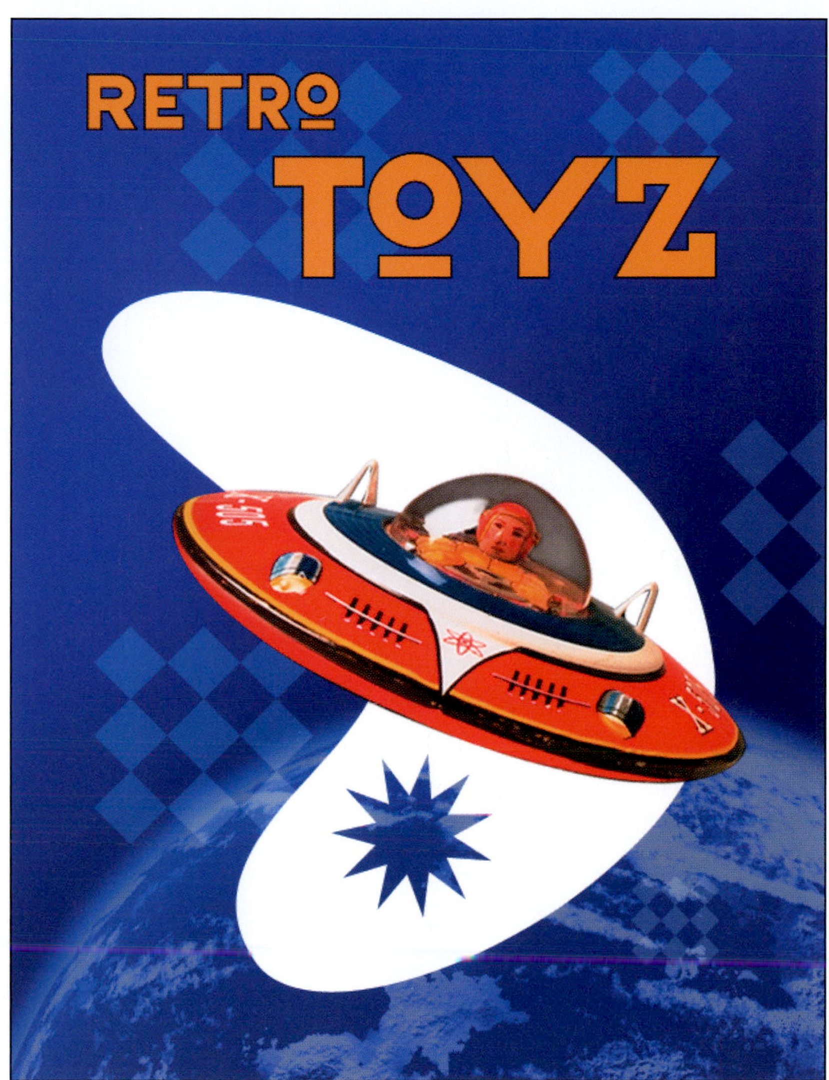
RETRO
TOYZ

Review

Review questions

1 How can the Pen tool be useful as a selection tool?

2 What is the difference between a bitmap image and a vector graphic?

3 What does a shape layer do?

4 What tools can you use to move and resize paths and shapes?

5 What are Smart Objects, and what is the benefit of using them?

Review answers

1 If you need to create an intricate selection, it can be easier to draw the path with the Pen tool and then convert the path to a selection.

2 Bitmap or raster images are based on a grid of pixels and are appropriate for continuous-tone images such as photographs or artwork created in painting programs. Vector graphics are made up of shapes based on mathematical expressions and are appropriate for illustrations, type, and drawings that require clear, smooth lines.

3 A shape layer stores the outline of a shape in the Paths palette. You can change the outline of a shape by editing its path.

4 You use the Path Selection tool (▸) and the Direct Selection tool (▹) to move, resize, and edit shapes. You can also modify and scale a shape or path by choosing Edit > Free Transform Path.

5 Smart Objects are vector objects that you can import from Adobe Illustrator and place and edit in Photoshop without a loss of quality. Regardless of how often you scale, rotate, skew, or otherwise transform a Smart Object, it retains sharp, precise edges. A great benefit of using Smart Objects is that you can edit the original object in Illustrator, and the changes will be reflected in the placed Smart Object in your Photoshop image file.

After you've learned basic layer techniques, you can create more complex effects in your artwork using layer masks, path groups, filters, adjustment layers, and more layer styles.

11 Advanced Layer Techniques

Lesson overview

In this lesson, you'll learn how to do the following:

- Create clipping groups so that an image on one layer can be a mask for artwork on other layers.
- Create layer sets to organize and manage layers.
- Add adjustment layers to an image, and use them to apply color and tonal adjustments without permanently changing pixel data.
- Create knockout layers to use one layer selectively to reveal others.
- Import layers from other Photoshop files.
- Work with type layers.
- Duplicate and clip layers.
- Add layer styles to a layer, and apply the effects to multiple layers.
- Rasterize layers.
- Convert clipping paths to masks.
- Liquify a layer, giving it a melted appearance.
- Flatten and save a layered file, greatly reducing its file size.

This lesson will take less than an hour to complete. If needed, remove the previous lesson folder from your hard drive, and copy the Lessons/Lesson11 folder onto it. As you work on this lesson, you'll overwrite the start files. If you need to restore the start files, copy them from the *Adobe Photoshop CS2 Classroom in a Book* CD.

Getting started

In this lesson, you'll work with an image that has two layers plus a background layer. You'll get more experience with adjustment layers, layer effects, layer masks, and layer filters. Beyond this lesson, there is no substitute for experimentation and creativity for learning what you can do by combining the many filters, effects, layer properties, layer masks, and layer properties in new ways.

1 Start Adobe Photoshop, and immediately hold down Ctrl-Alt-Shift (Windows) or Command-Option-Shift (Mac OS) to restore the default preferences.

2 When prompted, click Yes to confirm that you want to reset preferences, and Close to close the Welcome Screen.

3 Click the Go to Bridge button (icon) on the tool options bar to open Adobe Bridge.

4 In the Favorites palette in the upper left corner of Bridge, click the Lessons favorite, and then double-click the Lesson11 folder in the preview area.

5 Select the 11End.psd thumbnail and examine it in the Preview palette. If necessary, enlarge the Preview palette so that you can get a good look.

6 Double-click the 11Start.psd thumbnail to open the file in Photoshop.

7 Close (or minimize) the Navigator, Color, and History palette groups, and move the Layers palette group to the top of the work area. Drag the corner of the Layers palette group to elongate it so that you'll be able to see about ten layers without scrolling.

Currently, there are only three layers in the palette, and visibility for all three is on. However, only the opaque Metal Grille layer is visible in the image window. The Rust layer and the Background are stacked underneath it, so the metal grille image blocks your view of these underlying layers.

8 Using the eye icons (👁) in the Layers palette, examine the layers one by one, hiding each of the other layers so that you can see exactly what each layer image looks like.

9 Reset eye icons for all the layers so that all are on, as when you opened the file.

Creating paths to clip a layer

You can use a vector path to clip a layer, creating a sharp-edged mask on that layer. In this part of the lesson, you'll draw a circle and use it to knock out the holes in the metal grille image. This will let you see through the holes to the layers below.

Drawing the vector work path

You'll begin by drawing the basic path on the Metal Grille layer.

1 Click the Metal Grille layer in the Layers palette to select it.

2 Select the Ellipse tool (◯), hidden behind the Rectangle tool (▭). (Be careful not to select the Elliptical Marquee tool.) On the tool options bar, click the Paths option (▣).

3 Move the pointer to the center of one of the holes in the metal grille and start dragging. Then, hold down Shift-Alt (Windows) or Shift-Option (Mac OS) and continue to drag until the circle is the size of the hole. Carefully release the mouse button first, and then release the keyboard keys.

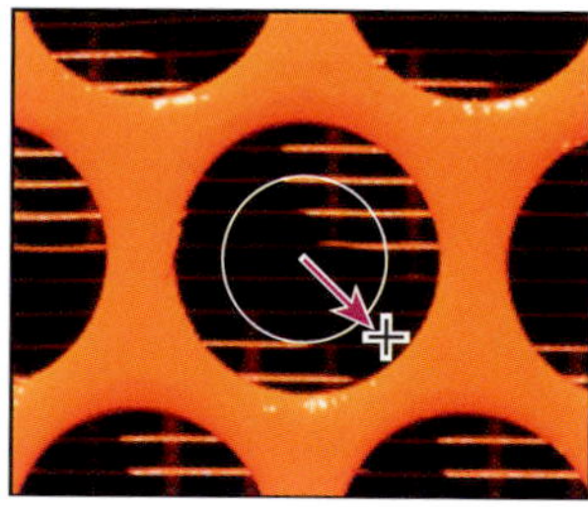

Note: If the circle is not exactly centered when you're done, hold down Ctrl (Windows) or Command (Mac OS) and drag the circle path into position. If the circle fills with black, choose Edit > Undo, and repeat Step 2, making sure that you select the Paths option on the tool options bar.

Next, you'll make copies of the circle for the rest of the metal grille.

4 In the toolbox, select the Path Selection tool (), which is beside the Type tool, and click to select the circle you just drew.

5 Hold down Alt (Windows) or Option (Mac OS) so that a small plus sign appears below the pointer icon (), and then drag the circle to place a copy of the path over another hole in the metal grille.

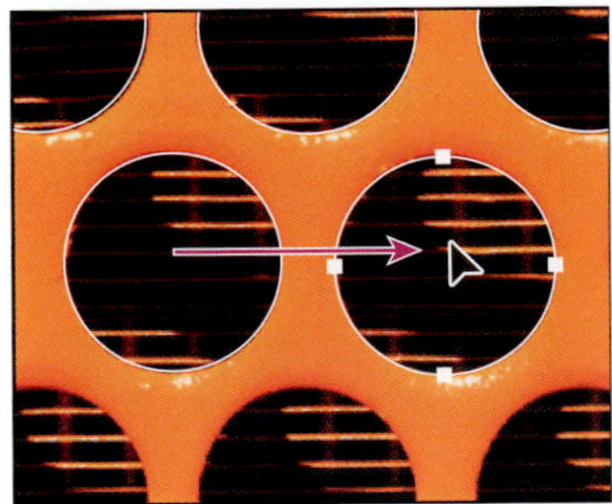

6 Repeat Step 5 to place copies over the remaining holes, including the holes that extend outside the edges of the image.

When you have copies of the circle path over several holes, you can Shift-click to select them all, and then Alt-drag or Option-drag to duplicate and move them.

Note: *You can adjust the position of a selected circle using the arrow keys on the keyboard. You may also find it helpful to choose View > Snap To, and deselect any of the commands that are checked on the Snap To submenu so that none of them are active.*

Creating a layer mask from the work path

You're ready to use these circles as a layer vector mask.

1 Shift-click to select all 16 circle paths.

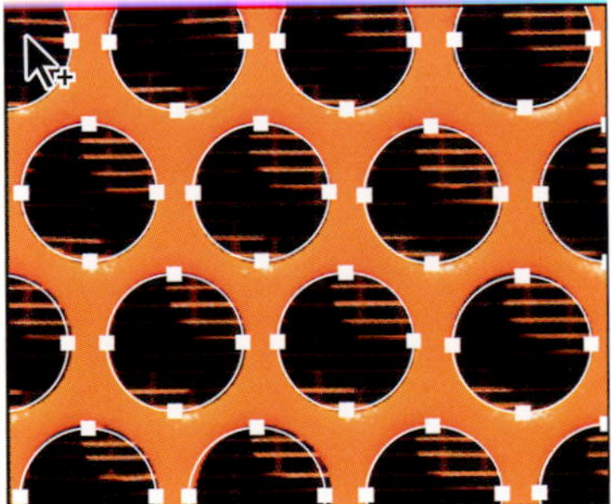

2 On the tool options bar, click the Subtract From Shape Area option ( ), or press hyphen (-) to select it with the keyboard shortcut.

The subtraction option sets up Photoshop to use the circle shapes to define where it will remove pixels from the layer, so those areas of the Metal Grille layer become transparent when you apply the path as a vector mask.

3 Choose Layer > Vector Mask > Current Path.

The Rust layer appears through the holes you cut in the Metal Grille layer. In the Layers palette, a thumbnail of the vector mask appears in the Metal Grille layer.

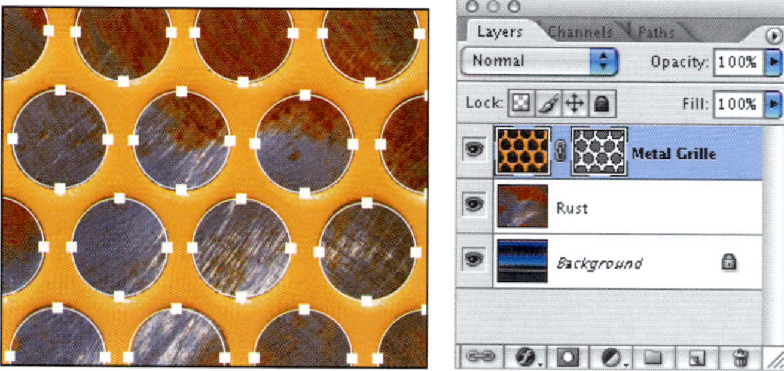

4 Click the Dismiss Target Path button (✓) on the tool options bar to deselect the multicircle path you created.

5 Choose File > Save to save your work.

Creating layer sets

Layer sets help you organize and manage individual layers by grouping them. You can then expand the layer set to view the layers contained in it, or collapse the set to simplify your view. You can change the stacking order of layers within a layer set.

Layer sets can function like layers in a number of ways, so you select, duplicate, and move entire sets of layers, as well as apply attributes and masks to the entire layer set. Any changes you make at the layer-set level apply to all the layers within the set.

In this section, you'll create two layer sets, one for type and another for the metal grille.

1 In the Layers palette, click the Create a New Group button (🗀) twice to create two layer sets.

2 Double-click the name *Group 2* and type **Words**, and then press Enter (Windows) or Return (Mac OS).

3 Double-click the name *Group 1* and type **Images**, and then press Enter (Windows) or Return (Mac OS).

4 In the Layers palette, drag the Metal Grille layer onto the Images layer set, and release the mouse button. The Metal Grille layer now appears indented in the Images layer set.

5 Drag the Rust layer to add it to the Images layer set, too. Notice that the Rust layer is also indented, and is below the Metal Grille sublayer in the set.

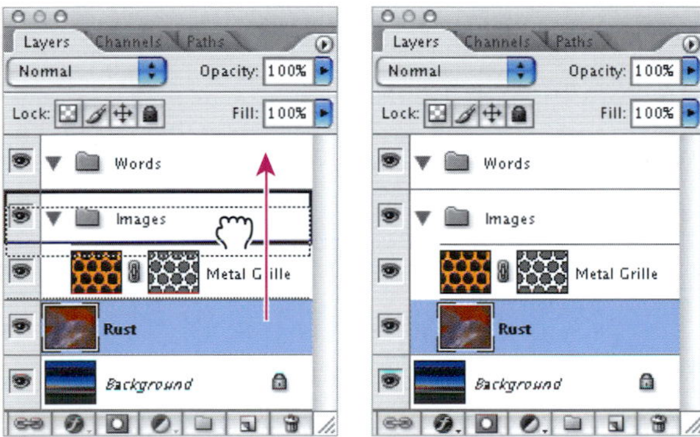

6 Choose File > Save.

Creating an adjustment layer

Adjustment layers can be added to an image to apply color and tonal adjustments without permanently changing the pixel values in the image. For example, if you add a Color Balance adjustment layer to an image, you can experiment with different colors repeatedly, because the change occurs only on the adjustment layer. If you decide to return to the original pixel values, you can hide or delete the adjustment layer.

Here, you'll add a Curves adjustment layer to create a greater contrast between the grille and the rust layer behind it. You'll do this by darkening the entire rust image. An adjustment layer affects all layers below it in the image's stacking order. Because you'll place the Curves adjustment layer below the Metal Grille layer, the adjustment will affect the Rust layer and the Background but not the metal grille.

1 Select the Rust layer in the Layers palette.

2 Click the Create New Fill or Adjustment Layer button (◐) at the bottom of the Layers palette, and choose Curves from the pop-up menu.

3 Click the middle of the diagonal line in the grid (the color curve) to add a control point on the curve that will adjust the midtones.

4 Drag the control point down and to the right, or enter values in the Input and Output text boxes. (We moved the control point so that the value in the Input text box is 150 and the value in the Output text box is 105.)

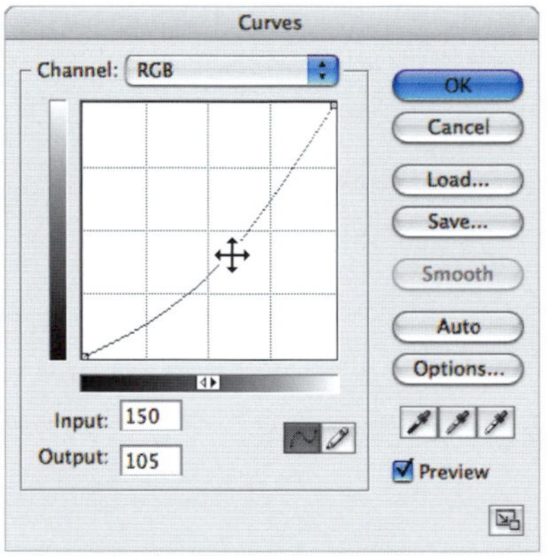

5 Click OK to close the Curves dialog box.

An adjustment layer named Curves 1 appears in the Layers palette. The thumbnails for the new layer include one of the Curves 1 graph and one of the layer mask.

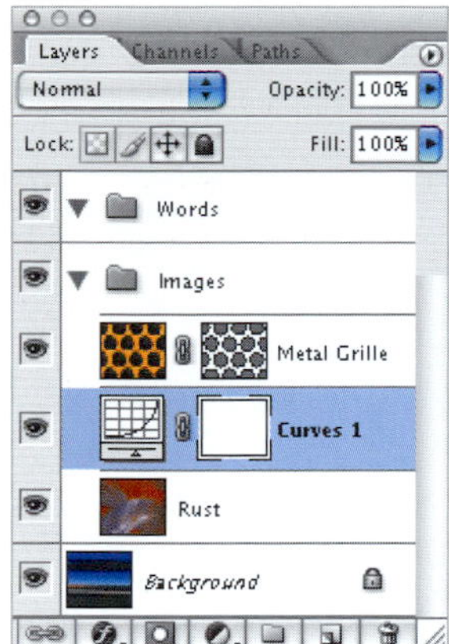

6 Choose File > Save.

You can experiment by clicking the eye icons for the Curves 1 and Rust layers off and on to see the effect of the adjustment layer on the other layers. When you finish, be sure to return all layers to their visible state.

Creating a knockout gradient layer

Knockout layer options specify how one layer reveals other layers. In this section, you'll create a knockout gradient layer so that the lower third of the image reveals the Background layer.

You'll begin by creating a new layer in the Images layer set.

1 Select the Images layer set in the Layers palette and click the Create a New Layer button (▣) at the bottom of the palette.

This creates a new layer (Layer 1) in the Images layer set, above the Metal Grille, Curves 1, and Rust layers.

2 Double-click the new Layer 1, and type **Knockout Gradient** to rename it. Press Enter (Windows) or Return (Mac OS), and keep the Knockout Gradient layer selected.

3 Select the Gradient tool (▣) in the toolbox.

4 If necessary, click the Default Foreground and Background Colors icon (▣) in the toolbox to set the foreground color to black and the background color to white.

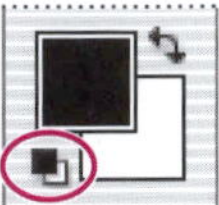

5 If necessary, click the Linear Gradient button (▣) on the tool options bar to create a linear gradient.

6 Click the arrow (▾) to the right of the gradient display on the tool options bar to open the gradient picker.

7 Click the arrow button (◉) to open the gradient-picker palette menu, and choose Small List. Then select Foreground to Transparent in the picker, and close it by clicking outside it or double-clicking the Foreground to Transparent option.

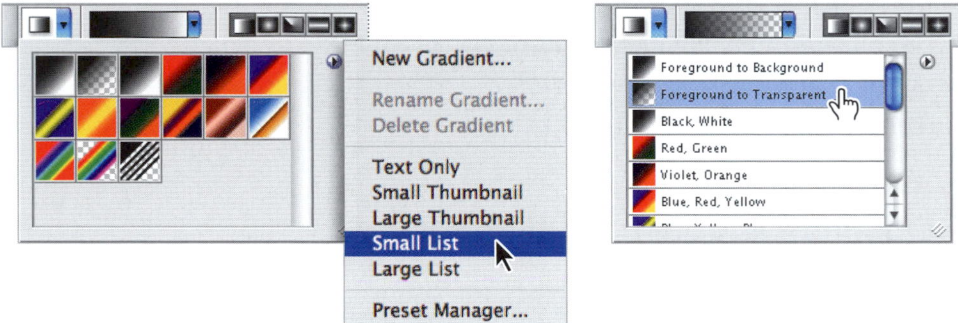

8 Shift-drag from the bottom of the image to slightly above the midpoint to create a gradient that goes from black at the bottom to transparent at the top.

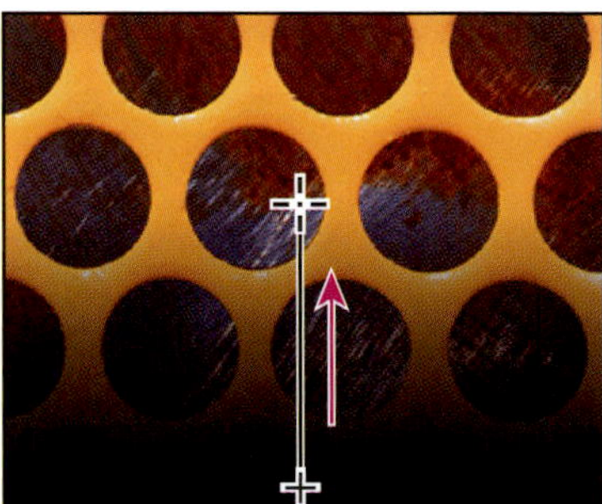

9 Click the Add a Layer Style button (◉) at the bottom of the Layers palette, and choose Blending Options from the pop-up menu.

10 In the Layer Style dialog box, do the following:

- Under Advanced Blending, drag the Fill Opacity slider all the way to the left, or type to enter **0** as the value. (Be careful to adjust the Fill Opacity, not the Opacity option under General Blending.)
- Choose Knockout > Deep.
- Click OK to close the dialog box.

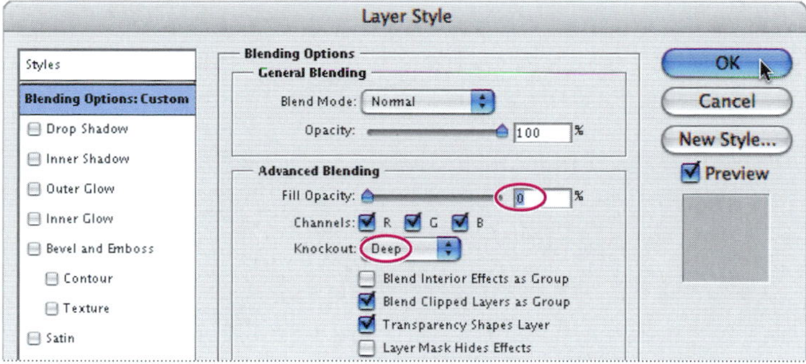

Now the horizontal stripes of gradient colors on the Background layer start to show through the layers in the Images layer set.

11 Choose File > Save.

Importing a layer from another file

In this part of the lesson, you'll import an existing layer from another file into your artwork. Although the imported layer contains the word *diesel* and was originally created with the Type tool, the text has been converted to a graphic. You can no longer edit it with the Type tool, but the advantage here is that you also don't have to worry about whether or not anyone who works on the file has the same font installed in order to see the image correctly.

1 Select the Words layer set in the Layers palette.

2 Use Bridge or the File > Open command to open the Diesel.psd file, located in the Lessons/Lesson11 folder, in Photoshop.

3 With the Diesel.psd file active, drag the Diesel layer from the Layers palette into the 11Start.psd image window.

Because the Words layer set was selected in the 11Start.psd image, the Diesel layer is added to that set.

4 Select the Move tool (▸✥) and drag the Diesel layer image to position it in the center of the 11Start.psd image and near the bottom.

5 Choose File > Save to save your 11Start.psd file.

6 Close the Diesel.psd image file without saving it.

Applying layer styles

Layer styles are automated special effects that you can apply to a layer.

Once you have the text arranged on the image, you can add layer styles to enhance the appearance of the type. Here, you'll add two different layer styles to the Diesel type layer.

1 With the Diesel layer selected in the Layers palette, click the Add a Layer Style button (Ⓕ) at the bottom of the palette and choose Drop Shadow from the pop-up menu.

2 In the Layer Style dialog box, make sure that the Preview check box is selected, or select it now so that you'll be able to see the changes as you work.

3 Examine the options for Drop Shadow in the Layer Style dialog box. You can either leave them at the default settings, or experiment with various changes until you like the results you see in the image window.

4 Click the words *Bevel and Emboss* in the Styles list at left so that they are highlighted and so that a checkmark appears in the Bevel and Emboss check box.

5 In the Structure area on the right side of the dialog box, adjust the sliders for Depth and Size until you achieve a fairly subtle, beveled look in the Diesel image. (We used 2% for Depth and 2 pixels for Size, but you may think this is too subtle. You can also leave them set at the default values: 100% and 5 pixels.)

Watch the square located directly below the Preview option as you adjust settings. This thumbnail image shows how the layer style options you select will look on a plain gray square.

6 Click OK to close the Layer Style dialog box.

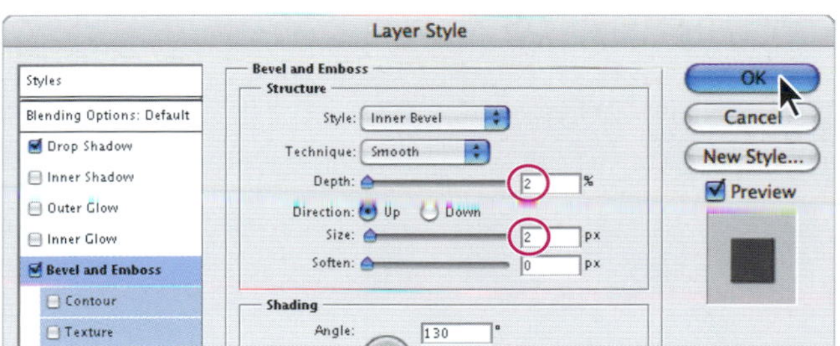

7 Choose File > Save.

Duplicating and clipping a layer

In this section, you'll learn how to copy the Rust layer and then use the compound shape of the Diesel layer to clip away some of the Rust layer.

First, you'll copy the Rust layer and move the copy above the Diesel layer.

1 Select the Rust layer in the Layers palette and drag it onto the Create a New Layer button (◻) at the bottom of the palette.

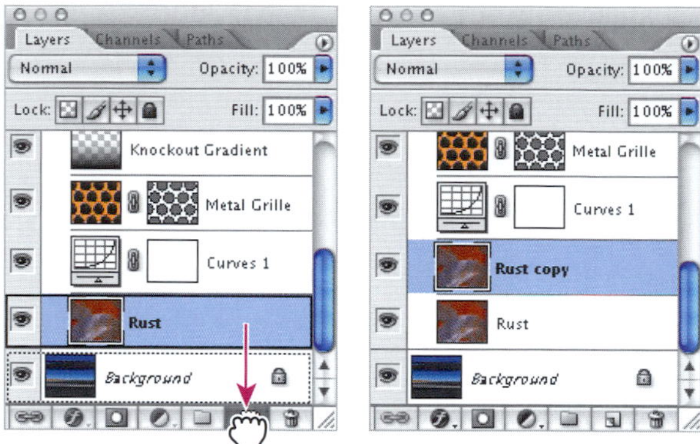

A new layer called "Rust copy" is created directly above the Rust layer in the palette.

2 Drag the Rust copy layer just above the Diesel layer inside the Words layer set.

Because Rust copy is the top layer, the rust image is all you can see in the image window.

3 Hold down Alt (Windows) or Option (Mac OS) and move the mouse pointer over the line dividing the Rust copy and Diesel layers in the Layers palette. When the pointer changes to two overlapping circles (◌), click the mouse button to create a clipping mask.

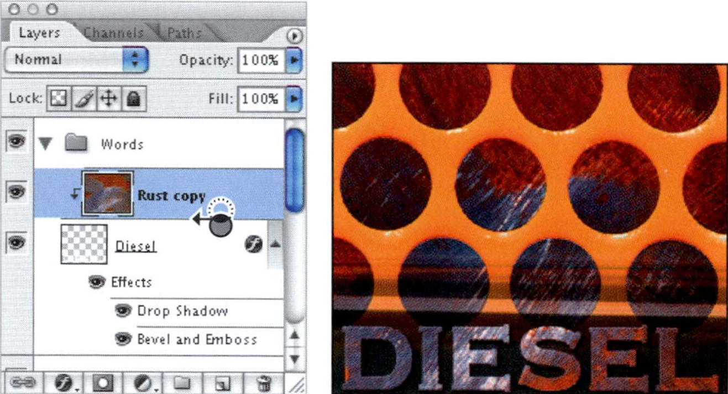

The Rust copy layer is clipped away so that it appears inside the Diesel shape and you can see the other layers in the other areas of the image.

4 Choose File > Save.

Note: *The rust layer that appears inside the Diesel lettering is separate from the rust that appears within the circular holes in the yellow grille. You can see this by clicking off the eye icon in the Rust copy layer. The rust disappears from the Diesel letters but remains visible behind the yellow metal.*

Liquifying a layer

The Liquify command adds a melted look to an image. Using it, you can interactively push, pull, rotate, reflect, pucker, and bloat any area of an image. The distortions you create can be subtle or drastic, which makes the Liquify command a powerful tool for retouching images as well as creating artistic effects. In this part of the lesson, you'll make the metal grille look as if it has melted from one side to the other.

Note: *The Liquify command is available only for 8-bit images in RGB, CMYK, Lab, and Grayscale image modes.*

Rasterizing the mask

Before you can apply the Liquify feature to the metal grille, you must rasterize its vector mask and merge the mask and image to create just one image.

1 In the Layers palette, select the Metal Grille layer in the Images layer set.

2 Choose Layer > Rasterize > Vector Mask. This converts the circles path, which is a vector graphic and resolution-independent, into a mask that is a raster image and resolution-dependent.

To view a mask by itself, Alt-click (Windows) or Option-click (Mac OS) the layer mask thumbnail in the Layers palette. Repeat to restore the view.

3 Choose Layer > Layer Mask > Apply to merge the layer with its mask, creating a single rasterized image on that layer. Notice that there is now only one thumbnail in the Layers palette for the Metal Grille layer, whereas before there were two: one for the image and one for the mask.

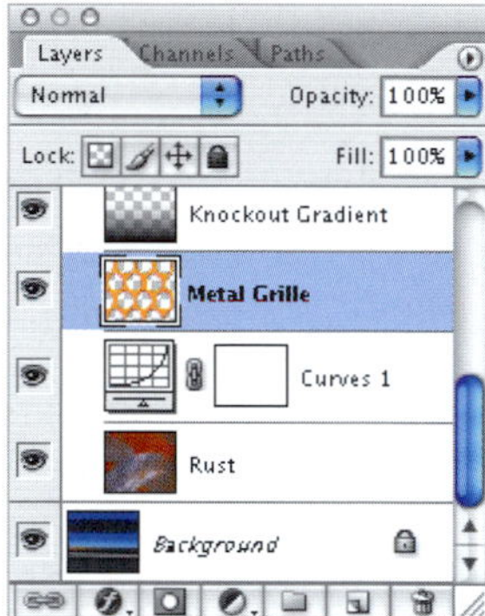

Applying the Liquify filter

The Liquify filter applies a hidden grid, or mesh, to the image. By dragging the handles of the mesh, you can distort the image. Turning on the mesh visibility can help you see more clearly how you're manipulating the grid as you use the various liquify tools.

1 With the Metal Grille layer selected in the Layers palette, choose Filter > Liquify.

2 In the Liquify dialog box, do the following:

• In the upper left corner of the dialog box, make sure that the Forward Warp tool ( ) is selected.

• On the right side of the dialog box under Tool Options, select a Brush Size that's the same size as the holes in the grille (we used 133). Then, for Brush Pressure, select a moderate value (we used 20).

• Under View Options, make sure the Show Image and Show Mesh boxes are checked, but that the Show Backdrop check box is *unchecked*.

Note: *Activating the Show Backdrop view option can be visually confusing because it shows the original, undistorted version of the Metal Grille layer in addition to the distorted version you're working on. So we will leave it unselected for this exercise.*

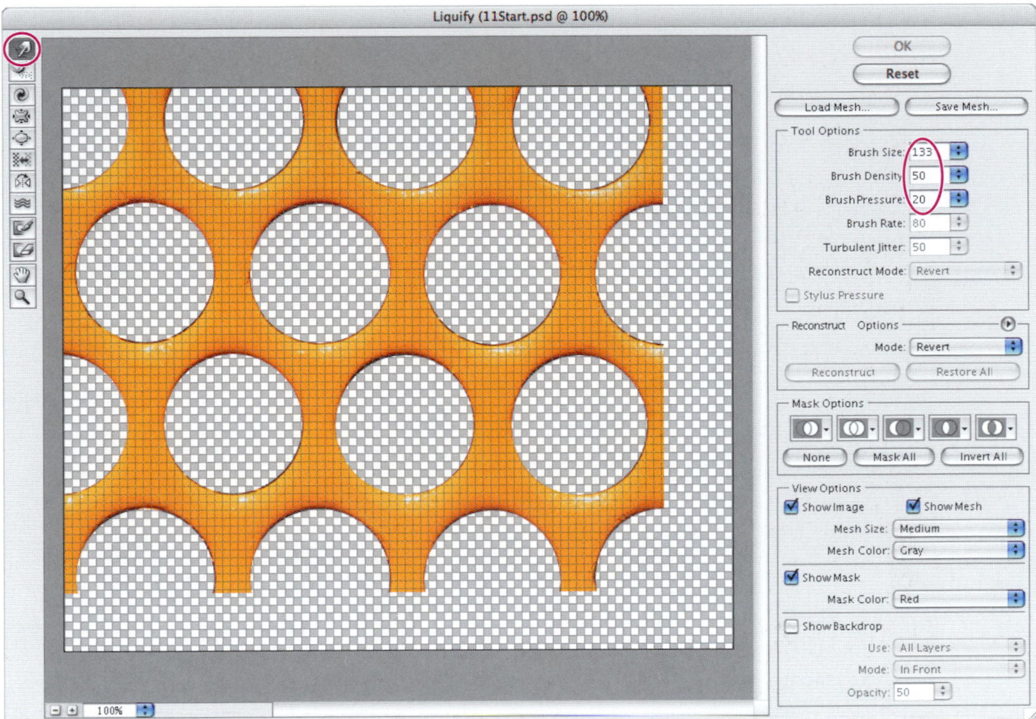

3 Drag the brush across and down the image in the Liquify dialog box to start applying the effect.

Notice how the mesh has been distorted by the Forward Warp tool. You can drag the Forward Warp Tool brush in the image some more to create different results.

Removing distortions in the Liquify dialog box

If you want to undo some or all of your distorting work, you don't have to cancel your efforts and start over completely. While the Liquify dialog box is open, you have several other choices for removing or reducing distortions from an area or from the entire image. The method you select depends on how much of your work you want to undo.

- Press Ctrl-Z (Windows) or Command-Z (Mac OS) to undo your most recent action, but only by one step.
- Select the Reconstruct tool at the left side of the dialog box and drag it across an area of the image that you want to restore to its original condition.
- Click the Reconstruct button at the right side of the dialog box to reduce the entire distortion by degrees.
- Use the Freeze Mask tool to protect an area of the image that you want to remain distorted, and then use either the Reconstruct tool or the Reconstruct button to remove or reduce the distortion of the areas that are not frozen.
- Click the Restore All button to revert to the original (undistorted) condition of the image. The Restore All button even restores frozen areas, so it is the equivalent of clicking Cancel, but it leaves the Liquify dialog box open.

You can also select different reconstruction modes in Reconstruct Options and in Tool Options. For more information, see Photoshop Help.

4 On the left side of the dialog box, select the Turbulence tool (≋), and drag the brush across another area of the metal grille image.

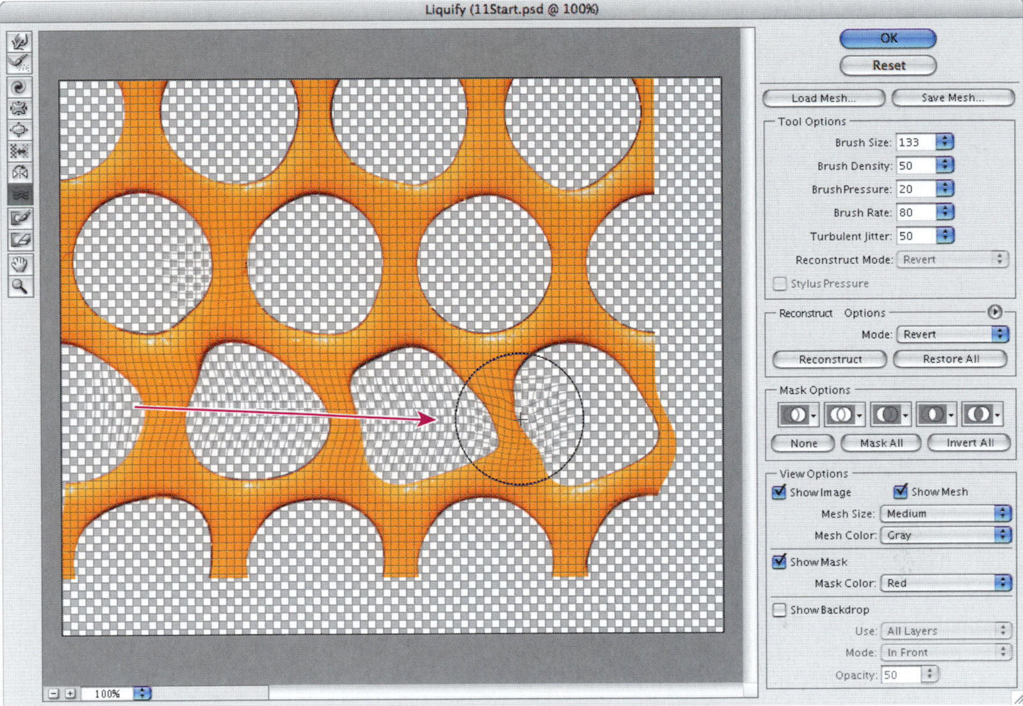

5 Move the Turbulence tool to an undistorted area of the image and hold down the mouse button for several seconds without moving the pointer.

As you hold down the mouse button, the grille appears to melt under the influence of the Turbulence tool. Look closely for other differences between the results created with the Forward Warp and Turbulence tools.

6 Continue to apply different effects to the metal grille. When you are satisfied with the results, click OK to close the Liquify dialog box, and then choose File > Save.

Creating a border layer

To give the image a finished look, you'll add a border to it.

1 Click the Create a New Layer button (▣) in the Layers palette. (It doesn't matter which layer is currently selected, because you're going to move the new layer a little later.)

2 Double-click the new Layer 1, and type **Image Border** to rename it. Then press Enter (Windows) or Return (Mac OS).

3 Drag the Image Border layer to the top of the Layers palette stack, until a black line appears immediately above the Words layer set, and then release the mouse button.

The Image Border layer is now the top layer in the image.

4 Choose Select > All to select the entire image in the image window.

5 Choose Edit > Stroke. In the Stroke area, enter **5 px** for Width and click OK. (Or, for a more dramatic black border, enter a larger number, such as **10** or **15** pixels.)
A 5-pixel-wide black stroke now appears around the entire image.

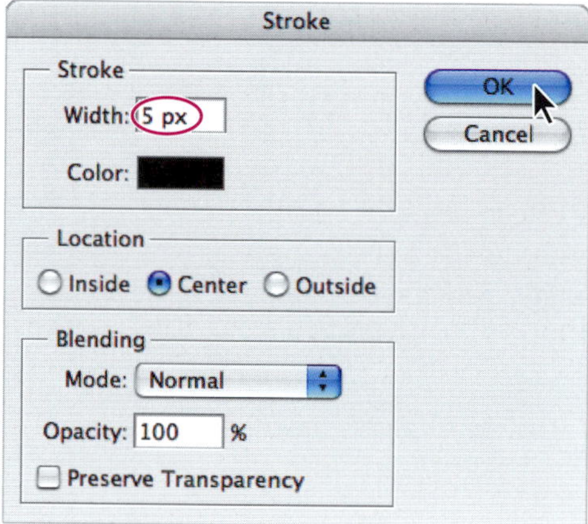

6 Choose Select > Deselect to deselect the entire image.

7 Choose File > Save.

Flattening a layered image

As you've done in previous lessons of this book, you'll now flatten the layered image. When you flatten a file, all layers are merged into a single background, greatly reducing the size of the file. If you plan to send a file out for proofs, it's a good idea to save two versions of the file—one containing all the layers so that you can edit the file if necessary, and one flattened version to send to the print shop.

1 First, note the values in the lower left corner of the image or application window. If the display does not show the file size (such as "Doc: 909K/6.4M"), click the arrow and choose Show > Document Sizes.

The first number is the printing size of the image, which is about the size that the saved, flattened file would be in Adobe Photoshop format. The number on the right indicates the approximate document size of the file as it is now, including layers and channels.

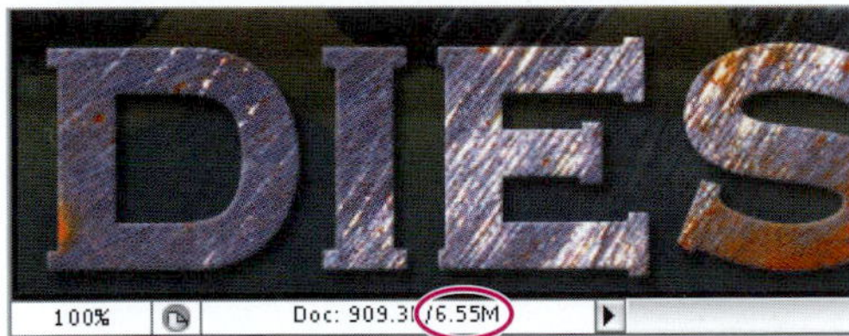

2 Choose Image > Duplicate, name the duplicate file **11Final.psd**, and click OK.

3 From the Layers palette menu, choose Flatten Image. The layers for the 11Final.psd file are combined onto a single background layer.

Now the file sizes shown in the lower left area of the work area or image window are the same smaller number that you saw earlier.

4 Choose File > Save. In the Save As dialog box that appears, click Save to save the file in Photoshop format.

Good work. You've completed the lesson.

Review

Review questions

1 Why would you use layer sets?

2 What are clipping path layers?

3 How do adjustment layers work, and what is the benefit of using them?

4 What are layer styles, and why would you use them?

Review answers

1 Layer sets allow you to organize and manage layers. For example, you can move all the layers in a layer set as a group and then apply attributes or a mask to them as a group.

2 A clipping path is when you configure the artwork on the base layer as a mask for the layer above it. In this lesson, you used the Metal Grille layer (which had holes in it created by the vector mask you created) as a clipping path for the Rust layer, so the rust appeared only in the holes in the grille. You also used the Diesel layer as a clipping path for the copy of the Rust layer, so it appeared only inside the shapes of the word.

3 An adjustment layer is a special type of Photoshop layer that works specifically with color and tonal adjustments. When you apply an adjustment layer, you can edit an image repeatedly without making a permanent change to the colors or tonal range in the image.

4 Layer styles are customizable effects that you can apply to layers. You can use them to apply changes to a layer, and you can modify or remove them at any time.

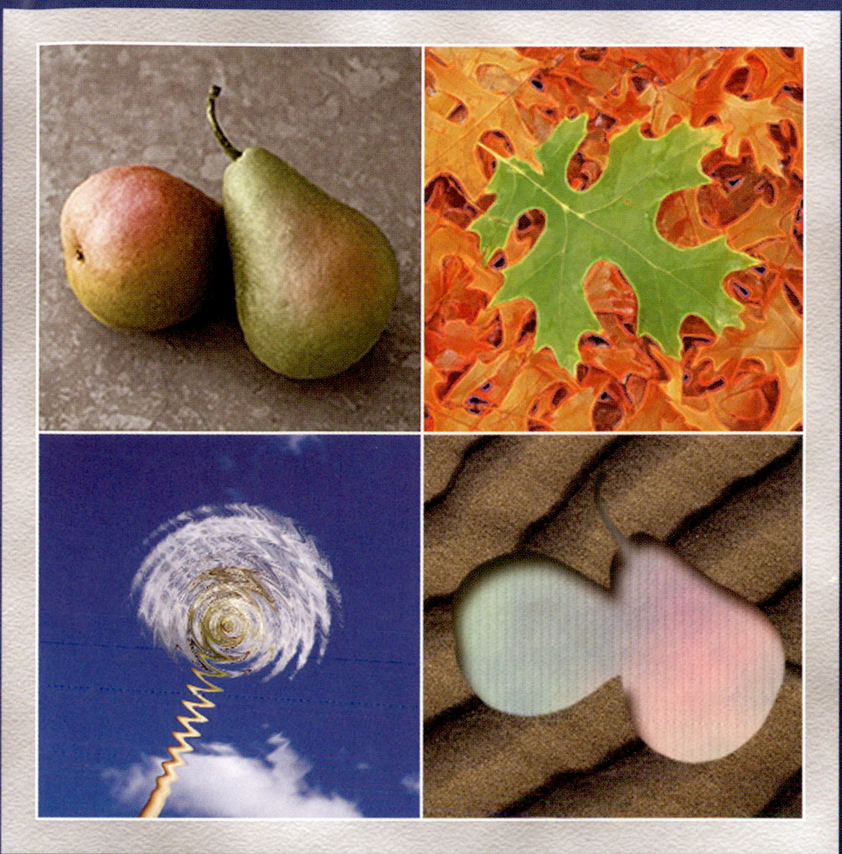

With the huge assortment of filters available for Adobe Photoshop, you can transform ordinary images into extraordinary digital artwork. You can select filters that simulate a traditional artistic medium—a watercolor, for example—or you can choose from filters that blur, bend, sharpen, or fragment images. In addition to using filters to alter images, you can use adjustment layers and painting modes to vary the look of your artwork.

12 Advanced Compositing

Lesson overview

In this lesson, you'll learn how to do the following:

- Record and play back an action to automate a series of steps.
- Add guides to help you place and align images precisely.
- Save selections and load them as masks.
- Apply color effects only to unmasked areas of an image.
- Add an adjustment layer to color-correct a selection.
- Apply filters to selections to create various effects.
- Add layer styles to create editable special effects.

This lesson will take about 90 minutes to complete. If needed, remove the previous lesson folder from your hard drive, and copy the Lessons/Lesson12 folder onto it. As you work on this lesson, you'll overwrite the start files. If you need to restore the start files, copy them from the *Adobe Photoshop CS2 Classroom in a Book* CD.

Getting started

You'll start the lesson by viewing the final lesson file, to see what you'll accomplish.

1 Start Photoshop and then immediately hold down Ctrl-Alt-Shift (Windows) or Command-Option-Shift (Mac OS) to restore the default preferences. (See "Restoring default preferences" on page 6.)

2 When prompted, click Yes to confirm that you want to reset preferences, and Close to close the Welcome Screen.

3 Click the Go to Bridge button ( ) on the tool options bar to open Adobe Bridge.

4 In the Favorites palette in the upper left corner of Bridge, click the Lessons favorite, and then double-click the Lesson12 folder in the preview area.

5 Select the 12End.psd thumbnail and examine it in the Preview palette. If necessary, enlarge the Preview palette so that you can get a good look.

This end file is a montage that comprises four pictures. Each quadrant has had a specific filter or effect applied to it.

6 Double-click the 12Start.jpg thumbnail to open it in Photoshop.

Automating a multistep task

An *action* is a set of one or more commands that you record and then play back to apply to a single file or a batch of files. In this exercise, you'll see how actions can help you save time by applying a multistep process to the four images you'll use in this project.

Using actions is one of several ways that you can automate tasks in Adobe Photoshop. To learn more about recording actions, see Photoshop Help.

Opening and cropping the files

You'll start by resizing four files. Since this part of the task involves aesthetic choices about where and how much of the image to crop, you'll do these steps manually rather than record them with the Actions palette.

1 Click the Info tab in the Navigator palette group to bring that palette forward.

2 In the toolbox, select the Crop tool (). Hold down Shift to constrain the shape to a square, and drag around the pears. When you finish dragging, be careful to release the mouse button first and then the Shift key.

Dragging and pressing Shift

Cropped image

3 Examine the width (W) and height (H) values in the Info palette. If you've drawn a perfect square, the pixel counts will be identical.

4 If necessary, make any adjustments to the selection so that the pears are centered in the cropping marquee and fit fairly snugly inside it:

- If the width and height are not equal, drag a corner until the W and H values in the Info palette are identical. (Do not hold down Shift.)
- To move the marquee, click inside it and drag until it is positioned properly.
- To resize the marquee, hold down Shift and drag one of the corners to make the marquee larger or smaller.

5 When you are satisfied with the crop selection, double-click inside the crop area, or press Enter (Windows) or Return (Mac OS) to apply the cropping.

Because you're working with a number of files, you'll rename the 12Start.jpg file with a descriptive name so that it will be easy to identify.

6 Choose File > Save As, and save the cropped image as **Pears.jpg** in your Lesson12 folder. If a dialog box appears with options for image quality, click OK to accept the default settings.

7 Repeat Steps 2 through 5 for the three other JPEG images in the Lesson12 folder: Leaves.jpg, Dandelion.jpg, and Sand.jpg, and then choose File > Save instead of Save As to save each of the files. (You don't need to rename them.)

Note: *It is not necessary to make all the cropped images the same size. You will adjust their sizes again later in this lesson.*

Cropped versions of the Leaves, Dandelion, and Sand JPEG files

Leave all the newly cropped files open for the next procedures.

Preparing to record an action

You use the Actions palette to record, play, edit, and delete individual actions. You also use the Actions palette to save and load action files. You'll start this task by opening a new document and preparing to record a new action in the Actions palette.

1 Click the Actions tab in the History palette group to bring the Actions palette forward, or choose Window > Actions to accomplish the same thing.

2 At the bottom of the Actions palette, click the Create New Set button ( ). Or, create a new set by choosing New Set from the Actions palette menu.

3 In the New Set dialog box, type **My Actions**, and click OK.

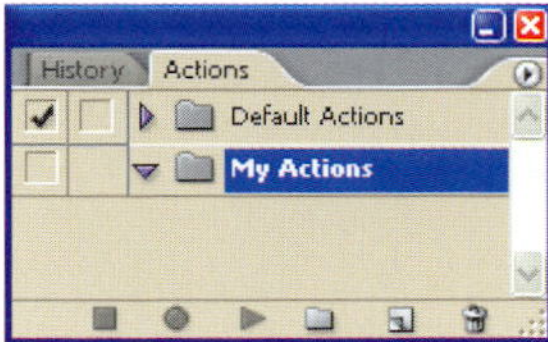

4 Choose Window > Dandelion.jpg to make that file active.

Recording a new action set

For this project, you'll want the images to be identical sizes and for each to have a narrow white border. You'll perform those tasks now on the dandelion image. You'll start by setting the image dimensions to a specific number of pixels, and then you'll apply a stroke to the image. As you work, you'll set up the Actions palette to record each step of the process.

Note: *It is important that you finish all the steps in this procedure without interruption. If you become distracted and need to start over, skip ahead to Step 10 to stop the recording. Then, you can delete the action by dragging it onto the Delete button (🗑) in the Actions palette, and start again at Step 1.*

1 In the Actions palette, click the Create New Action button (▣) or choose New Action from the Actions palette menu.

2 In the New Action dialog box, type **Size & Stroke** in the Name field and make sure that My Actions is selected from the Set pop-up menu. Then click Record.

Note: *Take all the time you need to do this procedure accurately. The speed at which you work has no influence on the amount of time required to play a recorded action.*

3 Choose Image > Image Size.

4 Make sure that both the Constrain Proportions and the Resample Image check boxes are selected at the bottom of the Image Size dialog box. For the Width, type **275**, and make sure that pixels is selected as the unit of measurement. Then click OK.

5 Choose Select > All.

6 Choose Edit > Stroke.

7 In the Stroke dialog box, make sure that the following options are selected, or select them now:

- Width should be **1** pixel.
- In the Color swatch, use white, or select it by clicking the swatch to open the Color Picker, selecting white (C, M, Y, and K = 0), and clicking OK to close the picker.
- For Location, leave Center selected.
- For Blending, leave Mode set to Normal and Opacity set at 100%.

8 Then click OK to close the Stroke dialog box.

9 Choose Select > Deselect.

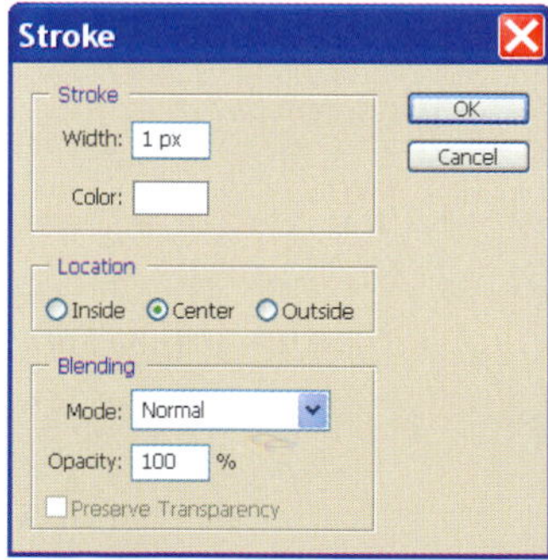

Stroke dialog box settings and resulting border on image

10 In the Actions palette, click the Stop button (■) at the bottom of the palette to stop recording steps. Save your work.

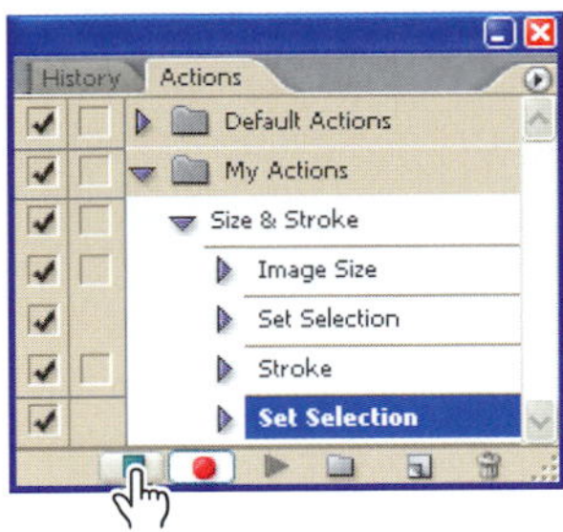

Your action is now saved in the Actions palette. You can click the arrows to the left of the My Actions set, the Size & Stroke action, and beside each step of that action to expand and collapse them at your convenience. With these expanded, you can examine each recorded step and the specific selections you made. When you finish reviewing the action, click the arrows to collapse the steps.

Playing an action on an individual file

Now that you've recorded the process of setting the image size and stroke characteristics for the dandelion image, you can use the action as an automated task. You'll apply the Stroke & Size action to one of the other three image files that you cropped earlier in this lesson.

1 If the Leaves.jpg, Pears.jpg, and Sand.jpg files are not still open, use Adobe Bridge or choose File > Open and open them now.

2 Choose Window > Document > Sand.jpg to make that image active.

3 In the Actions palette, select the Size & Stroke action in the My Actions set, and then click the Play button (▶), or choose Play from the Actions palette menu.

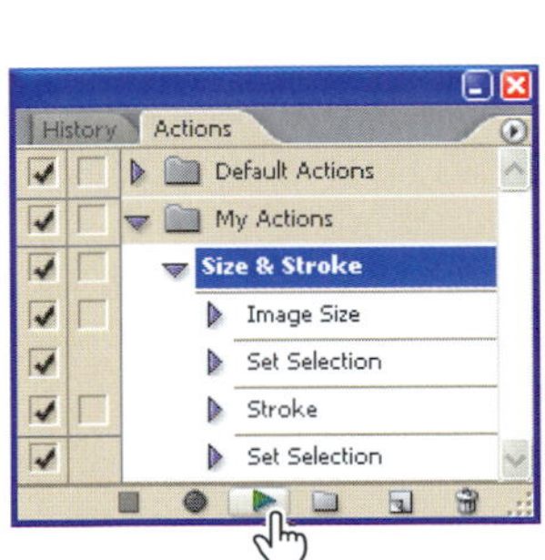

The Sand.jpg image is automatically resized and given a stroke so that it now matches the Dandelion.jpg image for these properties.

4 Choose File > Save.

Batch-playing an action

Applying actions is a time-saving process for performing routine tasks on files, but you can streamline your work even further by applying actions to all open files. Two more files in this project need to be resized and given strokes, so you'll apply your automated action to them simultaneously.

1 Close the Dandelion.jpg and Sand.jpg files, saving the changes if you're prompted. Make sure that only the Pears.jpg and Leaves.jpg files are open.

2 Choose File > Automate > Batch.

3 Under the Play section of the Batch dialog box, make sure that My Actions is chosen for Set, and that Size & Stroke is chosen for Action.

4 In the Source pop-up menu, choose Opened Files.

5 Leave Destination set as None, and click OK.

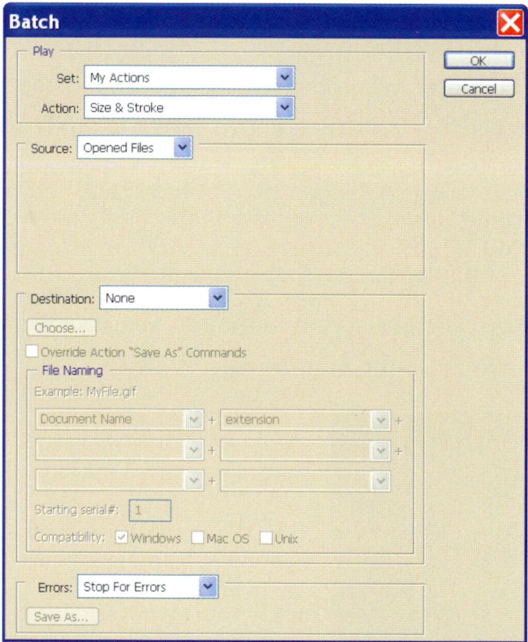

The action is applied to both the pears and leaves images, so the files have identical dimensions and strokes.

6 Choose File > Save and then File > Close for each of the two open files.

In this exercise, you batch-processed two files instead of making all the same changes in each of them; this was a mild convenience. But creating and applying actions can save significant amounts of time and tedium when you have dozens or even hundreds of files that require any routine, repetitive work.

Setting up a four-image montage

Now that you've finished preparing the four images, you'll place them together in a new composite image. Using guides, you'll be able to align the images precisely without a lot of effort.

Adding guides

Guides are nonprinting lines that help you align elements in your document, either horizontally or vertically. You can choose a Snap To command so that the guides behave like magnets: When you drag an object close to a guide, it will snap into place along the guide when you release the mouse button.

1 Use Bridge or choose File > Open to open the Montage.psd file in the Lesson12 folder.

2 Choose View > Rulers. A vertical ruler appears along the left side of the window and a horizontal ruler appears along the top of the window.

Note: *If the ruler units are not inches, choose Edit > Preferences > Units & Rulers (Windows) or Photoshop > Preferences > Units & Rulers (Mac OS); choose Rulers > Inches; and then click OK.*

3 If the Info palette is not visible, click the Info tab or choose Window > Info to bring it forward in its palette group.

4 Drag down from the horizontal ruler to the middle of the image window, watching the Info palette to see the Y coordinate as you drag. Release the mouse when Y = 3.000 inches. A blue guide line appears across the middle of the window.

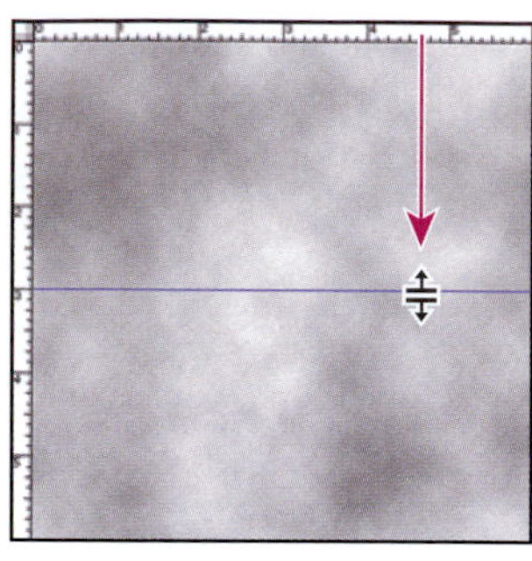

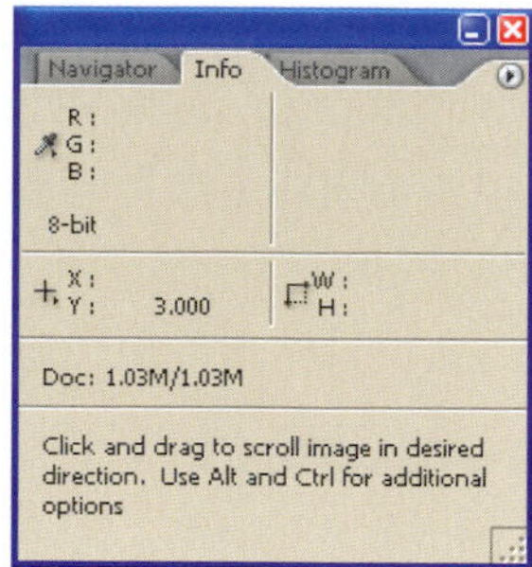

5 Drag another guide from the vertical ruler to the middle of the image and release the mouse when X = 3.000 inches.

6 Choose View > Snap To, and make sure that the Guides command is checked, or select it now.

7 Choose View > Rulers to hide the rulers again.

Snapping images into position

Your guides are in place, so you're ready to arrange your four cropped images in the montage.

1 Choose File > Open Recent > Pears.jpg. The pears image opens in a separate image window.

2 In the toolbox, select the Move tool (![Move tool icon]).

3 Click the Move tool anywhere in the pear image and drag from that image window to the larger Montage.jpg window, and then release the mouse button.

4 Still using the Move tool, drag the pears image into the upper left quadrant of the montage image so that its lower right corner snaps into place against the intersection of the two guides at the center of the window.

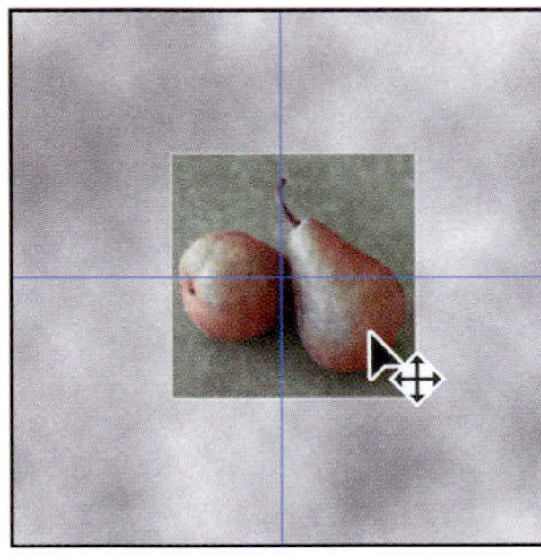

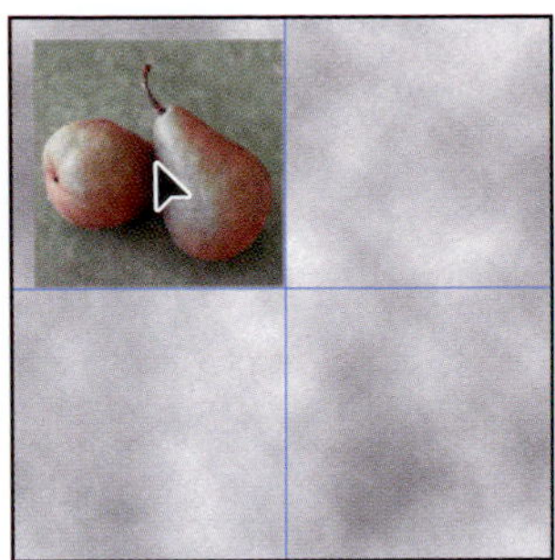

In the Layers palette, you'll notice that the pears image is on a new layer, Layer 1.

5 Choose Window > Pears.jpg to make it active again, and then close it, either by clicking the red Close button or by choosing File > Close.

6 Repeat Steps 1–5 for the three other cropped files, placing the leaves image in the upper right quadrant, the dandelion in the lower left quadrant, and the sand in the lower right quadrant. All the images should snugly abut the intersection of the guides in the center of the window.

7 Choose View > Show > Guides to hide the guides.

EXTRA CREDIT Precise alignment using Smart Guides. Although we were able to easily align the four images using centered guides, Smart Guides are an excellent way to align photos and objects with greater precision. Using your working file as it is after the "Snapping images into position" exercise, you can experiment with another way to align these photos, or you can continue with your lesson and try this technique some other time.

1 Select the dandelion layer. Drag in the image window with the Move tool to move it out of alignment. Repeat for the leaves and sand layers. (The images will have different layer numbers, depending on the order in which you created them.)

2 Choose View Show > Smart Guides.

3 Select the sand layer, and (still using the Move tool) drag to line up its left edge with the right edge of the dandelion layer. Pink Smart Guides appear when the images are aligned.

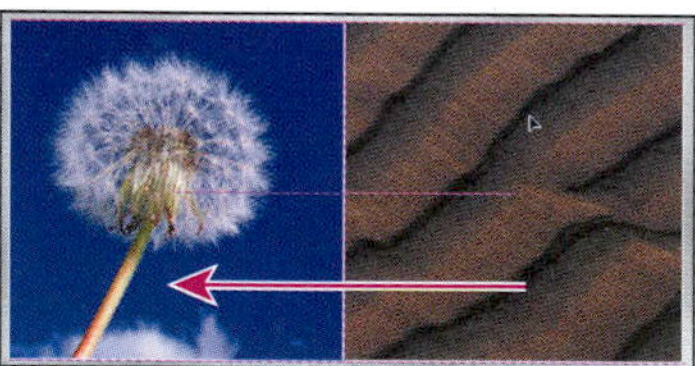

4 Next, select the dandelion layer and then Shift-click to also select the sand layer. Use the Move tool in the image window to move them together so that the top of the dandelion image aligns with the bottom of the pear image.

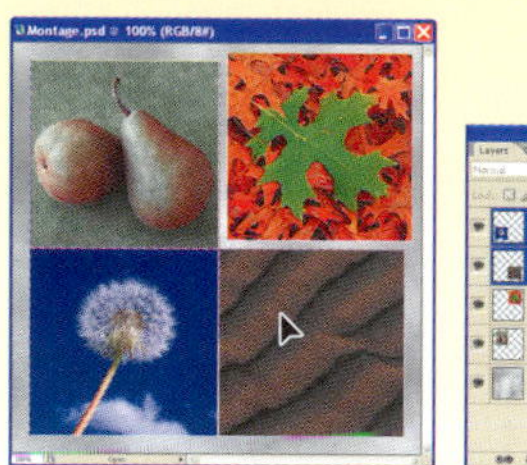

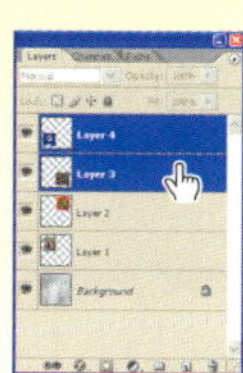

5 Select the leaves layer and drag to square it up with the other three images, as in the illustration below. Smart Guides will show you when each image is aligned in Steps 3, 4, and 5.

6 Choose View > Show > Smart Guides to turn off the Smart Guides when you're done.

Saving selections

Next, you'll select the two pears and save the selections. Later in this lesson, you'll use your saved selections to colorize the pears and to add a special effect.

1 In the toolbox, select the Zoom tool (), and drag a marquee around the pears to magnify your view. Make sure that you can see all of both pears in the image window.

2 Select the Magnetic Lasso tool (), hidden under the Lasso tool ().

For best results when tracing the pear stem with the Magnetic Lasso tool, decrease the tool's lasso Width and Frequency values on the tool options bar. For example, try tracing the pear using a Width of **1** or **2** pixels and a Frequency of **40**.

3 Click once to set a point on the edge of the pear on the right, and then move the pointer (you do not need to hold down the mouse button) around the pear to trace its outline.

As you move the pointer, the active segment snaps to the strongest edge in the image. Periodically, the Magnetic Lasso tool adds fastening points to the selection border to anchor sections. Try to make your selection a reasonably accurate outline of the pear, but don't worry if it's not perfect.

You can also click the Magnetic Lasso tool as you trace the outline to add your own fastening points. This might be especially helpful around the stem or where the highlights or shadows make the edge between the pear and the background less distinct.

4 When you get back to your starting point and a small circle appears in the lower right area of the Magnetic Lasso pointer (), click to close the segment.

If you want to fix any flaws in the selection, try switching to Quick Mask mode and using the techniques you learned in Lesson 7, "Masks and Channels."

5 Choose Select > Save Selection. Name the selection **Right Pear**, and click OK to save the selection in a new channel.

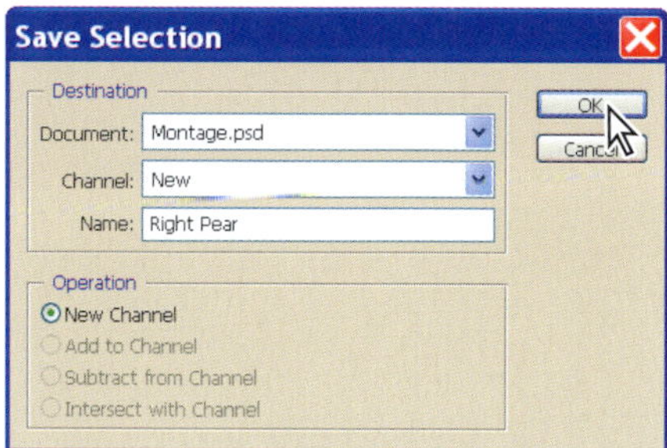

6 Choose Select > Deselect to deselect the right pear.

7 Repeat Steps 2–6, this time selecting the left pear and saving the selection as **Left Pear**. Then choose Select > Deselect, or press Ctrl-D (Windows) or Command-D (Mac OS).

8 To see your two saved selections, click the Channels tab to open the palette, and scroll down, if necessary. Click each pear channel name in turn to see the channel masks appear in the image window.

9 When you're ready to continue working, scroll to the top of the Channels palette and click the RGB channel to select it, and click to remove the eye icons from the Right Pear and Left Pear channels, if necessary. Then, click the Layers tab to bring that palette forward for the next procedure.

Hand-coloring selections on a layer

You'll start to add special effects to your montage by hand-coloring the pears, beginning with the pear on the right. To select it, you'll simply load the first selection you created in the previous procedure. Then, you'll remove the color from the selection so that you can color it by hand. Finally, after adding a layer above the pears, you'll be ready to apply new color by adding it to the new layer. In this way, you can simply erase the layer and start over if you don't like the results.

Desaturating a selection

You'll use the Desaturate command to remove the color from the selected pear area. Saturation is the presence or absence of color in a selection. When you desaturate a selection within an image, you create a grayscale-like effect without affecting the colors in other parts of the image.

1 In the Layers palette, select Layer 1, the layer with the pears image.

2 Choose Select > Load Selection.

3 In the Load Selection dialog box, choose Right Pear from the Channel pop-up menu, and click OK. A selection border appears around the right pear in your image.

Load Selection
Source
Document: Montage.psd
Channel: Layer 1 Transparency
Layer 1 Transparency
Right Pear
Left Pear
OK
Cancel
Operation
New Selection
Add to Selection
Subtract from Selection
Intersect with Selection

4 Choose Image > Adjustments > Desaturate. The color is removed from the selection.

5 Choose Select > Deselect.

6 Choose File > Save to save your work. If you get a compatibility warning, click OK.

Creating a layer and choosing a blending mode

Now, you'll add a layer and specify a layer blending mode for painting the desaturated pear image. By painting on a separate layer, you won't permanently alter the image. This makes it easy to start over if you aren't satisfied with the results.

Layer blending modes determine how the pixels in a layer blend with underlying pixels on other layers. By applying modes to individual layers, you can create a variety of special effects.

1 In the Layers palette, click the Create a New Layer button (▣) to add Layer 5 to the image, just above Layer 1 in the palette.

2 Double-click Layer 5, type **Paint** to rename the layer, and press Enter (Windows) or Return (Mac OS).

3 In the Layers palette, choose Color from the Blending Mode pop-up menu to the left of the Opacity text box.

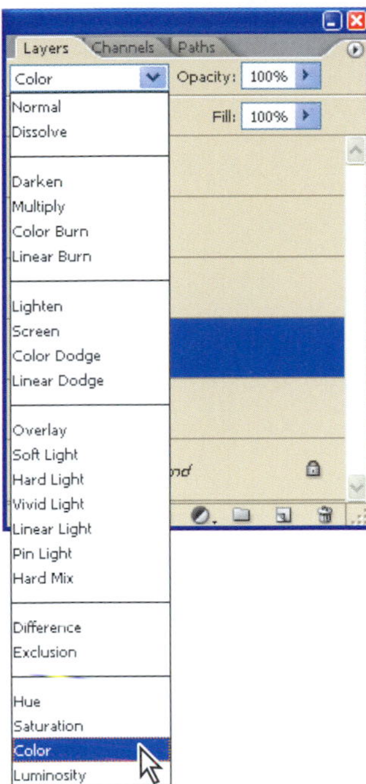

***Note:** If you ever want to delete a layer, you can drag it to the Trash button at the bottom of the Layers palette. Or, simply select the layer you want to delete and then click the Trash button and, when prompted, confirm that you want to delete the layer.*

You can use the Color mode to change the hue of a selection without affecting the highlights and shadows. This means that you can apply a variety of color tints without changing the original highlights and shadows of the pears.

Applying painting effects

To begin painting, you must again load the selection that you created earlier. By loading the Right Pear channel, you protect the unselected areas of the image as you apply colors, making it easy to paint within the lines.

1 Choose Select > Load Selection. In the Load Selection dialog box, choose Channel > Right Pear, and click OK.

Notice in the Load Selection dialog box that the color-mode change you just made also was saved as a selection, called *Paint Transparency*.

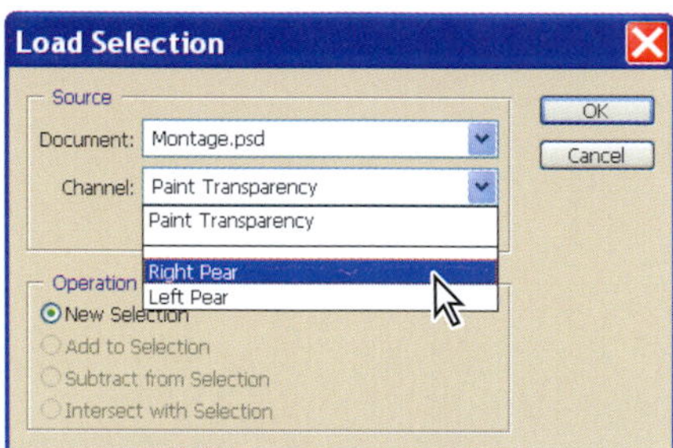

2 Select the Brush tool ( ). Then, on the tool options bar, type, scrub, or drag the slider to set the Opacity to about 50%.

Change the brush opacity by pressing a number on the keypad from 0 to 9 (where 1 is 10%, 9 is 90%, and 0 is 100%).

3 In the Brush pop-up palette, select a large soft-edged brush, such as the Soft Round 35-pixel brush. Click off the palette to close it.

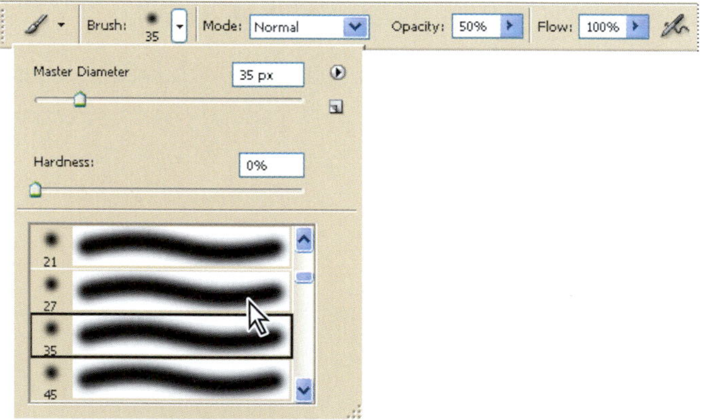

4 Choose Window > Swatches to bring the Swatches palette forward (or click its tab in the Color palette group), and then select any yellow-green color that appeals to you as your foreground color.

5 Drag the brush over the entire pear to apply the color.

Next, you'll use a darker and a lighter shade to add highlights and shadows.

6 Select a darker green from the Swatches palette. On the tool options bar, set the brush opacity to about 30%. Paint around the edges in the pear selection, avoiding the highlight area.

7 Select a rose color from the Swatches palette. On the tool options bar, select a smaller brush size and decrease the opacity to about 20%. Then, paint highlights on the pear.

8 When you are satisfied with your results, choose Select > Deselect, and then choose File > Save.

Adding a gradient

Now you'll use the Gradient tool to add a gradient to the other pear for a highlight effect. First, you'll need to load the selection of the left pear that you made earlier.

1 Choose Select > Load Selection. Choose Channel > Left Pear in the Load Selection dialog box, and click OK. A selection border appears around the left pear in your image.

2 Click the Color palette tab to bring it forward, and then select red as the foreground color by typing or dragging the R slider to **255** and the G and B sliders to **0**.

3 Click the Set Background Color icon in the upper left area of the Color palette and then select yellow as the background color by setting R and G at **255** and B at **0**.

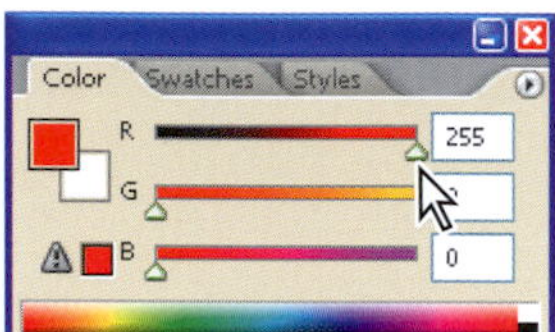

Foreground color

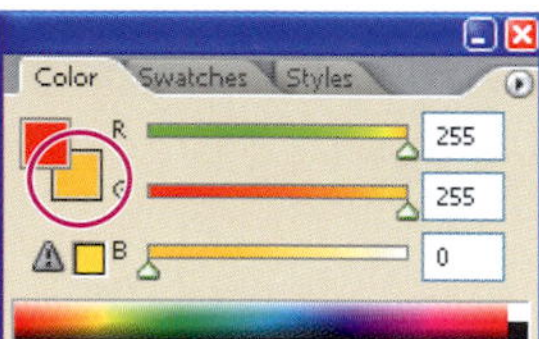

Background color

Note: *The alert triangle in the lower left corner of the Color palette indicates that the selected RGB color may not print. Since we're not printing, don't worry if you see this warning. For more information about color gamuts, see Lesson 16, "Producing and Printing Consistent Color," and Photoshop Help.*

4 Select the Gradient tool (). On the tool options bar, do the following:

- Select the Radial Gradient button.
- Open the gradient picker and make sure that Foreground to Background is selected, so the color blends from the foreground color (red) to the background color (yellow).
- Set the Opacity to **40%**.

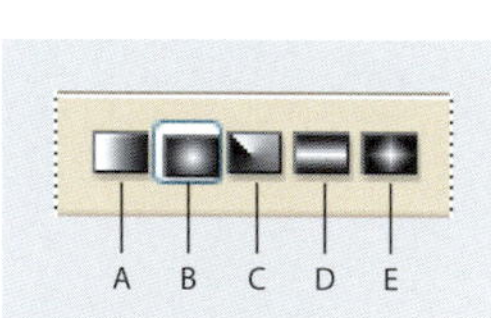

A. *Linear gradient*
B. *Radial gradient*
C. *Angle gradient*
D. *Reflected gradient*
E. *Diamond gradient*

Selecting Foreground to Background

5 Position the Gradient tool near the pear's highlight, and drag toward the stem end.

6 When you're satisfied with the results, choose Select > Deselect.

Merging layers

The next task, merging layers, helps you to keep the file size relatively small. However, after you merge, you cannot easily go back and restore the image or start the process over, so be sure that you are happy with your results before you choose a merge command.

1 In the Layers palette, make sure that the Paint layer is selected.

2 Choose Layer > Merge Down to merge the Paint layer with the pear-image layer (Layer 1) below it.

Now the two layers are fused as Layer 1.

3 Double-click the Hand tool (✋) so that the entire image fits in the image window, or double-click the Zoom tool (🔍) to set the view to 100%.

4 Choose File > Save.

Changing the color balance

Now, you'll use an adjustment layer to adjust the color balance on the leaves image.

Altering the color for a channel or a regular layer permanently changes the pixels on that layer. However, with an adjustment layer, your color and tonal changes reside only within the adjustment layer and do not alter any pixels in the layers beneath it. The effect is as if you were viewing the visible layers through the adjustment layer above them. By using adjustment layers, you can try out color and tonal adjustments without permanently changing pixels in the image. You can also use adjustment layers to affect multiple layers at once.

1 In the Layers palette, select the layer containing the leaves (in the upper right quadrant of the montage).

In our example this is Layer 2, but it may be on another layer in your file if you placed the images into the montage in a different sequence.

2 Choose Layer > New Adjustment Layer > Color Balance.

3 In the New Layer dialog box, select the Use Previous Layer to Create Clipping Mask check box, which ensures that your adjustment layer will affect only the leaves image, not the other three sections of the montage. Then click OK to create the adjustment layer with the default name, Color Balance 1.

The Color Balance dialog box opens, where you can change the mixture of colors in a color image and make general color corrections. When you adjust the color balance, you can keep the same tonal balance, which you'll do here. You can also focus changes on the shadows, midtones, or highlights.

4 Move the dialog box so that you can see the leaves in the image window and make sure that the Preview check box is selected.

5 Experiment with different Color Levels for the image, such as +10, –20, and –20.

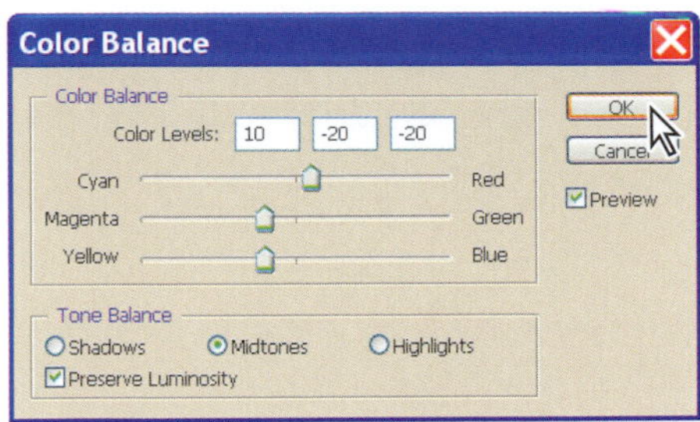

6 When you are happy with the result, click OK, and then save your work.

Adjustment layers act as layer masks, which can be edited repeatedly without permanently affecting the underlying image. You can double-click an adjustment layer thumbnail to display the last settings used, and you can adjust adjustment layers as often as you like. You can delete an adjustment layer by dragging it to the Trash button at the bottom of the Layers palette.

Applying filters

Next, you'll apply two filters to the leaves and dandelion images. Because there are so many filters for creating special effects, the best way to learn about them is to try out different filters and filter options.

Improving performance with filters

Some filter effects can be memory-intensive, especially when applied to a high-resolution image. You can use these techniques to improve performance:

- Try out filters and settings on a small portion of an image.
- Apply the effect to individual channels—for example, to each RGB channel—if the image is large and you're having problems with insufficient memory. (With some filters, effects vary if applied to the individual channel rather than the composite channel, especially if the filter randomly modifies pixels.)
- Free up memory before running the filter by using the Purge commands.
- Allocate more RAM to Photoshop (Mac OS). You can also close other open applications to make more memory available to Photoshop.
- Try changing settings to improve the speed of memory-intensive filters such as Lighting Effects, Cutout, Stained Glass, Chrome, Ripple, Spatter, Sprayed Strokes, and Glass filters. For example, with the Stained Glass filter, increase cell size. With the Cutout filter, increase Edge Simplicity, decrease Edge Fidelity, or both.
- If you plan to print to a grayscale printer, convert a copy of the image to grayscale before applying filters. However, applying a filter to a color image and then converting to grayscale may not have the same effect as applying the filter to a grayscale version of the image.

Applying the Accented Edges filter

The Accented Edges filter exaggerates the margins between areas with different colors.

1 In the Layers palette, select the layer with the leaves image. Make sure that you select the layer itself and not the adjustment layer.

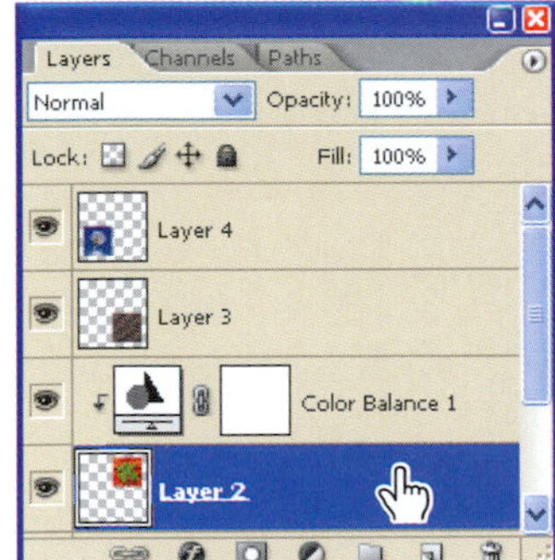

2 Choose Filter > Brush Strokes > Accented Edges. In the upper right corner of the Accented Edges dialog box, set Edge Width to 1, Edge Brightness to 30, and Smoothness to 3. Then click OK to close the dialog box.

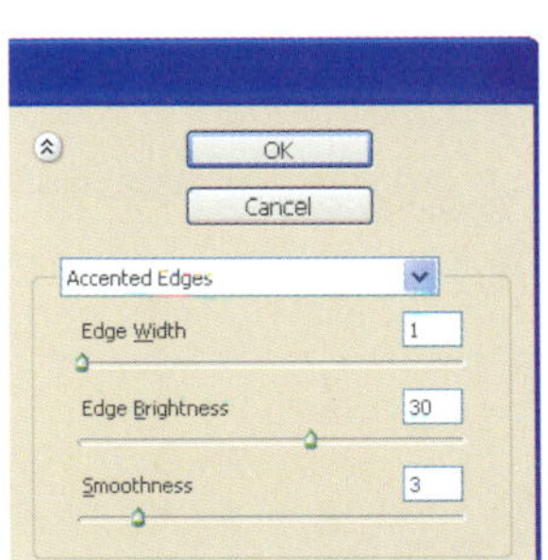

Using filters

To use a filter, choose the appropriate submenu command from the Filter menu. These guidelines can help you in choosing filters:

- The last filter chosen appears at the top of the Filter menu.
- Filters are applied to the active, visible layer.
- Filters cannot be applied to bitmap-mode or indexed-color images.
- Some filters work only on RGB images.
- Some filters are processed entirely in RAM.
- See "Using filters" in Photoshop Help for a list of filters that can be used with 16- and 32-bit-per-channel images.

Applying the ZigZag filter

Next, you'll use the ZigZag filter to create the impression that the dandelion is reflected on the surface of a rippled pool of water.

1 In the Layers palette, select the layer with the dandelion image.

2 In the toolbox, select the Elliptical Marquee tool (◯), which is hidden behind the Rectangular Marquee tool (⬚).

3 Drag across the dandelion image to select most of the seed head and stem, but do not extend the selection to the borders of the image.

The selection restricts the area that the filter will affect within the dandelion-image layer. If the selection is too large, the border will also be wavy and start to overlap the other quadrants of the montage image.

4 Choose Filter > Distort > ZigZag.

5 At the bottom of the ZigZag dialog box, make sure that Pond Ripples is selected in the Style pop-up menu. Then, experiment with different settings for Amount and Ridges by dragging the sliders. (The example uses 10% for Amount and 11 for Ridges.)

6 When you are satisfied with the result, click OK.

7 Choose Select > Deselect, and then File > Save to save your work.

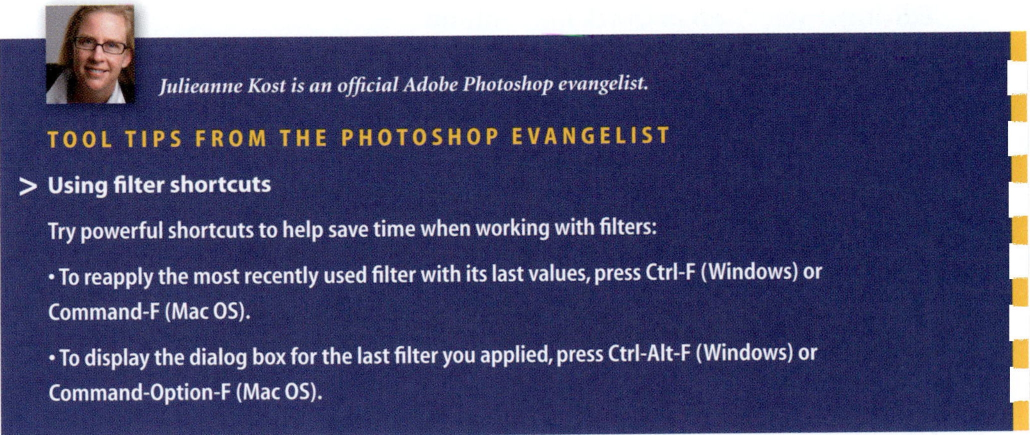

Julieanne Kost is an official Adobe Photoshop evangelist.

TOOL TIPS FROM THE PHOTOSHOP EVANGELIST

> Using filter shortcuts

Try powerful shortcuts to help save time when working with filters:

• To reapply the most recently used filter with its last values, press Ctrl-F (Windows) or Command-F (Mac OS).

• To display the dialog box for the last filter you applied, press Ctrl-Alt-F (Windows) or Command-Option-F (Mac OS).

Combining selections

Before you apply a filter to the remaining image quadrant—the sand—you'll load and combine the two selections you made earlier of the individual pears. By applying these selections to a different part of the image, you can create interesting and unusual results.

1 Choose Select > Load Selection.

2 In the Channel pop-up menu in the Load Selection dialog box, choose Right Pear and click OK.

3 Repeat Step 2, but this time select Left Pear as the Channel and select the Add to Selection option. Click OK.

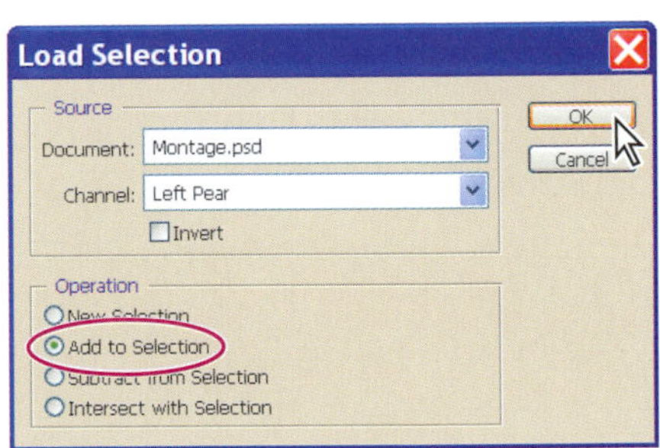

Now both pears are selected.

Editing a selection in Quick Mask mode

When you combine selections as you've just done, small unselected gaps may remain between the two loaded selections. In this exercise, you'll review the selection and repair any holes that may be there.

1 Using the Zoom tool (🔍), zoom in to the image so that the area where the two pears overlap fills the image window.

2 In the toolbox, click the Quick Mask Mode button (◙), or press Q to select it with the keyboard shortcut.

Areas in the image that are not included in the selection appear with a red tint.

You can double-click the Quick Mask Mode button to open the Quick Mask Options dialog box, where you can change the opacity and color of the tint that indicates the unselected areas.

3 Look closely at the area where the pears overlap to see if any red pixels are there.

4 In the toolbox, make sure that the foreground and background colors are black and white, respectively, or click the small Default Foreground and Background Colors button to reset them.

5 Select the Eraser tool (◪) and drag it over the area between the two pears to erase any red that appears there. If necessary, you can adjust the diameter of the Eraser tool on the tool options bar. Continue erasing until there are no more red pixels in that area.

Leave the selection active for the next procedure.

Moving a selection

Your next task is simple: Move the selection to another area of the image. This sets the stage for the final work, creating a different effect in the shape of the pears.

1 In the toolbox, click the Standard Mode button (), or press Q.

2 Double-click the Zoom tool () so that the image is at 100%.

3 Select the Rectangular Marquee tool (), which may be hidden under the Elliptical Marquee tool ().

4 Move the pointer inside the pear selection and then drag the selection marquee (not the pear images) into the lower right quadrant, centering it over the sand image.

If you want to move the selection at exactly a 45-degree angle, start dragging and then hold down Shift. Release the mouse button first, then the Shift key.

Be careful not to deselect yet, because you'll need this selection for the next exercise.

Creating a cutout effect

Next, you'll use your selection and some layer styles to create the illusion of a cutout in the sand image. Make sure that your combined-pears-shaped selection is still active. If you have accidentally deselected, you'll have to start this process over, beginning with "Combining selections" on page 363.

1 In the Layers palette, select the layer with the sand image.

2 Choose Layer > New > Layer via Copy to create a new layer above the original sand layer, based on your combined selection. The new layer automatically becomes the active layer in the Layers palette, and the pears-shaped marquee disappears.

You can quickly create a selection marquee around a layer by Ctrl-clicking (Windows) or Command-clicking (Mac OS) the layer thumbnail in the Layers palette. You can try this with the new Layer 5 to make the pear marquee reappear. Before you continue with this lesson, choose Select > Deselect.

3 At the bottom of the Layers palette, click the Add a Layer Style button (●) and then choose Pattern Overlay from the pop-up menu.

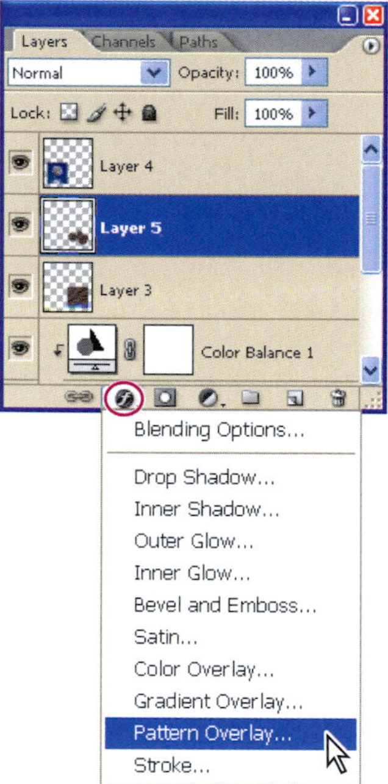

4 Drag the Layer Style dialog box aside, as needed, so that you can see both the dialog box and the image window.

5 Click the Pattern arrow (in the long, narrow button to the right of the thumbnail) to open the pattern picker, which displays smaller thumbnails of an assortment of patterns.

6 Click the arrow button (●) to open the palette menu for the pattern picker, and choose Load Patterns.

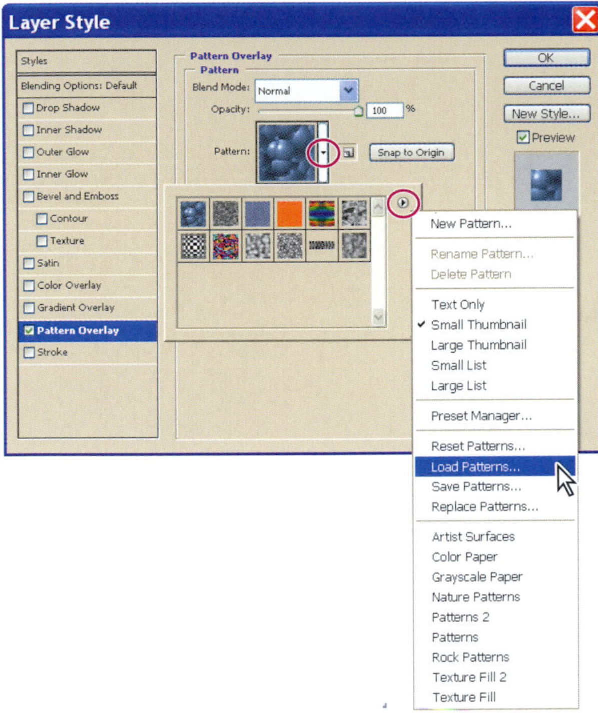

7 In the Load dialog box, go to the Lessons/Lesson12 folder and select the Effects.pat file. Click Load. When the dialog box closes, notice the new pattern that appears as the last thumbnail in the pattern picker.

8 Select the pattern thumbnail you added in Step 7. The pattern replaces the default pattern inside your pears selection. At this point, you can drag the pattern in the image window to adjust the area of the pattern that appears in the selection—even with the Layer Style dialog box open.

9 On the left side of the Layer Style dialog box, under Styles, select Inner Shadow to add that effect to the selection, and adjust the Inner Shadow options to your liking. (The example uses the default settings for Blend Mode, Opacity, and Angle, but uses 13 for Distance and 10 for Size.)

10 You can continue to experiment with other styles and settings until you create results that you think are interesting. When you are satisfied with the results, click OK.

11 Choose File > Save to save your work.

For specific information on individual filters, see Photoshop Help.

Matching color schemes across images

In this final task, you'll harmonize the color schemes in the four images by matching the target image to the dominant colors in a source.

1 Scroll down the Layers palette to the Background layer and click the eye icon () to hide that layer. If the Background layer is selected, select any other layer.

2 From the Layers palette menu, choose Merge Visible.

The Layers palette is reduced to two layers: Background and a merged layer with the same name as the layer that was selected at the end of Step 1.

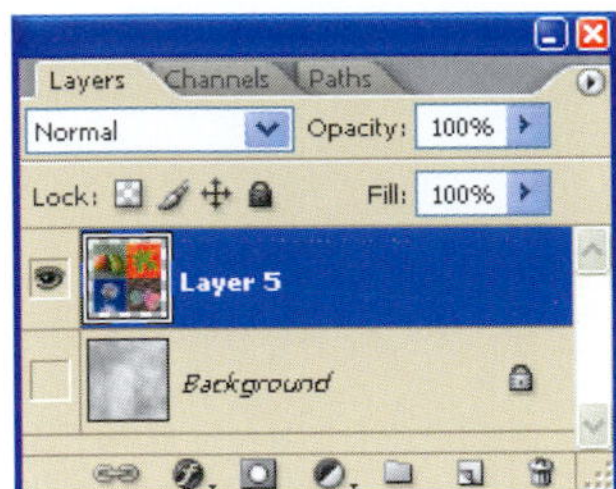

Next, you have to open the document that will be the source for the color match adjustment—the 12End.psd file that you previewed at the beginning of the lesson. It has all of the unmerged layers intact.

3 Use Adobe Bridge or the File > Open command to open the 12End.psd file, located in the Lesson12 folder.

4 Make Montage.psd the active image file, and then choose Image > Adjustments > Match Color. In the Match Color dialog box, do the following:

- Select the Preview option, if it is not already selected.
- Choose 12End.psd from the Source pop-up menu.
- From the Layer pop-up menu, choose the layer that contains the pears image; look at the thumbnail to the right of the menu to identify it. Observe the effect of your selection on the Montage.psd image window.

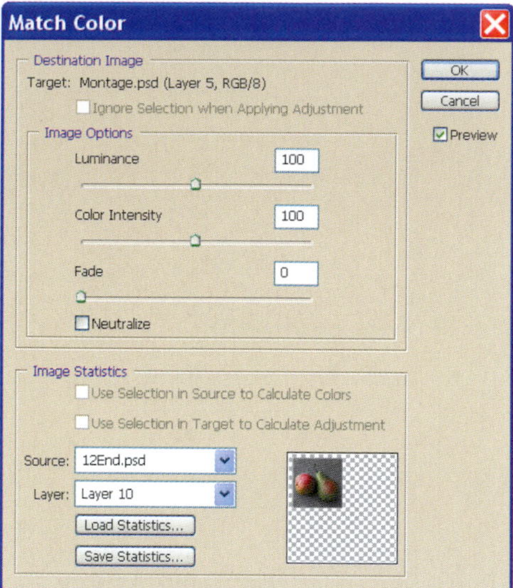

- One by one, choose the other layers and study the results in the image window. You can also experiment with the Image Options by adjusting the sliders for Luminance, Color Intensity, and Fade, with or without the Neutralize check box selected.

5 When you find the color scheme that you think does the best job of unifying the image and giving it the look you want, click OK to close the Match Color dialog box. (We used the pears-image layer and the default Image Options settings.)

6 In the Layers palette, make the Background layer visible again by clicking to set the eye icon (👁).

7 Choose File > Save.

You can use Match Color with any source file to create interesting and unusual effects. The Match Color feature is also useful for certain color corrections in some photographs. See Photoshop Help for more information.

You have completed Lesson 12, and you can close the Montage.psd and 12End.psd files.

Review

Review questions

1 What is the purpose of saving selections?

2 Describe one way to isolate color adjustments to an image.

3 Describe one way to remove color from a selection or from an image for a grayscale effect.

Review answers

1 By saving a selection, you can create and reuse time-consuming selections and uniformly select artwork in an image. You can also combine selections or create new selections by adding to or subtracting from existing selections.

2 You can use adjustment layers to try out color changes before applying them permanently to a layer.

3 You can choose Image > Adjustments > Desaturate to desaturate, or remove the color, from a selection.

why organic? | products | shop online | contact | help
Organic
Food
We're committed to producing fruit and vegetable products of the very highest quality through sustainable farming practices. Browse our site to see for yourself the beautiful and appetizing line of farm-to-you products we offer and learn what it takes to run a small family farm with a truly diversified output amidst the pressures and benefits of the information age.
Fresh Varieties
AVOCADO
HERBS
GRAPES
ASPARAGUS
PAPAYA

This lesson deals with basic slices and image maps—features that you can use to create multiple hypertext links within a single graphic. Web site visitors can click one part of your linked graphic on a Web page to open one site or page, and click another area to open a different site or page.

13 Creating Links Within an Image

Lesson overview

In this lesson, you'll learn how to do the following:

- Create image slices using the Slice tool.
- Distinguish between user slices and auto slices.
- Link user slices to other HTML pages or locations.
- Define image-map areas using three different methods.
- Link image-map areas to other HTML pages and locations.
- Generate an HTML page that contains the sliced image.
- Understand the differences between GIF and JPEG optimization.

This lesson will take about 90 minutes to complete. If needed, remove the previous lesson folder from your hard drive, and copy the Lessons/Lesson13 folder onto it. As you work on this lesson, you'll overwrite the start files. If you need to restore the start files, copy them again from the *Adobe Photoshop CS2 Classroom in a Book* CD.

In addition, for this lesson, you will need to use a Web browser application such as Netscape, Internet Explorer, or Safari. You do not need to connect to the Internet.

Getting started

In this lesson you'll work on graphics that are destined for a Web home page. Your goal is to embed multiple hypertext links within a complex image that is a single .psd file. Different areas, or *hotspots*, of the image map link to different files, so a Web site visitor can click one area of the home page to open a linked page, or click a different area of the home page to open a different linked page. There will also be unlinked areas of the home page that produce no change if the user clicks randomly or by accident.

Let's start now by viewing the finished HTML page that you will create.

1 Start Adobe Photoshop, holding down Ctrl-Alt-Shift (Windows) or Command-Option-Shift (Mac OS) to restore the default preferences. (See "Restoring default preferences" on page 6.)

2 When prompted, click Yes to confirm that you want to reset preferences, and Close to close the Welcome Screen.

3 Click the Go to Bridge button (icon) on the tool options bar to open Adobe Bridge.

4 In the Favorites palette in the upper left corner of Bridge, click the Lessons favorite, and then double-click the Lesson13 folder in the preview area, then double-click the 13End folder.

5 Right-click (Windows) or Control-click (Mac OS) on the 13End.html file, and choose Open With from the contextual menu. Choose a Web browser to open the HTML file.

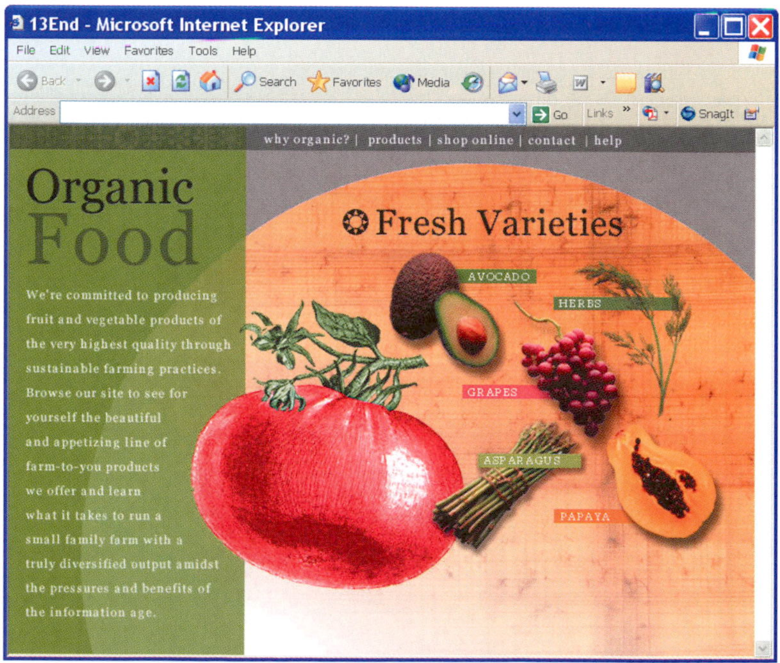
13End - Microsoft Internet Explorer
File Edit View Favorites Tools Help
Back Search Favorites Media
Address Go Links SnagIt
why organic? | products | shop online | contact | help
Organic Food
We're committed to producing fruit and vegetable products of the very highest quality through sustainable farming practices. Browse our site to see for yourself the beautiful and appetizing line of farm-to-you products we offer and learn what it takes to run a small family farm with a truly diversified output amidst the pressures and benefits of the information age.
Fresh Varieties
AVOCADO
HERBS
GRAPES
ASPARAGUS
PAPAYA

6 Click the "why organic?" button at the top of the page.

A new Web browser window opens to a new page. (It's not a fully developed page; it's just a placeholder page to show that the things you click really do represent links.)

7 Close the Why page instance of the Web browser.

8 At the top of the Organic Food Web page, click the "products" button. Then, close the new instance of the Web browser that shows the Products page.

9 Again in the Organic Food Web page, move the pointer over the picture of asparagus on the right side of the page. Notice that the pointer changes to a pointing-finger icon (☝), indicating that this area is linked. Move the pointer around the page and notice when it appears as an arrow and when as a hand.

10 Click the asparagus to jump to its linked Web page. Then, close the linked Asparagus page and return to the Organic Food home page. Try some of the other links you find on the page.

11 When you finish viewing the Organic Food Web site, quit your browser and return to Bridge.

In the preceding steps, you experienced two different types of links: slices (in the menu buttons at the top of the page) and image maps (the asparagus, papaya, and herbs image areas).

Slices are rectangular areas in an image that you define based on layers, guides, or precise selections in the image, or by using the Slice tool. When you define slices in an image, Photoshop creates an HTML table or Cascading Style Sheet to contain and align the slices. If you want, you can generate and preview an HTML file that contains the sliced image along with the table or Cascading Style Sheet.

An *image map* is also an image area that supports a hypertext link. In an image map, different areas of the image, called *hotspots*, link to different files. As a result, a Web site visitor can click one area of the image to open a linked page, or click a different area of the image to open a different linked page. Unlike slices, which are always rectangular, image maps can be any shape. The controls for making image maps are available only in Adobe ImageReady, so you will jump to ImageReady to do this work when the time comes in this lesson.

In this lesson you will embed multiple hypertext links—by creating both slices and an image map—within a complex image that is a single .psd file. You'll start by working with slices, which are always rectangular.

Slicing an image in Photoshop

The basic way to define slices in Photoshop is to use the Slice tool to drag over an area of the image that you want to make a slice. You can also create slices in ImageReady, but for simplicity, we'll just use Photoshop in this exercise.

About designing Web pages with Photoshop and ImageReady

When designing Web pages using Adobe Photoshop and Adobe ImageReady, keep in mind the tools and features that are available in each application:

- Photoshop provides tools for creating and manipulating static images for use on the Web. You can divide an image into slices, add links and HTML text, optimize the slices, and save the image as a Web page.
- ImageReady provides many—but not all—of the same image-editing tools as Photoshop. In addition, it includes tools and palettes for advanced Web processing and creating dynamic Web images such as animations and rollovers.

Preparing to create slices

Before you start working in your file, you'll customize the work space so that everything is ready to go.

1 In Bridge, click the "Go up" button ( ) to go up one level to the Lesson13 folder, and then double-click the 13Start.psd thumbnail to open it in Photoshop.

If a notice appears asking whether you want to update the text layers for vector-based output, click Update.

The start file includes blue guides. You'll use the guides and the Snap To commands when you draw marquees so that they are tightly aligned.

2 Make sure that the following commands are selected (checked), or select them now if they are not:

- View > Show > Guides.
- View > Show > Slices.
- View > Snap.

- View > Snap To > Guides.
- View > Snap To > Slices.

The blue guides have been created to help you draw slices accurately. As you create slices close to the guides, the edges of the slices will snap to the guides so that your slices are uniform and precise.

Using the Slice tool to create slices

You might wonder why the heading for this topic uses the word "slices" instead of "a slice." The answer is that unless you create a slice that includes the whole image—which would be a fairly useless thing to do, especially since that slice is created automatically—you can't create just one slice. Any new slice within an image (a *user slice*) also causes the creation of other slices (*auto slices*) that cover all the area of the image outside the user slice you create.

Notice the small gray rectangle in the upper left corner of the image. The rectangle contains the number 01 and a small icon, or *badge*, that resembles a tiny mountain. The number indicates slice 01, which includes the entire image. The gray color tells you that it is an auto slice. The symbol indicates that the slice contains image content.

1 In the toolbox, select the Slice tool (✂).

2 Drag the Slice tool diagonally across the *why organic?* text area, starting and ending close to the guides surrounding the text.

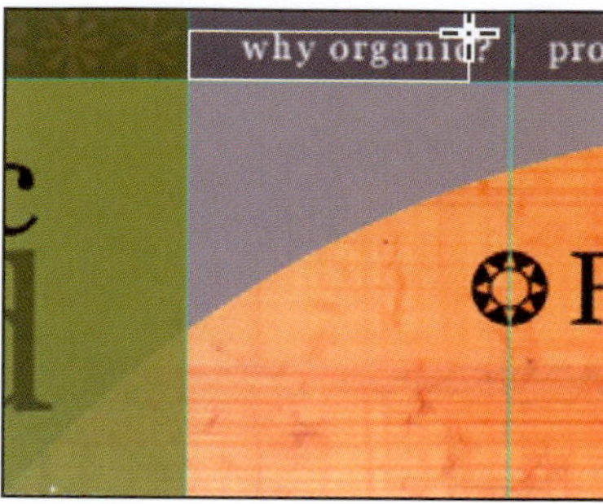

A blue rectangle, similar to the one for slice 01, appears in the upper left corner of the slice you just created, slice 02. The blue color tells you that this is a user slice, not an auto slice.

The original gray rectangle for auto slice 01 remains unchanged, but the area included in slice 01 is smaller, covering only the left side of the page.

Slice 03—another auto slice, as indicated by its gray color—covers the remaining area of the menu bar to the right of slice 02. A third auto slice, slice 04, covers the area below the menu bar and to the right of slice 01.

Creating more user slices

Now you'll slice the rest of the text in the menu bar into four more buttons.

1 With the Slice tool still selected in the toolbox, drag across the *products* text to create another user slice.

The new slice becomes slice 03. The number of each slice after slice 03 automatically increases by one.

2 One at a time, draw slice marquees around each of the other text items in the same row—around the words *shop online*, *contact*, and *help*—to create three slices for those menu buttons.

Your image should have a total of eight slices: five user slices and three auto slices. If your numbers are different, don't worry, because you'll fix that now.

3 In the toolbox, select the Zoom tool (🔍) and click the area of your button slices to enlarge the view to 300% or 400%.

4 Carefully examine the user slices you created to see if there are any gaps between them. (If there are, these gaps will be auto slices.) If there are no gaps between your user slices, you can skip to Step 7.

Gaps between slices

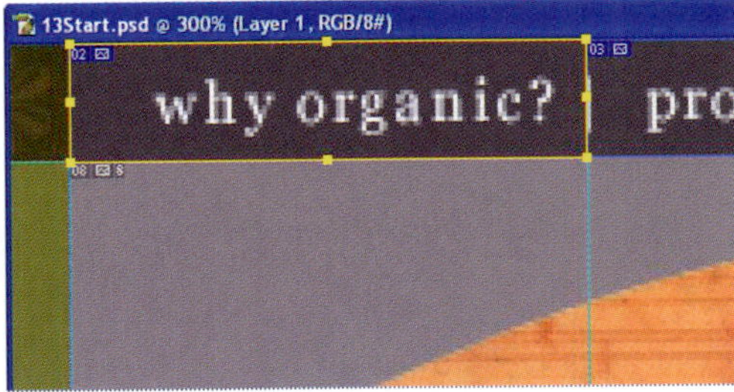

No gaps between slices

5 In the toolbox, select the Slice Select tool (), hidden behind the Slice tool, and select one of the user slices that did not snap to the guides—that is, a slice with a gap between it and the adjacent user slice.

6 Drag a selection handle for the selected slice until the slice boundaries snap into position against the guides and the other slices.

Note: *You can also use the Slice Select tool to drag the slice from one position to another.*

7 Double-click the Zoom tool to return to 100%, and choose File > Save.

If you find the indicators for the auto slices distracting, select the Slice Select tool and then click the Hide Auto Slices button on the tool options bar. You can also hide the guides by choosing View > Show > Guides, because you won't need them again.

Setting slice options

Slices aren't particularly useful until you set options for them. Slice options include the slice name and the URL that opens when the user clicks the slice.

Note: *You can set options for an auto slice, but doing so automatically promotes the auto slice to a user slice.*

1 Select the Slice Select tool (), and use it to select slice 02, the *why organic?* text.

2 On the tool options bar, click the Slice Options button (), or double-click the slice itself, to open the Slice Options dialog box.

By default, Photoshop names each slice based on the filename and the slice number, so the current filename appears as "13Start_02," representing slice 2 in the 13Start.psd file.

3 In the Slice Options dialog box, enter the following information: In Name, type **Why_button**; in URL, type **pages/why.html**; and in Target, type **_blank**. (Make sure to include the underscore before the letter "b.") Then click OK.

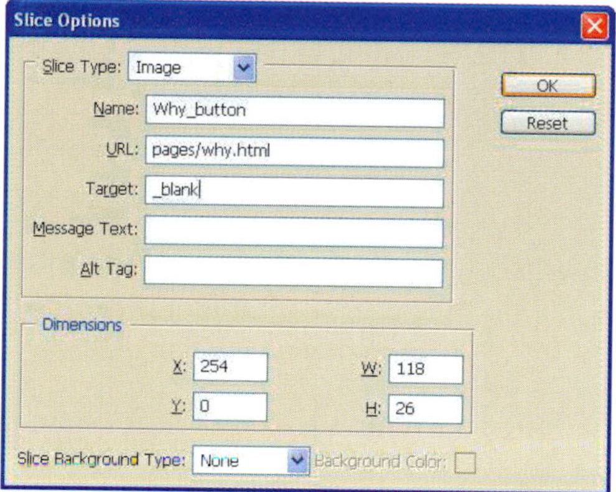

Note: The Target option controls how a linked file opens when the link is clicked. The _blank option opens the linked page in a new instance of the Web browser. If you wanted the link to open in the original Web browser window, you would type a different code. For more information, see Adobe Photoshop Help or an HTML reference book.

4 Using the Slice Select tool, select slice 03, the *products* text, and then click the Slice Options button () on the tool options bar.

5 In the Slice Options dialog box, enter the following information: In Name, type **Products_button**; in URL, type **pages/products.html**; and in Target, type **_blank**. Then click OK.

6 Select slice 04 with the Slice Select tool, open the Slice Options dialog box, and enter the following: In Name type **Shop_button**; in URL, type **pages/shop.html**; and in Target, type **_blank**. Then click OK.

7 Select slice 05 with the Slice Select tool, open the Slice Options dialog box, and enter the following: In Name type **Contact_button**; in URL, type **pages/contact.html**; and in Target, type **_blank**. Then click OK.

8 Select slice 06 with the Slice Select tool, open the Slice Options dialog box, and enter the following: In Name type **Help_button**; in URL, type **pages/help.html**; and in Target, type **_blank**. Then click OK.

9 Choose File > Save.

Leave the file open for the next procedure.

You may have noticed that there are more options in the dialog box than the three you specified for these slices. For more information on how to use these options, see Photoshop Help.

More about creating slices

You've finished the slices work for this lesson. You've created basic slices and set slice options in Photoshop. There are other methods of creating slices that you can try on your own. For example:

- You can create slices based on layers. A layer-based slice includes all the pixel data in the selected layer. When you edit the layer, move it, or apply a layer effect to it, the layer-based slice adjusts to encompass the new pixels. To unlink a layer-based slice from its layer, you can convert it to a user slice.

- You can create No Image slices, and then add text or HTML source code to them. No Image slices can have a background color and are saved as part of the HTML file. The primary advantage of using No Image slices for text is that the text can be edited in any HTML editor, saving you the trouble of having to go back to Photoshop to edit it. However, if the text grows too large for the slice, it will break the HTML table and introduce unwanted gaps.

- If you use custom guides in your design work, you can instantly divide up an entire image into slices with the Slices From Guides button on the Photoshop Slice tool options bar. This technique should be used with caution, however, because it discards any previously created slices and any options associated with those slices. Also, it creates only user slices, and you may not need that many of them.

- When you want to create identically sized, evenly spaced, and aligned slices, try creating a single user slice that precisely encloses the entire area. Then, use the Divide button on the Slice Select tool options bar to divide the original slice into as many vertical or horizontal rows of slices as you need.
- If you have selected an area with the ImageReady selection marquee tools that you want to designate as a slice, you can use the Create Slice from Selection command. Be aware that even if the selection is an irregular shape, the slice will always be a rectangle.

Jumping to ImageReady

It's time to start getting acquainted with ImageReady. You'll use the Jump To button to switch to it. The Jump To button not only launches ImageReady but also "jumps" the file that is open in Photoshop, transferring control to ImageReady until you either close the file or jump back to Photoshop.

1 Make sure that you have saved the 13Start.psd file. Then, in the Photoshop toolbox, click the Jump to ImageReady button ().

ImageReady opens and displays the 13Start.psd file. Notice that ImageReady has a Slices menu and a Slices palette, neither of which appears in Photoshop.

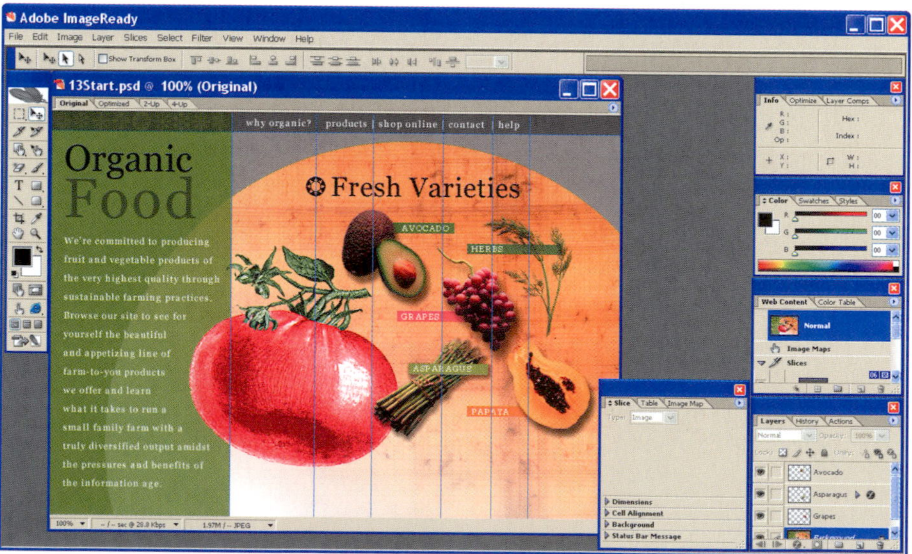

You can set slice options in ImageReady using the Slice palette. Just select any slice using the Slice Select tool (), and enter the information into the fields in the Slice palette. This actually is a bit faster than defining slice options in Photoshop, because it doesn't require the extra actions of opening and closing a dialog box.

Now that ImageReady is open, let's arrange the workspace a bit for this lesson.

2 Choose Window > Workspace > Interactivity Palette Locations to close some of the palettes you won't need.

3 Close the Animation palette and the Web Content palette group by clicking the red Close buttons on the palette title bars, or close them by selecting those palettes from the Window menu.

4 Drag the Slice palette group to the right until it snaps into place at the edge of the work area, and then click the Image Map tab to bring that palette forward. Your work area should now resemble the following illustration:

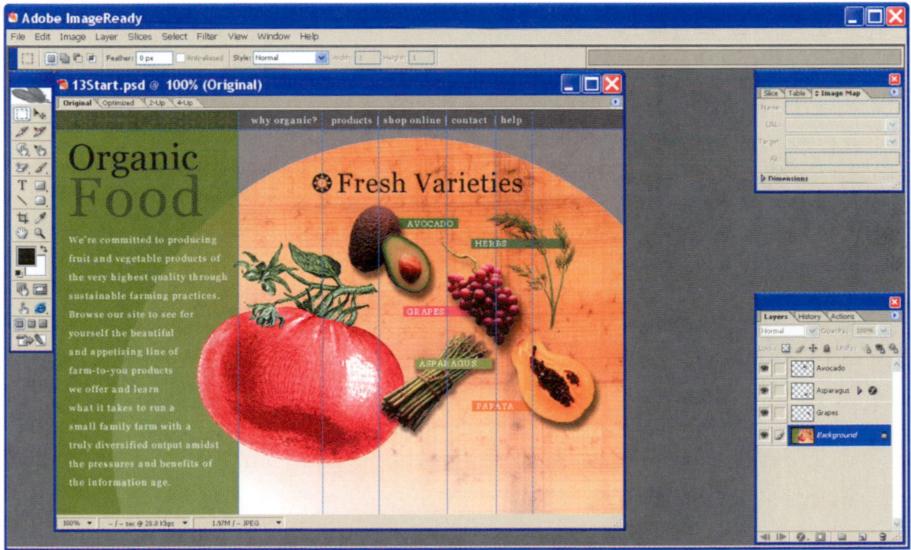

Creating image maps in ImageReady

Creating image maps is one of the few functions that you must do in Adobe ImageReady. You can use Photoshop to create slices, which share certain functionality with image maps, but you cannot create image maps with Photoshop.

In this section, you'll create an image map within the same image that you've been working on in this lesson, the Organic Food home page. Your task is to create links to different Web pages that match the shapes of the pictured produce items—something that would be difficult to do with slices, because slices are always rectangular.

Using layers to create image maps

You'll define image-map areas based on some of the layers in the home page design. Using layers is an efficient way to define the hotspots, letting you easily gain control over the shapes of those areas.

1 In the Layers palette, select the Asparagus layer.

Notice that a layer style, the Drop Shadow effect, has already been applied to this layer.

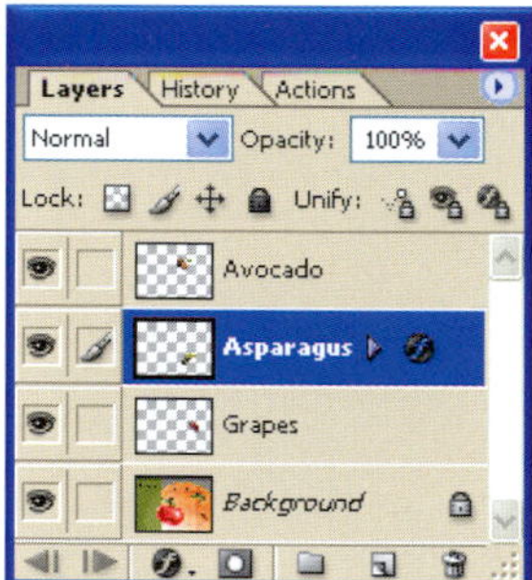

2 Choose Layer > New Layer Based Image Map Area.

A ghosted rectangular area surrounded by a red line appears in the image window, enclosing the asparagus. The line and ghosting define the hotspot in the image map. In the Layers palette, a pointing-finger icon indicates that the layer now has a layer-based image map.

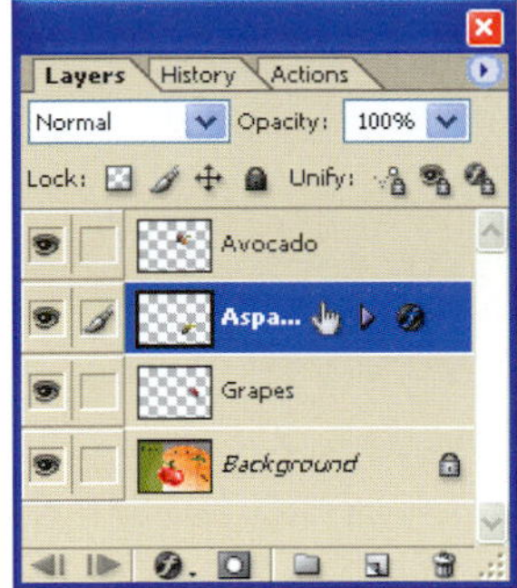

3 In the Image Map palette, click the arrow to view the Layer Based Settings option (if necessary), and choose Polygon from the Shape pop-up menu.

Now the red outline in the image window approximates the shape of the asparagus bunch, including the drop shadow layer style.

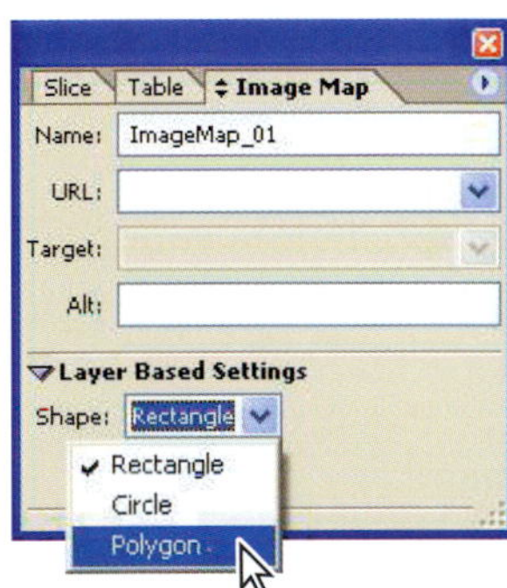

4 Set the Quality option to **90** to make the red line more closely conform to the asparagus shape.

5 Still in the Image Map palette, type **Asparagus** in Name, type **pages/asparagus.html** for URL, and choose _blank from the Target pop-up menu.

6 Click a blank area of the Layers palette to deselect the Asparagus layer, and then choose File > Save.

Using the image-map tools

When the elements you want to use for image maps are conveniently located on separate layers, it's simple to define those image-map areas, as you saw in the previous procedure. This procedure and the next show you a couple of techniques for defining image maps within a single layer.

The first method is similar to using the Pen tool in Photoshop. Before you begin working, you'll turn off the Snap To options, which will make it easier to position anchor points exactly where you want them.

1 Choose View > Snap to deselect (uncheck) that command.

2 In the toolbox, select the Polygon Image Map tool ( ), which is hidden behind the Rectangle Image Map tool ( ).

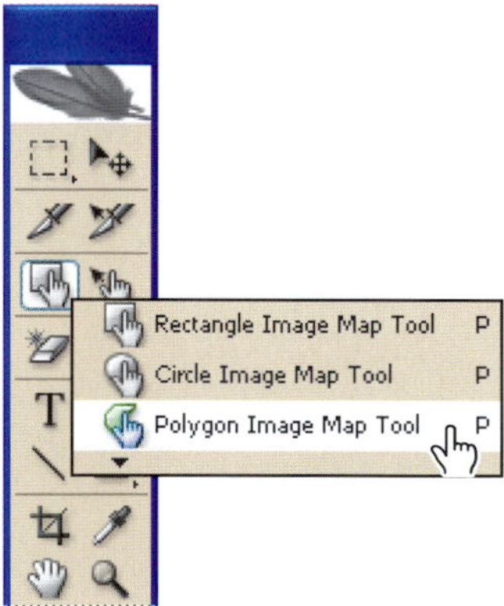

3 Zoom in to the papaya in the image window if necessary (but keep it all in view onscreen), and then reselect the Polygon Image Map tool and click the edge of the papaya to set an anchor point.

4 Move along the outside edge of the papaya and the Papaya label, clicking frequently to set more anchor points.

Press Shift as you drag around the Papaya label to constrain your dragging motion to a straight horizontal or vertical line.

5 When the anchor points are almost completely around the papaya, click the original anchor point to close the image-map shape. (The pointer icon changes when you're at the right spot, showing a little circle that indicates a click will close the shape.)

The red image-map boundary appears around the papaya, with anchor points where you set them.

6 Specify the following in the Image Map palette: type **Papaya** for Name, type **pages/papaya.html** for URL, and choose _blank for Target.

7 Choose Select > Deselect Image Maps, and then double-click the Zoom tool (🔍) to change the view to 100%.

8 Choose File > Save.

Using selections to create image maps

You can also convert selections to image maps. You'll try that now with the fennel herb, selecting it with the Magic Wand tool.

1 Zoom in on the fennel herb until you have a good close-up view (about 300%), making sure you can see it all onscreen.

2 In the Layers palette, select the Background layer.

3 Select the Magic Wand tool (), which is hidden behind the Marquee tool (). Then, on the tool options bar, type **42** in the Tolerance option and make sure that the Contiguous check box is selected, or select it now.

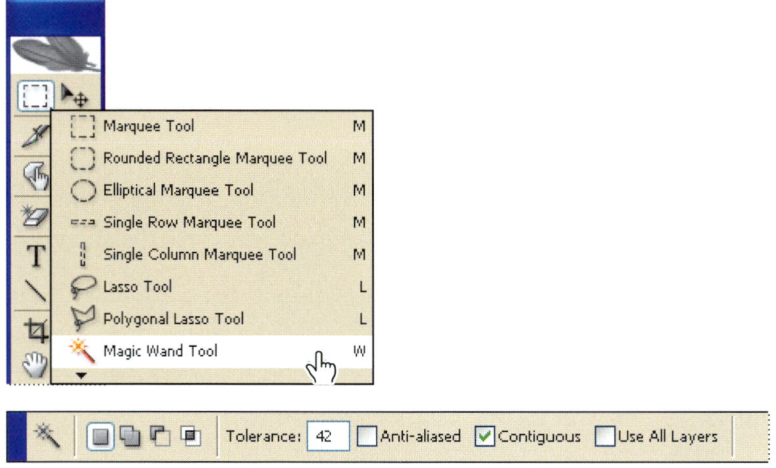

4 Click the fennel branch where the Herbs label crosses it.

5 Hold down Shift so that the Magic Wand tool pointer has a plus sign, and carefully click an unselected area of the fennel branch. Repeat a few more times until most of the fennel is selected—the selection doesn't need to be perfect.

***Note:** If the selection marquee seems to disappear after a click, you may have accidentally clicked the wood grain, so the marquee includes a very large area. In that case, choose Edit > Undo and try again.*

6 Choose Select > Create Image Map from Selection. The Create Image Map dialog box opens. Select the Polygon with Quality 80 option, and click OK.

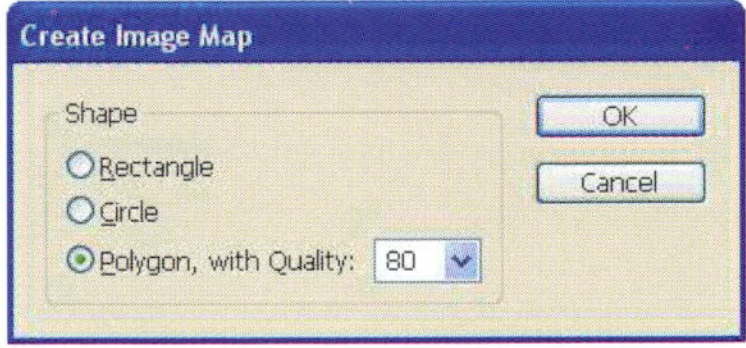

In the image window, the fennel image appears ghosted. A red line indicating the shape of the image map surrounds the fennel.

7 Choose Select > Deselect to remove the selection marquee.

8 In the Image Map palette, type **Herbs** for Name, type **pages/herbs.html** for URL, and choose _blank for Target.

9 Choose File > Save.

***Note:** If you want to see your image without the light blue image-map lines and ghosting, click the Toggle Image Maps Visibility button ( ) in the toolbox, or press A. Click the button or press A again to see the image-map indicators.*

So far in this lesson you have created five slice links and three image-map links on your Web page image. You can go ahead and create additional image maps for the avocado and grapes if you want to practice on your own, or you can proceed to the next topic. (We have included these HTML pages on the CD for you if you decide to practice.)

***Note:** The previous procedures did not attempt to create image-map shapes that were perfect matches for the items pictured. You can improve the shapes by using the Image Map Select tool and dragging the anchor points to better positions until you're satisfied with the shape of the image map. To add anchor points, press Shift-click; to delete anchor points, Alt-click (Windows) or Option-click (Mac OS).*

Saving linked images in an HTML file

When you save an image with linked slices and image maps in an HTML file, the basic HTML tags needed to display the image on a Web page are generated automatically. The easiest way to do this is to choose the HTML and Images option when you save the optimized image. Once you have created the HTML file, it can easily be updated to reflect any changes, such as new or modified image-map areas or URLs.

Before saving the HTML file, however, quickly check your links in the Web Content palette.

1 Choose Window > Web Content to open that palette. If necessary, click the arrows to expand the Image Maps and Slices categories, and drag the lower right corner of the palette down so that you can see all the items listed.

2 Review the Web Content listings, which include thumbnails of the slices and image maps. Notice that the image-map thumbnails include the boundary lines of the image-map areas. Click to select any slice or image map, and the Slice or Image Map palette, respectively, displays the relevant information about the slice or image map.

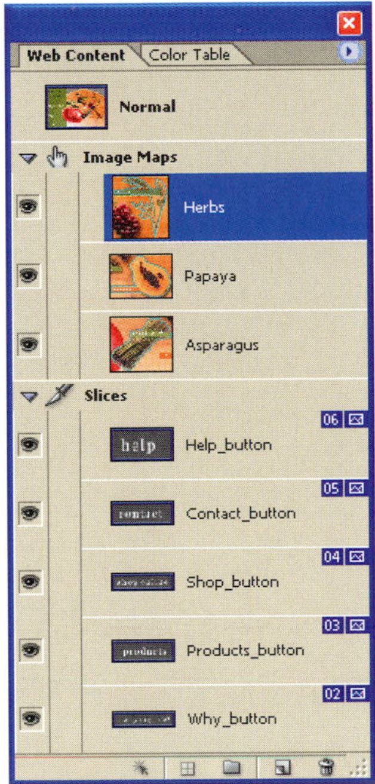

3 Close the Web Content palette or move it out of the way.

4 Choose File > Save Optimized As. (Do *not* select Save As.)

5 In the Save Optimized As dialog box, accept the default name, 13Start.html; choose HTML and Images from the Save As Type pop-up menu (Windows) or Format pop-up menu (Mac OS); and specify the Lessons/Lesson13/13MyPage folder as the destination. Then, click Save.

Note: *In Photoshop, create an HTML file by choosing File > Save for Web. Optimize the image, and then click Save. The Save Optimized As dialog box will appear, and you can specify the HTML information.*

Optimizing images for the Web

Optimizing is the process of selecting format, resolution, and quality settings so that an image has the efficiency, visual appeal, and utility for Web browser pages. Simply put, it's balancing file size against good looks. No single collection of settings can maximize the efficiency of every kind of image file; optimizing requires human judgment and a good eye.

Compression options vary according to the file format used to save the image. You should be familiar with the two most common formats: JPEG and GIF. The JPEG format is designed to preserve the broad color range and subtle brightness variations of continuous-tone images such as photographs. It can represent images using millions of colors. The GIF format is effective at compressing solid-color images and images with areas of repetitive color, such as line art, logos, and illustrations with type. It uses a palette of 256 colors to represent the image and supports background transparency.

Photoshop and ImageReady offer a range of controls for compressing image file size while optimizing onscreen display quality. Typically, you optimize images before saving them in an HTML file. In Photoshop, you use the Save for Web dialog box; in ImageReady, you use the Optimize palette. Both methods let you compare the original image to one or more compressed alternatives and interactively change settings as you compare. To experiment as described in the following captions, use the images in the Lessons/Lesson13 folder. And for more on optimizing GIF and JPEG images, see Photoshop Help.

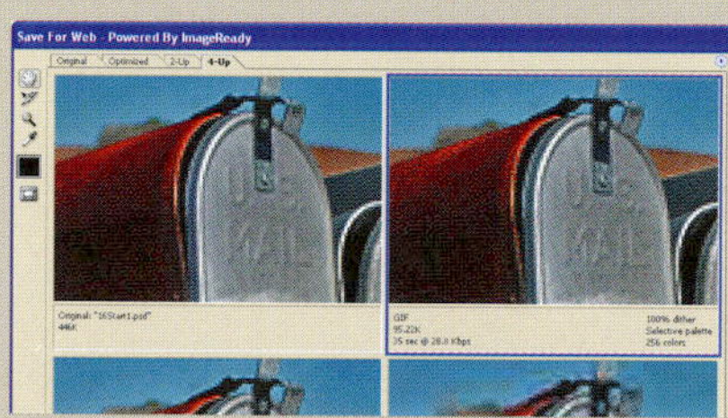

JPEG compression preserves broad color ranges and is suitable for continuous-tone photographic images. With the mailbox .psd file open in Photoshop, choose Save for Web, and click the 4-Up tab. (In ImageReady, click the 4-Up tab and make sure the Optimize palette is open.) The upper left preview area displays the original image; Photoshop automatically renders high-, medium-, and low-quality JPEG previews. Compare the quality and size differences, and then click any optimized version to experiment with format and quality settings, continuing to judge quality vs. file size.

GIF compression uses a palette of 256 colors to represent an image, making it suitable for artwork with areas of solid or repetitive color. With the landscape.psd image open in Photoshop, choose Save for Web, and click the 4-Up tab. (In ImageReady, click the 4-Up tab and make sure the Optimize palette is open.) The original image appears in the upper left corner; Photoshop renders three GIF alternatives. Compare the quality and size differences, and click any optimized version to experiment with format, color-reduction method, and other options. The Color Table palette shows exactly which colors are used in the optimized file.

Before ending this lesson, preview your Web site in a browser.

6 Switch to Adobe Bridge and navigate to the Lessons/Lesson13/13MyPage folder. Right-click (Windows) or Control-click (Mac OS), and choose Open With. Choose a Web browser to open 13Start.html file.

7 Click several of the areas with slices or image maps that you created and examine them to see that they link properly (they should).

why organic? | products | shop online | contact | help
Organic
Food
We're committed to producing fruit and vegetable products of the very highest quality through sustainable farming practices. Browse our site to see for yourself the beautiful and appetizing line of farm-to-you products we offer and learn what it takes to run a small family farm with a truly diversified output amidst the pressures and benefits of the information age.
Fresh Varieties
AVOCADO
HERBS
GRAPES
ASPARAGUS
PAPAYA

If some of the links in the HTML file don't work properly, you can return to ImageReady, fix the links in the 13Start.psd file's Image Map or Slice palette, and then choose File > Update HTML. In the Update HTML dialog box, navigate to and select the 13Start.html file, and click Open. Click Replace when the Replace Files dialog box appears, and click OK in the update message. Then, preview the HTML page again in a Web browser.

Congratulations! Now that you know how to create interactive slices and image maps, it's time to start a new project to learn how to create image rollovers.

Review

Review questions

1 What are slices?

2 Describe three ways to create image slices.

3 What are the differences and similarities between slices and image maps?

4 What is image optimization and how do you optimize images for the Web?

Review answers

1 Slices are rectangular areas of an image that you can define in Photoshop or ImageReady for individual Web optimization. With slices, you can create animated GIFs, URL links, and rollovers.

2 You can create image slices by dragging to define areas in the image with the Slice tool. You can also convert layers into slices using the Layer menu in Photoshop, or convert selections into slices using the Select menu in ImageReady. Auto slices are created automatically for areas in the sliced image that are left undefined when you create user slices.

3 Slices can be created in either Photoshop or ImageReady; image maps must be created in ImageReady. Slices are always rectangular in shape; image maps can have any shape. Both slices and image maps can be configured as hotspots with links to other pages. Both also can be configured with rollover states, which you can learn more about in Lesson 14, "Creating Rollover Web Visuals."

4 Image optimization is the process of choosing a file format, resolution, and quality settings for images that will be published to the Web. When optimizing, it is necessary to balance a small file size with the visual appearance of the compressed image. Continuous-tone images are typically optimized in JPEG format; solid-color images and images with repetitive areas of color are typically optimized as GIF. To optimize images in Photoshop, choose File > Save for Web. In ImageReady, use the Optimize palette.

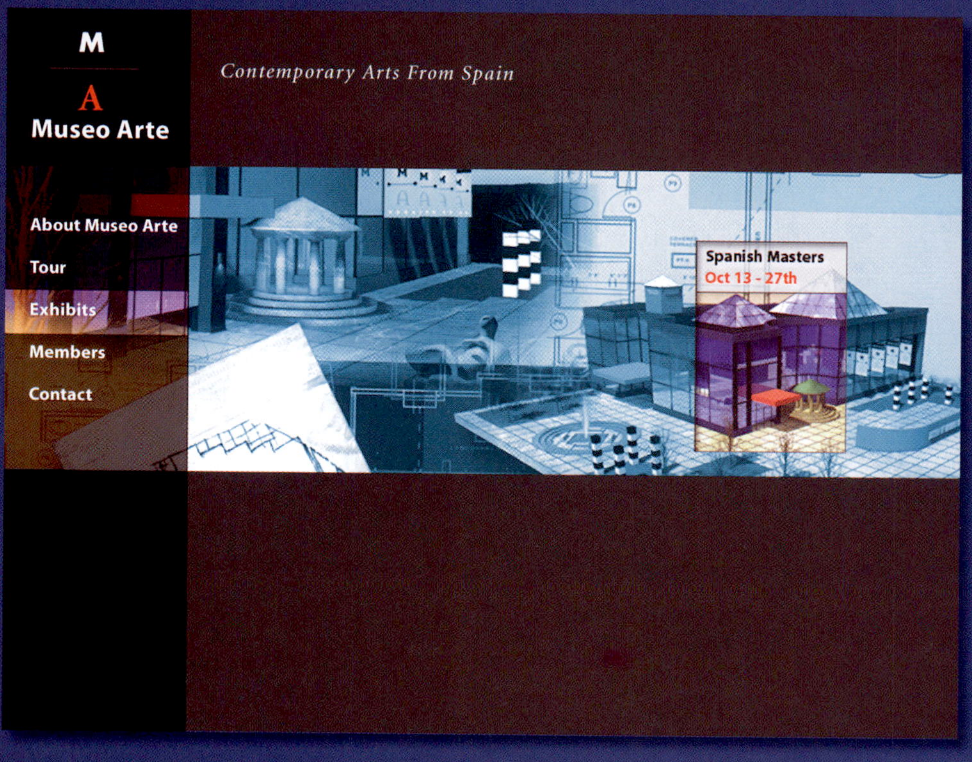

Rollovers animate slices of an image on a Web page with visual changes that occur in response to mouse actions. Rollovers can go a long way toward making your Web pages more user friendly. They give even casual visitors clues about links and other items that are available to them on your Web site.

14 Creating Rollover Web Visuals

Lesson overview

In this lesson, you'll learn how to do the following:

- Define a rollover state that results in warped text.
- Define rollover states that affect layer visibility.
- Preview rollover effects.
- Create a remote rollover.
- Generate an HTML page that contains the sliced image in a table.

This lesson will take about an hour to complete. If needed, remove the previous lesson folder from your hard drive, and copy the Lessons/Lesson14 folder onto it. As you work on this lesson, you'll overwrite the start files. If you need to restore the start files, copy them again from the *Adobe Photoshop CS2 Classroom in a Book* CD.

In addition, for this lesson, you will need to use a Web browser application (such as Netscape, Internet Explorer, or Safari). You do not need to connect to the Internet.

About rollovers

Rollovers are Web effects that alter the usual appearance of the Web page without switching the user to a different Web page. The primary example is the namesake behavior: When a user rolls the mouse so that the pointer passes over a defined area of a Web page, that same area of the page changes appearance in some way. Usually, this is done as a visual cue, emphasizing that the area is a hotspot that the user can click to make something happen, such as open another Web page.

There are other kinds of rollovers. Some rollovers are tied to other types of user actions, such as clicking or holding down the mouse button. Some rollovers triggered by a user action in one area of the Web page can cause another part of the Web page to change.

Rollover effects or states represent different conditions in the Layers palette. These conditions may involve layer visibility, layer position, layer styles, and other options for formatting. This lesson is devoted to exploring a representative sampling of what you can do with rollovers.

Note: *This lesson assumes that you have a basic knowledge of slices either from your work in Lesson 13, "Creating Links Within an Image," or from your own experience.*

Getting started

You'll start the lesson by viewing an example of an HTML page that you'll create based on a single .psd file. Several areas of the artwork react to mouse actions. For example, some areas of the image change appearance when the pointer "rolls over" them, or when you click one of the hotspots.

1 Launch Adobe Bridge and click Lessons in the Favorites palette in the upper left corner of the browser window. Then double-click the Lesson14 folder in the preview area, then double-click the 14End folder.

2 Right-click (Windows) or Control-click (Mac OS) the 14End.html file, and choose Open With from the contextual menu. Choose a Web browser to open the HTML file.

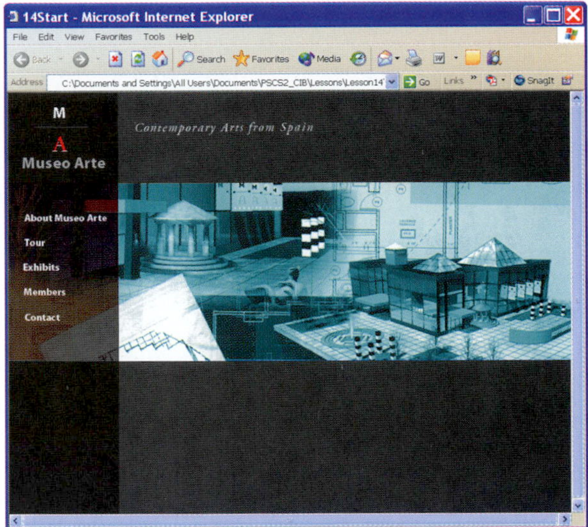

3 Move the mouse pointer over the Web page, especially over the left side. Look for changes in the appearance of the image, and changes in the appearance of the pointer (from an arrow to a pointing hand).

Note: Links have not been configured for this page, so clicking these buttons will not open other Web pages.

4 When you finish viewing the Web page, quit the Web browser.

Creating rollover states

A *rollover state* is named by the event, such as a click or rolling the pointer over an area of the image, that triggers a change in the image or part of the image. ImageReady automatically assigns one of the following eight states to new rollovers: Over, Down, Click, Custom, None, Selected, Out, or Up. (For complete definitions of these states, see ImageReady Help.)

Remote rollovers tie a rollover state in one slice to changes in a different slice. For example, the user could click a button (the activating slice) that would make a previously hidden graphic or text block (the remote slice) visible in another area of the Web page.

Only user slices can have rollover states. However, you can choose Slices > Promote to convert an auto slice into a user slice, and then assign rollover states to that slice.

Preparing the workspace and work options

If you've already completed other lessons in this book, then you've had some experience customizing the workspace. ImageReady has several predefined workspaces that you can use for specific kinds of work, one of which you'll use for this exercise.

1 Launch Adobe ImageReady, holding down Ctrl-Alt-Shift (Windows) or Command-Option-Shift (Mac OS) to restore default preferences. (See "Restoring default preferences" on page 6.) Click Erase when the alert asks if you're sure you want to erase all ImageReady preferences.

2 Choose Window > Workspace > Interactivity Palette Locations.

3 In the Slice palette group, select the Table tab to bring it forward, and then click the double arrows (⬍) on that tab to fully expand the palette. Then drag it to the upper right corner of the work area, and switch its location with the Web Content palette.

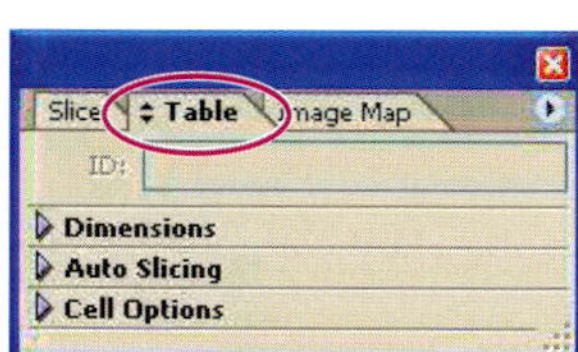

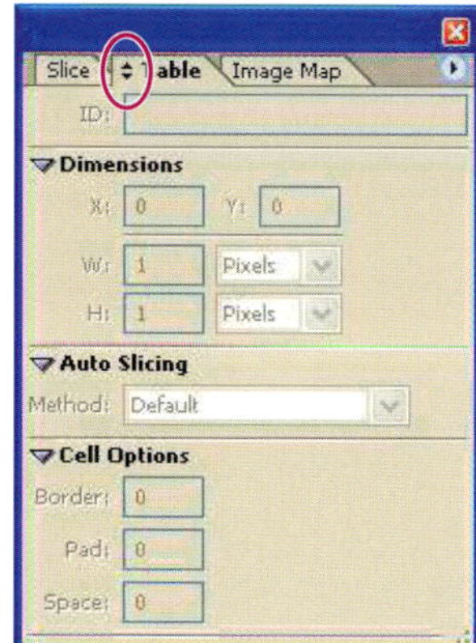

4 Drag the lower right corners of the Layers and Web Content palettes so that they take full advantage of the available space below them.

5 Close the Animation palette in the lower left corner of the work area.

Your workspace should look like the following image.

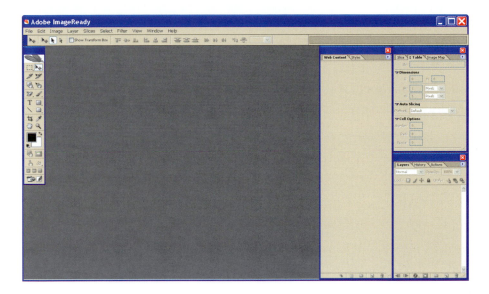

Another important preparation is to make sure that the work settings for ImageReady are configured properly. Some of these can't be configured unless a file is open, so you'll open your start file now.

6 Choose File > Open, navigate to the Lessons/Lesson14 folder on your hard drive, select the 14Start.psd file, and click Open.

7 If necessary, resize the image window and zoom in or out so that you can see the entire image.

8 Examine the View menu and submenus to make sure that the following commands are selected (checked), or select them now:

- Extras
- Snap
- Guides and Slices on the Show submenu
- Guides and Slices on the Snap To submenu

Now you're ready to get to work.

Creating a rollover with warped text

One of the fun things you can do in ImageReady is to warp text shapes. For example, you can make the words appear as if they were painted on a three-dimensional object.

In this exercise, you'll apply that warp as well as a rollover state to some text. The resulting text will appear on the final HTML image only when the user performs a specific action.

1 Select the Slice tool (), and drag a rectangle around the words "Museo Arte," using the guides as a reference so that the slice borders snap to them.

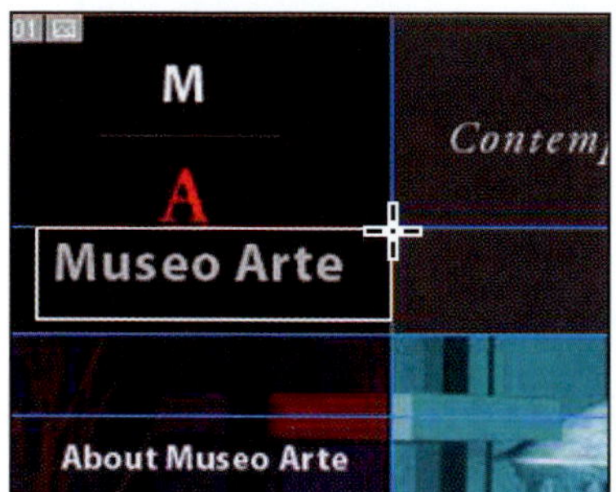

2 In the Web Content palette, double-click your new user slice, named 14Start_02 by default, type **Museo Arte**, and press Enter (Windows) or Return (Mac OS) to rename it.

3 Click the Create Rollover State button () at the bottom of the Web Content palette. A new Over state rollover appears nested below the Museo Arte slice in the palette.

The Over state activates the image when a user rolls the mouse cursor over the hotspot.

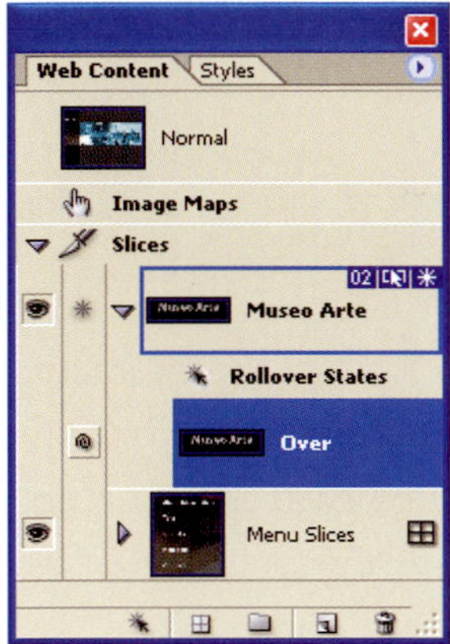

4 In the Layers palette, select the Museo Arte layer.

5 In the toolbox, select the Type tool (T). On the Type tool options bar, click the Create Warped Text button (). (If a dialog box appears warning you that editing will cause the layout to change, click OK.)

Note: *You do not need to use the Type tool or select the text. The warping effect applies to the entire text layer, not to individual words or characters.*

6 In the Warp Text dialog box, choose Style > Fisheye, and drag the Bend slider to 30%. Leave the Vertical and Horizontal Distortion sliders at 0%, and click OK. Notice the distortion of the Museo Arte text.

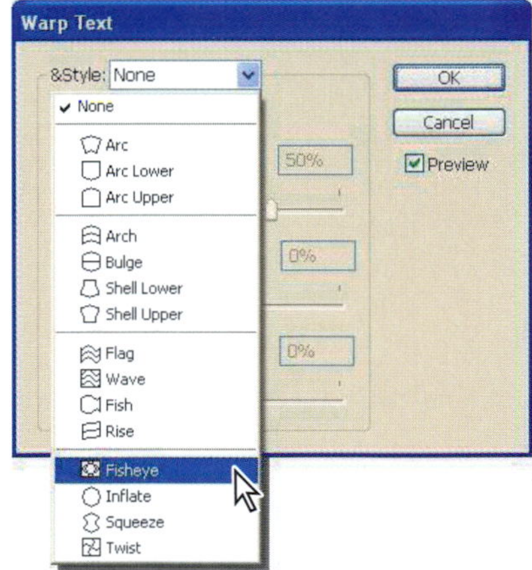

7 In the Web Content palette, click Normal to deactivate the rollover-state display in the image window.

Note: Warping text is not the same as placing type on a path, which is a Photoshop feature. For information on how to arrange characters on geometric or freeform paths, see Photoshop Help. (That feature is not available in ImageReady.)

Previewing a rollover

Although the end result of this project is a Web page, you can test the interactive behaviors of your slices in ImageReady. You do this by stepping out of working mode into preview mode. While you are previewing, some palettes, such as the Layers palette, are dimmed because you cannot select layers or make adjustments in those palettes in preview mode.

1 In the Layers palette, click a blank area to deselect the Museo Arte layer.

2 In the toolbox, first select the Toggle Slices Visibility button ( ) or press Q to hide the slice boundaries and remove the ghosting appearance over the image.

3 Click the Preview Document button ( ) or press Y to activate preview mode.

Note: The guides are still visible in the image window. You can either ignore them as you preview, or hide them by choosing View > Show > Guides or using the keyboard shortcut Ctrl-; (Windows) or Command-; (Mac OS). If you hide them now, be sure that you make them visible again after you finish previewing, because you'll need them for the next procedure.

4 Move the pointer over the Museo Arte text in the image window, and then move it away so that you can see the effect of the Over rollover state with the warped text applied.

Notice the effect the pointer position has on the highlighting in the Web Content palette. As you move the pointer over and then away from the Museo Arte slice in the image window, the slice selection in the Web Content palette shifts from Normal to the Museo Arte Over state.

5 Click the Preview Document and Toggle Slices Visibility buttons again to exit preview mode and to restore slice visibility in the image window.

The slice boundaries and the ghosted overlay reappear in the image window.

6 In the Web Content palette, select Normal (if it isn't already selected), and click the arrow on the Museo Arte slice to hide the rollover listing.

Try to keep the Web Content and Layers palettes as tidy as possible for your rollover work. By avoiding visual clutter, you'll make fewer mistakes, do less scrolling, and more easily find and focus on the item that requires your attention. To this end, you should always collapse grouped items when you finish working with them, even though this doesn't affect the end result of your work.

In this lesson, you won't go on to the next logical step for a Web page designer—associating a hypertext link to another Web page with the Museo Arte slice. It's something you can do later on your own, if you'd like, using the techniques in Lesson 13, "Creating Links Within an Image."

Creating rollovers that affect layer visibility

Perhaps one of the most common methods of animating a file is to change the visibility of different layers.

In this design, the original version of the central image was fully colored instead of the heavily blue-toned version that you see in Normal state. Sections of the original version have been copied onto layers in this file, above the blue-version Background layer. The original-color sections line up perfectly with the blue image, so making them visible appears to brighten just that area of the image by removing the blue color cast.

1 In the Web Content palette, locate the Menu Slices slice and toggle it open by clicking the arrow next to the thumbnail. Notice that the slice has a small grid icon next to its name (). This means Menu Slices is part of an HTML table.

Tables produce cleaner, more manageable HTML code. Each cell in a table can contain an image slice, as in our Menu Slices slice. The slices within the Menu Slices slice are called *nested slices*.

2 Select the About nested slice, and then click the Create Rollover State () button at the bottom of the palette to create a new Over state for it.

3 In the Layers palette, expand the Menu Color Bkgds layer set, and click the visibility box to set an eye icon () by the Cell_1 layer.

The background behind the About Museo Arte text is now more brightly colored.

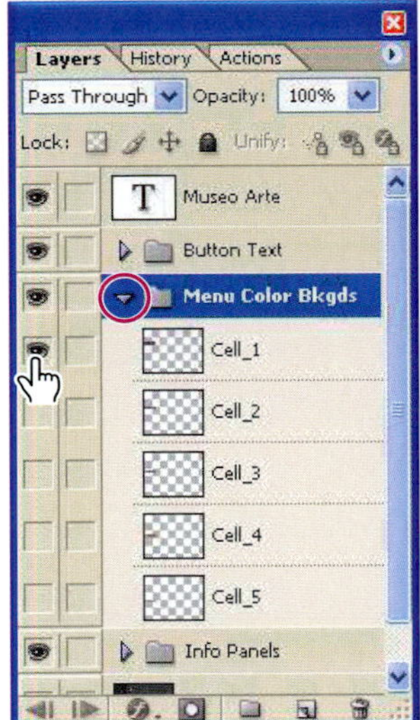

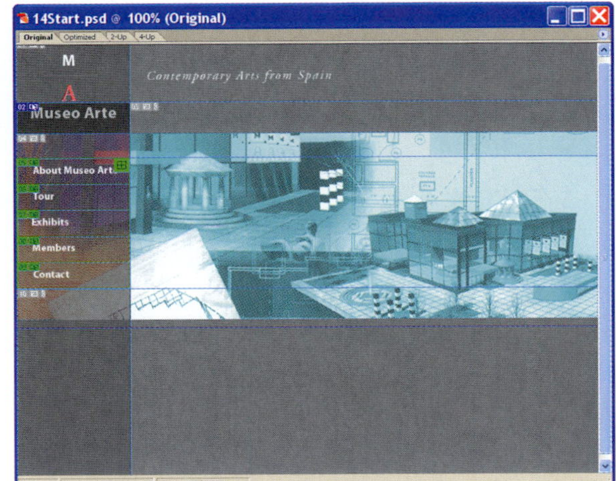

4 In the Web Content palette, click Normal, and click the arrow by the About slice to collapse its contents.

The eye icon disappears from the Cell_1 layer, and the About button in the image window returns to its monochromatic blue coloring.

5 Using the same process as Steps 2–3, create rollover states for each of the remaining four table slices:

- Select the Tour slice, create a new rollover, and make the Cell_2 layer visible.
- Select the Exhibits slice, create a new rollover, and make the Cell_3 layer visible.
- Select the Members slice, create a new rollover, and make the Cell_4 layer visible.
- Select the Contact slice, create a new rollover, and make the Cell_5 layer visible.

6 Hide all the rollover-state listings for the slices by clicking the arrow for each slice.

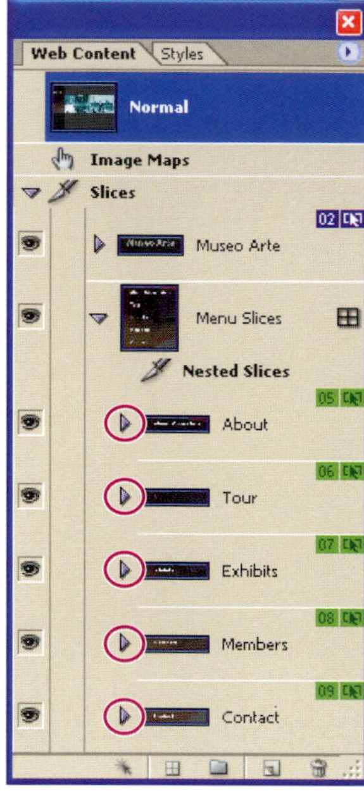

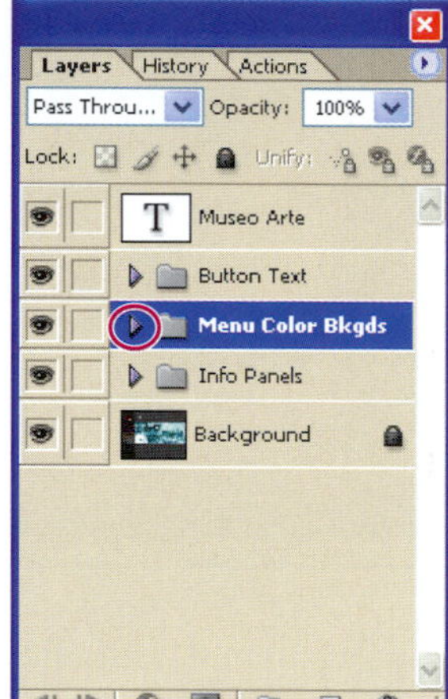

7 In the Layers palette, collapse the Menu Colored Bkgds layer set.

Previewing layer-visibility rollovers

Now it's time to test your rollovers by previewing them.

1 Click a blank area of the Layers palette to ensure that no layers are selected. Then click the Preview Document button (☝) in the toolbox.

Note: Do not *click the Toggle Slices Visibility button this time. Keep slice boundaries and symbol boxes visible as you preview.*

2 Slowly move the pointer up and down over the different buttons in the table and notice the following:

- The changes in background coloring as the pointer moves over the button areas.
- The Active Slice badge (✳) that appears in the symbol sets in the image window and slice listings in the Web Content palette, and also in the boxes next to the slice visibility symbols (👁).

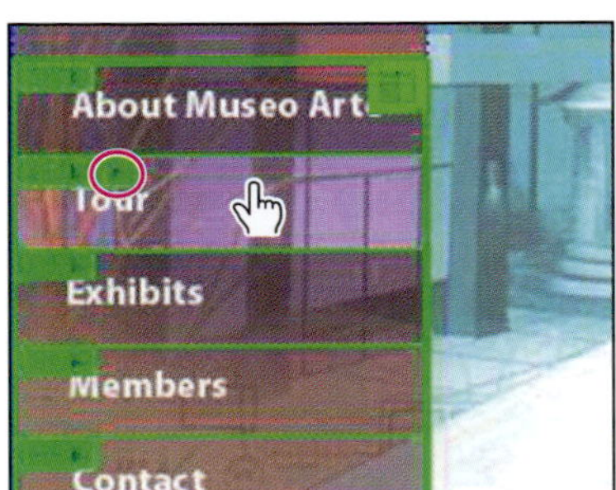

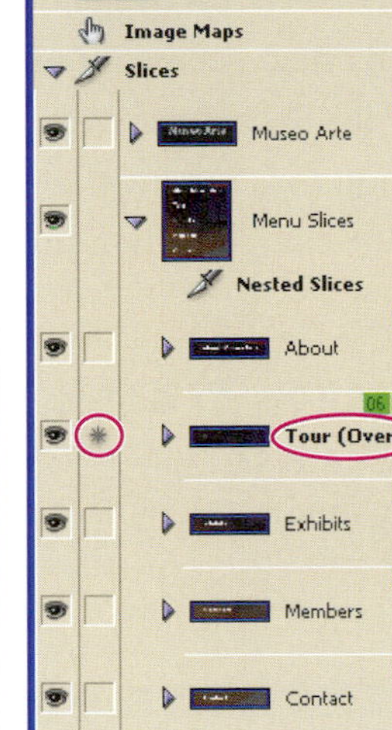

3 Click the Preview Document button again to deactivate it.

4 Choose File > Save to save your work.

About slice symbols

The blue, green, and gray slice symbols, or badges, in the Web Content palette and in the image window can be useful reminders if you take the time to learn how to read them. Each slice can contain as many badges as are appropriate. The following badges appear under the stated conditions:

(01) The number of the slice. Numbers run sequentially from left to right and top to bottom of the image.

( ) The active rollover state is in this slice.

( ) The slice contains image content.

( ) The slice contains no image content.

( ) The slice is layer-based (that is, it was created from a layer).

( ) The slice includes at least one rollover effect.

( ) The slice is a nested table.

( ) The slice is a remote trigger (causes a change in a remote slice).

( ) The slice is a remote target (changes in response to a user action in an associated remote trigger slice).

( ) The slice is linked to other slices (for optimization purposes).

Creating remote rollovers

A remote rollover is the association of one slice with another one so that an action in one slice affects the visibility or effects in the other slice. In this exercise, you will create a remote rollover in which an effect occurs on one part of the screen (in the center image) when the Web site visitor rolls the mouse over a different part of the screen (over the Exhibits slice). In preparation for creating that rollover, you will first create the slice that will appear in the center of the screen when the mouse action occurs.

1 In the Layers palette, select the Exhibit_info layer in the Info Panels layer set, and then click its visibility box. An eye icon (👁) appears in the Layers palette, and the layer becomes visible in the image window. The layer contains a graphic that says "Spanish Masters" and provides the dates of the exhibit.

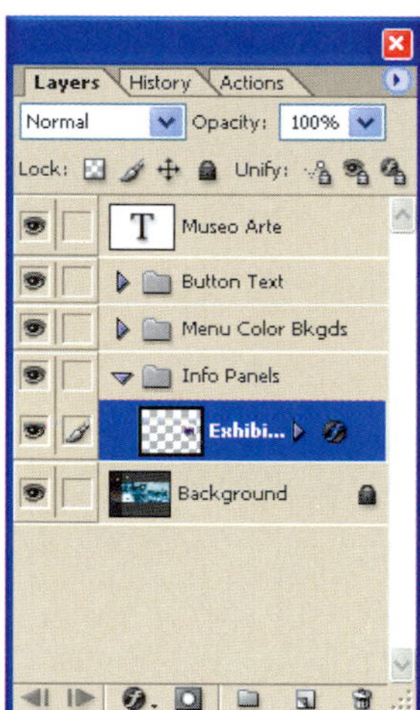

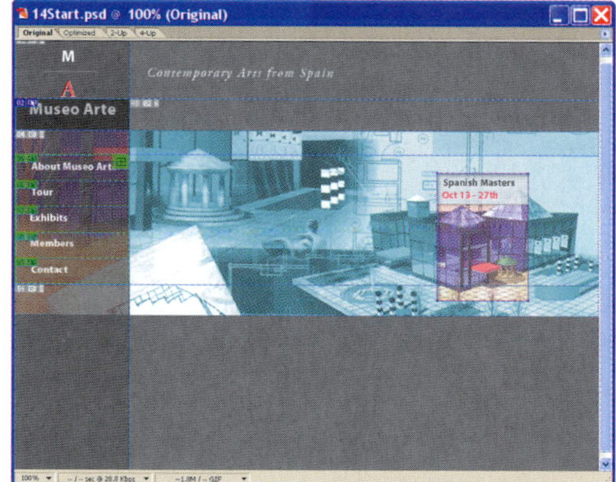

You will create a slice of that graphic from a selection.

2 Choose Select > Load Selection > Exhibit_info Transparency.

An animated selection border appears around the layer contents.

3 Choose Select > Create Slice from Selection.

A solid yellow border indicates that the layer is now also a slice, but the selection border is also visible.

4 Choose Select > Deselect, or press Ctrl-D (Windows) or Command-D (Mac OS).

5 In the Web Content palette, notice the appearance of your new slice, which was given a sequential number by default.

6 Double-click the new slice name, type **Exhibit Info**, and press Enter (Windows) or Return (Mac OS) to rename it.

7 In the Web Content palette, select Normal, and then click the eye icon (👁) next to the Exhibit_info layer in the Layers palette to hide it.

Associating slices using the pickwick feature

When creating remote rollovers, it is not enough to change the visibility settings in the Layers palette for the remote slice. You must also create the relationship between the two slices. The pickwick (◉) feature makes it easy and intuitive to accomplish this task.

1 In the Web Content palette, expand the Exhibits slice so that you can see the Over rollover state identified with the slice. Then, click to select the rollover state.

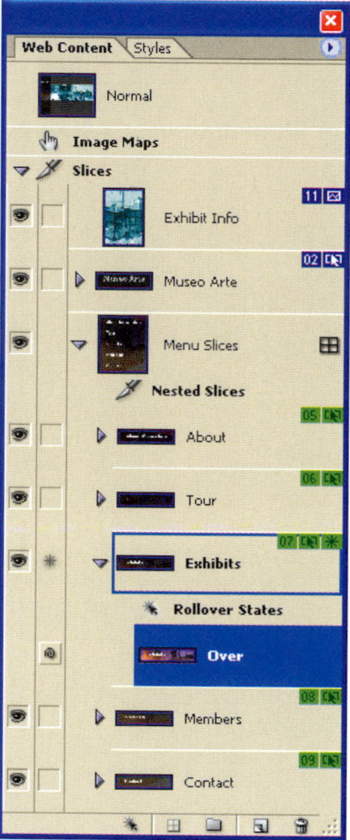

2 In the Layers palette, click the visibility box for the Exhibit_info layer. An eye icon (👁) appears for that layer, and it becomes visible in the image window.

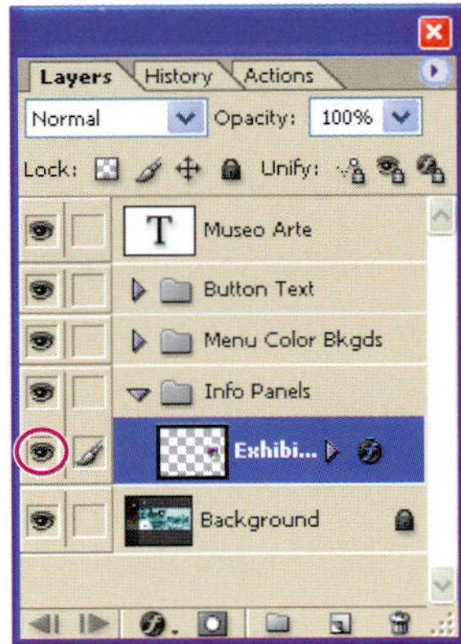

3 In the Web Content palette, drag the pickwick (◉) from the Over rollover state of the Exhibits slice to the Exhibit_info layer in the image window so that the slice boundary is highlighted by a dark border.

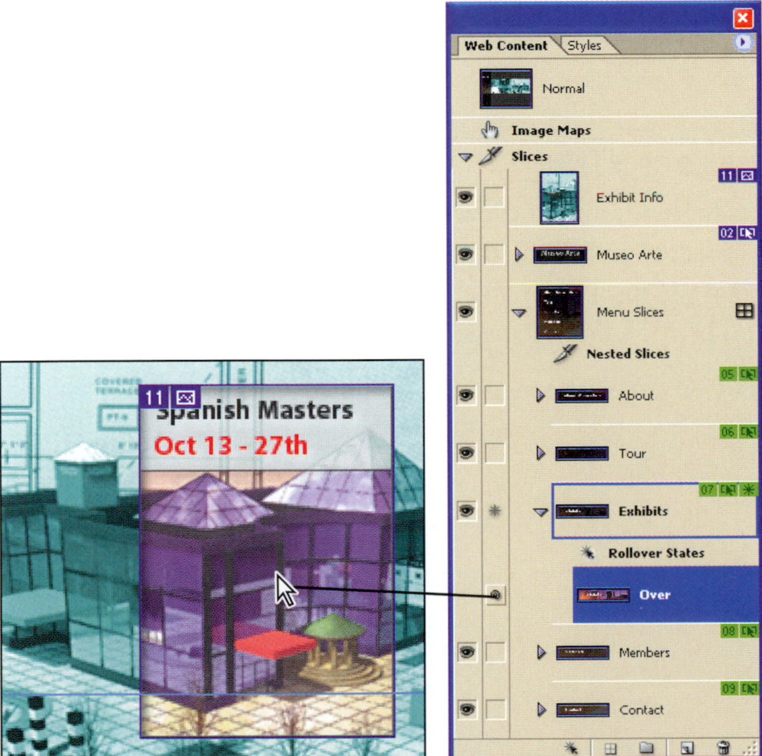

When you release the mouse button, notice the new remote trigger badge ( ) in the symbol sets for the Exhibits slice in the image window. Also notice the remote target badge ( ) for the Exhibit Info slice in the image window.

Note: *Instead of dragging the pickwick to the target slice in the image window, you can drag it to that slice in the Web Content palette. The result is the same with either method.*

4 Select Normal in the Web Content palette, and click the arrow on the Exhibits slice to hide its associated rollover.

5 In the Layers palette, click the arrow to collapse the Info Panels layer set.

If you accidentally release the pickwick over the wrong slice or decide later that you don't want to use the remote rollover, you can remove it. To do this, select the rollover state you want to edit, such as an Over or Down state nested under the triggering layer. Then click the remote target badge ( ) for the target slice in the Web Content palette to delete it, which dissolves the remote rollover relationship.

Saving the page as HTML

ImageReady does the hard work of converting your image-file information to a Web page that consists of an HTML file and supporting folders of files. There is one important step that you must do in order for the Web page to recognize the rollovers so that they work properly on the Web page. You'll do that step first.

1 From the Web Content palette menu, choose Find All Remote Slices.

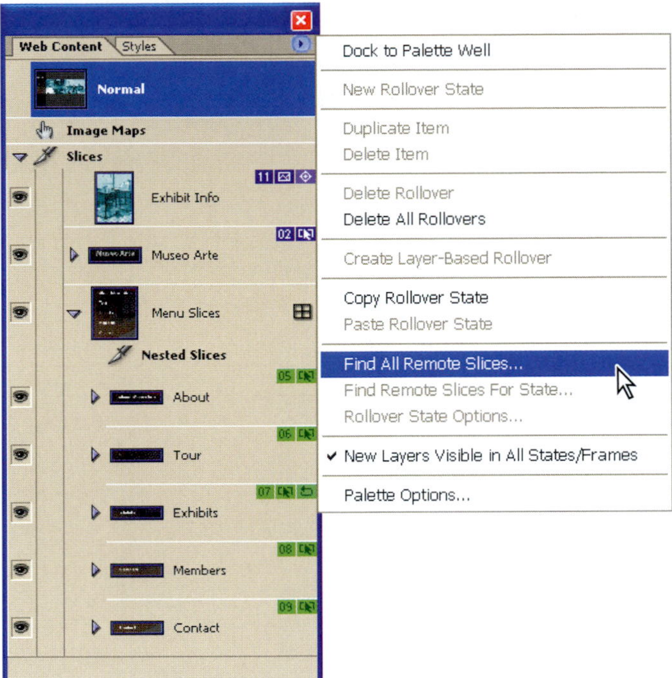

2 When a message appears reporting the changes that ImageReady has made to the file, click OK.

3 Choose File > Save Optimized As.

4 In the Save Optimized As dialog box, do the following:

- Navigate to the location where you want to save the file, or save it in the Lessons/Lesson14 folder.
- Leave the filename as it is.
- Choose HTML and Images for Save as Type (Windows) or Format (Mac OS).
- Choose Settings > Default Settings.
- Choose Slices > All Slices.
- Click Save.

5 Switch to Adobe Bridge, locate the 14Start.html file you just saved, and right-click (Windows) or Control-click (Mac OS). Choose Open With from the contextual menu, and choose a Web browser to open the HTML file and view your rollovers. When you're done, quit the browser.

Nice job! You have finished your work on Lesson 14.

Review

Review questions

1 Name two common rollover states and the mouse actions that are associated with them.

2 How many rollover states can a slice have?

3 What is a remote rollover?

4 Can rollovers do more than cause changes in appearance?

Review answers

1 Normal and Over are probably the two most common rollover states. Normal is the default appearance of the Web page, as it opens and before the user performs any mouse actions. Over is the state when the pointer tip is within the defined area but the user doesn't press the mouse button in any way. There are eight rollover states you can create in ImageReady, including Custom and None.

2 A slice can have multiple rollover states, but only one of each type. For example, a slice cannot have two Over states, but one Over state can trigger multiple changes in the slice and also in one or more remote slices.

3 A remote rollover is when a mouse action taking place in one slice affects the appearance of another slice in the image. These have sometimes been called *secondary* rollovers.

4 Yes. Properly configured, you can use remote rollovers to do other things, such as launch an application or run an animation. For more information, see ImageReady Help.

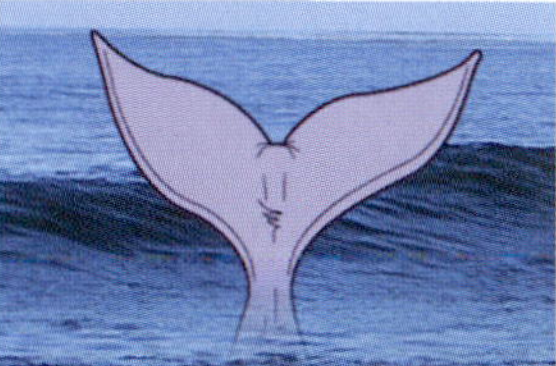

To add dynamic content to your Web page, you can use Adobe ImageReady to create animated GIF images. Compact in file size, animated GIFs display and play in most Web browsers. ImageReady provides an easy and convenient way to create imaginative animations.

15 Animating GIF Images for the Web

Lesson overview

In this lesson, you'll learn how to do the following:

- Use a multilayered GIF image as the basis for an animation.
- Use the Layers and Animation palettes to create animation sequences.
- Create animations based on changes in position, layer visibility, and layer effects.
- Make changes to single frames, multiple frames, and an entire animation.
- Use the Tween command to create smooth transitions between different settings for layer opacity and position.
- Preview animations in ImageReady and in a Web browser.
- Optimize the animation using the Optimize palette.

This lesson will take about an hour to complete. The lesson must be done in Adobe ImageReady, not Adobe Photoshop.

If needed, remove the previous lesson folder from your hard drive, and copy the Lessons/Lesson15 folder onto it. As you work on this lesson, you'll overwrite the start files. If you need to restore the start files, copy them from the *Adobe Photoshop CS2 Classroom in a Book* CD.

In addition, for this lesson, you will need to use a Web browser application (such as Netscape, Internet Explorer, or Safari). You do not need to connect to the Internet.

Creating animations in Adobe ImageReady

In Adobe ImageReady, you create animations from a single image using animated GIF files. An *animated GIF* is a sequence of images, or frames. Each frame varies slightly from the preceding frame, creating the illusion of movement when the frames are viewed in quick succession—just like movies. You can create animation in several ways:

- By using the Duplicate Current Frame button in the Animation palette to create animation frames, and then using the Layers palette to define the image state associated with each frame.
- By using the Tween feature to quickly create new frames that warp text or vary a layer's opacity, position, or effects to create the illusion of an element in a frame moving or fading in and out.
- By opening a multilayer Adobe Photoshop or Adobe Illustrator file for an animation, with each layer becoming a frame.

When creating an animation sequence, it's best to select the Original tab in the image window, because this view doesn't require ImageReady to re-optimize the image as you edit the frame contents. Animation files are output as either GIF files or QuickTime movies. You cannot create a JPEG or PNG animation.

About working with layers in animations

Working with layers is an essential part of creating animations in ImageReady. Placing each element of an animation on its own layer allows you to change the position and appearance of the element across a series of frames.

Frame-specific changes Some changes you make to layers affect only the active animation frame. By default, changes you make to layers using Layers palette commands and options—including layer opacity, blending mode, visibility, position, and style—are frame specific. However, you can apply layer changes to all frames in an animation by using the unity buttons in the Layers palette.

Global changes Some changes affect every frame in which the layers are included. Changes you make to layer pixel values using painting and editing tools, color- and tone-adjustment commands, filters, type, and other image-editing commands are global.

Each new frame starts out as a duplicate of the preceding frame—you edit the frame by adjusting its layers. You can apply layer changes to a single frame, a group of frames, or the entire animation.

Getting started

In this lesson, you'll work with a set of images designed to appear on the Web page of a fresh-juice company. Use a Web browser application to preview the finished animations.

1 Launch Adobe Bridge and click Lessons in the Favorites palette in the upper left corner of the browser window. Then double-click the Lesson15 folder in the thumbnail preview area.

2 Right-click (Windows) or Control-click (Mac OS) the 15End.html file, and choose Open With from the contextual menu. Choose a Web browser to open the HTML file.

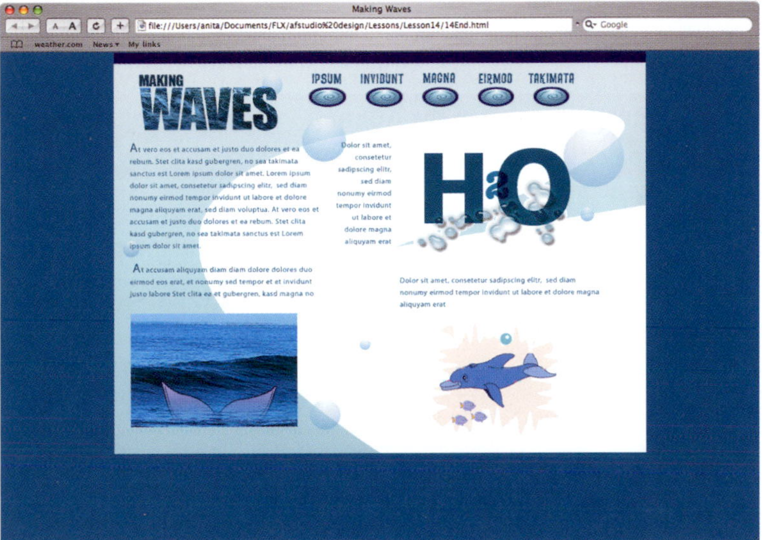

The page includes three animated areas: the "Making Waves" text, the chemical formula for water moving into the image, and a dolphin swimming along and releasing bubbles that pop into the air. (The text and buttons are merely placeholders.)

3 When you have finished viewing the file, quit the browser.

4 Start Adobe ImageReady while holding down Ctrl-Alt-Shift (Windows) or Command-Option-Shift (Mac OS) to restore the default preferences. (See "Restoring default preferences" on page 6.)

5 When prompted, click Erase to erase preferences.

Defining a workspace for animation tasks

Before you start working on the file, you'll define a new workspace especially for animation work. Having the right workspace available at any time reduces screen clutter and makes your task more efficient and more enjoyable.

1 Choose File > Open, navigate to the Lessons/Lesson15 folder, and double-click the Dolphin.psd file to open it. (The artwork for the animation has been completed for you, so you won't need to enlarge the image window or zoom in for the tasks in this lesson.)

Note: *Double-clicking the image thumbnail in Bridge opens the file into Photoshop.*

2 Close the Color, Web Content, and Slice palette groups.

3 In the Info palette group, select the Layer Comps tab to bring it forward.

4 Choose Window > Animation to open the Animation palette. Drag the lower right corner of the Animation palette to expand it so that you take advantage of available horizontal space in the work area.

(Optional) You can also move the Animation palette closer to the image window, to keep elements in the work area close together.

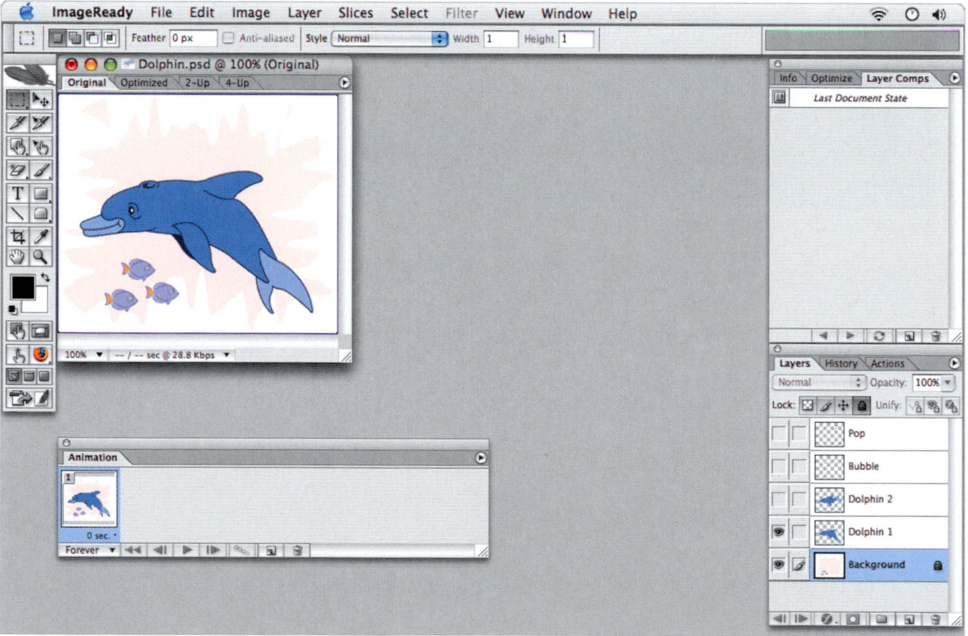

5 Choose Window > Workspace > Save Workspace.

6 Type **Animation** in the Save Workspace dialog box, and click OK.

Now you can quickly restore these palette sizes and positions by choosing Window > Workspace > Animation at any time.

Animating by hiding and showing layers

Perhaps the simplest way to create a two-step animation is by toggling the visibility of two layers by changing the eye icons (👁) in the Layers palette. For example, you can make an animated character alternate between different expressions or make an object move back and forth in a simple pattern.

The Dolphin.psd image file includes five layers, as you can see by examining the Layers palette. You'll create your first animation with the two Dolphin layers.

Preparing layer comps

You learned about layer comps in Photoshop in Lesson 6, "Layer Basics." ImageReady offers the same capabilities, which can make animations much easier to create.

1 In the Layers palette, make sure that eye icons (👁) appear in the visibility boxes for the Background and Dolphin 1 layers and that the visibility boxes for the three other layers are empty.

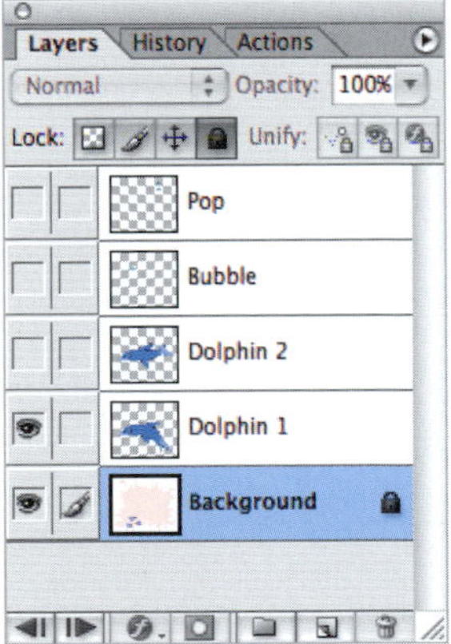

2 In the Layer Comps palette, click the Create New Layer Comp button (▣).

3 In the New Layer Comp dialog box, type **Dolphin 1**, make sure that Visibility is selected (checked), and click OK.

Now a new layer comp, Dolphin 1, appears in the Layer Comps palette.

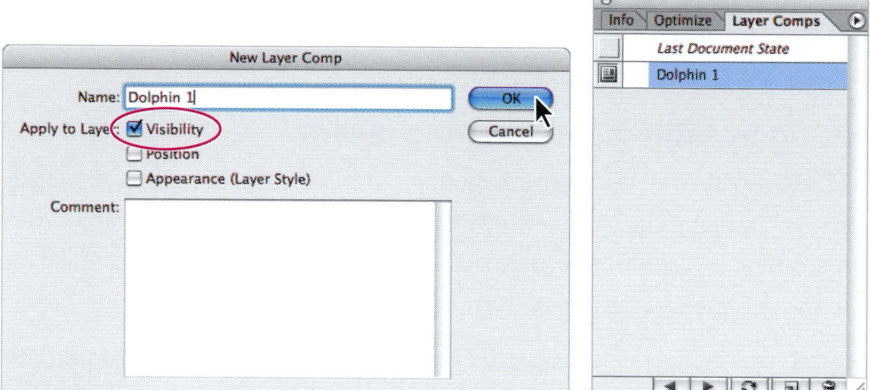

4 In the Layers palette, click to hide the eye icon for the Dolphin 1 layer, and then click to set an eye icon for the Dolphin 2 layer.

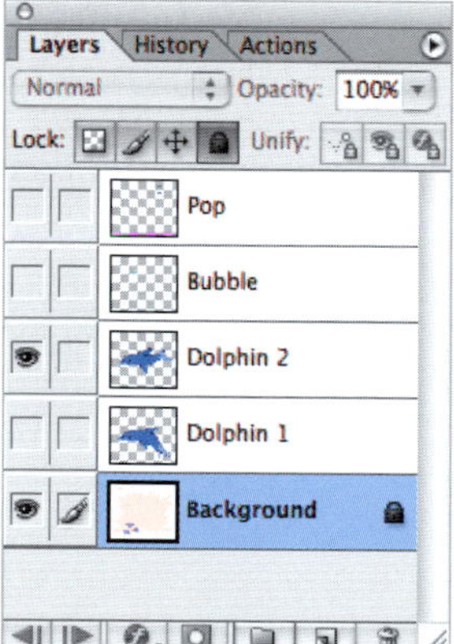

5 Create a new layer comp, Dolphin 2, using the techniques in Steps 2 and 3.

6 Click the box on the left of the Dolphin 1 layer comp to apply those visibility conditions to the image. A badge (▤) appears in the box, indicating that this is the current layer comp.

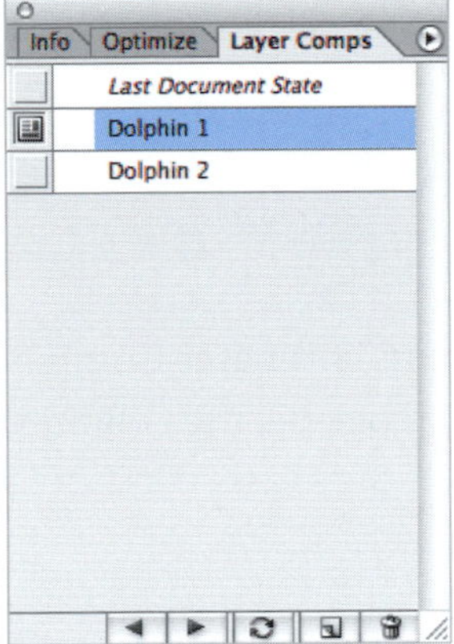

You now have two layer comps that you can use as starting points for the frames you'll create in the animation.

Beginning the animation process

As you begin, only one frame, the default, appears in the Animation palette. This frame shows the current visibility settings in the Layers palette, with only two layers visible: Dolphin 1 and Background. The frame is selected (outlined with a border), indicating that you can change its content by editing the image.

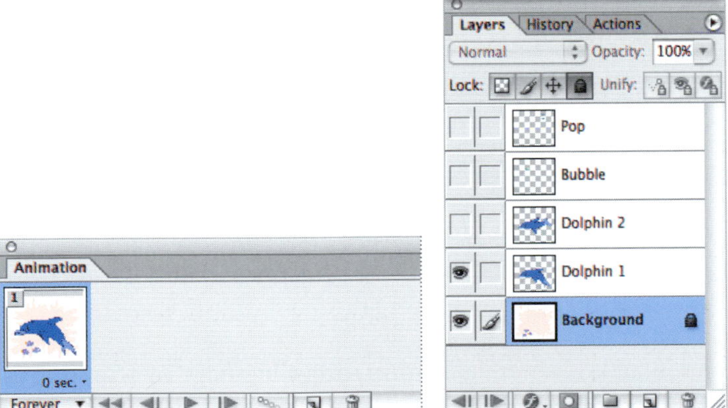

1 In the Animation palette, click the Duplicate Current Frame button ( ) to create frame 2.

2 In the Layer Comps palette, click the box to set the Apply This Layer Comp badge (▤) for the Dolphin 2 layer comp. Notice that in the Layers palette, the Dolphin 1 layer is now hidden and the Dolphin 2 layer is visible.

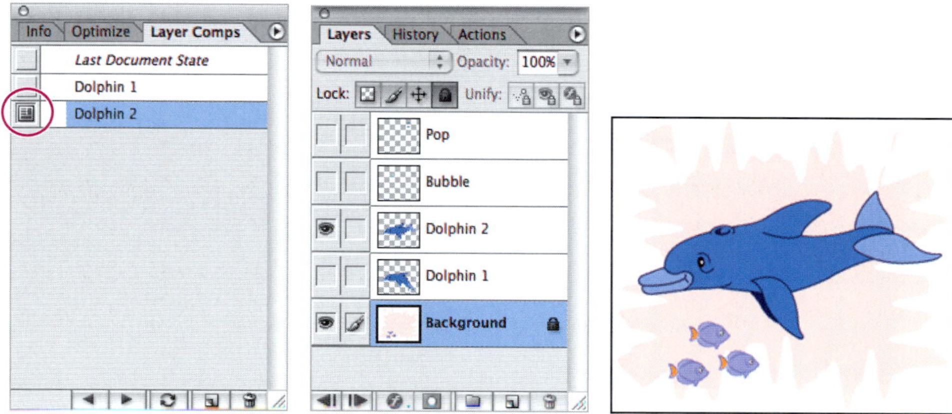

3 In the Animation palette, select frame 1. In the image window, the dolphin resumes its original appearance, with only Layer 1 visible.

4 Select frame 2 and then frame 1 repeatedly to manually animate the image.

Navigating animation frames and previewing the animation

You can use a number of techniques to preview and scroll through your animation frames. Understanding the controls available on the Animation and Layers palettes is essential to mastery of the animation process.

You've already experimented with manually animating the image by selecting each of the frames in turn. In this exercise, you'll try out other ways to preview an animation in ImageReady and in a Web browser.

Note: *To use the Preview In command, you must have a browser application installed on your system. For more information, see the topic "Previewing an image in a browser" in ImageReady Help.*

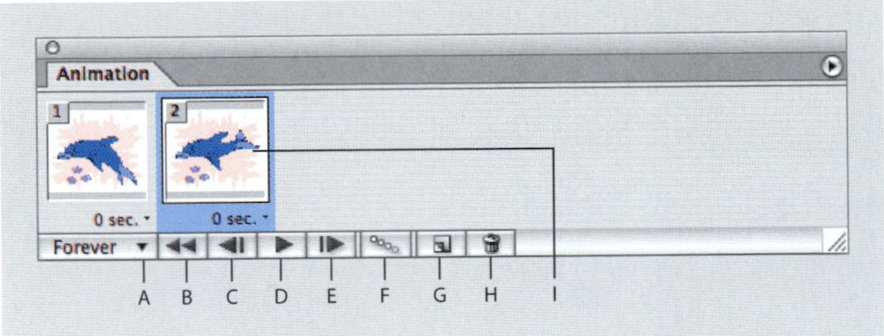

A. Looping pop-up menu B. Select First Frame button C. Select Previous Frame button D. Play/Stop Animation button E. Select Next Frame button F. Tween button G. Duplicate Current Frame button H. Trash I. Selected frame

1 In the Animation palette, make sure that Forever is chosen in the Looping pop-up menu in the lower left corner of the palette.

2 Click the Select Previous Frame button (◀▮) to move to the other frame. (Try clicking the button repeatedly in quick succession, and watch the manual playback of the animation in the image window.)

3 In the Layers palette, click the Backward or Forward button in the lower left corner of the palette, and notice results similar to the previous step.

A. Layers palette Backward button
B. Layers palette Forward button

4 Click the Play button (▶) in the Animation palette to preview the animation. The Play button becomes the Stop button (■), which you can click to stop the playback.

5 Choose File > Preview In, and choose a browser application from the submenu. When you finish previewing the animation, quit the browser window and return to ImageReady.

You can also press Ctrl-Alt-P (Windows) or Command-Option-P (Mac OS) to launch a browser preview quickly, or click the Preview In button in the toolbox.

6 Choose File > Save Optimized As.

7 In the Save Optimized As dialog box, open the Lessons/Lesson15 folder and click the icon for Create New Folder. Type **My_GIFs** to name the new folder, and then open it. Still in the Save Optimized As dialog box, name the file **Dolphin.gif** and click Save.

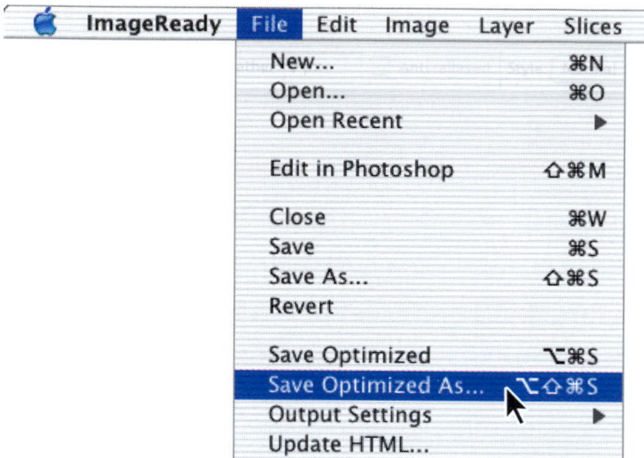

Preparing layer copies for an animation

Now you'll animate a different element in the dolphin image, adding to the existing animation. In this procedure, you'll use the same basic technique—hiding and showing layers in different frames—to create your animation, but this time you'll also create the different layers by copying and transforming a single layer.

Before adding layers to an image that already contains an animation, it's a good idea to create a new frame. This helps protect your existing frames from unwanted changes.

1 In the Animation palette, select frame 2 and click the Duplicate Current Frame button (▣) to create a new frame (frame 3) that is identical to frame 2. Leave frame 3 selected.

2 Open the Animation palette menu and choose the New Layers Visible in All States/ Frames command to deselect it (remove the check mark).

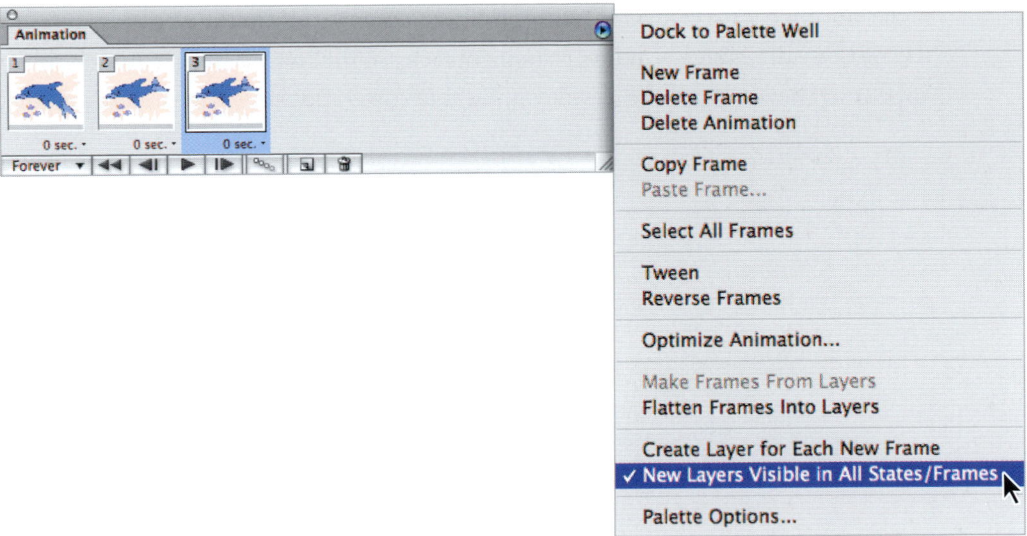

3 In the Layers palette, select the Bubble layer and click the box for the eye icon (👁) to make the layer visible. Leave the Bubble layer selected.

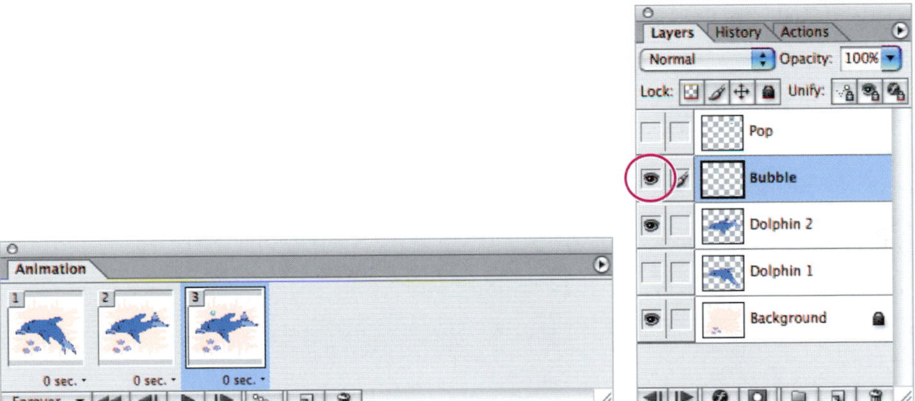

In the image window and in the frame 3 thumbnail, notice the bubble that appears above the dolphin's blow hole.

4 Choose View > Snap to deselect it so that no check mark appears by this command.

5 Select the Move tool (▸✥) in the toolbox.

6 Hold down Alt (Windows) or Option (Mac OS) and drag the bubble up and to the right in the image window. When you release the mouse button, two bubbles now appear in the image, and a new layer, Bubble copy, appears in the Layers palette.

7 Again hold down Alt (Windows) or Option (Mac OS) and drag to create a third bubble, a little above and to the right of the second bubble.

You now have three bubble layers in the image window and the Layers palette: Bubble, Bubble copy, and Bubble copy 2.

***Note:** The duplicate layers would be visible in all three frames in the Animation palette if New Layers Visible in All States/Frames were selected in the Animation palette menu.*

Transforming layers for an animation

Now that you've prepared the duplicate bubble layers in the Dolphin.psd file, you'll apply a scale transformation to the two copies so that the bubble appears to grow as it trails behind the swimming dolphin.

1 If the Move tool () is not still selected, select it now, and then make sure that the Layer Select tool () is selected on the tool options bar.

2 In the image window, select the middle bubble, the Bubble copy layer object.

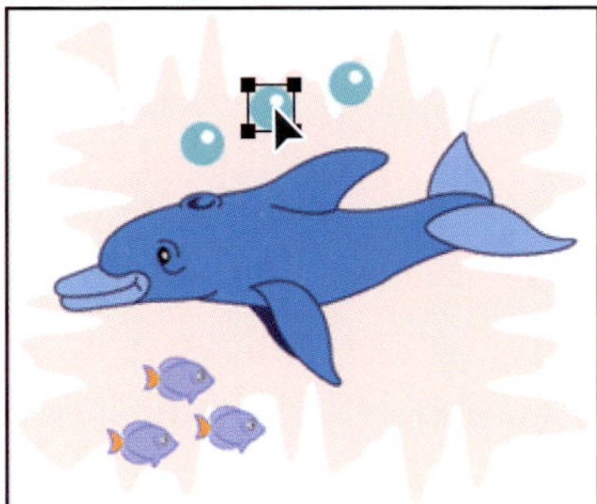

3 Choose Edit > Transform > Scale.

In the image window, the transformation bounding box appears around the Bubble copy layer.

4 On the tool options bar, select the Constrain Aspect Ratio button (), and type **24** px for width (W:). Click anywhere outside the width text box and notice that the bubble assumes its new size, but the transformation bounding box remains on the Bubble copy layer object.

5 Press Enter (Windows) or Return (Mac OS) to commit the transformation.

6 Select the third bubble and repeat Steps 3–5, but this time type **26** px as either the width or height dimension.

7 Still using the Move tool and the Layer Select tool option, refine the locations of the three bubble layers by dragging them in the image window, as needed.

Make sure that the third bubble does not extend beyond the tip of the dolphin's dorsal fin and that the three bubbles are nearly evenly spaced. Refer to the following illustration as a guide.

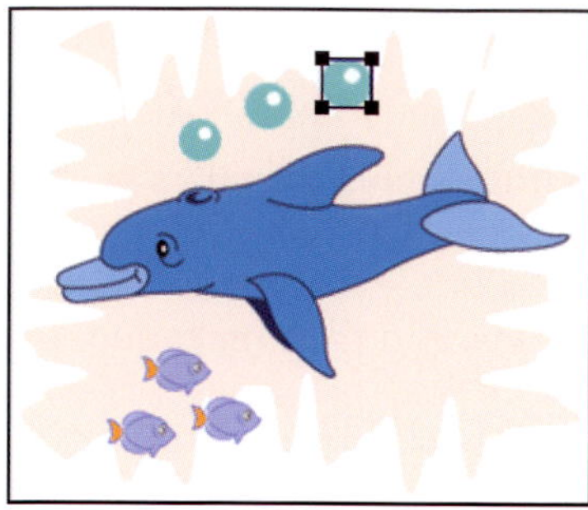

8 Choose File > Save.

Creating the simultaneous animations

Now you'll define the rising-bubble animation by successively hiding and showing the layers of the Dolphin.psd file. You'll combine this rising bubble with the swimming dolphin animation by duplicating frames and coordinating settings in the Layers and Animation palettes.

1 In the Animation palette, make sure that frame 3 is selected, or select it now.

2 In the Layers palette, click the visibility boxes to set or remove eye icons (👁) so that the Background, Dolphin 1, and the original Bubble layer are visible and the other layers are hidden.

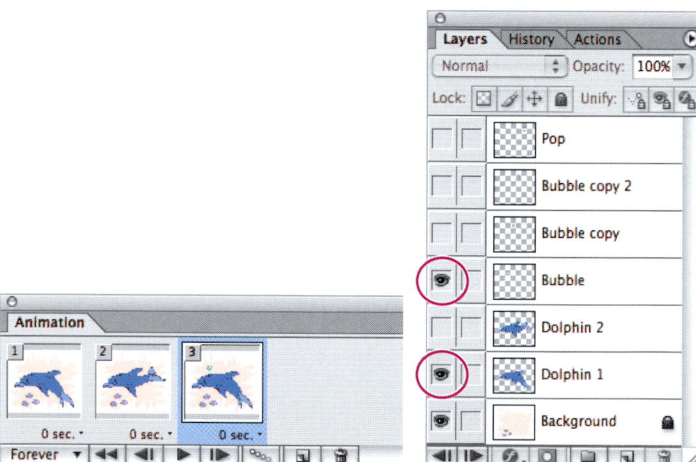

***Note:** When you hide or show a layer in a frame, the visibility of the layer changes for that frame only.*

3 In the Animation palette, click the Duplicate Current Frame button (▣) to create frame 4. Leave frame 4 selected in the Animation palette.

4 In the Layer Comps palette, select Dolphin 2 by clicking its Apply this Layer Comp button. Then, in the Layers palette, set an eye icon (👁) for the Bubble copy layer.

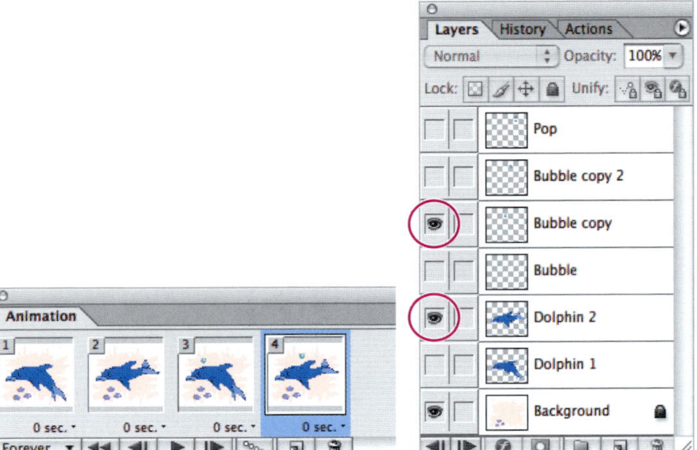

5 Click the Duplicate Current Frame two more times, and then use the Layer Comps and Layers palettes as follows:

- For frame 5, apply the Dolphin 1 layer comp and make the Bubble copy 2 layer visible.
- For frame 6, apply the Dolphin 2 layer comp and make the Pop layer visible.

6 Click the Play button (▶) on the Animation palette to preview the results. When you are finished, click the Stop button (■) to stop the playback.

As the animation moves from frame to frame, the dolphin's tail moves up and down with each step. In each full cycle, the bubble emerges from the dolphin, rises, and pops in a four-step sequence.

If your results are different from what is described here, review the visibility settings on the Layers palette for each successive frame and make any necessary corrections.

Setting and previewing the timing sequence

Earlier, when you previewed your animation in the browser, you probably noticed that the rate at which the dolphin is swimming is nothing short of frenetic. You can calm the dolphin's motion by setting a delay between each frame in the animation. Then, you'll play the animation again to review the speed of the apparent action.

In your own projects, you can specify pauses for all frames or different pauses for various individual frames in your animation. For this file, you'll apply the same time delay between each pair of frames in the complete animation.

1 From the Animation palette menu, choose Select All Frames.

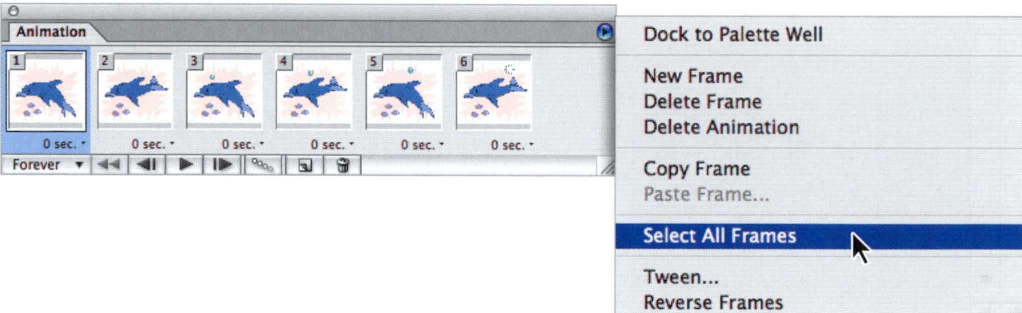

2 Click the time (0 seconds, which is the default) beneath any one of the frames to open the Frame Delay pop-up menu, and choose 0.2 seconds.

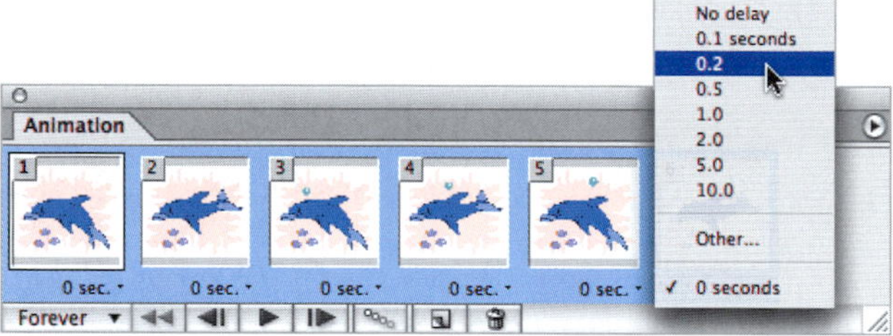

The new value appears below each frame thumbnail, indicating that the time delay applies to all the frames in the palette.

3 Click the Play button (▶) in the Animation palette to view your animation, and then click the Stop button (■) when you're ready to halt the playback.

4 Choose File > Preview In, and choose a browser from the submenu to play back the animation with accurate timing. When you finish previewing, return to ImageReady.

5 Choose File > Save Optimized As.

6 In the Save Optimized As dialog box, make sure that the image is named **Dolphin .gif** and that the location is your My_GIFs folder. Then click Save, and click Replace to replace the existing file.

The Save Optimized As command saves a file in the GIF, JPEG, or PNG format for use in your Web pages. GIF is the only format that supports animations, so that's the format you need for this project.

7 Choose File > Close to close your original image without saving changes.

You've finished your work on the dolphin animation for the Web-page project. Next, you'll continue with work on other animated elements for the project.

Animating with layer opacity and position

You'll use a slightly different method for animation in the next part of the project. This time, you'll animate a fly-in of a text logo, using a multilayered Photoshop image.

The good news is that you don't have to manually create more layers for each change in position, and you don't have to painstakingly create and adjust each individual frame. As soon as you create the beginning and end frames for the sequence, you can relax and let ImageReady do all the work for the frames in between them.

Opening the image file and starting the animation process

To get started, you'll open the new art file and review its current settings.

1 In ImageReady, choose File > Open, and open the H2O.psd file from the Lessons/ Lesson15 folder on your hard disk.

The logo consists of four components that reside on separate layers. You'll compose animation frames that show the characters of the logo appearing and moving into their final position from different areas. The initial state reflects how you want the image to appear at the end of the animation.

2 Make sure that the Animation and Layers palettes are visible, or choose Window > Workspace > Animation to open them.

3 In the Animation palette, click the Duplicate Current Frame button ( ) to create a new animation frame.

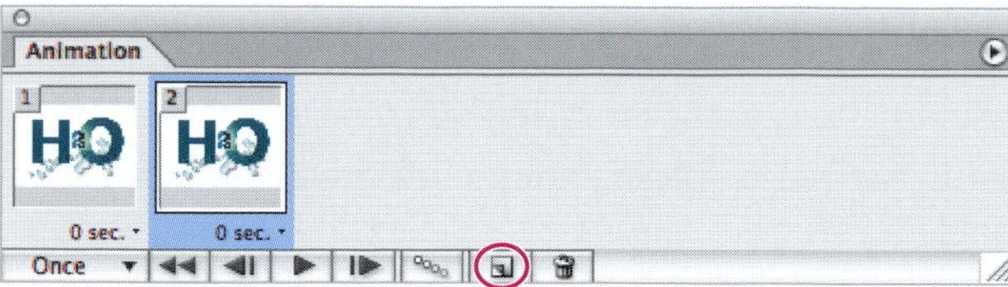

Now that you have two frames, you've paved the way for a new animation. Your next task will be to change the status of various layers for the different frames.

Setting layer positions and opacity

Next, you'll adjust the position and opacity of layers in an image to create the start and end frames of an animation sequence. Changing the order in which frames appear in the animation is as simple as dragging the thumbnails in the Animation palette.

1 In the Animation palette, make sure that frame 2 is selected. Then, in the Layers palette, select the H layer.

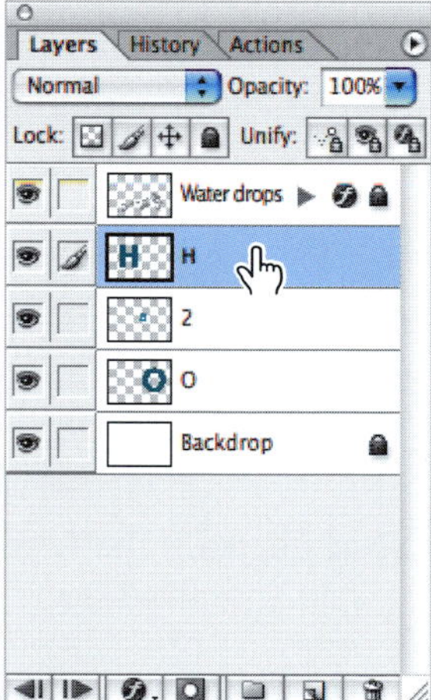

2 Select the Move tool (▸✢) and begin to drag the "H" to the left side of the image window. After you start dragging, hold down Shift to constrain the movement. When only a portion of the "H" is visible, release the mouse button and then the Shift key.

3 In the Layers palette, select the O layer, and drag the "O" to a similar position on the right side of image window, using Shift again to constrain the movement.

***Note:** Be careful not to drag the letters completely out of the image window and onto the desktop, which might create an ImageReady clipping file there.*

4 Repeat Step 3, but this time select the 2 layer and drag the "2" to the upper edge of the image window. The three layers should be arranged as shown in the following illustration.

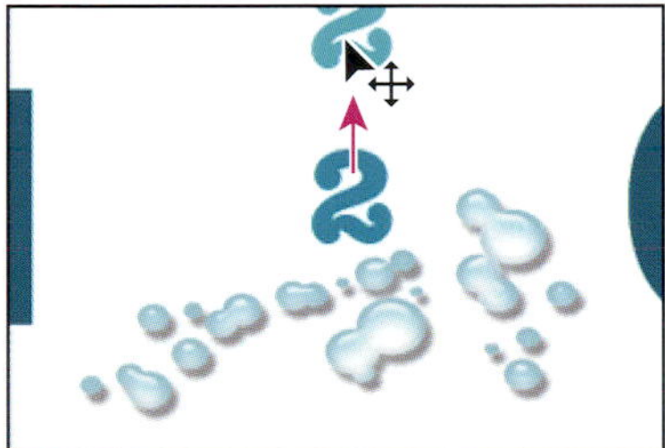

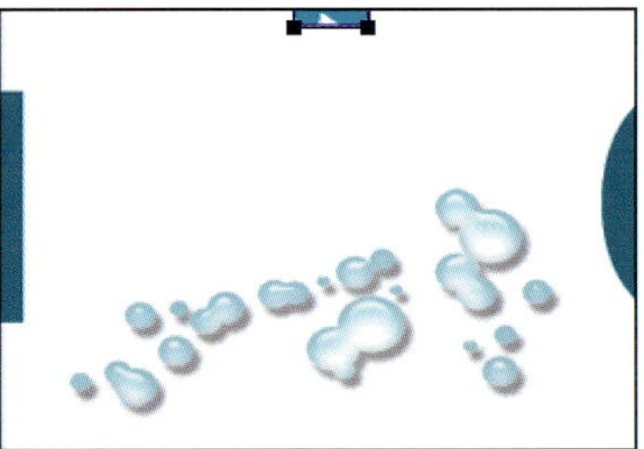

5 In the Layers palette, select the H layer and drag the Opacity slider to 20%. Repeat this action to reset the opacity of the 2 and O layers at 20% as well.

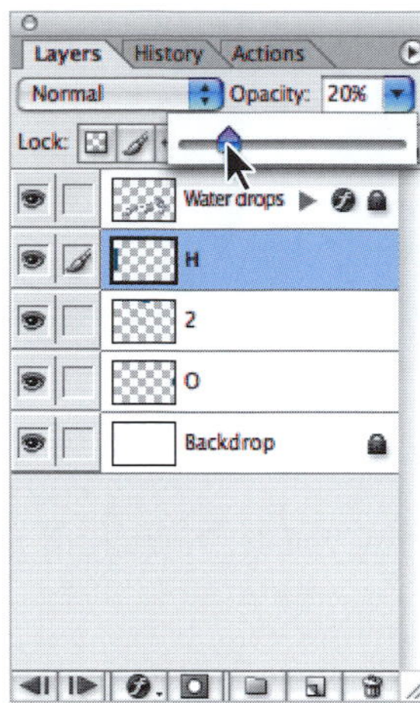

In the Animation palette, notice that frame 2 has updated to reflect the current image state. To make frame 2 the starting state of your animation, you'll switch the order of the two frames.

6 In the Animation palette, drag frame 2 to the left, releasing the mouse when the black bar appears to the left of frame 1.

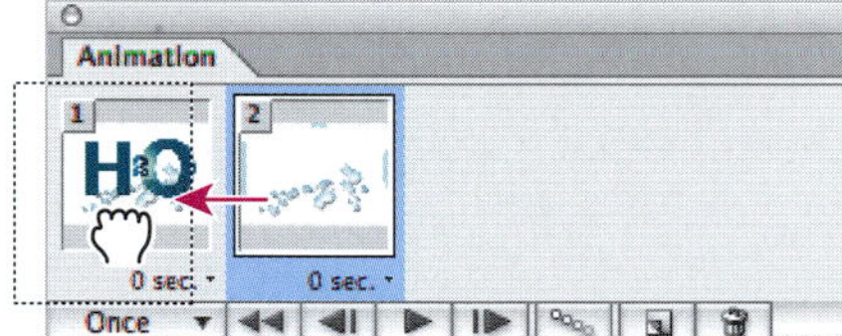

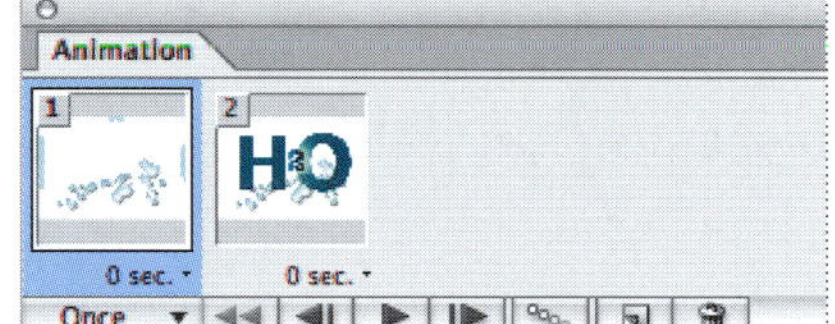

Tweening the position and opacity of layers

Next, you'll add frames that represent transitional image states between the two existing frames. When you change the position, opacity, or effects of any layer between two animation frames, you can instruct ImageReady to *tween,* which automatically creates as many intermediate frames as you specify.

1 In the Animation palette, make sure that frame 1 is selected and then choose Tween from the Animation palette menu.

2 In the Tween dialog box, set the following options (if they are not already selected):

- Choose Tween With > Next Frame.

- For Frames to Add, type **4**.
- Under Layers, select All Layers.
- Under Parameters, select Position and Opacity, as needed, so that check marks appear for those options. (You could select Effects if you were going to vary the settings of layer effects evenly between the beginning and ending frames. You won't choose this option now, because you haven't applied any layer effects.)

3 Click OK to close the dialog box.

ImageReady creates four new transitional frames, based on the opacity and position settings of the layers in the original two frames.

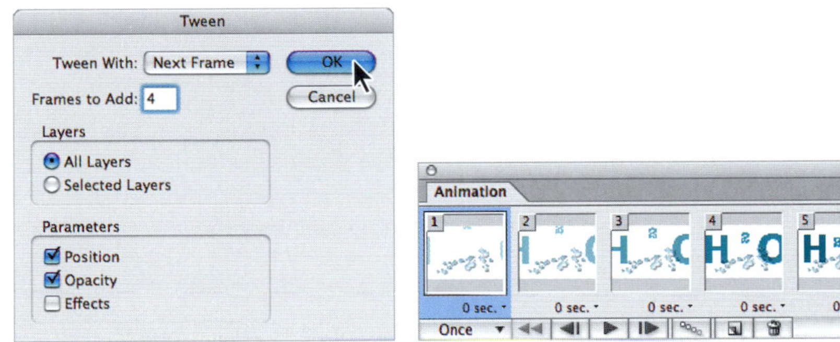

4 Choose Once from the Looping pop-up menu in the lower left corner of the Animation palette.

***Note:** In the 15End.html file that you previewed at the beginning of this lesson, the looping is configured differently from what you're instructed to do here. In the end file, the Looping option is Forever, but there is also a long delay after the final frame of the animation, which has not yet been created.*

5 In the Animation palette, click the Play button (►) to preview your animation in ImageReady.

Tweening frames

You use the Tween command to automatically add or modify a series of frames between two existing frames—varying the layer attributes (position, opacity, or effect parameters) evenly between the new frames to create the appearance of movement. For example, if you want to fade out a layer, set the opacity of the layer in the starting frame to 100%, and then set the opacity of the same layer in the ending frame to 0%. When you tween between the two frames, the opacity of the layer is reduced evenly across the new frames.

The term *tweening* is derived from "in betweening," the term used in traditional animation to describe this process. Tweening significantly reduces the time required to create animation effects such as fading in or fading out, or moving an element across a frame. You can edit tweened frames individually after you create them.

If you select a single frame, you choose whether to tween the frame with the previous frame or the next frame. If you select two contiguous frames, new frames are added between the frames. If you select more than two frames, existing frames between the first and last selected frames are altered by the tweening operation. If you select the first and last frames in an animation, these frames are treated as contiguous, and tweened frames are added after the last frame. (This tweening method is useful when the animation is set to loop multiple times.)

Note: You cannot select discontiguous frames for tweening.

Animating a layer style

When you tweened to create the four new frames in the previous procedure, you noticed the Effects check box in the Tween dialog box. In this procedure, you will animate a layer effect, or *layer style*. The final result will be a little flash of light that appears and then disappears behind the 2 image.

1 In the Animation palette, select frame 6, and then click the Duplicate Current Frame button to create a new frame with all the same settings as frame 6. Leave frame 7 selected.

2 In the Layers palette, select the 2 layer, and then choose Outer Glow from the Layer Style pop-up menu at the bottom of the palette.

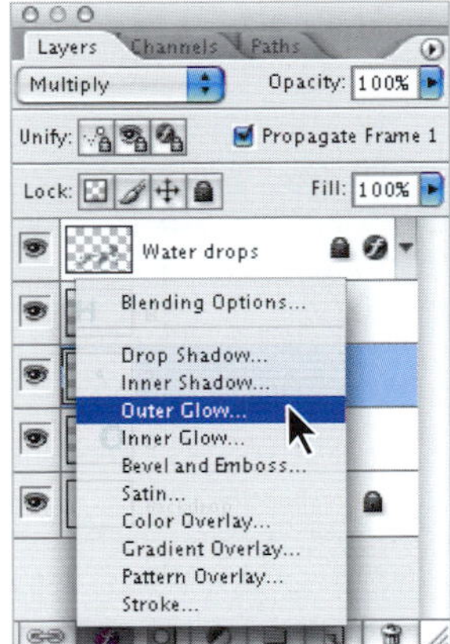

3 When the Layer Style dialog box opens, click OK to accept the default settings.

A subtle, light halo is created around the edges of the 2 image.

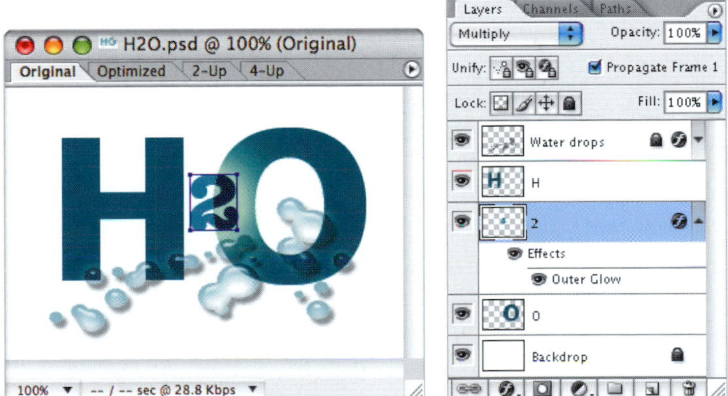

4 Duplicate frame 7 by clicking the Duplicate Current Frame button (icon) in the Animation palette.

5 In the Layers palette, double-click the Outer Glow effect for the 2 layer to open the Layer Style dialog box. Make sure that the Preview box is checked, and then set Spread to **20%** and Size to **49** pixels. Then click OK.

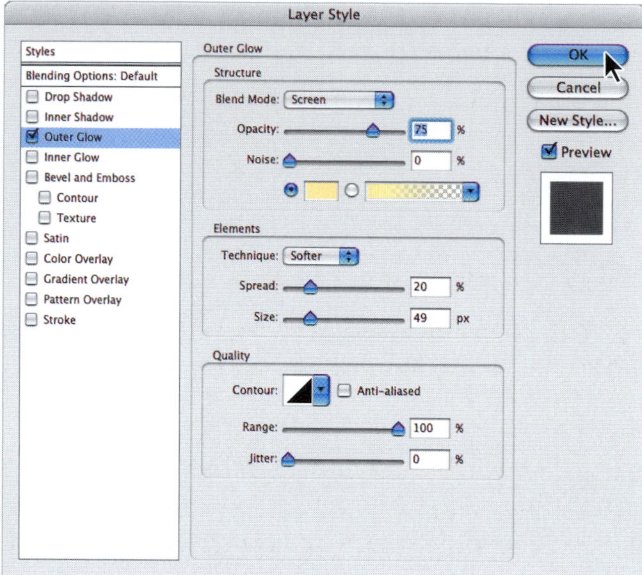

6 Choose File > Save.

Tweening frames for the layer-style changes

As you've seen, the Tween feature can save you lots of time you might have spent doing tedious and exacting work. You'll use the Tween command again now to animate the change in layer style. You'll also complete the glow effect by duplicating one more frame and moving it to the end of the animation. The resulting animation gives the impression of a little "pop" of light behind the 2 image as it comes into place.

1 In the Animation palette, select frame 7.

2 Choose Tween from the Animation palette menu.

3 In the Tween dialog box, specify the following options:

- For Tween With, choose Next Frame.
- For Frames to Add, type **2**.
- Under Layers, select All Layers.
- Under Parameters, select Effects.

4 Click OK to close the dialog box.

5 In the Animation palette, select frame 6, and then click the Duplicate Current Frame button (▣) to create a new frame 7, which will renumber the frames following 7.

6 Drag the new frame 7 to the end of the Animation palette so that it is to the right of (after) frame 11.

7 Choose File > Save.

Preserving transparency and preparing to optimize

Next, you'll optimize the H2O image in GIF format with background transparency, and then preview your animation in a Web browser. Remember that only the GIF format supports animated images.

We included the Backdrop layer in the H2O.psd file to make it easier to see the results as you work. That layer is not necessary for the final Web page, because you're going to optimize the file with a transparent background. Your first step, then, is to hide the Backdrop layer.

1 From the Animation palette menu, choose Select All Frames.

2 In the Layers palette, click the eye icon (👁) for the Backdrop layer to hide it in all frames.

3 In the Optimize palette, set the following options:

- For the Format, choose GIF.
- Under Color Table, choose Perceptual for Reduction and **256** for Colors.
- Under Transparency, select the Transparency check box (to preserve the transparency of the original image).
- For Matte, choose the white swatch from the pop-up palette if it is not already selected.

Making good GIF optimization choices

One of the most important aspects of making efficient GIF images—whether still or animated—is to reduce file size as much as possible without degrading image quality. To that end, when you optimize GIF images, you need to choose the most appropriate color-reduction algorithm, reduce the color palette as much as possible, and control application and browser dither.

ImageReady (and Photoshop) can calculate the most-needed colors for you based on any of several color-reduction algorithms: Perceptual, Selective, Adaptive, Web, Custom, and Windows or Mac OS. Typically, you'll want to choose between Perceptual, Selective, and Adaptive.

Perceptual creates a custom color table by giving priority to colors for which the human eye has greater sensitivity. Selective works similarly, but favors broad areas of color and the preservation of Web colors. Selective usually produces images with the greatest color integrity. Adaptive creates a custom color table by sampling colors from the spectrum appearing most commonly in the image.

Once you've chosen a color-reduction method, the colors in the file are displayed in the Color Table. You can further reduce the number of colors in the file using the Color pop-up menu. This often preserves good image quality while dramatically reducing the file space required to store extra colors.

Application dither occurs when ImageReady or Photoshop attempts to simulate colors that appear in the original image, but not in the optimized palette that you specify. To control application dither, zoom in to transition areas of your image and see if they are smooth or abrupt. If there are harsh borders or bands of color, drag the Dither slider up to 100%.

Browser dither occurs when a Web browser using a 256-color display simulates colors that appear in the optimized image's palette, but not in the system palette used by the browser. You can control browser dither by shifting selected colors to Web-safe colors in the Color Table palette.

For more information on these and other optimization settings, see ImageReady Help.

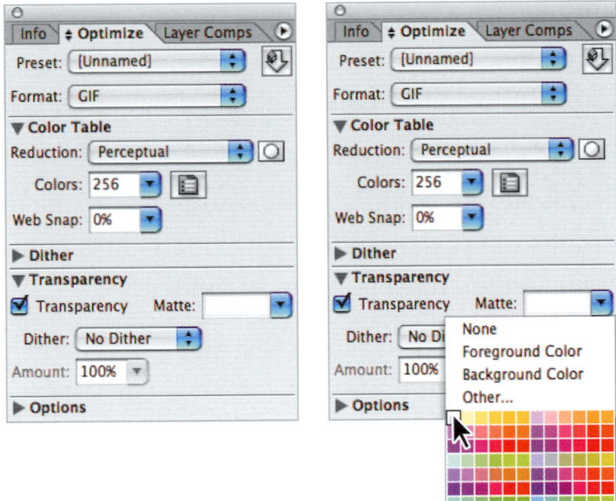

4 With all frames still selected in the Animation palette, right-click (Windows) or Control-click (Mac OS) one of the frames in the Animation palette to open the Disposal Method contextual menu, and choose Restore to background.

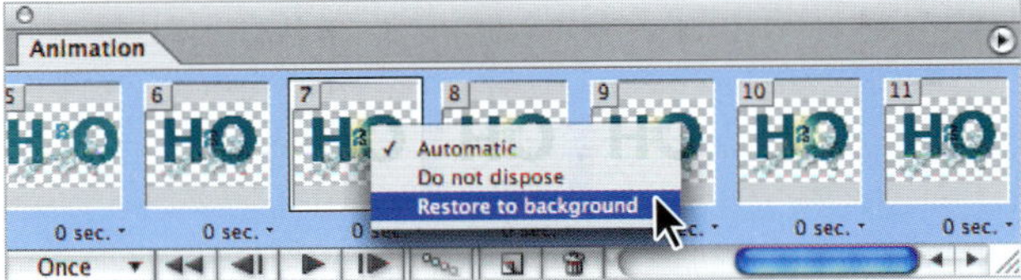

The frame-disposal method specifies whether to discard the current frame before displaying the next frame. The disposal options "Restore to background" ( ) and Automatic clear the selected frame before the next frame is played, eliminating the danger of displaying remnant pixels from the previous frame. The "Do not dispose" option ( ) retains the frames. The Automatic option is suitable for most animations. This option selects a disposal method based on the presence or absence of transparency in the next frame, and discards the selected frame if the next frame contains layer transparency.

5 With all frames selected, use the Frame Delay pop-up menu at the bottom of any one of the frame thumbnails and choose 0.1 sec.

6 From the Animation palette menu, choose Optimize Animation.

7 In the Optimize Animation dialog box, make sure that both the Bounding Box and Redundant Pixel Removal check boxes are selected, and then click OK.

The Bounding Box option directs ImageReady to crop each frame to preserve only the area that has changed from the preceding frame. Animation files created using this option are smaller but are incompatible with GIF editors, which do not support the option.

The Optimize by Redundant Pixel Removal option makes all pixels in a frame that are unchanged from the preceding frame transparent. When you choose the Redundant Pixel Removal option, the Disposal Method must be set to Automatic.

In addition to the optimization tasks applied to standard GIF files, several other tasks are performed for animated GIF files. If you optimize the animated GIF using an Adaptive, Perceptual, or Selective palette, ImageReady generates a palette for the file based on all of the frames in the animation. A special dithering technique is applied to ensure that dither patterns are consistent across all frames, to prevent flickering during playback. Also, frames are optimized so that only areas that change from frame to frame are included, greatly reducing the file size of the animated GIF. As a result, ImageReady requires more time to optimize an animated GIF than to optimize a standard GIF.

For more information about optimizing images for the Web, see Photoshop Help.

Viewing the optimized GIF file

You've almost completed your work in the H2O.psd file that you'll use to save as an animated GIF image.

1 In the image window, click the Optimized tab.

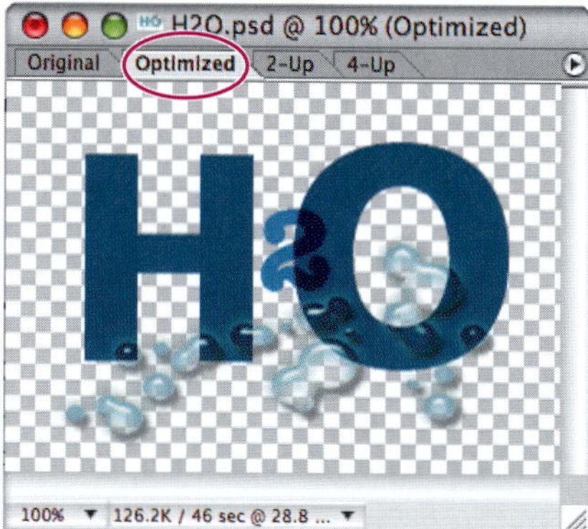

ImageReady rebuilds the image according to the options you entered.

2 In the image window, click the 2-Up tab and compare the information for the original and optimized versions of the animated image.

3 Choose File > Save Optimized As, name the image **H2O.gif**, select the My_GIFs folder, and click Save.

If you want to preview your animation in your default Web browser, do that now by clicking the Preview In button in the toolbox. Then close the browser.

4 In ImageReady, choose File > Close to close the original file, and don't save changes.

You have finished your work on the fly-in logo.

Using vector masks to create animations

The last part of this lesson deals with masks, as they apply to animations. You will use a vector mask to create the effect of an ocean wave rising and falling inside the characters of the word *Waves*. The vector mask will partially block the Wave layer so that the ocean appears only inside the word, and then you'll use position changes to define the frames of the animation.

1 Choose File > Open, and open the Waves.psd file from the Lessons/Lesson15 folder.

2 In the Layers palette, make sure that all the layers are visible. If not, click the visibility boxes so that eye icons appear for each of the layers.

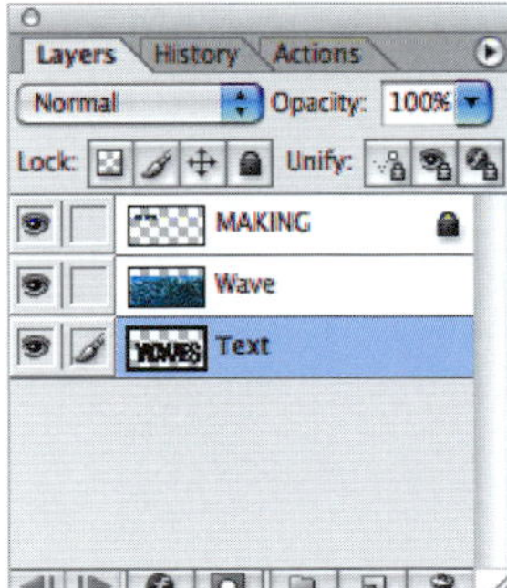

3 In the Layers palette, select the Wave layer.

4 Hold down Alt (Windows) or Option (Mac OS) and move the pointer (without clicking) over the solid line dividing the Wave and Text layers in the Layers palette until the pointer changes to two overlapping circles (). Then click the dividing line between the layers to link the two layers together.

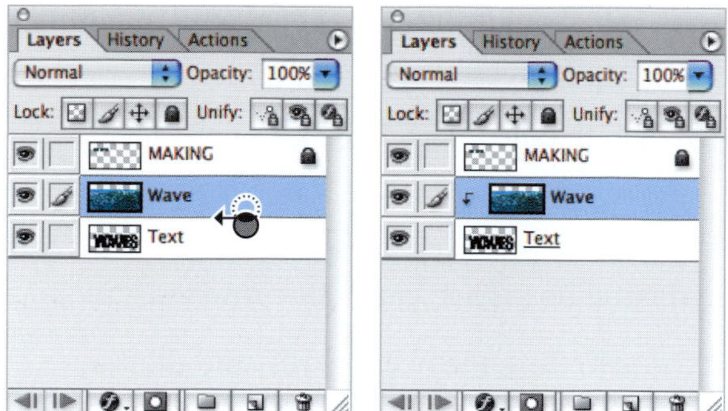

Notice that the waves now appear masked by the logo text. A downward-pointing arrow (↲) appears in front of the Wave layer name and thumbnail in the Layers palette, indicating that the layer is grouped with the layer below.

Animating position changes within a vector-mask layer

Although the Wave and Text layers are linked, you can still make position changes to individual layers.

1 In the Animation palette, click the Duplicate Current Frame button to create a new frame, frame 2.

2 If necessary, select frame 2 in the Animation palette. In the Layers palette, make sure the Wave layer is the only layer selected.

3 Select the Move tool (▸✥) in the toolbox.

4 Begin to drag the Wave layer downward in the image window, and then press Shift after you start to drag to constrain the movement. Drag until the top of the wave image rests just above the top of the WAVES text. (As you drag, the entire Wave layer is ghosted so that you can see the position of the wave as you move it.)

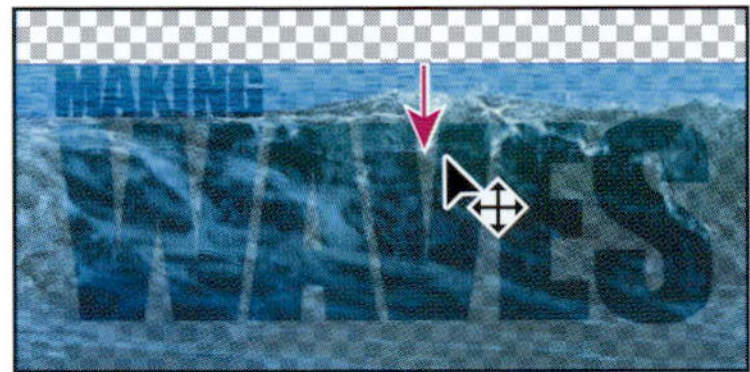

5 Click the Play button (►) to play the animation. The wave moves up and down inside the logo. Click the Stop button (■) to stop the playback.

Smoothing the wave action

To make the wave action look a little more natural, you'll use the now-familiar tweening feature to add more frames to the animation.

Before you begin, make sure that frame 2 is selected in the Animation palette.

1 Choose Tween from the Animation palette menu, and in the Tween dialog box, do the following:

- For Frames to Add, type **2**.
- For Tween With, choose Previous Frame.
- Under Layers, select All Layers.
- Under Parameters, select Position.
- Click OK to close the dialog box.

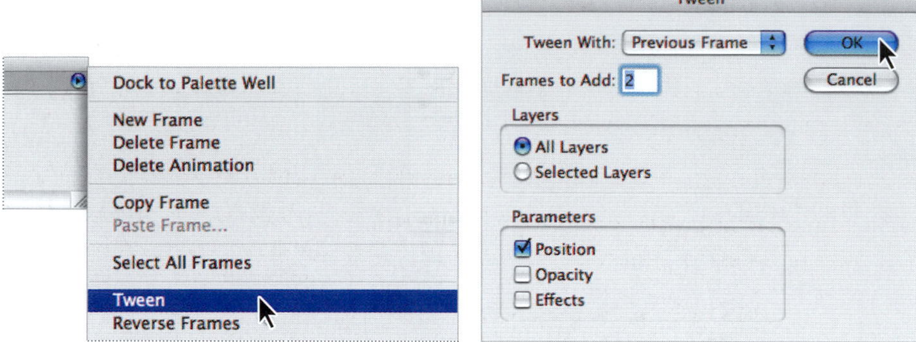

2 In the Animation palette, choose Forever from the Looping pop-up menu.

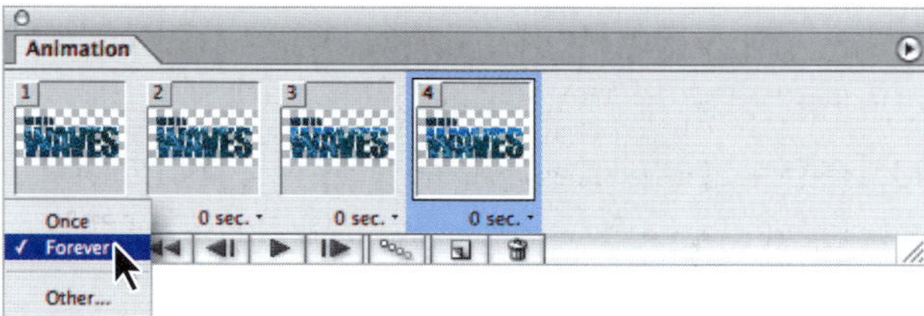

3 Choose Select > Deselect Layers, and then click the Play button (►) in the Animation palette to preview the animation. When you've seen enough, click Stop (■).

The animation is still bumpier than ideal, so you'll fix that next using the same or similar techniques as ones you used with the previous two animations in this lesson.

4 Select frame 2 and then Shift-click frame 3 to select both frames. Then choose Copy Frames from the Animation palette menu.

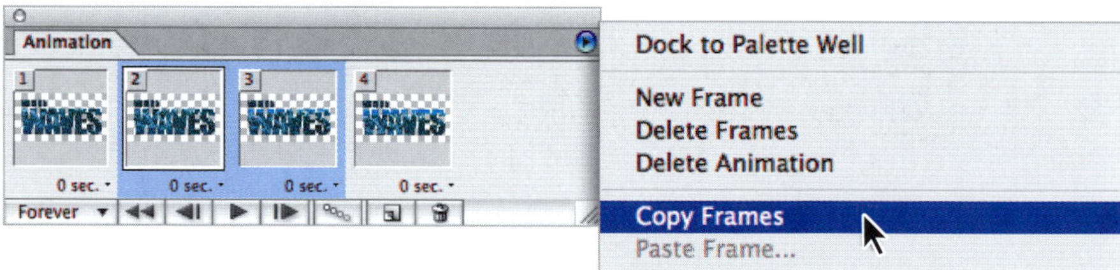

5 Select frame 4, and then choose Paste Frames from the Animation palette menu to open the Paste Frames dialog box, and select Paste After Selection. Then click OK.

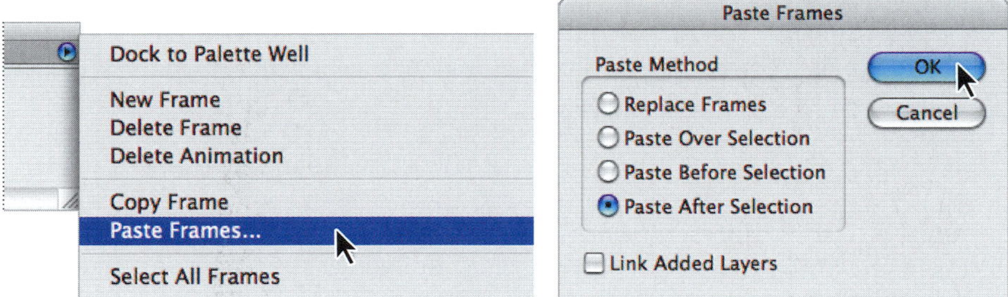

6 Click frame 5 so that it is the only frame selected, and drag it to the right so that it becomes the last frame in the animation.

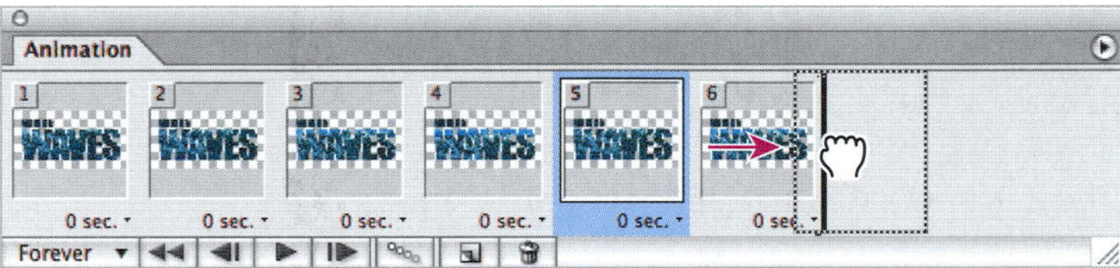

7 With frame 6 selected, hold down Shift and click frame 1 to select all the frames, and then select 0.2 from the Frame Delay pop-up menu for any one of the frames. Then, choose File > Save.

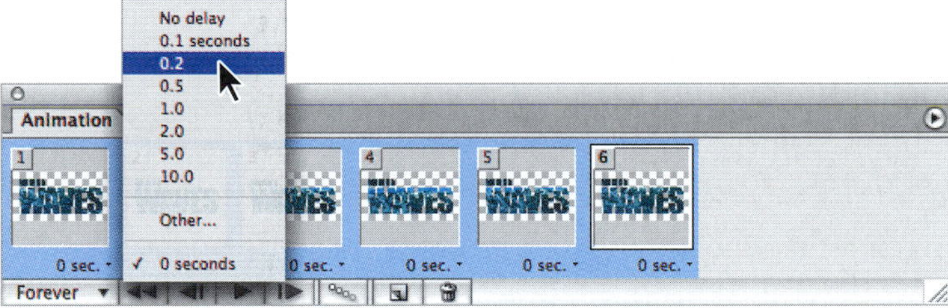

Previewing and saving the vector-mask animation

Now, you'll put your animation to the test by previewing it to see if the wave action meets your standards.

1 In the Animation palette, click the Play button (▶). When you are ready, click the Stop button (■) to halt the playback.

2 If necessary, make any adjustments to the delay or the order of the frames to correct errors or set the timing the way you want it.

3 Preview the animation again and continue to make adjustments until you are fully satisfied with the results.

4 (Optional) Click the Preview In button in the toolbox to preview the animation in your default Web browser. Or choose File > Preview In, and choose your preferred Web browser. When you finish, close the Web browser and return to ImageReady.

5 Choose File > Save Optimized As, specify the My_GIFs folder location, and type **Waves.gif** as the filename. Then click Save.

ImageReady saves the animation as a GIF file using the current settings in the Optimize palette.

6 Choose File > Close to close the original file, and don't save your changes.

Give yourself another pat on the back—you've finished all three animated elements in this Web-page project.

If you want to test your images in the Web page you viewed at the beginning of this lesson, you can go to the desktop and drag contents of the My_GIFs folder into the Lessons/Lesson15/images folder to overwrite the GIF files inside. (Click Yes when messages appear asking you to confirm this action.) Then double-click the 15End.html file. When the page opens in your default Web browser, it will use your GIF images rather than the samples provided for this lesson.

Review

Review questions

1 Describe a simple way to create an animation.

2 When can you tween animation frames? When can't you tween frames?

3 How do you optimize an animation?

4 What is frame disposal? Which frame-disposal method should you usually use?

5 What file formats can you use for animations?

Review answers

1 A simple way to create an animation is to start with a layered Photoshop file. Use the Duplicate Current Frame button in the ImageReady Animation palette to create a new frame, and then use the Layers palette to alter the position, opacity, or effects of one of the selected frames. Then, create intermediate frames between the two frames either manually, by using the Duplicate Current Frame button, or automatically, by using the Tween command.

2 You can instruct ImageReady to tween intermediate frames between any two adjacent frames. Tweening can change layer opacity or position between two frames, or add new layers to a sequence of frames. You cannot tween discontiguous frames.

3 After using the Optimize palette, choose File > Save Optimized As to optimize animations. Choose Optimize Animation from the Animation palette menu to perform optimization tasks specific to animation files, including removing redundant pixels and cropping frames according to the bounding box.

4 A frame-disposal method specifies whether to discard the selected frame before displaying the next frame when an animation includes background transparency. This option determines whether the selected frame will appear through the transparent areas of the next frame. Generally, the Automatic option is suitable for most animations.

5 Files for animations must be saved in GIF format or as QuickTime movies. You cannot create animations as JPEG or PNG files.

SEASON'S GREETINGS!
FROM The Center of the City

Print

Position
Top: 3.222 inches
Left: 1.125 inches
Center Image

Scaled Print Size
Scale: 100% Scale to Fit Media
Height: 3.75 inches
Width: 5.736 inches
Show Bounding Box
Print Selected Area

Print...
Reset
Remember
Page Setup...
Fewer Options

Color Management

Print
Document (Profile: U.S. Web Coated (SWOP) v2)
Proof (Profile: N/A)

Options
Color Handling: Separations
Printer Profile: Working RGB – Adobe RGB (19...
Rendering Intent: Relative Colorimetric
Black Point Compensation
Proof Setup Preset: Working CMYK
Simulate Paper Color
Simulate Black Ink

Description

To produce consistent color, you define the color space in which to edit and display RGB images, and in which to edit, display, and print CMYK images. This helps ensure a close match between onscreen and printed colors.

16 Producing and Printing Consistent Color

Lesson overview

In this lesson, you'll learn how to do the following:

- Define RGB, grayscale, and CMYK color spaces for displaying, editing, and printing images.
- Prepare an image for printing on a PostScript CMYK printer.
- Proof an image for printing.
- Create and print a four-color separation.
- Understand how images are prepared for printing on presses.

This lesson will take less than an hour to complete. If needed, remove the previous lesson folder from your hard drive, and copy the Lessons/Lesson16 folder onto it. As you work on this lesson, you'll overwrite the start files. If you need to restore the start files, copy them from the *Adobe Photoshop CS2 Classroom in a Book* CD.

This lesson requires that your computer be connected to a PostScript color printer. If it isn't, you can do most, but not all, of the exercises.

Reproducing colors

Colors on a monitor are displayed using combinations of red, green, and blue light (called RGB), while printed colors are typically created using a combination of four ink colors—cyan, magenta, yellow, and black (called CMYK). These four inks are called *process colors* because they are the standard inks used in the four-color printing process.

RGB image with red, green, and blue channels

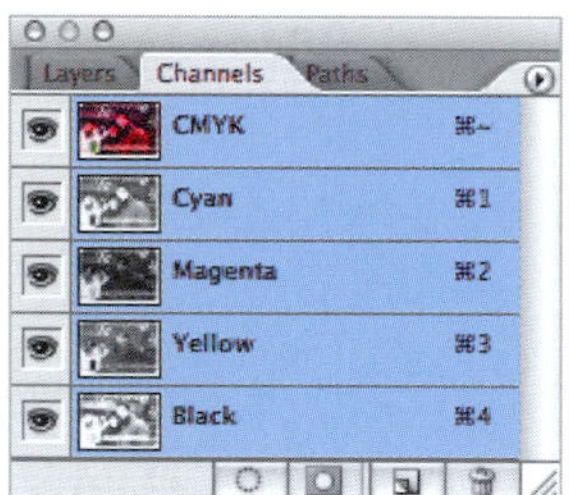

CMYK image with cyan, magenta, yellow, and black channels

Because the RGB and CMYK color models use different methods to display colors, they each reproduce a different *gamut*, or range of colors. For example, because RGB uses light to produce color, its gamut includes neon colors, such as those you'd see in a neon sign. In contrast, printing inks excel at reproducing certain colors that can lie outside the RGB gamut, such as some pastels and pure black.

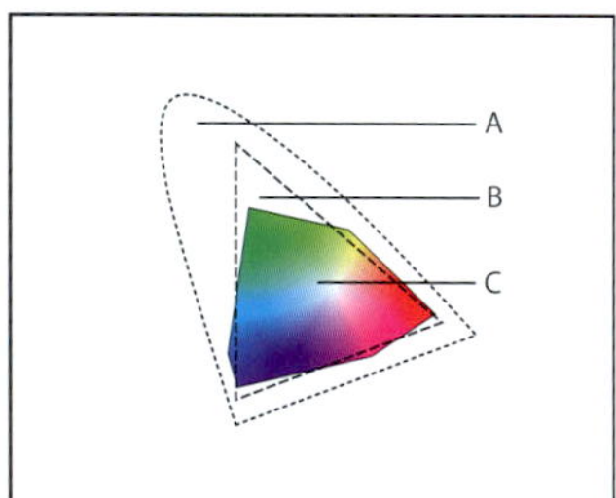

A. *Natural color gamut*
B. *RGB color gamut*
C. *CMYK color gamut*

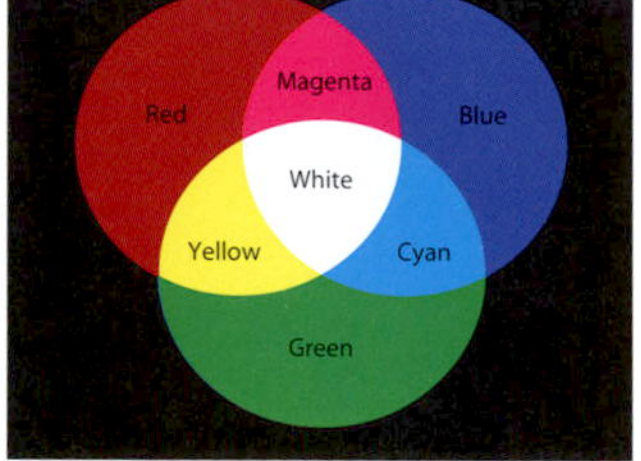

RGB color model

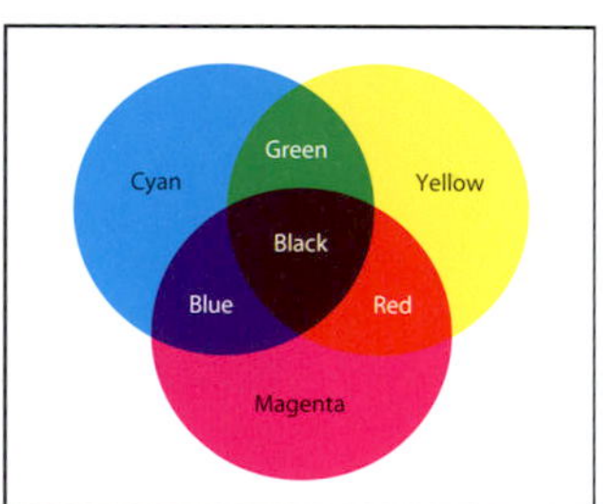

CMYK color model

But not all RGB and CMYK gamuts are alike. Each model of monitor and printer is different, and so each displays a slightly different gamut. For example, one brand of monitor may produce slightly brighter blues than another. The *color space* for a device is defined by the gamut it can reproduce.

RGB model

A large percentage of the visible spectrum can be represented by mixing red, green, and blue (RGB) colored light in various proportions and intensities. Where the colors overlap, they create cyan, magenta, yellow, and white.

Because the RGB colors combine to create white, they are also called *additive* colors. Adding all colors together creates white—that is, all light is transmitted back to the eye. Additive colors are used for lighting, video, and monitors. Your monitor, for example, creates color by emitting light through red, green, and blue phosphors.

CMYK model

The CMYK model is based on the light-absorbing quality of ink printed on paper. As white light strikes translucent inks, part of the spectrum is absorbed while other parts are reflected back to your eyes.

In theory, pure cyan (C), magenta (M), and yellow (Y) pigments should combine to absorb all color and produce black. For this reason, these colors are called subtractive colors. Because all printing inks contain some impurities, these three inks actually produce a muddy brown and must be combined with black (K) ink to produce a true black. (*K* is used instead of *B* to avoid confusion with blue.) Combining these inks to reproduce color is called *four-color process printing*.

An ICC profile is a description of a device's color space, such as the CMYK color space of a particular printer. In this lesson, you'll choose which RGB and CMYK ICC profiles to use. Once you specify the profiles, Photoshop can embed them into your image files. Photoshop (and any other application that can use ICC profiles) can then interpret the ICC profile in the image file to automatically manage color for that image.

For information on embedding ICC profiles, see Photoshop Help.

Getting started

Unlike other lessons in this book, this lesson does not require that you preview a final image to see what you will be creating. However, you do need to launch Photoshop and restore default preferences.

1 Start Photoshop and then immediately hold down Ctrl-Alt-Shift (Windows) or Command-Option-Shift (Mac OS) to restore the default preferences. (See "Restoring default preferences" on page 6.)

2 When prompted, click Yes to confirm that you want to reset preferences, and Close to close the Welcome Screen.

Note: *Be sure that your monitor is calibrated before continuing. If your monitor does not display colors accurately, the color adjustments you make to an image displayed on that monitor may be inaccurate.*

Specifying color-management settings

In the first part of this lesson, you'll learn how to set up a color-managed workflow. To help you with this, the Color Settings dialog box in Photoshop contains most of the color-management controls you need.

For instance, by default Photoshop is set up for RGB as part of a Web workflow. If you are preparing artwork for print production, however, you would likely change the settings to be more appropriate for images that will be printed on paper rather than displayed on a screen.

You'll begin this lesson by creating customized color settings.

1 Choose Edit > Color Settings to open the Color Settings dialog box.

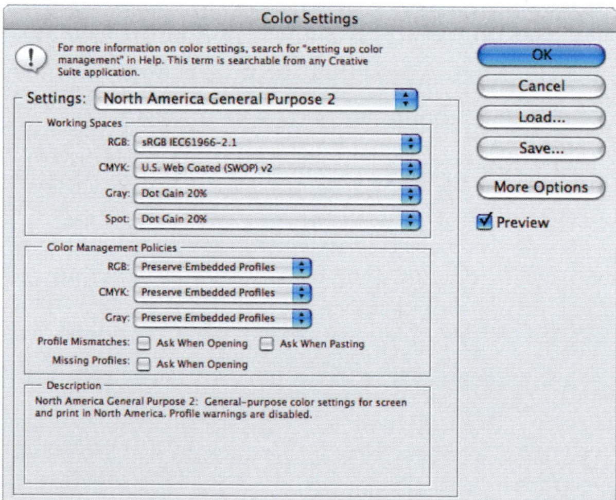

Note: By default, the Settings menu should show North America General Purpose 2. If it doesn't, you must have changed it at some point. Choose it now.

The bottom of the dialog box interactively describes each of the various color-management options, which you'll review now.

2 Move the mouse pointer over each part of the dialog box, including the names of areas (such as Working Spaces) and the options you can choose (such as the different menu options), returning the options to their defaults when you're done. As you move the mouse, view the information that appears at the bottom of the dialog box.

Now, you'll choose a set of options designed for a print workflow, rather than an online workflow.

3 Choose Settings > North America Prepress 2. The working spaces and color-management policy options change for a prepress workflow. Then, click OK.

Proofing an image

In this part of the lesson, you'll work with a typical file of the kind you might scan in from a printed original. You'll open it, convert its color profile, and set it up so that you can see a close onscreen representation of what it will look like when printed. This will let you proof the printed image on your screen for printed output.

You'll begin by opening the file.

1 Click the Go to Bridge button ( ) on the tool options bar to open Adobe Bridge, or choose File > Open, to open the 16Start.tif file from the Lessons/Lesson16 folder.

The Missing Profile notice appears, offering three options: Leave as is (don't color manage); assign the Adobe RGB working space (which is specified in your North American Prepress 2 Color Settings); or assign a profile from a pop-up menu of profile choices and optionally convert the document to the working RGB space.

2 Select the "Assign profile: Adobe RGB (1998)" option, select the "and then convert document to working RGB" check box, and click OK.

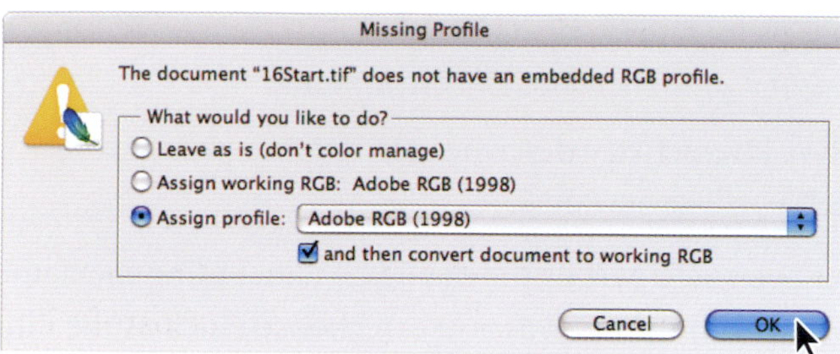

An RGB image of a scanned postcard opens.

When you choose to convert a document's color to the Photoshop working space, Photoshop compares the color space in the image file's embedded color profile (if any) with the color space you defined in the Color Settings dialog box. Photoshop then converts the image file's colors as necessary to display the image onscreen as accurately as possible.

Note: *Depending on what you specify in the Color Settings dialog box and what image you're opening, you might encounter the Embedded Profile Mismatch notice. If so, select the "Convert document's colors to the working space" option, and then click OK.*

Before soft-proofing—that is, proofing onscreen—or printing this image, you'll set up a proof profile. A proof profile (also called a *proof setup*) defines how the document is going to be printed, and adds those visual properties to the onscreen version for more accurate soft-proofing. Photoshop provides a variety of settings that can help you proof images for different uses, including print and display on the Web. For this lesson, you'll create a custom proof setup. You can then save the settings for use on other images that will be output the same way.

3 Choose View > Proof Setup > Custom. The Customize Proof Conditions dialog box opens.

4 Make sure that the Preview box is checked.

5 From the Device to Simulate menu, choose a profile that represents a final-output source color profile, such as that for the printer you'll use to print the image. If you don't have a specific printer, the profile Working CMYK - U.S. Web Coated (SWOP) v2 is generally a good choice.

6 Make sure that Preserve Color Numbers is *not* selected. Leaving this option off simulates how the image will appear if colors are converted from the document space to their nearest equivalents in the proof profile space.

Note: *This option is not always available, and it is grayed out and unchecked for the U.S. Web Coated (SWOP) v2 profile.*

7 From the Rendering Intent menu, choose a rendering intent for the conversion, such as Relative Colorimetric, which a good choice for preserving color relationships without sacrificing color accuracy.

8 If they're available for the profile you chose, select the Simulate Ink Black and Simulate Paper Color check boxes.

Notice that the image appears to lose contrast. Ink Black simulates the dynamic range defined by an image's profile. Paper Color simulates the specific shade of white for the print medium defined by an image's profile. That is, the whites in the image are now simulating the white of paper.

Normal image

Image with Ink Black and Paper Color options checked

9 Click OK.

To turn the proof settings off and on, choose View > Proof Colors.

Identifying out-of-gamut colors

Most scanned photographs contain RGB colors within the CMYK gamut, and changing the image to CMYK mode (which you'll do later in order to print the file) converts all the colors with relatively little substitution. Images that are created or altered digitally, however, often contain RGB colors that are outside the CMYK gamut—for example, neon-colored logos and lights.

Note: *Out-of-gamut colors are identified by an exclamation point next to the color swatch in the Color palette, the Color Picker, and the Info palette.*

Before you convert an image from RGB to CMYK, you can preview the CMYK color values while still in RGB mode.

1 Choose View > Gamut Warning to see out-of-gamut colors. Adobe Photoshop builds a color-conversion table and displays a neutral gray in the image window where the colors are out of gamut.

Because the gray can be hard to spot in the image, you'll now convert it to a more visible gamut-warning color.

2 Choose Edit > Preferences > Transparency & Gamut (Windows) or Photoshop > Preferences > Transparency & Gamut (Mac OS). Then click the color sample in the Gamut Warning area at the bottom of the dialog box.

3 Choose a vivid color, such as pink or a saturated clear blue, and click OK.

4 Click OK again to close the Transparency & Gamut dialog box. The bright, new color you choose appears instead of the neutral gray as the gamut warning color.

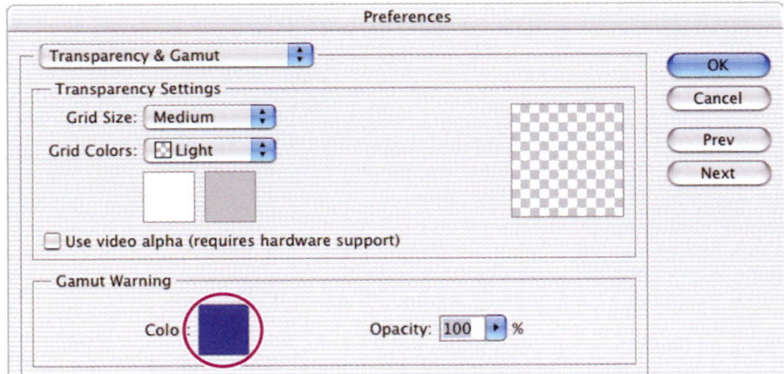

5 Choose View > Gamut Warning to turn off the preview of out-of-gamut colors.

Photoshop will automatically correct these out-of-gamut colors when you save the file in Photoshop EPS format later in this lesson. Photoshop EPS format changes the RGB image to CMYK, adjusting the RGB colors as needed to bring them into the CMYK color gamut.

Adjusting an image and printing a proof

The next step in preparing an image for output is to make any color and tonal adjustments that are necessary. In this exercise, you'll add some tonal and color adjustments to correct an off-color scan of the original postcard.

So that you can compare the image before and after making corrections, you'll start by making a copy.

1 Choose Image > Duplicate and click OK to duplicate the image.

2 Arrange the two image windows in your workspace so that you can compare them as you work.

Now you'll adjust the hue and saturation of the image. There are various ways to adjust color, including using the Levels and Curves commands. You'll use the Hue/Saturation command.

3 Select 16Start.tif (the original image) and choose Image > Adjustments > Hue/Saturation.

4 Drag the Hue/Saturation dialog box aside so that you can still see the 16Start.tif image, make sure the Preview box is checked, and then do following:

- Drag the Hue slider until the colors, especially the flesh tones, look more natural. (We used +20.)

- Drag the Saturation slider until the intensity of the colors looks normal (we used –17).
- Leave the Lightness setting at the default value (0), and click OK.

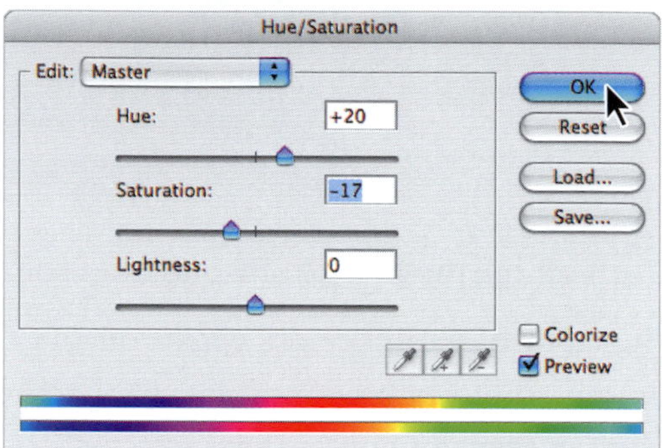

***Note:** Before going on to print this image, try toggling the gamut warning back on, and you should see that you have removed most of the out-of-gamut colors from the image.*

5 With 16Start.tif still selected, choose File > Print with Preview.

6 In the Print with Preview dialog box, click the More Options button (in the upper right corner) if necessary to see all of the print options available. Then do the following:

- Choose Color Management from the pop-up menu under the image preview.
- In the Print area, click the Proof button to select your proof profile.
- Under Options, choose Color Handling > Let Printer Determine Colors, and then choose Proof Setup Preset > Working CMYK.
- (Optional) Press Alt (Windows) or Option (Mac OS) to change the Done button to Remember, and click Remember to save these settings for the next time you print.
- Click Print to print the image to a color printer, and compare it with the onscreen version.

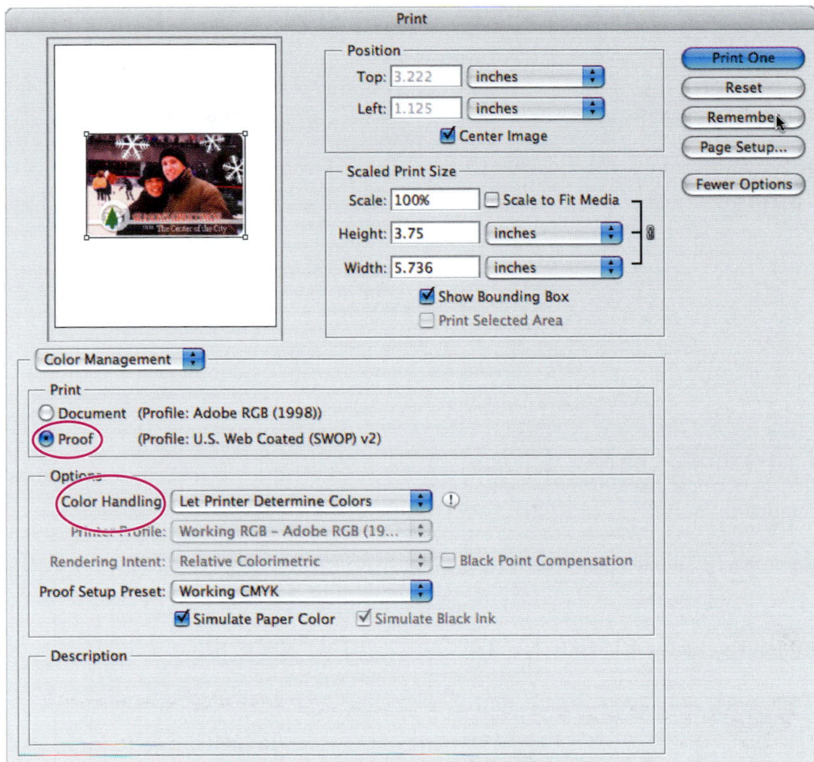

7 Choose File > Save to save your work.

Saving the image as a separation

In this exercise, you'll learn how to save the image as a separation so that it can print out on separate cyan, magenta, yellow, and black plates.

1 With 16Start.tif still selected, choose File > Save As.

2 In the Save As dialog box, do the following:

• Choose Format > Photoshop EPS.

• Under Color, select the Use Proof Setup: Working CMYK check box. Don't worry about the save-a-copy warning icon that appears.

Note: *These settings cause the image to be automatically converted from RGB to CMYK when it is saved in the Photoshop Encapsulated PostScript (EPS) format.*

• Accept the filename 16Start.eps, and click Save.

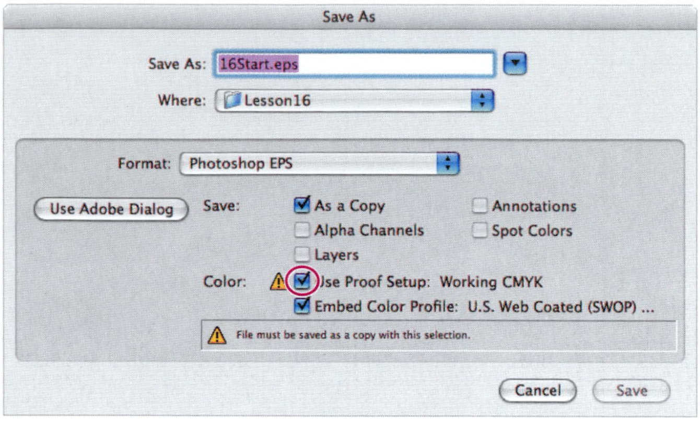

3 Click OK in the EPS Options dialog box that appears.

4 Save and then close the 16Start.tif and 16Start copy.tif files.

5 Choose File > Open, navigate to the Lessons/Lesson16 folder, and select and open the 16Start.eps file.

Notice in the image file's title bar that 16Start.eps is a CMYK file.

Printing

When you're ready to print your image, use the following guidelines for best results:

- Print a *color composite*, often called a *color comp*. A color composite is a single print that combines the red, green, and blue channels of an RGB image (or the cyan, magenta, yellow, and black channels of a CMYK image). This indicates what the final printed image will look like.
- Set the parameters for the halftone screen.
- Print separations to make sure the image separates correctly.
- Print to film or plate.

Printing halftone separations

To specify the halftone screen when you print an image, you use the Screen option in the Print with Preview dialog box. The results of using a halftone screen appear only in the printed copy; you cannot see the halftone screen onscreen.

When you print color separations, you print four grayscale screens, one for each process color. Each screen contains halftone information for the respective channel, including screen frequency, screen angle, and dot shape.

The *screen frequency* controls the density of dots on the screen. Since the dots are arranged in lines on the screen, the common measurement for screen frequency is lines per inch (lpi). The higher the screen frequency, the finer the image produced (depending on the line-screen capability of the printer). Magazines, for example, tend to use fine screens of 133 lpi and higher, because they are usually printed on coated paper and on high-quality presses. Newspapers, which are usually printed on lower-quality paper, tend to use lower screen frequencies, such as 85 lpi.

The *screen angle* used to create halftones of grayscale images is generally 45 degrees. For best results with color separations, select the Auto option in the Halftone Screens dialog box (which is accessible through the Print dialog box, as you'll see in a minute). You can also specify an angle for each of the color screens. Setting the screens at different angles ensures that the dots placed by the four screens blend to look like continuous color and do not produce moiré patterns.

Diamond-shaped dots are the most commonly used in halftone screens. In Photoshop, however, you can also choose round, elliptical, linear, square, and cross-shaped dots.

***Note:** By default, an image will use the halftone screen settings of the output device or of the software from which you output the image. You usually don't need to specify halftone screen settings unless you want to override the default settings. And you should* always *consult your prepress partner before specifying halftone screen options.*

In this exercise, you'll adjust the halftone screens for the postcard image, and then print the color separations.

1 With the 16Start.eps image open from the previous exercise, choose File > Print with Preview.

2 Choose Output from the pop-up menu under the preview (click the More Options button in the upper right corner of the dialog box if you don't see the menu).

3 Click the Screen button.

4 In the Halftone Screen dialog box, do the following:

- Deselect the Use Printer's Default Screen check box.
- Toggle through the Ink menu to see the Frequency, Angle, and Shape information for each color channel.
- For the Cyan ink, choose Shape > Ellipse.
- Toggle through the Magenta, Yellow, and Black Ink menus again, and notice that all of the Shape menus now show Ellipse. We could change other options, but we'll leave them as they are for this exercise.
- Click OK to close the Halftone Screen dialog box.

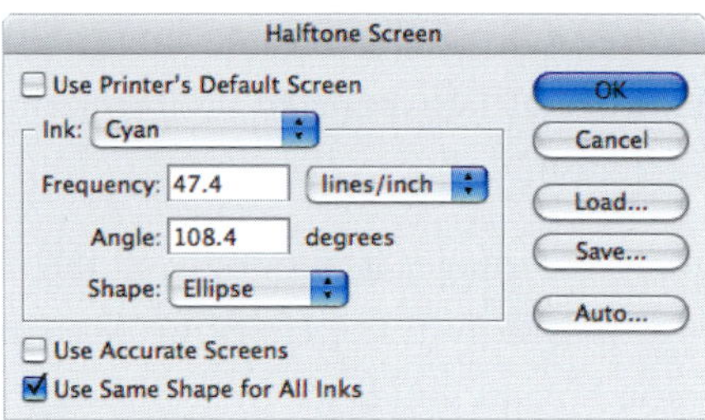

By default, Photoshop prints a CMYK image as a single document. To print this file as separations, you need to explicitly instruct Photoshop in the Print with Preview dialog box.

5 Back in the Print with Preview dialog box, do the following:

- Choose Color Management from the pop-up menu under the image preview.
- In the Print area, click the Document button.
- In the Options area, choose Color Handling > Separations.
- Click Print.

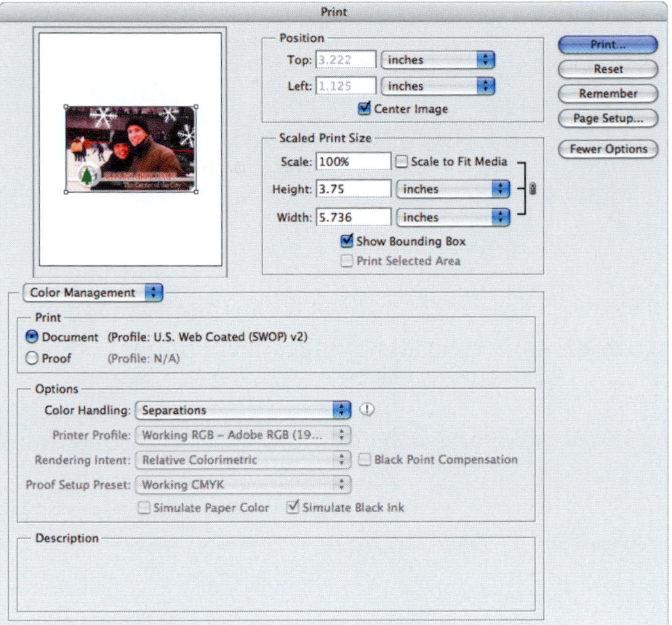

6 Choose File > Close, and don't save the changes.

This completes your introduction to printing and producing consistent color using Adobe Photoshop. For more information about color management, printing options, and color separations, see Photoshop Help.

Review

Review questions

1 What steps should you follow to reproduce color accurately?

2 What is a gamut?

3 What is an ICC profile?

4 What are color separations? How does a CMYK image differ from an RGB image?

5 What steps should you follow when preparing an image for color separations?

Review answers

1 Calibrate your monitor, and then use the Color Settings dialog box to specify which color spaces to use. For example, you can specify which RGB color space to use for online images, and which CMYK color space to use for images that will be printed. You can then proof the image, check for out-of-gamut colors, adjust colors as needed, and—for printed images—create color separations.

2 A gamut is the range of colors that can be reproduced by a color model or device. For example, the RGB and CMYK color models have different gamuts, as do any two RGB scanners.

3 An ICC profile is a description of a device's color space, such as the CMYK color space of a particular printer. Applications such as Photoshop can interpret ICC profiles in an image to maintain consistent color across different applications, platforms, and devices.

4 A color separation is created when an image is converted to CMYK mode. The colors in the CMYK image are separated into the four process-color channels: cyan, magenta, yellow, and black. An RGB image, by contrast, has three color channels: red, green, and blue.

5 You prepare an image for print by following the steps for reproducing color accurately, and then converting the image from RGB mode to CMYK mode to build a color separation.

Index

C

L

M

T

U

V

W

Z